Higgling

Higgling

Transactors and Their Markets in
the History of Economics

Annual supplement to volume 26

History of Political Economy

Edited by Neil De Marchi and
Mary S. Morgan

Duke University Press

Durham and London 1994

Contents

Introduction

Neil De Marchi and Mary S. Morgan

Fairness versus Reasoned Efficiency in Exchange

Economics knows two traditions with respect to market transactions. One has grown out of a concern for fairness, the other, for efficiency. In the conventional history of the discipline, economics narrowed its scope late in the nineteenth century and focused on elucidating the laws governing exchange and efficient allocation. In the process, questions of fairness were pushed out to the margins, or into other fledgling social sciences. But this search for *efficiency in exchange* could also be said to have had its roots in a felt need to *make fairness objective,* and in this sense the change had been building for centuries.

If the change was not swift, neither was it straightforward. A host of individuals and groups struggled, over an extended period, to reconcile the claims of the two traditions, claims of *justness* and of *well-reasoned allocation.* Think, for example, of the seventeenth-century compiler of the Law Merchant, Malynes, who settled upon a formulation for price that was founded upon, and therefore expressed, both reason and consensus. He spoke of price as "a certain equality in the value of things, permuted by a true reason grounded upon the commodious use of things. So that equality is nothing else but a mutual voluntary estimation of things made in good order and truth" (1685, cited by Lowry, this volume). An awareness of the joint claims can also be read in Smith's equivocal use of the term "natural." On the one hand, he stressed that the natural rates of wages and profit, and of rent, are those rates "which must be paid" if supply is to be maintained where individuals are at liberty to change their trade; on the other, he held open the door to customary or social influences by also referring to the natural rates as the "ordinary or average rates . . . at the time and place in which they commonly prevail" (*Wealth of Nations,* 1.7 [1976], 72–73). A century later, J. B. Clark, in the midst of the so-called marginal revolution, was driven by the problem of finding a fair division of the gains from trade, and his work may be seen as an ongoing exploration of alternative resolutions of this problem. In his early work, Clark emphasized moral economic man; in his later writings, he thought the problem of fairness would be solved rationally (objectively or according to reason) if factors received the value of their marginal product; yet his formulation of the problem itself hardly altered between these two proposed solutions.

Similarly, tensions are apparent at the group level. One example is the British classical economists' agonized analyses of the effects of Poor Laws, of the Factory Acts, and of trades unions. Recall too the various groups which arose to defend fairness once it began to seem that the efficient allocation perspective might take over: the Fabians, for example; or the social Christianity that inspired many of the founders of the American Economic Association.

The essays in this collection, in their several ways, are reminders of aspects of this struggle, and of the fact that it has been going on a long time. They were produced for a conference on "higgling" held at Duke University, 25–28 March 1993, and organized by Mary Morgan and Neil De Marchi. The connection between higgling, best known perhaps from Smith's phrase "the higgling and bargaining of the market" (*Wealth of Nations,* 1.5, para. 4; Glasgow ed., 49), and the more abstract issue of justness versus efficient allocation, may not be obvious. It probably wasn't obvious to many of those who responded to an open call for papers, or to the ultimate participants, and wasn't to the organizers either, at the start. What became clear, however, as papers were submitted, presented, and discussed, was that what past economists have said on the role and significance of higgling is a reliable clue to how they resolved the tension caused by the competing claims of the two traditions. Broadly speaking, those opting for efficient allocation have also viewed higgling as a process through which equilibrium, or allocatively rational prices, may be discovered. Once the discovery is made, however, higgling becomes irrelevant. Those for whom fairness was a main concern tended, on the other hand, to focus precisely on these practices and processes and on the structure of rules and conventions through which particular markets actually work.

This division is plainly visible in modern economics. Intellectually, there are those who claim that once a true equilibrium has been identified, how learning may have occurred along the way, or *what* institutions may have been in existence, add no information to what the equilibrium conditions can tell us about economic performance. Free competition and efficient outcomes subsume learning, subsume institutions, and thereby make actual history irrelevant (Lucas 1987, 218; North 1990, 11, 16). Opposing this stance is an array of claims centering on the view that economic outcomes are, in theory and in fact, and indeed unavoidably so, path dependent (David 1975, 1986, 1991; Mirowski 1989a, 1989b; Langlois 1986; North 1990). This division is itself an outcome: the arguments have long since been clarified and positions taken, and there is no real discussion between the protagonists.

The histories of economics in this volume, by contrast, show this contrast being formulated, where arguments are still tentative and individuals struggle with themselves to find a way to retain something of both fairness and allocative efficiency. They also serve to remind us that the modern sharp division obscures and even distorts the history of both traditions. Todd Lowry, in a draft version of his contribution to this volume, expressed this in the form of a strong thesis: "It is the burden of this essay to question the premise that the essential building blocks of modern market theory, namely voluntarism and rational choice, were framed as either observations of, or ethical mandates for, nascent market processes or primitive political structures." They were, instead, "originally *distributive* concepts" (emphasis added). Lowry's and the other essays printed here invite reconsideration of how the modern division came to be. They give researchers a base from which to recover more of the specific contexts in which the struggle has been expressed, and they suggest in the process other ways of viewing it, even alternative outcomes— those which might have been—so that we can see the particularity of the formulation and resolution (or rather, separation) that we encounter in the recent literature.

One way to trace the struggle between the two traditions concerning exchange is to focus somewhat more narrowly, on pricing. Many (not all) of the essays presented here, though not designed with that in view, may be read as offering traces of a history of thought about pricing. As a device to draw attention to, without exaggerating, the commonality of these traces, we have thus used as one of the volume's uniting themes the hypothesis—hinted at once already—that the history is a "search" for a price which combines fairness with allocative efficiency. But on the evidence presented here, there are two phases of that search. In the first, which begins in ancient Greece, the starting point is fairness in the *division* of goods, and the movement is toward ways of incorporating efficiency into that division. This was accomplished by the time of Smith and Say, when the focus had already moved toward the *pricing* of goods in such a way as to incorporate both fairness and efficiency in varying elements. The last part of the nineteenth century and perhaps the early decades of the twentieth saw something of a reversal of this movement: with efficiency in pricing well understood, the movement was to recover or retain the earlier successful incorporation of fairness. At the same time, disciplinary developments led to increasing specialization within the social sciences, and more detailed study of market processes and conventions began to occur largely in other fields. Thus many of the analyses surrounding this question of fairness disappeared from economics to surface elsewhere, under different guises, while raising also a range of different questions about the higgling problem.

Fairness, Efficiency and Language in the Analysis of Higgling

The Elements of Fairness

In his essay, Lowry is concerned with both fairness and rationality in pricing. "Rationality" makes reference both to the notion of efficient allocation (rationing) of *goods* carried out by "experts" in the system and to the notion that the *pricing* of goods might be linked to some objective reasoning (rationale) about the value of the goods. He suggests that the concept of rationality must date back to the need for "coherent and systematic record keeping and uniform allocation" in administering grain and water supplies in Mesopotamia and the valley of the Nile, but he finds positive evidence of the reasoning element of rationality in discussions of pricing only in the seventeenth century (as in the passage from Malynes cited above). The principle that justice is implicit in voluntary exchanges, however, is present in the records of Greek culture, in both mythology and ethical writings. There is further ratification from practice, both in the divide-and-choose rule sometimes used for apportioning the spoils of war and in the Athenian practice of designating some wealthy citizen to pay for public festivals, any designee having the option to swap his property with another if he thought that person better able to pay.

Justice stemming from voluntariness in the exchange of goods, however, does not necessarily mean objectivity in the price agreed upon, for after all, there may have been no "price" in the exchange (other than that implied in the barter ratio). To ratify individual voluntary agreements and at the same time establish a publicly accepted standard of value, the Romans transposed private transactions into the public arena. A special institutional form, using auction techniques, was applied to the sale of some agricultural produce and of certain other goods. Prior notice of a sale was given; it was held in a public place; and an official (a banker) was present to apply the rules of sale and manage any credit arrangements necessary.

Lowry stresses that Roman auction sales resulted in a managed price, and that in this and the other conditions surrounding the sales they differed considerably from the self-regulating market of later economic theory, whose assumed conditions, he notes, include ease of comparison of the goods, full and shared information, and stability of commercial supply and distribution channels.

In the wider world of transactions across borders or across political regimes, the "local" authority wielded by the officials at a Roman auction obviously needed to be supplemented in various ways. Mutual trust, reinforced by threat of ostracism, worked for selected merchant communities united by ties of family or religion (Greif 1989); merchant guilds and the Law Merchant evolved to create something akin to Roman conditions in medieval fairs (Greif, Milgrom, and Weingast 1990; Milgrom, North, and Weingast 1990); and the Church's teachings on "just" price and against usury reinforced pragmatic and private safeguards over much of Europe. These are areas where economic historians are producing intriguing reconstructions, but where historians of economics have made less progress. Practical considerations kept us from widening the conference to include economic historians' contributions in this area. As a result there is a yawning temporal gap between Lowry's treatment of classical and medieval evidence and the group of essays closest in time to his, those by De Marchi and Harrison, Schabas, and Brown, which deal with seventeenth- and eighteenth-century themes and figures.

The Regulator's Need for a Reference Price

Neil De Marchi and Paul Harrison look at a particular problem in the mercantile culture of seventeenth-century Holland: how to regulate share-trading practices. One sort of transaction proved especially troublesome: short selling, or selling shares one did not have—trading in the wind, as Dutch contemporaries referred to it. This was viewed as harmful, whereas futures contracting in commodities was not. It is not obvious that the differences warranted any such special attitude or attention; but taking that phase of bother about short selling at face value, one can see in it elements of what we are calling the struggle to reconcile fairness with "rationality" in pricing.

The fairness issue here was the more prominent, and it was much the same as the problem confronting the Roman auctioneer, namely, how to see to it that prices agree with those that the public will judge fair or appropriate. By the seventeenth century, consensus about appropriateness had come to mean "reasonable"; and as Malynes made clear in his definition of price (quoted earlier), reasonable meant equality "permuted by a true reason grounded upon . . . a mutual voluntary estimation of things made in good order and truth." What this seems to exclude is coercion, and the sort of prices that might result from "speculative" behavior, where the latter involved the manipulation of supplies or the exploitation of unequally shared information about them. But if it is correct to infer that such elements probably were excluded from the notion of "reasonable" price, any contemporary would-be price controller would have had to find ways of identifying and dealing with them (though the "reasonableness" of a fair price involving justice to both buyer and seller would also have been kept in mind).

Conceptually, the modern notion of the rational price of a share is the discounted value of expected true earnings; seventeenth-century Hollanders seem to have held something like that conception. Was it any more difficult, in the conditions of the time, to make that notion operational for shares than to estimate the proper prices of commodities? Probably not, but contemporaries made heavy weather of reconciling speculation in shares with what they judged to be a reasonable or rational pricing process. The essay by De Marchi and Harrison charts their unsteady progress.

We simply followed Lowry in portraying the Roman auctioneer's primary problem as that of finding a way of translating notions of fairness and justice into going market price. If we combine his insights with what we know from the Dutch encounter with short selling in the seventeenth century and attempt a more general formulation of the price setter's problem, we come up with something that Adam Smith would have had no difficulty recognizing. The price setter, we may say, must (1) find practical ways to distinguish proper or normal prices from actual prices (those actually ruling in the absence of any official intervention), (2) discover or judge whether deviations of actual from normal prices are due to manipulation, and (3) work out ways of guarding against or getting rid of the effects of manipulation (on prices, but also perhaps on qualities and quantities). The first element here matches Smith's suggestion that "natural" price should be understood as the ordinary or average price. The second matches Smith's concern to draw attention to the ways in which long-standing privilege, or coercive power, can affect price. Smith's way of meeting the third condition, of course, was to get rid of the legal basis for such privileges and to warn the public to beware the inclinations of those of identifiable economic interest: when they meet together, even if only for merriment, they invariably end up in a scheme to defraud others.

It should not surprise us to find this correspondence between Smith's views and what we have identified as the problem of the price setter. As Lange made clear in the course of the Socialist Calculation Debate, the informed, rational planner and the freely competitive market will home in on the same set of prices. Introducing Smith into our schematic history of the search for a balance between fairness and objectivity in pricing, however, also means that we have moved beyond the Greek and Roman formulation of the problem. For them fairness, stemming naturally from the voluntariness of private exchanges of goods, was a given, and the practical problem was to find ways of ensuring an expression of that fairness in market prices. By the late eighteenth century the balance had shifted: a reasoned basis for the pricing of the goods (rather than fairness in their distribution) was the primary focus, and the fairness issue had come to be subsumed under the larger question of how to secure abundance.

In Smith's view of exchange and higgling, provided that individuals voluntarily choose to specialize, the market for talent works its product-increasing miracle and all may share in the larger product that will follow: "Among men . . . the most dissimilar geniuses are of use to one another; the different products of their respective talents, by the general disposition to truck, barter, and exchange, being brought, as it were, into a common stock, where every man may purchase whatever part of the produce of other men's talents he has occasion for" (*Wealth of Nations,* 1.2; Glasgow ed., 1:30). No question of equality here, but deprivation too is absent. Fairness in this context meant simply meeting the third condition above: excluding coercion in exchange, eliminating privilege, facilitating liberty in the allocation of resources, and thereby ensuring that prices would reflect measurable component elements, such as prime costs—a rationale for pricing which carried associated claims for efficiency and objectivity.

Three Meanings of Higgling

Merchants in the early modern period understood prime costs as materials plus ordinary charges such as transport, tolls, and, eventually, interest. But this applied only to ordinary (common) or easily substitutable goods. The artisan, it was allowed, charged on a somewhat different basis, "by reckoning the Cost of the Materials, with the Time of Art," as Nicolas Barbon put it (1690, 19–20). The "time of art," he further explained, means "the value of the Art, and the Skill of the Artists," that is, the contribution due to particular training and its application. That required a way to estimate economic rent, which is more problematic than dealing with ordinary costs. As Smith noted, speaking of how to reckon wages for "different sorts of hardship endured, and of ingenuity exercised": "it is not easy to find any accurate measure" of either (*Wealth* 1.5; Glasgow ed., 48). It is in just this context, as Vivienne Brown notes in her essay, that he introduces higgling. The needed measure is found, in a rough and ready but usable way, Smith allows, through the higgling and bargaining of the market (49).

Brown draws a distinction between two sorts of higgling. Higgling of the Smithian sort is a way through which an objective fact—here differences in training and ability—is made manifest in market exchange ratios (to provide a "rational," that is, objectively reasoned basis for price). The market outcome itself is "inevitable and necessary" in the sense that under competitive conditions prices must be congruent with relative prime (mostly labor) costs; hence the higgling is "theoretically immaterial as it does not affect the values of the final outcome." This finding is exactly in line with the focus on outcomes rather than processes that, as we noted earlier, characterizes modern neoclassical analysis, and not surprisingly Brown is able to offer quotes from Edgeworth and Marshall that show them supporting this position. Brown's second sort of higgling is, by contrast, a denial of the objective conditions of the market. It embraces all those forms of persuasion that are used to subvert "proper outcomes" to the *interests* of one party to a transaction.

Brown finds a parallel to the way these two sorts of higgling are regarded in economic discourse—the one appropriate to economists' concerns because it reflects the "objective conditions of the market" (if of merely heuristic value), the other not appropriate (but effective in moving the market away from its "true" outcome to some "false" one)—in the classical contrast between language as the means of conveying truth and language as the mode of persuasion.

Although our next paper comes out of chronological sequence, it continues Brown's theme of the role of language and offers a third sense of higgling. Michael Hutter argues that higgling is the noise of markets in action. Economists do not hear this noise, because they think and observe within the confines of equilibrium as their organizing principle (that is, within Brown's first sense of the term). Hutter argues that if economists were to conceptualize money as a communication medium, we should begin to hear and recognize the importance of higgling, for we would perceive money as the flow of language which makes communication (exchange) possible.

Hutter uses the texts of early twentieth-century German and Austrian economists to help him validate these ideas in terms of self-reference, self-reproduction, and self-observation. He offers a social theory about the importance of higgling and, more centrally, of the overwhelming role of money in any analysis of market exchange in which we could recognize higgling as "the central process by which a money economy comes about."

Brown's and Hutter's discussions of the relevance of language and its importance to exchange outcomes are made more concrete for us in Clark and Pinch's fascinating study (with which we end our volume) of modern-day market rhetoricians at work, in particular those known as "patter merchants." They bring to life what Locke may have had in mind when referring to "vulgar discourses," and interested readers may find comparable eighteenth-century examples of persuasion in the market in Mandeville—the interaction between a mercer and his lady customer as described in the "Essay on the Nature of Society" ([1714] 1924, 1:349–53)—and in Thomas Mortimer's *Every Man His Own Broker: Or, A*

Guide to Exchange Alley (1762, 72–79), where the patter of a stock jobber is reported.

Economic Order Supersedes Market Disorder

The contrast identified by Brown between persuasive discourse and truth telling, in which the former mode was disparaged, alerts us to a further shift that occurred in the eighteenth century. Locke, for example, representing the skeptics of persuasion and oratory, disparages "all the artificial and figurative application of words eloquence hath invented," not least the "obscurity, doubtfulness . . . [and] equivocation" practiced in the marketplace (Locke, *Essay,* cited by Brown). But whereas Locke derogates the language of public places, it was precisely by bringing transactions into a public arena that the Romans had thought to add a measure of objectivity to private notions of fairness. It is possible, however, that Locke was in part commenting on a growth of disreputable higgling in the markets he knew. In the Roman food auction, buyers and sellers confronted each other without middlemen intervening. In England from the mid-sixteenth century, and also in the France of Louis XIV and Louis XV, regulation of the grain trade became both extensive and quite complex, and much of the law had as its end the restraining of middlemen (Kaplan 1976; Thompson 1971).

Middlemen not only helped form a market but were in a position to forestall, engross, and regrate, as well as to buy by sample direct from the grower rather than in the open marketplace, where amounts and terms could be seen and controlled. In all these ways middlemen could and did interfere with market forces, preventing grain prices from reaching their "correct" level. Contemporaries in France often dubbed this sort of behavior "monopolizing"; and, as if to ratify Locke's concern, we also find in the English context a proclamation by the Exeter town clerk, dated 28 March 1795, forbidding "hucksters, higlers, and retailers" from participation in the corn market between the hours of 8 A.M. and noon (Thompson 1971, 84). Thompson argues that these attempts to control marketplace trading were already, by Adam Smith's time, being subverted by the economic forces of the "free market."

With Smith's elaboration of a "system of natural liberty," in which labor, capital, and land are free to shift to more productive uses and will do so unless hampered by laws based upon sectional interest, there was acquired an understanding of price as rational in the sense of being both efficient and objectively justified. Prices might also be social, consensual, fair in some sense, but this aspect began to take second place in the hierarchy of concerns. That altered balance, to which we already called attention, was facilitated by the positive public welfare implications of specialization and division of labor. The increased productivity stemming from specialization and exchange meant that all might benefit, with none in principle having to suffer loss. This did not eliminate the problem of just division of the gains from exchange, but it surely lessened the pressing need to resolve that issue for each and every particular market and transaction. Attention thus also shifted to the level of society as a whole—a level of thinking made acceptable, even to those such as Hume who were skeptical towards the idea of a social contract, by the notion that the gains from specialization and exchange are potentially available to all. Hence we find treatments of exchange and of pricing also being situated in a new discourse, about social and economic order. Two papers pick up on this further shift.

Margaret Schabas focuses on higgling in the sense of argument over the terms of an exchange, and suggests that higgling is a temporary phenomenon which arose when the institutions which regulated prices had broken down, and disappeared when the market economy prevailed. Her interest is in Hume and, more particularly, in those features of the spread of commerce that, to him, seemed conducive to economic and political order. The story she tells is one in which nonbarter exchange has become extensive; traders have both lowered the general level of prices and produced something like price uniformity (so higgling is redundant); money, like a vital spirit, has infused and nourished the body politic; there is a commitment to keeping promises, hence security of contracts and justice prevail, selfishness has waned, and social order is established. The primacy of the economic in this set of related conditions is striking, as is the strong presumption that various processes tend to orderly outcomes. Here, too, is a different sort of argument for the irrelevancy of higgling: it is merely a feature of the transition to a moneyed and market economy and of the process by which actual market phenomena come into conformity with the natural economic order. That process in turn depends on the presence and active expression of civility, trust, and consent as epitomized in commercial agreements. (Such elements appear again among the norms of buying behavior in retail stores as described later by our resident sociologists, Clark and Pinch.)

Market Order and Efficient Prices

Evelyn Forget shows J.-B. Say to have entirely absorbed the sort of reasoning that impressed Hume and Smith. Prices, Say believed, will be objective if left to themselves. That is to say, they would then fully reflect the operation of allocative efficiency, with its incentives and constraints. Interference with these incentives and constraints by legislators was necessarily misguided, and "disequilibrium" trade was invariably associated with social disorder. This was the opposite side of the coin chosen and polished by Hume, for whom economic order was a precondition for social and political order. Say, somewhat in the manner of Smith, warns instead of what may be expected if the economic order is tampered with by legislators. Forget shows how Say, perhaps anticipating Quetelet, elected to dispense with real people in actual markets, in favor of a representative ("mean") agent and a description of fortunes that might be reduced to a normal distribution.

Michael White's paper by contrast focuses on a late nineteenth-century dissident, William Thornton. Thornton attacked exactly this neglect by Say and others of the process of price formation in real markets. He drew attention to phenomena such as multiple prices and unsatisfied demands at the going price, insisting that the law of supply and demand, and market clearing, do not always obtain and are therefore not essential and ineluctible forces. Thornton's, however, was a lone stand against the mechanistic model of demand and supply determinants of price, which encroached steadily and received ever more finely specified articulation. As that model increased its hold, so higgling and market processes decreased and soon ended up marginalized out of scientific economics.

If Market Prices Are Efficient, What Should Their Level Be?

To recap, our stylized history to this point runs as follows. The Greeks institutionalized the notion that exchanges of goods that are voluntarily undertaken must be fair. The Roman public auction, conducted under official supervision, imparted a sense of objectivity to the prices agreed to by private transactors. Could the going market price be relied upon to convey something too that was rational? In a partial way this problem could be, and probably was, addressed by making sure that market prices reflected normal or average conditions, and seeing to it that no built-in distortions (privilege, for example) altered normal prices away from costs. The rationality problem was more fully solved in the eighteenth century, with the recognition that under a regime of freely transferable resources, prevailing prices would have to reflect allocative efficiency. By the nineteenth century, efficiency prices became the norm, and when the system of natural liberty was at one with economic markets, higgling, along with all other actual market institutions and higgling processes that belonged to the level of the empirical, became epistemologically as well as methodologically irrelevant.

Nevertheless, these efficiency prices did not solve all the questions; there was still the regulators' problem. Michael Lawlor's paper returns us to that subtheme: the question of what is the appropriate level for the price of particular products seems to press for attention at various points in the history, even if the dominant concern is to understand prices— relative prices—as related to efficiency. The reason for this is obvious in the case of basic necessities, which is where discussions of the "just price" notion are usually located. But some of the factors that were ob- served to play a role in grain prices, for example, such as rumor and panic, could be observed also to affect share prices. One concern over this in seventeenth-century Holland was that if speculators deliberately played on such factors they could cause harm to others. Lawlor adds another dimension. He shows Keynes's approach to financial markets evolving from an early Marshallian disinterest in higgling—it could add nothing to the more fundamental forces determining equilibrium—to the mature conviction that efficiency considerations do not tell us at what level asset prices will settle. This latter position is of course familiar as Keynes's insistence that the rate of interest is determined by a fundamen- tal psychological factor, liquidity preference. Lawlor, however, presents fresh evidence on the source of the conviction, suggesting that Keynes's shift to a thoroughgoing acceptance of the importance of market psy- chology rested less on his grapplings with economic theory and rather more on his reflections on his personal experiences, often rude, in the financial markets. Between 1914 and the early 1930s Keynes switched from a belief in stockbrokers as price-smoothing market makers to view- ing them as pawns or at least willing participants in a game of chance rigged by people in the know. All the ethical concerns of the seventeenth- century Dutch here reemerge, unresolved. If *mutual* gain in exchange is possible with goods, shares still seemed disturbingly different.

American Economists Recover Fairness and Market Process

It is among American economists of the late nineteenth and early twentieth centuries that we find some of the most explicit discussions and analyses of higgling. Surprisingly, even two Americans with such strong credentials for neoclassicism as John Bates Clark and Frank Knight figure in this history, along with their less orthodox countrymen Veblen and Commons. They shared a concern for ethical issues in the process of exchange, and in their work we can trace attempts to recover the Greek concern with fairness in exchange.

J. B. Clark's main concern about fairness was located in how the gains from trade are divided. This division was discussed not in terms of the outcome but in terms of the social process by which the division is decided. In Clark's account, the outcome of higgling depended on the particularities of the individuals involved and the context in which the exchange took place. Mary S. Morgan's analysis shows that for Clark, the important elements which determined fairness in the process of exchange (and so in the division of the gains) included not only familiar conditions known or hinted at earlier, such as the existence of other buyers and sellers in the market (later to be codified in the conditions for perfect competition; see Stigler 1957), but other important social dimensions such as the relative economic power of the individuals, the context of exchange, and the changing customary mores and laws surrounding any exchange of goods and services.

Malcolm Rutherford's account of Veblen reflects both the similarities of analysis between the early Clark and Veblen and also the gap that divided them. They shared a common historical analysis in which fairness was associated with the personal relations of the individuals in exchange, and Veblen's account of the "bargain" seems to owe much to Clark's earlier account of how unequal power relations subvert the benign outcomes of classical economics. Yet Veblen's cynical and pessimistic account of the predatory nature of modern economic processes of exchange was far removed from Clark's optimistic portrayal of the moral elements which will ultimately redeem economic man.

Fairness in exchange is revealed, in Morgan's account of Clark and his contemporaries in the 1880s and 1890s, not as an unobtainable ideal but as the practical aim of good government. The regulator's role was not to fix the fair price, but to assure fairness through legal requirements to ensure equality in the conditions of exchange or to ensure fairness in individual cases of higgling through the process of expert arbitration (rather as Lowry suggested for earlier times, and Edgeworth for modern times). As Rutherford's account shows, Commons believed that the state—or the law—acts as an explicit (or implicit) party in all transactions, both in enforcing fairness through the "rules of bargaining" and by setting the legal rights for the transfer of ownership. Evolving rules, either explicitly or implicitly, either legal or customary, are an important part of the process in Commons's account of exchange.

Commons's innovation was to take the analysis of fairness further, by making the transaction the unit of analysis in order to categorize and systematically examine the different sorts of power relationships involved in the higgling process. Within this context, he also developed an explicit account of the "negotiational psychology" of exchange relations far removed from the simple pain-pleasure utility-maximizing psychology of exchangers in marginal economics. His rejection of the narrowness of behavioral content in the orthodox accounts of exchange by rational economic man was shared, not only with Clark and Veblen who came before him, but with Knight after him.

Ross Emmett's account of Knight makes explicit his contrast between the rational economic man of the exchange relations in neoclassical theory—portrayed as a "slot machine" man—with the real economic man who is a "good sport" game player, facing uncertainty with skill and chance yet still playing within the rules of a game. Where Veblen and Commons had looked back to history for validation of their analyses, and to the slow, grinding changes in the law or to the just arbitrator for their appeal to fairness in practice, Knight appealed to a contemporary portrait of American characteristics. His good sport was close to Clark's moral man in personifying the ethics of competition. Being a good sport involved being a better man: learning the game, developing the rules of the game, and making the game better.

These American accounts of fairness in exchange share some fundamentals. They all focus on how the higgling process and conditions of an exchange determine the fairness of the outcome, and they depend on economic man as a well-rounded individual for the process to have the desired results. Though grounded in individualism, all these accounts portray the individual in the social realm, interacting with other individuals and the rules which make economic society cohere. The higgling process may have fair outcomes, but only if many conditions surrounding market exchange are met, or if regulations and social mores act to replicate those conditions.

The late nineteenth-century American writers aimed to create a social science based on the social realm and located their accounts of higgling within that context. Knight continued the tradition, in his writings on ethics. He saw both the possibilities and the limitations of economic *science* limited to the mechanical model. In his idealized utility-maximizing theory he portrayed exchange as a meeting between two preprogrammed slot machines in which prices and quantities are fixed (unless the machines break down!) and higgling is irrelevant. That was just one extreme; but it was also the approach that came to dominate twentieth-century economic thinking about exchange.

The Nature of Exchange:
In the Wild and in the Laboratory

Disciplinary Distinctions

The meeting of two slot machines, the economic account of exchange offered by Knight, is at one end of a continuum describing how individuals interact in a market as discussed within the various social sciences. At the other end, we might place the accounts of the anthropologists, who describe and analyze markets out in the wild. Anne Mayhew's discussion of the differences in the disciplinary concerns of anthropologists compared to those of economists focuses in part on the issue of process. Each group is interested in process, but economists tend to be concerned with preconditions and outcomes, and the list of characteristics which alter the latter are severely restricted. For anthropologists the list is open-ended, for it is the characteristics of the exchangers, and the process and context of the exchanges, which form the substance of their disciplinary discussions.

Thus both the market*place* and the higgling *process* feature as important elements in anthropological accounts of market exchange. Economists by contrast are concerned exclusively with markets abstracted from place, in which buyers and sellers do not actually seem to meet face to face. Here Mayhew raises the issues of standardization of quantity and quality, which seem to be preconditions for "modern" economic markets and, she suggests, also for the development of modern economic thinking too (a point which echoes Schabas's account of Hume's eighteenth-century economics). In the sense that once quality and quantities are standardized, all higgling becomes an argument over price, we at least have a reason for understanding why these other dimensions of exchange bargaining do not figure in economists' discussions of retail markets, though, no doubt, they do still figure largely in active intercompany higgling over the terms of contracts.

Mayhew recounts one clash between the anthropologists and the economists, over the portrayal of the individual: Are the stylized "individuals" that appear in modern neoclassical economic accounts of markets more rounded, because they only incorporate general features of humankind, than the highly specific and fully characterized individuals who appear in the anthropologists' accounts of market activity? Philip Mirowski's essay takes up another interaction between the two disciplines, this time over the forms of exchange. Here the continuum focuses not on the individual but on the meaning of exchange, ranging from the utilitarian economic notion of "pure trade" through to the anthropologists' discussion of the gift, or "something for nothing."

Whereas anthropologists have looked for the meaning of exchange in form, and seen the latter as a reflection of the social structure which unites the two parties and determines the extent and manner of higgling, economists have looked for the meaning of exchange within their dominant concern with the source of economic value. These two seemingly incommensurable interpretations have in fact been the cause of some not entirely fruitful interactions between the two fields over the last century, some of which Mirowski relates. For our purposes, however, they extend our questions about the importance of social relations in exchange. From the myth of Prometheus's tricking Zeus (reported by Lowry) to Commons's problem of power relations in exchange (discussed by Rutherford), many of our contributors recognize the role of social relations in determining exchange outcomes and in whether and how higgling is conducted. This is made quite explicit, if not central, in the anthropological literature on exchange which Mirowski discusses.

Laboratory Experiences

Two papers dealing with practical social science studies of markets complete this collection. One, by Robert Leonard, discusses the history of modern experimental work in the laboratory, contrasting the studies of psychologists and economists. Here we find another reflection of the open-ended list, and the concern with process, seen in Mayhew's anthropologists, but now also evident in Leonard's psychologists. By contrast, Colin Clark and Trevor Pinch's laboratory, as befits sociologists who observe and sometimes participate, is out in the wilds of the late twentieth-century street markets.

Leonard's paper continues the theme raised by Lowry in our first paper, but here we are given the nitty-gritty of experimental economics to contend with. Experimental subjects, even when they are "trained" economics students, seem determined to raise doubts about economists' stories of rational and efficient market exchange and behavior. Often they prefer to go for fairness in division, even when higgling (in this literature, "bargaining") should beckon them on to selfishness. The game theories of the current generation of economic scientists seem less adept at capturing economic behavior in the laboratory than the gamesmanship that Knight envisaged as endemic in real economic behavior.

In his interesting comparison between economists' and psychologists' experiments on bargaining (higgling) behavior, Leonard points to the difficulty the "open-ended" list of characteristics holds for the psychologists' experiments, compared to the "successful" narrowing strategy of the economists' concern with preconditions and outcomes. On the other hand, economists are confounded by those variables in the list: some are not supposed to be important (according to economic theory) but turn out to be so in the laboratory; others are supposed to be important (according to theory) but turn out not to be. Despite their best attempts, economists have had to admit to cultural or social norms in bargaining behavior and in determining outcomes, in order to understand their own experimental results (or else retreat to another experimental design).

Our final paper is the nearest we can get to providing the reader with a live example of market higgling. Clark and Pinch's interactional study of street market selling techniques gives us a direct report from their "laboratory." The authors provide a wonderful account of "pitching" in English street markets, which differs from "higgling" in that the seller determines the price and controls the exchange situation through clever rhetoric and a reliance on (and perhaps manipulation of) social norms of behavior in the buyers. This is patently different from their "higgling" example drawn from the interaction of a tourist and a street seller in India, though both still rely on rhetorical skills and social norms. Their comparative analysis of market "pitching," "higgling," and normal retail "buying" provides a fascinating insight into the differences in social norms involved in these three forms of exchange interaction and, at the same time, into the way sociologists approach an analysis of higgling. In this analysis, issues of fairness and rational economic pricing are both, *apparently*, equally superfluous. Bargaining follows set patterns, language is important (but is remarkably stable), and higgling *is* the process by which a price is agreed upon.

Conclusion

Our account of the papers in this volume has been couched for the most part in terms of a history of economics pulled between the competing demands of fairness and efficiency pricing. And now, it seems, anthropology, psychology, and sociology, between them, deal with many other aspects which determine exchange prices. But this is a recent development; economists too have concerned themselves with these over the years. The papers we have discussed here touch often upon the role of the social (conventions, norms of behavior, and other more obvious institutional factors such as legal systems), as well as the role of the human (morality, ethics, personal variety, and the well-rounded person) and of course the interpersonal element (power, strategic behavior in exchange, and so on). It may well be that the professionalization and separation of the social sciences at the end of the nineteenth century is in part responsible for economists' rather narrow current conception of the role of higgling in exchange relations.

In part, also, the fairness versus efficiency dualism is itself located in our modern understanding of economics. Fairness might have been the guiding principle of the economic analysis of exchange, and the rationale for efficient division might then be based on how far fairness was achieved, or perhaps measured by various different notions of fairness. As it is, we have the reverse: efficiency is the leading notion, and because of its primary position, we rationalize and measure the outcomes as more or less fair according to how far they are from efficient outcomes.

References

Barbon, Nicolas. [1690] 1905. *A Discourse of Trade*. Facsimile edition. Baltimore: Lord Baltimore Press.

David, Paul A. 1975. *Technical Choice, Innovation, and Economic Growth: Essays on American and British Experience in the Nineteenth Century*. New York: Cambridge University Press.

———. 1986. Understanding the Economics of QWERTY: The Necessity of History. In *Economic History and the Modern Economist*, edited by W. N. Parker. Oxford: Blackwell.

———. 1991. The Hero and the Herd in Technological History: Reflections on Thomas Edison and the Battle of the Systems. In *Favorites of Fortune: Technology, Growth, and Economic Development since the Industrial Revolution*, edited by Patrice Higonnet, David S. Landes, and Henry Rosovsky. Cambridge: Harvard University Press.

Greif, Avner. 1989. Reputation and Coalitions in Medieval Trade: Evidence on the Maghribi Traders. *Journal of Economic History* 49:857–82.

Greif, Avner, Paul Milgrom, and Barry Weingast. 1990. The Merchant Guild as a Nexus of Contracts. Mimeo. Stanford University.

Kaplan, Steven L. 1976. *Bread, Politics and Political Economy in the Reign of Louis XV*. 2 vols. The Hague: Nijhoff.

Langlois, Richard N. 1986. *Economics as a Process: Essays in the New Institutional Economics*. Cambridge: Cambridge University Press.

Lucas, Robert E., Jr. 1987. Adaptive Behavior and Economic Theory. In *Rational Choice: The Contrast between Economics and Psychology*, edited by Robin M. Hogarth and Melvin W. Reder. Chicago: University of Chicago Press.

Malynes, Gerard de. [1662] 1981. *Consuetudo, vel Lex Mercatoria: Or, the Ancient Law-Merchant*. 3d ed. London: F. Redmayne, 1685. Facsimile reprint, Oxford: Professional Books Ltd.

Mandeville, Bernard. [1714] 1924. *The Fable of the Bees: Or, Private Vices, Publick Benefits*. Edited by F. B. Kaye. 2 vols. Oxford: Clarendon Press. Facsimile reprint, Indianapolis: Liberty Press, 1988.

Milgrom, Paul R., Douglass C. North, and Barry R. Weingast. 1990. The Role of Institutions in the Revival of Trade: The Law Merchant, Private Judges, and the Champagne Fairs. *Economics and Politics* 2.1 (March): 1–23.

Mirowski, Philip. 1989a. *More Heat than Light: Economics as Social Physics, Physics as Nature's Economics*. Cambridge: Cambridge University Press.

———. 1989b. 'Tis a Pity Econometrics Isn't an Empirical Endeavor: Mandelbrot, Chaos, and the Noah and Joseph Effects. *Ricerche Economiche* 43:76–99.

Mortimer, Thomas. 1762. *Every Man His Own Broker: Or, A Guide to Exchange-Alley*. 5th ed. London: S. Hooper.

North, Douglass C. 1990. *Institutions, Institutional Change and Economic Performance*. Cambridge: Cambridge University Press.

Smith, Adam. [1776] 1926. *An Inquiry into the Nature and Causes of the Wealth of Nations.* Glasgow Edition of *The Works and Correspondence of Adam Smith,* vol. 2. Edited by R. H. Campbell, A. S. Skinner, and W. B. Todd. Facsimile edition, Indianapolis: Liberty Press, 1981.

Stigler, George J. 1957. Perfect Competition, Historically Contemplated. *Journal of Political Economy* 65:1–17.

Thompson, E. P. 1971. The Moral Economy of the English Crowd in the Eighteenth Century. *Past and Present* 50:76–136.

Part 1   Fairness, Efficiency, and Language in the Analysis of Higgling

The Market as a Distributive and Allocative System: Its Legal, Ethical, and Analytical Evolution

S. Todd Lowry

The search for evidence of the origins of modern ideas about the character and justice of market exchange requires a careful examination of the socioeconomic setting from which these ideas emerged. In addition, special attention must be given to the problems that policies or practices were presuming to solve. Considering the intensity of the flowering of naturalism in the late seventeenth century and the eighteenth, when modern market theory emerged—natural rights, natural reason, natural law, and natural price—it is easy to understand the strong temptation to approach ancient accounts of allocative processes with an eye to discovering the initial stages of natural processes.

It is, of course, this anachronistic temptation that we must systematically eschew by examining the accounts and policies from antiquity and extant primitive cultures in terms of their own milieux. As we seek to understand the specific elements in the chain of economic and legal ideas that extend from the ancient Mediterranean to modern Western thought, some new insights may become apparent. In this context it is very important to emphasize that the overt agenda in this presentation focuses on the role of human ideas, customs, legal institutions, and analytic structures in the development of legal and economic processes. We must, of course, concede the complex interaction between the development of ideas and the crystallization of behavior patterns into customs and institutions. Most would agree, however, that allocative and exchange activities fall into the category of *folkways*—to use a sociological distinction—and the influence of ideas in framing cultural perspectives on these matters must be contrasted with the naturalistic or alleged empiricist search for material conditions in history and among primitives that generated these patterns of social organization, giving substance to abstract principles of natural economic law.

The most fundamental ideas that we find in antiquity relevant to the emergence of modern market theory relate to the notion of a pervasive rationality and the importance of voluntary choice. While the first of these elements, a pervasive rationality, has an intriguing intellectual influence that is important for understanding modern equilibrium theory, we can only generalize it briefly before directing our attention to the elements of volition and choice that are central to both ancient and modern concepts of the higgling and bargaining process.

Social correlations with mathematics have been part of a continuous line of Western thought since Pythagoras presumed to project his expertise in arithmetic and geometry into his political regime in Crotona in the sixth century B.C. The pedigree of our rationalistic tradition was aptly generalized by Isaiah Berlin, attributing it to Pythagoras and Plato, whose ideas he framed in terms of three "unquestioned dogmas":

(a) that to all genuine questions there is (only) one true answer . . . all others being . . . false, and that this applies to questions of conduct . . . , to practice, and . . . theory . . . to questions of value no less than those of fact;

(b) that the true answers to such questions are in principle knowable;

(c) that these true answers . . . cannot be incompatible . . . ; that together these true answers must form a harmonious whole. (1991, 209)

This rationalistic absolutism in Plato was accompanied by a nearly theological commitment to the possibility of efficient decision making and order. It was clearly coordinated with the powers and policies of the great administrative empires in Mesopotamia and Egypt. These absolutist empires aggregated and redistributed vast resources, human and material, with systematized or bureaucratized patterns of rationing or allocation that gave substance to the concept of rationality (Lowry 1987, 23ff.). However, we find the framing of the concept of voluntary choice emerging from a different and probably more primitive context that provided an arena for the play of pure rationality.

Divide and Choose

In his *Theogony* (555–60), a seventh-century B.C. recounting of Greek mythology, Hesiod set forth a structure for formalizing volition and choice. The titan Prometheus, patron of mankind, out of a desire to match wits with Zeus, the king of the Gods, divided a slaughtered ox with him. The account is inconsistent on a number of points, suggesting the braiding together of several tales. Nevertheless, an ancient tradition from the earliest stages of social and economic organization is quite clear (Lowry 1991a; 1987, 125ff.). To appreciate the setting of this story about structured choice, the basic passage should be read as a whole. Prometheus,

> eager to try his wits, cut up
> a great ox, and set it before Zeus,
>> to see if he could outguess him.
> He took the meaty parts and the inwards
>> thick with fat and set them
> before men, hiding them away
>> in an ox's stomach,
> but the white bones of the ox he arranged,
>> with careful deception,
> inside a concealing fold of white fat,
>> and set it before Zeus.

Although the myth has some difficulty rationalizing Zeus's alleged omniscience with his apparent poor choice, the presumption that this distributive technique had to be honored seemed to be above question. There was also some room for higgling or manipulation implicit in the division of a nonhomogeneous asset such as a slaughtered animal, despite its bilateral symmetry.

In the mythic presentation of the system, there is a subplot indicating that Zeus was fooled into taking a portion composed of the major bones covered with some layers of fat, but he nevertheless honored the distribution, and it was enforced as a binding commitment in temple sacrifice reflected in both Greek and Judaic traditions. The bones and fat being flammable, Zeus's or Jehovah's portion was sent up to him as a burnt offering:

> Ever since that time the races of mortal men
>> on earth have burned
> the white bones to the immortals
>> on the smoky altars.

Aside from its religious implications, both the abstract principle and the functional use of this economic technique were proliferated.

We find in Aesop's *Fables* a verification of the utility of this division system to settle a joint hunting enterprise, replete with a wry commentary on how raw power overrules the customs of fair distribution. It seems that a lion, a donkey, and a fox were successful in a joint hunt. The lion ordered the donkey to divide the kill into three portions. Upon seeing the three equal portions, the lion became enraged and killed the donkey. He then ordered the fox to divide the game into two portions. The fox divided the meat into one very large portion and one very small one. As the lion chose the larger portion (the lion's share), he asked the fox, "Who taught you to divide things so well?" The fox replied, "What happened to the donkey" (trans. Hanford 1954, 13).

The ingenuity of this bit of social or economic technology for avoiding disputes in two-party distributions is readily apparent. Within the larger society, where occasional or temporary nonfamily common ventures were developed, a system for negotiating a mutually satisfactory division of goods would be needed. The abstract principle is quite obvious. The dividers are committed to the fairness of their division. If they honestly make the two piles of meat equal from their own perspective, they cannot complain about the unfairness of the residual portion when the other party makes the first choice. By the same token, with access to perfect information, the chooser cannot complain about the outcome, since the chooser has the freedom to inspect and choose either pile, thus implementing the purest of rational choices—evaluating the ratio of one pile of meat to the other, just as the divider did. The parties cannot complain without each asserting their own folly or frustrated connivance within the context of the broader socially prescribed or privately arranged joint venture.

Inheritance, Booty, and Antidosis

Two very important distributive problems in the ancient world drew on the tradition of implicit fairness in separating the divider from the chooser. The first of these was dividing inheritances among two or more heirs. The second was dividing booty, from piratical raids as well as major military ventures.

There are references to the "divide and choose" technique having been used in ancient Near Eastern cultures as well as in the Greek tradition. If there were only two heirs, the routine could follow the meat-division pattern; but in the case of several heirs, one, possibly the eldest, could divide and choose last, or an outside arbitrator would make the division and the heirs would choose in order of age. A problem arises in this type of division, however, that is also implicit in the original meat division. Unless the assets being divided are absolutely uniform, such as grain or money, there is room for some subtle bargaining under the umbrella of this apparently direct distribution system. If, as in the Promethean division, it is known that Zeus had a high preference for large bones and fat—a point made by some scholars—and that Prometheus, representing mankind, preferred the lean meat, then the division could be loaded in favor of these subjective preferences and a subtle form of exchange would be administratively promoted. This system of division of inheritance, by its very nature, seems to have resulted in no notable legal wrangles that produced a famous oration, but Finley (1951, 66–67) records an estate settled by this technique.

The distribution of booty also presents a complex valuation problem. It was one of the most important sources of nonagricultural income in antiquity. The spoils of war had to be parceled out on some basis of equality among men of common rank, with double measures for conspicuous valor and appropriate tithes to the temple and king. How goods were distributively allocated among the troops is a matter of speculation, but one can envision a primitive auction system in which shares were proffered and volitional acceptance was relied upon to minimize dissatisfaction. At the higher level, where two cities were participating in a joint campaign, a common practice was for the total booty to be divided into two portions by one city, and the other to choose. In one instance, captives that were to be enslaved or ransomed were gathered in one place and material goods in another; representatives of the other city chose which they wanted (Pritchett 1971, 83; Lowry 1987, 131–39). However, even here, the decision was apparently loaded by the differential potential of one city or the other to make optimum use of slaves as opposed to household plunder.

Finally, the most intriguing implementation of this theoretical perspective was in the civic resort to mandatory support of public functions where reliance on pure philanthropy had failed. This amounted to the system of private taxation followed by Athens during its heyday in the fifth and fourth centuries B.C. In a tradition paralleling the "potlatch" of the Pacific Northwest Indians, public festivals and athletic games were customarily sponsored and financed by the wealthiest citizen of the city. As these major events became increasingly burdensome, it was necessary for city officials to designate "the wealthiest citizen of the state" to finance specific events each year. To neutralize the protestations of poverty with which many designees responded to the "honor," a system called *antidosis* was provided that permitted anyone designated to put on the festivals to escape the responsibility by identifying some other citizen who was wealthier than himself. To successfully implement this defensive claim, he must offer to trade all his property with the proposed substitute (Andreades 1933, 293–94; Lowry 1987, 284 n. 11, for other citations). Under these circumstances, if the unhappy initial designee was actually the wealthiest man in the city, any other citizen he tapped would accept the challenge and trade property with him, accepting also the duty to perform the service out of his increased wealth. If, however, he did not want to change property, he would have to accept the burden and finance the festivals out of his own assets. The system eventually became too cumbersome, and people had to resort to the courts for comparative evaluations (Demosthenes 42).

These procedures evolved in significant sectors of ancient life involving major assets. Some ingenuity in solving valuation problems by structuring nominal voluntarism and individual choice was demonstrated. They dealt with wealth that was not easily evaluated in an economy where markets were not as intricately involved in everyday life as today, and where wide variations in handmade goods made the idea of a general market price somewhat elusive. Valuations could best be handled when turned back on subjective choice in some form or other, and a volitional commitment was considered a validation of the justice of the decision or allocation.

It may be of some interest to note that aspects of this form of higgling are preserved in many modern partnership agreements. The arrangement is that if either party wishes to dissolve the partnership, he or she must set a value on a half-interest in the enterprise. The other partner then has the option of buying out the dissenter at his or her named price, or selling to the dissenter at that price.

At the political level, in the mid-seventeenth century, James Harrington drew on this principle of "divide and choose" as the basis for part of his political theory. He argued for a bicameral legislative system with a senate "dividing" or allocating and a popular house "choosing." He illustrated the virtues of this process with an outline of the nuances involved when two little girls undertake to divide a cake, one dividing and the other choosing (Harrington 1965, 46–48).

Can One Be Voluntarily Unjust to Oneself?

The theoretical implications of this principle, namely that what someone voluntarily chooses to do could not be defined as an injustice to that person, became a critical tenet in Athenian philosophy and jurisprudence. In Plato, it evolved into an argument that people would not behave in a manner contrary to their own best interest, except through ignorance. This led to a rationalization for respect for authority, illustrated by the role of the medical doctor and the ship captain (*Republic* 6.488; Protagoras 358b–c; Lowry 1987, 165). Plato wanted to make moral values, as well as efficiency, matters for rational expertise. Thus the ship captain should decide where the passengers should go as well as how best to get there. This attitude was extended further into a theory that no person would damage the harmony of his or her soul or inner self by immoral or inefficient actions—thus laying a foundation for our tradition of unregulated professional responsibility (*Republic* 4.442–43d–e; Lowry 1991b). The ultimate point is that when two or more parties come together as part of a mutually beneficial process, the fair allocation of the benefits of the union can be conceived as a rationally knowable matter, best administered by an expert. In her contribution to this volume, Mary Morgan presents John Bates Clark's formulation that a zone of moral discretion and guidance is retained within the family core of a community, with rational negotiations applying to the more distant social relationships. There is some parallelism between this view and the more Platonic view of Immanuel Kant, who took the position that within a zone or arena of individual control, free will and pure moral rationality could be exercised (Berlin 1991, 217; Kant 1990, 50–57). Kant's treatment of "a realm," in which free will, action, morality, and rationality dominate, perpetuates an individualistic zone of internal debate that obviates interpersonal negotiations or higgling in the achieving of rational conclusions. This concept of a zone of free will and choice in social interactions must be separated as applicable to expert administrators on the one hand and free participants on the other. Under the assumption of a value-free rationality, their optimum positions would not differ.

However, we see variations on the latter view expressed in the ideas of Frank Knight, who came from philosophy to economics. In his paper later in this volume, Ross Emmett explains Knight's view that sportsmanship participates in the interaction between parties in the zone of choice and decision making, avoiding a natural mechanical or rational market process. The question of rationality in the Platonic tradition is implicit in the issue of whether human interactions can be analyzed as "game theoretic" or whether individuals tend to "play fair" according to rules (see Leonard, this volume). These discussions echo issues raised in antiquity in struggling to distinguish between the level of negotiating, that is, higgling, that takes place in political interactions and in personal distributions and exchanges. The way in which the principle of voluntary choice became embedded in the legal tradition and eventually into the legal treatment of sales agreements is revealing.

The thesis that a voluntary choice could not give rise to an injustice to the chooser appeared in Athenian tort law in the latter half of the fifth century B.C. It was not, however, limited by modern jurisprudential distinctions between forms of action. The classic issue was presented in a formal study piece, the second of the *Tetralogies* of Antiphon, in which a set of four speeches was given to illustrate ways of arguing a case (Sprague 1972, III(i)6, III(iv)3; Lowry 1987, 197, 310 n. 52). In that case a boy ran across the practice field into the path of a thrown javelin and was killed. One line of analysis of this incident was that a person is absolutely responsible for the results of his or her acts, and the killing of someone constitutes an injustice to that person. The counter-argument was that if someone voluntarily does something that results in his or her own death, there is no injustice to that person and no liability. One cannot voluntarily do an injustice to oneself. The issue is the point of departure for analyses of culpability, contributory negligence, and duress. In regard to this latter element, the limits of exchange were laid down in a story recounted in Xenophon's romanticized biography of Cyrus the Great. As a boy, Cyrus was allowed to judge disputes among his playmates as training for his adult life. A dispute came before him in which a tall boy with a short tunic had forcibly traded tunics with a short boy with a long one. Cyrus ruled that since they were consequently both better off with properly fitting tunics as a result of the exchange, there was no injustice done. He was reprimanded by his tutor because the exchange was not voluntary, which made it unjust (Xenophon *Cyropaedia* 1.3.15–18).

The high point of the implementation of this principle of voluntary choice in the analysis of exchange is found in Aristotle's *Nichomachean Ethics* (5.5). The general awareness that trade in the agora is between individuals who respectively place a lesser value on what they offer than on what they receive is amply documented in literary references. In law, then, any trade voluntarily entered into is prima facie just to both parties, since no injustice was done. Since this was a principle that applied to any "isolated exchange," it did not constitute a market theory, but rather a theory of individual exchanges whether they occurred in the public marketplace or elsewhere. The problem arose when a jurist or ethicist attempted to distinguish between the mutual benefits of exchange that drew parties together for trade and the conflicting interests that arose from the distribution or allocation of this mutual gain from exchange. This distribution tended to be settled by higgling or by judicial arbitration.

Exchange: Process, Voluntarism, and Arbitration

To understand how a theory of market process grew out of the principles of isolated individual exchanges, we must consider the origin of a concept of interactive process in the political arena that was peculiar to the Greek and Roman heritage. It is embedded in the vitality of the tradition of the *polis,* or community, as a participative decision-making body with special reference to its assembly in the Greek agora or Roman forum. These open areas served as the political center of the community, where debate and consensus building were recognized as a dynamic process generating stability and unanimity. Simultaneously, goods had to be brought to this central point to be taxed at a percentage of estimated value by officials such as the Agoranomoi and Metronomoi (Stanley 1979). Private transactions, therefore, took place in the setting of a public arena that provided a sense of publicly recognized value combined with an endorsement of individual voluntarism in exchange. The image of a bargaining process was clearly framed in the tradition of public debate and, at the individual level, in the dialectic of argument in the law courts, where contending sides approached justice, and rhetoric anticipated many modern economic nuances (Lowry 1987, 139).

The mathematical dyad designed to approach irrational numbers had even been drawn upon to support this notion of interaction. Dyads, made up of Eudoxan number ladders, closing on the square roots of 2, 3, 5, etc., and the better known Fibonacci series (1, 2, 3, 5, 8, 13 . . . in which fractions composed of consecutive numbers in the cumulative series are alternately "a little more and a little less" but always approaching the irrational "golden mean," approximately 0.618) were an important dynamic image in a rationalistic tradition (Lowry 1969; Thompson 1929).

It was this mathematical tradition that François Quesnay drew upon in his less well known mathematical work, in which he introduced the term *tâtonnement* into French economic discourse (Bae 1992). Philip Wicksteed, a classicist before becoming an economist, also drew on the dyadic image of "a little more and a little less," as does an anthropological writer (Jonathan Parry) cited by Mirowski (this volume).

In tracing the evolution of ideas about subjective interactions over exchange (higgling), it is clear that transactions were primarily analyzed as individual occurrences. This was implicit in the types of cases that gave rise to disputes that required formal resolution. Under Greek law, no sale was just unless voluntary. This meant that up to the moment of execution of the sale, when property changed ownership, a party could decide that the transaction was not advantageous and repudiate it. This made contracts—commitments to execute a sale at some future time—unenforceable and made precise individual economic planning impossible in the absence of direct personal ownership of all relevant assets. It was left to Roman law, with its development of enforceable contracts, to make an objective notion of market price important in evaluating the justice of an individual contractual commitment. In Greek law, if a party was unhappy with the intended transaction, it could be repudiated up to the point of consummation. After the transaction was executed, then fraud or duress were needed to overturn the presumption of volition in the completed exchange. In a voluntary exchange, one could not be unjust to oneself, given free choice.

Nevertheless the Greeks' analytic ability led them to recognize that there is mutual benefit in exchange, and even though both parties voluntarily entered into the transaction, one party may have benefited excessively compared to the other. Does equity demand the equal distribution of the excess derived from the mutual benefits of exchange or other interactions such as partnership ventures? The mathematical dyad and tâtonnement suggest that free bargaining will come to rest at a halfway point, and the principle of "divide and choose" embraced a format for the justice of a negotiated equality of portions. The problem was the difficulty of formulating the "two-phase" aspect of isolated exchanges which were dealt with as individual cases or controversies in the legal system. The willingness to make the deal for mutual benefit means that the transaction is fundamentally fair. The bargaining over the surplus or mutual benefit may result in a skewed "distribution" of "the benefits of the bargain" that may justify "rectification" as a matter of equity (Lowry 1969).

There is an implication that exchanges were evaluated as joint ventures with the obligation to share equally the "benefits of the bargain," in the tradition of the joint hunt and consequent meat division. At least this was the premise in the formally organized partnership venture of antiquity and the Middle Ages that was at the heart of much commercial activity and produced a significant body of records of mercantile transactions.

The dominant commercial organization in the Mediterranean region from very early times was a kind of partnership in which one party put up the capital and the other provided the trading expertise and embarked upon the venture. With such obviously incommensurable contributions, how should the profits be divided at the end of the venture? I would contend that the most plausible explanation of the standard rule is that tradition dominated. The initial arrangement was separated from the issue of bargaining over the division of the profits (that is, the benefits of the hunt). Fairness would dictate an equal sharing of the profits based upon the premise of a common participative venture. This basic system was crystallized in Roman law as *societas* and had Judaic and Muslim forms. As the *commenda* contract, it was used across southern medieval Europe, perpetuating the distinction between basic commitment and division of profits (Pryor 1977). Although Byzantine, Jewish, Muslim, and southern European variations on this contract evolved, and the adjustment of profit sharing to variations in capital contribution by the trader developed, the system still retained a dependence upon trust, good faith, and a sense of fraternal obligation among merchants (Greif 1989; Udovitch 1970). What is particularly striking is that this tradition of the presumption of equal division of profits between partners, regardless of the proportionate value of their contributions, persists to this day in commercial law. In the absence of any special agreements, "Each partner shall be repaid his contributions, . . . and share equally in the profits and surplus remaining . . ." (U.S. Uniform Partnership Act, 18, a).

The clarity with which this Mediterranean tradition of partnership contracts has perpetuated the basic concept of mutual benefit is illustrated in an appraisal by an eleventh-century Muslim jurist, Sarakhsi. It is this contract concept with the presumption of fair sharing of the benefits that made this arrangement a conduit for a perspective on proper pricing:

> Because people have a need for this contract. For the owner of capital may not find his way to profitable trading activity, and the person who

can find his way to such activity may not have the capital. And profit cannot be attained except by means of both of these, ... By permitting this contract, the goal of both parties is attained. (Pryor 1977, 32, from Udovitch's translation)

Kibitzing the Higgled Price

As has been discussed above, the Greeks thoroughly assimilated the view that one could not, by definition, voluntarily commit an injustice to oneself. While this made the simple sale unquestionably fair as long as it was freely entered into, questions of fraud, duress, and lack of full information constantly produced complications that led to protestations about the fairness of transactions. There was a steady evolution in the systems for reappraising the validity of the bargain. First was the public oath in the temple denying any injustice to the other party. This relied on the fear of divine retribution for perjury and on the concern members of a close-knit community held for the respect of their peers (Plescia 1970). The idea of a public standard is implicit in this system. Second, as sophistication reduced the level of religious awe, disputes were referred to a respected individual, a private arbitrator. Such decisions could be appealed to a public official who arbitrated the dispute (Plescia 1970). This process referred the dispute to a superior or trained individual whose rationality and insight refined and reflected the "public standards." The ultimate resort was to a public trial before one of the large Athenian juries, where a mass vote by secret ballot guaranteed an effective representation of the public standard. As more complex problems arose in Roman law associated with consensual contracts (the enforcement of promises rather than of completed transactions), the parameters became more clearly defined. As long as there was consideration moving to both parties, a *quid pro quo,* mutual benefit could be presumed, and within the broad scope of the various specific details of the contract, the principle that no one could voluntarily be unjust to himself was honored. This principle that a fair price is one freely arrived at between a willing buyer and a willing seller survives to this day, particularly in referring to real estate transactions, where the unique substance of the transaction makes market appraisal somewhat speculative. The Romans, however, institutionalized a very important addition to the judicial tradition, namely, the role of the jurisconsult. Magistrates, burdened with the responsibility of ruling on cases where subtle nuances of traditional concepts of justice had to be applied, adopted the custom of referring the case to a prominent legal scholar or teacher who brought unbiased rationality and cumulative learning to the decision. One can easily see how this tradition of the impartial rational jurist coincided with Stoic philosophy in the Roman world, where a studied indifference to the pressures of daily life was presumed to permit one to be conversant with pure or natural rationality and justice. A good illustration of the application of this formal rationality to a legal problem was the framework for the settlement of damages in the case of "delicts," or torts. The injured party was presumed to have the right to inflict the same injury reciprocally on the offender; then the two parties could negotiate a damage award in exchange for the forgoing of this right (Watson 1970, 15ff.).

Among the qualifications that emerged from this tradition was the limitation on the zone of free bargaining—a delineation of the proper arena for higgling—to the effect that the price arrived at must not deviate more than 50 percent from some notion of general market value (Justinian Code 4.44.2, 4.44.8; see Watson 1970, 68).

One nagging problem with the rationality and clarity of the volitional perspective on "just price" was raised initially in book 5 of Aristotle's *Nicomachean Ethics* and repeated in the Justinian Digest and in medieval writings. This was the question of the fair price for ransoming or purchasing a slave. In warfare, captured prisoners were ransomed to their families. Also, if a man had a child by the slave woman of a neighbor and wished to buy the child to liberate it, what would be a fair price? This problem necessarily posed "market value" against "special concern," be it ever so willing or free (Digest 9.2.33). The Justinian Code and Digest, compiled under the auspices of the Byzantine emperor between A.D. 530 and 540, preserved Roman law and made it common property for the Schoolmen and jurists of the Middle Ages and their heirs. If the scholastic moralists and even the merchants had some difficulty with a simplistic formula for the justice of freely bargained price, Hobbes, Grotius, and Pufendorf embraced it wholeheartedly. Hobbes quoted the Latin maxim *Volenti non fit injuria,* "The willing man receives no injury" (*Phil. Rud.* 3.7) and further opined that "as both the buyer and the seller are made judges of the value, and are thereby both satisfied: there can be no injury." Pufendorf echoed the same thesis, as did Grotius. (For these and other extensive citations on this matter see Langholm 1982, 261; Lowry 1987, nn. 47–52.)

The practical views of merchants as expressed through their body of customary law enforced in merchants' courts, the courts of "pie poudre" (the dusty foot), are expressed in Gerard de Malynes's manual and other writings. He suggests that mutual exchange of surpluses brings countries together and builds friendship. Market price is subjectively based upon "the estimation of concent after the pleasure and sensualitie of man" (1603, 9). Fair exchange was based upon need and taste evaluated under the doctrine of "Commutatio Negotiativa" (Malynes 1622, 62). The use of the goods and the cost of their manufacture must be considered (63). His full pronouncement on fair exchange touches bases with Stoic rationalism and Aristotelian theory. Goods are exchanged after a price is reached "according to a certain equality in the value of things, permuted by a true reason grounded upon the commodious use of things. So that equality is nothing else but a mutual voluntary estimation of things made in good order and truth, wherein inequality is not admitted or known. And the seller is to sell his wares according to the common estimation" (67). The reference to the "common estimation" and the emphasis on "truth" and knowledge incorporate both the Averroist tradition and the Patristic moral line followed by many Scholastics; but first let us explore Malynes's understanding of "rational price" and its ramifications as determinable by experts or magistrates pursuing "provisions policies" to protect the standard of living of the urban poor, or in administering monopolies to foster the expansion of trade.

Malynes contended that most sellers believed their goods to be worth about 20 percent more than their rational price, and most buyers thought they were worth about 20 percent less. He was dealing with wholesale trade—transactions between merchants—and he understood that these deals partook of isolated exchange to the degree that no clear and conspicuous market price was evident. He therefore advised the merchant to buy through a broker who was an expert in the particular market and knew the "rational" price. These brokers were called *alcavalla* (more precisely, *alcaballeros* in Spanish) (1622, 143). One should note the indications of an Arabic origin in the spelling of the term.

Langholm (1982, 65–68) surveys the consternation caused among medieval Scholastics as they wrestled with the implications of some six different passages from the Digest that more or less said that goods were worth what they could be sold for. The prestige of Justinian's Digest and of Roman law made it necessary to try to rationalize this principle with morality, but when one said that things were worth what they could be *justly* sold for, the result was to change the problem from a debate over value to one over justice. What needs to be considered is that the Roman maxim is probably oriented toward conditions of isolated exchange, where there is little reference for defining a "rational" price. The Scholastic moralists tended to solve the problem by adding the qualifications that the buyer must not suffer from ignorance or lack of understanding. The various expansions and ramifications of this tendency to withdraw from the full implications of unfettered bargaining in open markets was, surprisingly enough, fully matched and even exceeded by Malynes. He summarized the fraternal protection offered by the merchants' courts in pursuit of rules of fair play (as indicated in Emmett's paper, this volume, on the views of Frank Knight). In summarizing the standard requirements for an enforceable sale, Malynes added three provisos, namely, that the buyer must not be lacking in expertise, that he must not be taken advantage of because he is needy, and that the seller must not use unreasonable persuasion (1622, 143). There is no reason to believe, however, that anyone presumed to extend these principles to sales made to consumers who were outside the consensual jurisdiction of the merchants' fraternal courts. For consumers there were few if any commercial remedies until Lord Mansfield brought the Law Merchant into the body of the Common Law of England during his long tenure as chief justice of the Court of King's Bench from 1756 to 1788 (Lowry 1974).

Finally, Malynes's identification of rational, true, and voluntary fair price with "common estimation" recognized a major stride in the development of market theory, moving from a perception tied to isolated transaction to a view of a market process. Early moves in this direction were made by Averroists (those influenced by the Muslim nominalist Ibn Rushd, latinized as Averroes). The argument was made that merchants, buying in a market, planned to gain by reselling, so that excessive gain by the seller was not an injustice to the buyer and raised no moral questions (Langholm 1982, 272). A definition of "common estimation" was finally developed in a commentary on Digest 13.1.14. Bartolus wrote, "A thing is worth what it can be sold for, that is, commonly and in a public place, to many people, over several days" (Langholm, 279). Others cited by Langholm expanded their commentaries on this particular rule in the Digest and others at about the same time, and this marks the intellectual crossing of the threshold into a conceptual framing of a market setting that brings extended public participation into the theory of determinable rational, natural, or just price. Despite his obvious eclecticism, Malynes clearly put his money on informed rationality as the safest source of price information from the point of view of a practicing merchant. Buying "at the market price" for resale was not the path of a shrewd merchant.

The establishment of a clear idea of the acceptability of market price from a public policy and moral standpoint (with perhaps a "provisions policy" exception) led to the abandonment of interest in the nagging problem of the two potential layers or zones in contract analysis. The problem is how to distinguish the process of mutually advantageous attraction to form a contract from higgling over the division of the surplus that is generated by the "combination." In modern commercial law, if there is clear evidence that the parties intended to make a contract, and if a quantity term is determinable, the courts will revive the rationalistic tradition of the jurisconsults and provide a price term and other details based upon principles of fairness and reason [Uniform Commercial Code (U.S.) sec. 2-305(1): The parties if they so intend can conclude a contract for sale even though the price is not settled. In such a case the price is a reasonable price at the time of delivery . . .]. In economic theory, the analysis of the zone or arena for higgling was not rigorously framed until analyzed in Edgeworth's Box with the contract curve. There is a zone of potential benefit that can be divided in different proportions. The Aristotelian heritage of this theory of a zone of overlap of the terms of trade that parties are willing to accept was recently surveyed by William Jaffé (1974). This theoretical perspective has been implicit in foreign trade where barter figures in the image of exchange. It leaves a zone or an arena in which the specific terms of the bargain can be negotiated or higgled. Ideally, bargaining and fairness should result in the equal or reasonable division of this mutual benefit of the bargain. When this is being settled by arbitration, an informal legal device, modern lawyers frequently resurrect the cliché that arbitrators tend to "cut the baby in half" rather than apportioning the benefits of the bargain in terms of ethics or commercial rationality. The tenor of this image suggests that the famous biblical account of Solomon's proffered settlement of the dispute between two women over a baby was a parody of the simplistic principle of justice as equal division or equal sharing of the quantity in contention. At the very minimum, this concept of a "surplus" or "benefit of the bargain" opens the door to a clearer formulation of a rational basis for arbitrating disputes arising out of business relationships.

Modern contract theory has evolved a picture of the specific commercial "transaction" as taking place in the temporal context of ongoing commercial "relations" reinforced by previous mutually beneficial transactions and anticipated future benefits (Macneil 1974, 720–26). Economic theory has tended to perpetuate the image of a sequence of discrete commercial transactions taking place in a market setting which operates as an information center that refines and perfects the individual bargains. This tends to be a theory of specific sales. You just buy or sell at the "going market price," and the cumulative consensual wisdom of informed market participants regulates the economy—there is little room for bargaining or higgling. What Macneil has done in his long, eclectic leading article is to point out that "when goods became more complex and more complexly produced, more extensive planning was required than could be supplied by relying on contemporaneous exchange transactions." Plans had to be firmed up before production and in anticipation of distribution: "It [promise] provided the degree of certainty necessary to both exploit and control change." The usefulness of enforceable commitments grew in response to and led to the more extensive enforcement of contract (765). In elaborating this relational or planning theory of contract, Macneil identifies the distributive aspect of *higgling:* "Purely allocative planning is a zero-sum game, and hence conflict laden. But planning for the relational enterprise itself . . . need involve no conflict . . . among the participants; . . . but . . . [be a game] in which all hope to, and quite normally do, gain" (778).

To the extent that modern industrial and commercial activity is built on complex and unique systems of relational contracts, the arena for bargaining or higgling takes on a more clearly defined distributive tone, characteristic of isolated exchange. The role of the market as a public selling place takes on aspects of the auction process. It is, of course, beyond the scope of this discussion to explore how the relational theory of contract as a system of planning undercuts the image of the market process as an impersonal regulator of the productive and distributive process.

The Auction: An Aggregate Transaction

From the perspective fostered by modern economic theory, the auction is a sales transaction partaking of the characteristics of the general market process. On closer inspection, however, it has some administrative elements, and the centralized control exercised by the auctioneer has a distributive flavor, placing the buyers in a responsive position, be it ever so voluntary. Also, the antiquity of the auction seems to suggest that it originated as a special kind of distributive institution rather than an institution that grew out of a perfected market process. The earliest references seem to be to the use of an auction system for farming out tax collections in fifth-century B.C. Greece. The auction was primarily a public sales device, and one can see possible parallels in procedures for inviting volition in the allocation of shares in booty distributions.

The Roman auction had a specially developed institutional form providing for the sale of agricultural produce by small farmers. In our modern auction, under rules of Common Law, the goods are placed on the block "with reserve," or "without reserve." In the former case, they can be withdrawn if no bid is considered adequate to support a sale. In the latter case, the goods are committed to the sale and will go to the highest bidder, no matter how low. The bid is treated as an offer that can be withdrawn before it is accepted, and is erased by a subsequent bid. The outstanding bid is accepted by "the fall of the hammer." This delicate system of "rules of the game" creates a sense of excitement that helps generate an optimum sales price that suggests the epitome of the market process. However, the Roman private auction just mentioned involved a more complex structure:

> Intimation of the intended auction was given both by public announcement by a *praeco* (herald) and by written *proscriptio* (notice). The sale would be held in an *atrium auctionarium* . . . under the auspices and control of an *argentarius* (banker), . . . who was responsible for the arrangements and conditions of sale, e.g., whether credit would be allowed to the buyer, whether goods might be delivered before payment, etc. (Thomas 1957, 43)

The bid could apparently not be withdrawn, once made, unless superseded or disqualified in some way, and the *dominus* (seller) owed the banker his commission if he collected directly from the buyer, while the banker, in turn, guaranteed the payment (Thomas, 65–66). This complex formal institution structuring the sale of produce by small farmers with a guarantee from a banker has market characteristics in that it arrives at an open market price with many sellers and many buyers, but we are not able to know what the limits were on participation by sellers, buyers, and bankers. The primary role of the *argentarius* in this procedure creates a set of limits and controls on the transaction that distinguishes it from an open market sale.

In his compendium on the Law Merchant of 1622, Malynes describes two kinds of auctions. One is called "the Dutch Auction," in which goods are offered to a crowd of prospective buyers. A high price is invited initially. The auctioneer continues to call out prices, successively lower and lower, until one buyer accepts, and the auction is completed. The other system is called "Sale by the Candle." In this system, a stub of a candle is lighted and the goods put up for sale. The last bid made before the candle flickers out takes the merchandise at that price. In the event of a tie, the candle is relit (Malynes 1622, part 1, 143–44). This is obviously the origin of the folk expression, when referring to a bad deal or shoddy merchandise, that "it is not worth the candle." Eli Heckscher (1935, 43) mentions Indian goods, held by the East India Company, being "sold by the candle" in the seventeenth century. The system appears to be tied to the use of a "time candle" or calibrated candle to keep track of time in certain circumstances, converted to the special use of promoting rapid sales/distributions. The Mediterranean background of this institution deserves further exploration, and the contexts in which it was used may be enlightening.

Conclusion

The essence of the problem raised in this essay is the distinction between individual transactions made in a public place, provided to encourage the buying and selling of goods, on the one hand, and the modern economist's concept of a self-regulating market process on the other. The latter requires uniformity, or at least ease of comparison of merchandise, high levels of information, and general stability of commercial channels so that flows of goods and production can respond to higher or lower prices. In the absence of such smoothly working processes, there is no *arena* in which the higgling or bargaining process can effectively serve a *market function*. Outside such an institutional arena, bargaining or higgling over individual transactions is just that, so much negotiating over isolated transactions in a public gathering place. In the absence of an elasticity in the flow of goods, either through stimulus of production or expanded commercial aggregation, information about short-term shortages is merely an invitation to "regrating" (buying for resale in the same market), or "engrossing" (cornering) of markets. The extremely high costs of overland transport, risky maritime shipping, and poor communications characterized ancient as well as early modern trade. There was a common tradition in the ancient Mediterranean and the medieval commercial towns of northern Europe. This tradition maintained complex systems of price regulation and laws against forestalling, regrating, and engrossing. (Forestalling was the buying of goods on the road, before they reached the public marketplace.) Such laws were attempts to make markets function as efficient distribution systems. Towns specifically engaged in "provisions policies" under which prices were regulated on basic necessities and, in time of shortage, subsistence goods were imported by the municipality.

In this setting, the originally distributive concepts of the critical role of voluntarism and rational choice could function in a legally defined arena to facilitate a rational formulation of justice in individual transactions. The most apparent legal concern was conspicuous inequality of information or misrepresentation. The principles of voluntarism and rational choice could not be credited with a justifying role in the market process until after the Industrial Revolution. It was only after advances in agriculture, transportation, and information systems made markets capable of orchestrating respectable responses to basic needs on a more spontaneous level that market processes could be considered superior to the informed rational judgment of responsible magistrates and policy makers. This allowed individual volition and choice to be envisioned as provocative of productive response. It was then that the legal emphasis upon volition and choice—*caveat emptor* (let the buyer beware)—could be ideologically enshrined as the limiting rule in settling individual legal cases. It then could become an economic principle supporting the implicit justice of unregulated market price that transcends individual transactions.

In the course of this transition, the historic formulations of compartmentalized zero-sum higgling or bargaining have been obscured, as has been the consciousness of a distinguishable structure of mutually beneficial relations. By surveying the history of theory and practice in distributive and exchange negotiations (higgling), we can perhaps benefit from a variety of insights into the ways in which aspects of individualized negotiations are intertwined with economically constructive aggregative processes, frequently occurring as multiple facets, zones, or levels in a single transaction or extended relationship. The need for broader perspectives on the negotiative process is, of course, highlighted by the emphasis of modern contract theory on the new levels of uniqueness and relational continuity that are essential to current business planning.

Another example of the theoretical recognition of the obsolescence of the allocative role of the market is the analysis of increased corporate administrative control and concentration through "vertical integration." It was Ronald Coase's (1937) analysis of this corporate assimilation of uncontrollable resource and distribution markets that contributed to his exaltation as a Nobel laureate.

References

Aesop. 1954. *Fables of Aesop*. Translated by S. A. Hanford. Illustrated by Brian Robb. Edinburgh: R. & R. Clark.

Andreades, A. M. 1933. *History of Greek Public Finance*. Rev. ed. Vol. 1. Cambridge: Harvard University Press.

Bae, S. Zin. 1992. [Privately circulated working paper on Quesnay.] Paris.

Berlin, Isaiah. 1991. The Apotheosis of the Romantic Will: The Revolt against the Myth of an Ideal World. In *The Crooked Timber of Humanity: Chapters in the History of Ideas,* edited by Henry Hardy. New York: Knopf.

Coase, Ronald. 1937. The Nature of the Firm. *Economica*, n.s. 4:386–405.

Finley, M. I. 1951. *Studies in Land and Credit*. New Brunswick: Rutgers University Press.

Greif, A. 1989. Reputation and Coalitions in Medieval Trade: Evidence on the Maghribi Traders. *Journal of Economic History* 49.4:857–82.

Harrington, J. 1965. The Commonwealth of Oceana. Excerpted in *Sources in British Political Thought, 1593–1900,* edited by W. Harrison. New York: Free Press.

Heckscher, Eli F. 1935. *Mercantilism*. Translated by Mendel Shapiro. Vol. 1. London: George Allen & Unwin.

Hesiod. 1959. *Theogony*. Translated by Richmond Lattimore. Ann Arbor: University of Michigan Press.

Jaffé, William. 1974. Edgeworth's Contract Curve: Part 2, Two Figures in Its Protohistory: Aristotle and Gossen. *HOPE* 6:381–404.

Kant, Immanuel. 1990. *Foundations of the Metaphysics of Morals*. 2d ed. New York: Macmillan/Library of Liberal Arts.

Langholm, Odd. 1982. Economic Freedom in Scholastic Thought. *HOPE* 14.2:260–83.

Lowry, S. Todd. 1969. Aristotle's Mathematical Analysis of Exchange. *HOPE* 1.1:44–66.

———. 1973. Lord Mansfield and the Law Merchant: Law and Economics in the Eighteenth Century. *Journal of Economic Issues* 7:605–22.

———. 1976. Bargain and Contract Theory in Law and Economics. *Journal of Economic Issues* 9:1–22.

———. 1987. *The Archeology of Economic Ideas: The Classical Greek Tradition*. Durham: Duke University Press.

———. 1991a. Distributive Economics and the Promethean Meat Division: Myth, Folktale, and Legal Precedent. In *Ancient Economy in Mythology East and West*, edited by Morris Silver. Savage, Md.: Rowman & Littlefield.

———. 1991b. Understanding Ethical Individualism and the Administrative Tradition in Pre–Eighteenth Century Political Economy. In *Perspectives on the History of Economic Thought*, edited by W. J. Barber. Brookfield, Vt., and Aldershot, U.K.: Edward Elgar.

Macneil, I. R. 1974. The Many Futures of Contracts. *University of Southern California Law Review* 47.3:691–816.

Malynes, Gerard de. [1603] 1972. *England's View, in the Unmasking of Two Paradoxes*. London: Richard Field. Facsimile reprint, New York: Arno Press.

———. [1662] 1981. *Consuetudo, vel Lex Mercatoria: Or, the Ancient Law-Merchant*. 3d ed. London: F. Redmayne, 1685. Facsimile reprint, Oxford: Professional Books Ltd.

Plescia, J. 1970. *The Oath and Perjury in Ancient Greece*. Tallahassee: University of Florida Press.

Pryor, J. H. 1977. The Origins of the Commenda Contract. *Speculum* 52:5–37.

Pritchett, W. K. 1971. *The Greek State at War*. Part 1. Berkeley and Los Angeles: University of California Press.

Sprague, Rosamund K., ed. 1972. *The Older Sophists*. Columbia: University of South Carolina Press.

Stanley, Philip V. 1979. Agoranomoi and Metronomoi: Athenian Market Officials and Regulations. *Ancient World* 11:13–19.

Thomas, J. A. C. 1957. The Auction Sale in Roman Law. *Juridical Review: The Law Journal of the Scottish Universities* 2:42–66.

Thompson, D. W. 1929. Excess and Defect: Or, the Little More and the Little Less. *Mind* 38:43–55. Reprinted in his *Science and the Classics*. London: Oxford University Press, 1940.

Udovitch, A. L. 1970. The "Law Merchant" of the Medieval Islamic World. In *Logic in Classical Islamic Culture*, edited by G. E. von Grunebaum. Wiesbaden: Otto Harrassowitz.

Watson, A. 1970. *The Law of the Ancient Romans*. Dallas: SMU Press.

Trading "in the Wind" and with Guile: The Troublesome Matter of the Short Selling of Shares in Seventeenth-Century Holland

Neil De Marchi and Paul Harrison

This essay examines legitimation issues attaching to one particular sort of market transaction, in one historical context. Lowry (this volume) has suggested that the problem faced by market officials in the ancient world was to ensure that the price arrived at in the marketplace, by higgling, captured (1) the voluntariness of a private exchange agreed to between two free and willing individuals but (2) was more "objective," in that it reflected underlying conditions governing supply and was acceded to by the many. He describes the public auction, in the presence of an official and with direct confrontation between buyers and sellers, as the form adopted in ancient Rome to secure objectivity in this sense. Something like this form operated as a model for many centuries in the trade in grain, even though the controls, notably to exclude "middlemen," became more direct and detailed (see Kaplan 1976; Thompson 1971). But it is not obvious that a market in grain, with the wares displayed in full and intermediaries carefully excluded, yields a general rule for achieving objectivity in pricing.

To what degree, for example, are parallel necessary conditions fulfilled in the commissioning of a work of art? In that case, the multitude is reduced to one (or a committee), and "normal" conditions governing supply cannot be easily observed: there is no "price current"; and materials costs comprise only a small part of the inputs. In addition, if the work really is commissioned, the agreement embodies promises on the one side and an expectations element on the other—neither of them tied, except in prospect, to a concrete object.

The case we examine embodies comparable, though not identical, departures from the case of grain. In seventeenth-century Amsterdam, a lively trade in shares occurred in and around the commodities *beurs* (cf. French *bourse*) or exchange. As an outgrowth of this, the short selling of shares—contracting forward to deliver shares not in the possession of the seller—made its appearance at various times. For a variety of reasons, many at the time found short s⸀ies of shares suspect, and we shall be concerned with their reasons. The way the matter was addressed in contemporary complaints to the authorities, in official edicts, and in published memoranda (pamphlets) suggests a revival of ancient questions, such as what is appropriate behavior in a market, and whether intentionality has any place in judging of market outcomes. It also showed that there were newer ones: In particular, just how objective could market price be in the case of short sales in shares, where there was no physical commodity that could be set down for viewing in a public marketplace, and relevant information, far from being equally shared, was readily distorted, even fabricated, to give the seller an advantage? In these circumstances, it seemed, price could not be much more than something agreed to between two parties, even if, in this case, voluntariness was not a guarantee of fairness.

A Modern Perspective on Short Selling

Before we address these matters, it is worth trying to sort out, without reference to any particular historical context, how short selling compares with more familiar forms of market transaction. In the view of modern finance theory, used here as a frame of reference, short selling is no different in principle from ordinary forward contracting. Think for the moment not of shares but of commodities; contracting forward to supply goods that one does not actually possess at the time the agreement is made is not at all unusual. Not having the goods in hand is often unavoidable; moreover, part of the convenience of the forward contract lies exactly in this, that it acts as a hedging device for the risk averse— the small farmer who does not want to take a chance on prices falling and who therefore sells a crop yet to ripen and be harvested, at a fixed price. A more refined instrument of insurance is the option. With both basic forward contracts and options, someone accepts a risk that another wishes *not* to bear. This—so the modern viewer contends—should not give rise to questions about equity, since a free exchange is involved. Even although one party must lose—the seller forward, if prices rise after the contract is signed; the buyer, otherwise—different individuals are simply giving expression to their different attitudes toward risk, and in this sense no injustice is done to the losers. (For a summary statement embodying this perspective see CGO 1991.)

What if the seller never intends to deliver, hoping instead to sell the contract again before the due date? This, too, need not involve questions of equity; to the modern finance theorist it simply indicates that there is a developed secondary market for risk. It is only when we take this a step further that serious questions begin to be asked. The extra step is taken when the sale and resale of contracts forms part of a deliberate speculative maneuver, and one, moreover, designed to move prices in a particular direction. Short selling then takes on the character of insider trading and similar moves which are designed to shift more risk onto others than they realize or would willingly accept if information were fully shared.

At this point resistance to the practice of short selling begins to show itself. Even if players in markets open to speculative movements are supposed to look out for themselves, regulators in modern financial markets typically have taken the view that their job is to maintain a level playing field and, as part of this, to guard the unwary small player against the impositions of the experienced, the better capitalized, and above all those with inside information (see Burk 1992 on the reforms adopted after the 1929 crash; and King and Roel 1988 on British regulation of insider trading).

To summarize, then, in modern finance theory short selling, whether of commodities or shares, is not in principle any different from a hedging operation; and even where deliberate risk taking is involved, short selling is merely one practice among many for enabling market players to give expression to their different judgments and attitudes toward risk. Only where manipulation of information asymmetries, or the propagation of misinformation, forms part of short selling does the regulator feel an obligation to step in.

Seventeenth-Century Concerns

The practice of short selling in *commodities* dates from at least the sixteenth century and probably much earlier. Flemish contracts of the sixteenth century survive which describe sales of grain yet to be harvested, while Dutch sales of herring before they had been caught were also common (Van Dillen 1927). Familiarity notwithstanding, the practice gave rise to problems and was looked upon with some suspicion. Buyers and sellers were not always happy to go through with agreements made earlier. It sometimes happened that buyers, foreseeing a scarcity, obtained contracts for future delivery, which the sellers subsequently, seeing that prices were in fact rising, sought to have annulled. Conversely, sellers were at times accused of creating an artificial fear of scarcity by offering grain forward at prices higher than those currently prevailing (Van Dillen, 507–9). Since one party or the other *had* to lose if the current price differed from the contract price, forward contracts put in question the convention, dating from Greek times, that voluntary agreements implicitly are fair (cf. Lowry, this volume).

Interestingly, in the matter of short sales of *shares,* such hints as we have from the seventeenth century do not suggest that failure to go through with a contract, even in the event of loss, was a problem—quite the opposite, in fact (de la Vega [1688] 1939, 159; *Request van eenige actiehandlaren* 1610, in Van Dillen 1930, document no. 9, 56). On the other hand, the trade in shares, when this took the form of short selling, caused contemporaries more trouble than in the case of commodities.

For convenience we divide the arguments encountered in contemporary literature—requests for official intervention; ordinances; and privately published pamphlets—into three groups: (1) complaints against and defenses of short selling as it affected the market status of and other participants in the major joint-stock trading companies (the Verenigde Oostindische Compagnie [VOC], or Dutch East India Company, founded 1602, and the West India Company [WIC], founded 1621), (2) cautions about the moral consequences of avarice, and (3) hints, unrelated to religious arguments, that short selling in shares too often involves breaches of normal business practice.

Short Selling and the Joint-Stock Companies

During VOC's first ten years, shareholders received just one small cash dividend, while the company several times engaged in costly military actions in the East, as well as diverting funds to construct expensive fortifications. Not all the military interventions were successful, and shareholders became restless; from a high of 300 percent (of par) in July 1607, VOC share prices fell to less than 140 percent in November 1608 and stayed in the 130 to 180 percent range for two years. In 1608 five participants registered a protest with a notary against what they felt were improper and noncommercial uses of shareholders' capital (Steensgaard 1982, 246). Then, in early 1609, a bear ring was formed to challenge the company on the exchange (Van Dillen 1930). It is not clear that the ring did more than help to hold down the already slumping prices, but the company lodged a request with the States of Holland and West Friesland in the summer of 1609 to have a ban placed on the sale of shares "in blanco." A ban was duly issued, and repeated in 1621, at the founding of WIC, and again in 1623, just after the East India Company's charter was renewed. The occasion of renewal brought out anew sentiment for and against VOC, as occurred yet again in the mid-1640s, when a further renewal was necessary. Bans on short selling were republished in 1624, 1630, 1636, and 1677 (see Bianchi and De Marchi 1993).

Expressions of concern about short selling (trading "in blanco," also called "selling in the wind" or *windhandel*) were sporadic, and except in 1609 and 1610 there was nothing that could be called a public debate on the practice. Nonetheless, traces of unease show through at various times in privately issued pamphlets and in the repeated official ordinances banning it. VOC's request of 1609 compiled a whole list of the negative effects of short selling, arguments which were heard again and again, without much variation, throughout the century. The practice of the short sellers was outlined in the following terms. First, forward sales are made for many times the value of shares actually registered in the names of the sellers. The shares are not delivered, on the pretext that, for security, the sellers prefer to retain them until the date of agreed delivery. As that date approaches, the sellers put out negative rumors about the company; then, as share prices begin to fall, they offer some shares for sale at a still lower price. While a downward momentum builds, accomplices then secretly buy back at low prices much larger amounts than those initially offered, and so fulfill their sales contracts, at a profit (*Request* 1609a, in Van Dillen 1930, document no. 2).

Three groups were alleged to suffer by this practice (ibid.). One was widows and orphans, who might be forced by circumstances to shed their shareholdings just when shares had been brought low. A second was unsuspecting merchants; for should shares rise despite the false rumors spread by the sellers, many sellers would themselves be ruined and unable to supply the shares they had earlier contracted to provide on the day of settlement. Third, the company, not to say the government of the Republic itself, was subject to disrespect by the short sellers' open

challenges to both company procedures, which called for share transactions to be registered and restricted sales to amounts actually held, and
to the notion, embodied in official support for VOC, that the interests
of the state were inseparable from the "India trade." In making this last
argument the supplicants insinuated that the Republic's enemies were
among the short sellers, a reference to the fact that Isaac le Maire, who
had started the bear ring in 1609, had been secretly negotiating with the
French king to set up a rival company (see Van Dillen 1927, 511–12).

VOC's directors were here appealing to concepts of legitimacy that
operated through a variety of channels. A notion of fairness, especially
toward the weak, is invoked in the reference to widows and orphans.
Market participants, including, we must infer, those dealing in shares,
were indirectly held to be accountable according to this standard. The
unsuspecting merchants, on the other hand, stand for the ideal of honest trade. Since theologians, Catholic and Calvinist alike, held that it
was immoral to gain at another's expense (see below), the contemporary
reader would here understand that the implicit opposition posited between short seller and unsuspecting merchant was a reference to moral
turpitude versus propriety. There is also a hint in this argument, when it
is taken together with the third, with its talk about the importance of the
India trade, of the Aristotelian distinction between trade for the mutual
venting of surpluses, which is natural, and mere trade for gain (unnatural) (Aristotle *Politics* 1.8–9). For the less philosophically minded,
plausible links were forged between private traffic in goods and the common weal, by making the security of the state appear to be bound up in
the success of the trade in goods.

VOC's request evoked a detailed response by some share traders (*Request van eenige actiehandelaren* 1609b, in Van Dillen 1930, document
no. 3). The traders reconstructed a history of the company since its start,
designed to show that share price movements could be fully accounted
for by well-founded, if fluctuating, estimates of its performance. The
company's fortunes had risen and fallen, but the reconstructed history
stressed mostly those military ventures that had failed, losses of ships
that had been suffered, equippage that was said to have been excessive,
the largeness of loans taken up at interest, and the uncertainties induced
by the failure of the directors to produce a financial report. In the light
of such information as we have about share price movements at the
time, the traders' account is not entirely compelling, but in their view
it served to excuse them, and by implication short sellers among them,

from any role in the share price slump of 1608–9. For surety, however, they added two more general arguments to their case. First, it had never been questioned that the freedom of trade in goods, so essential to the well-being of the Republic, extended to the advance purchases of goods and to share transactions. Second, if the freedom were removed to dispose of shares purchased but not yet paid for, this would amount to a loss of the opportunity to profit from price increases that might occur in the meantime.

There is no direct mention of short selling in this response. The last argument, which is the only one even to allude to the practice, is careful to present it from the viewpoint of buyers, not sellers, and to refer to a situation of price rise, not decline. All three arguments, moreover, seek to legitimate share transactions (including, though never more than implicitly, short selling) by linking them directly either to common wisdom or to accepted practices.

To start with common wisdom, it is no modern notion, but was self-evident wisdom among contemporaries that share prices should reflect company performance. A *memorie* giving an even more detailed company history and account of price movements in its shares, possibly written by the "bear" Isaac le Maire, himself at one time a VOC director (*Memorie* 1609, in Van Dillen 1930, document no. 4), argued that at their height VOC shares were "above their value." The very use of such a phrase suggests that readers shared a sense of how the true value of shares was to be estimated. A somewhat later pamphlet confirms this, even spelling out in so many words that a "well founded" price is one that reflects "apparent profits" (*Naerder Aenwijsinghe,* no date, probably ca. 1622). The need for the qualifier "apparent" here probably derives from the fact that, no annual balance being available, the outsider could only infer company earnings from dividends. The author of *Naerder Aenwijsinghe* (literally *Further Indications,* in this case of bad management by the directors of the company) goes on to argue that dividends at the time were an unreliable measure of company health and performance; but that does not affect the point here, which is simply that some idea of how to estimate share prices as to their true worth was part of contemporary discourse.[1]

---

1. This is *not* to say that contemporaries explicitly formulated a discounting or present value relation. This can be found in American books from at least the 1930s, but it is not to be read into seventeenth-century texts. Discounting was a common business practice and well understood, yet so far as share prices are concerned, a writer of 1645 expresses the widely

Two accepted practices gave added plausibility to the supplementary arguments used by the share traders in their 1609(b) *Request*. One was the convention of forward buying of goods. Here, once again, selling is carefully *not* mentioned. It is also interesting that the argument here is one of association: the authors proceed from free trade in goods (perfectly conventional and defensible from a common weal point of view), move on to the freedom to make forward purchases of commodities (accepted practice for at least several decades), and end with the freedom to trade in shares. This bundling, as well as the progression itself, may have been intended to persuade the reader that (all) share trading practices should unquestionably be regarded as no different in principle from trade in goods. A second *Request,* of early 1610, this time addressed by share traders to the High Court of Holland, of whom the States of Holland had asked advice, repeats this argument by association, only somewhat elaborated and without the same reticence about mentioning short selling by name.[2] It has never been the case, they urged, that restrictions were placed on "forward purchases or sales of commodities, nor of shares . . . [even] forward . . . provided both parties enter into the contract with good will and freely . . . just as herring, before they are caught, and grain and other commodities, before they are harvested or in hand, are sold 'on delivery' " (*Request van eenige actiehandelaren* 1610, in Van Dillen 1930, document no. 9).[3]

This later *Request,* we might add, also introduced a quite new argument. Referring to the decline in prices between 1607 and 1609, the traders argued that without them, prices might have been even lower. In other words, without those in need of shares to fulfill prior sales contracts, there is nothing sure to stop a downward slide once it is under way.

A second convention invoked by the traders who wrote the first *Request*—that of 1609(b)—was the accepted practice of paying interest. Interest was paid between merchants for credit extended, long before the

held view. Share prices, he stated, move "solely in response to presupposed and hoped-for profits and hence without basis, simply reflecting guesses" (*Discours* 1645). Far less should one infer that seventeenth-century Dutch pamphleteers had anything like the rational expectations "improvement" upon 1930s present value formulations. On the twentieth-century notions see Lehmann 1992.

2. It is not clear that this second *Request* was written by the same group of traders as the one of 1609, though it seems likely. The difference in tone and explicitness may reflect a growing sense that they had nothing to lose.

3. The mention of voluntariness in contracting is a new twist in the presentation and recalls the Greek tradition (see Lowry, this volume).

church accepted arguments distinguishing such payments from usury. By the second quarter of the seventeenth century a Jesuit named Lessius, who knew the practices of the Antwerp *beurs,* was able to argue that being without one's money meant being unable to take advantage of profitable opportunities, and that this should be compensated, whether or not the possessor of the money intended to employ it in some productive alternative. This opened the way for financiers to charge interest openly and respectably.[4] But existing merchants' practices inspired the argument; and it is not surprising to find its equivalent being used in the traders' response to VOC's *Request* of 1609: restricting the right to dispose of shares acquired though not paid for would cause buyers "to lose in the meantime the opportunity for gain through a price increase that may occur" (*Request van eenige actiehandelaren* 1609a, in Van Dillen 1930, 39).

We have concentrated on pamphlets published in 1609 and 1610 and on arguments dealing primarily with VOC. Little new was added in later pamphlets that we have encountered, or in discussions concerning WIC, though the later accusations by dissatisfied participants against VOC directors at times came close to accusing the directors of buying and selling shares on their own behalf and with an insider's advantage, the books of the company being closed to the general public (see, e.g., *Nootwendich Discours* 1622; *Discours op verscheyde voorslaghen* 1645, 11).

In the second half of the century share trading came to take on a life of its own, somewhat distanced from the activities of the companies and of merchants in general (Bianchi and De Marchi 1993). The discussion of trading "in blanco" therefore ceased to be linked to a discussion of the goods trade (see below). An exception is a pamphlet that appeared in 1687 (Muys van Holy, *Middelen en motiven*), in which the charges made in 1609 against share traders were repeated detail for detail, as well as the argument being made that selling "in the wind," which was not more substantial than smoke, was nonetheless driving the trade in goods from the land because it was both more profitable and as yet untaxed. Options, which had become popular during the 1680s, were judged also damaging and proper objects for a tax.

4. Lessius accepted the common judgment that it would be illegitimate to charge interest to a single borrower if one had not first intended to invest in a productive enterprise. At the same time, "since many need present money and there is not easily found anyone who wishes to lend freely," those with capital who choose to withhold it from business in order to meet the demands of the many are serving the collective good and may charge interest to individual borrowers in proportion to the benefit they receive. (See Noonan 1957, 263, 349.)

Windhandel, Avarice, and Harm to Others

Calvinist *predikanten* (preachers) held that gain is not in itself to be refused; rather, it may be honest or "foul." The laborer is worthy of his hire; and since trade undergirds the Republic's well-being, so the honest merchant too should enjoy a reward for his risk and trouble. Net profit indeed—something over and above a reward for risk and trouble—is also not unacceptable, so long as it does not arise through damage done to another, is put to a good use, and is not an expression of avarice (Cloppenburgh 1637; Udemans 1637, 1655). Even interest on money was selectively approved, on the basis of the argument we have identified with Lessius, provided a sort of balance was maintained, benefit to the borrower on the one hand being set off against a provision to ensure that the lender suffered no loss through forgoing the use of the money (Cloppenburgh 1637, 8, 41).

Notice that, unlike Aristotle in the *Politics* (1.8–10), these preachers did not express qualms about money itself generating gain, nor about there being no natural upper limit on gains made through trade. Indeed, Cloppenburgh for one was aware that an important avenue for the merchant to realize gains lay in *wissels* (bills of exchange). Here the gains were uncertain, reflecting unpredictable exchange rate movements, but they could be large. He hypothesizes cases where such gains would be foul, including successful efforts to engineer changes in the price of money away from ruling values.[5] Since those who produce such shifts impose costs on others, they must do it stealthily, slyly (1637, 9–10).

Cloppenburgh also explored numerous forms of borrowing and lending, including the *lijfrent,* or annuity for life. This did cause him some uneasiness, since there seemed to be an element of the gamble involved, the seller of such an annuity betting as it were that the buyer will not live long to enjoy the payments (155). But it was not the gamble as such that he seemed ready to condemn—the pervasiveness of uncertainties in life at the time made the line between prudent calculation and gambles a difficult one to draw (see Daston 1988, chapter 3). It was rather the lust for gain (the hope for extraordinary returns if the buyer should die quickly) combined with the lack of love for the other displayed in the act of taking the bet.

5. We are assuming that what is meant here is the exchange rate, though it is not entirely clear in the original. For a discussion of the way in which merchants could profit through *wissels* see De Roover 1948, 61–63.

What, then, of trade "in the wind," *windhandel?* Cloppenburgh seems to have been relatively sophisticated in his knowledge and discussion of these matters. The more straightforward path was simply to cite the practice, quote selected biblical texts dealing with what was translated as "overprofit" (e.g., Ezekiel 18:9, 18:13) and leave the reader to conclude that *windhandel* was akin to usury and, as such, an abomination in the sight of God. One such pamphleteer described a scheme for making money via short selling under the title *The Sly Trade of the Sharetraders* (*Den Loosen Handel* 1642) and made no bones about his conviction that it was fraudulent and godless (6). Another author, who assembled a whole collection of pamphlets after the South Sea Bubble and other crises—Holland had its share of companies which crashed in 1720— entitled it *A Collection to Warn Those Who Come After. . . (Verzameling* 1721–22). Noting how little effect a succession of bans on short selling had had during the preceding century, he commented that forbidding the practice was to no avail, "given the irrepressible passion of men to take advantage of each other, so as to derive profit, with no care for the means, even if they extend to robbery" (2:289).

We have not made a special study of religious writings on *windhandel* and cannot generalize on the basis of the few texts we are able to cite. But the principles governing acceptable trade are clearly laid down in works such as those by Udemans and Cloppenburgh, and it is no accident that the official ordinances prohibiting short selling themselves argue in effect that the guiding rule espoused by the preachers—no harm to others—was invariably broken by the share traders. Starting with the first, in 1610, the ordinances repeat the arguments initially adduced by the VOC directors: *windhandel* harms the reputation of the company, makes a mockery of the state, and disadvantages widows and orphans and any who cannot sit out a period of low prices. Even if share trading had the dubious status of gambling (see *Discours* 1645, 11), what caused the practice to incur moral censure (e.g., *Den Loosen Handel* 1642, 6) was, over and above that, (1) the ruin that often ensued for losers, especially those who allowed themselves to become leveraged beyond their means (*Den Loosen Handel,* 7); (2) the shady tricks employed; (3) the strong sense (which necessarily held true for options trades) that in all such dealings one party must lose; and (4) the idea that the short seller must fervently pray for prices to go against the buyer.

Windhandel and Normal Business Practice

Aristotle had concluded that exchange merely for gain, as distinct from the mutual exchange of surpluses to satisfy natural needs, was unnatural in that it borrowed any means, whether in a way appropriate to their nature or not, and knew no limit (*Politics* 1.8–10). Traces of this thinking are detectable in seventeenth-century Holland: ethical and moral considerations aside, some still clearly felt that short selling was an aberration. But we should be careful: the aberration lay not in its unnatural character, strictly understood, but in its practitioners' challenges to business conventions.

This poses a problem of interpretation in certain instances. The editor of the *Collection to Warn Those Who Come After,* for example, drew a contrast between *windhandel,* on the one hand, and "true and real trade" on the other (*Verzameling* 1721–22, title page). One's first thought, perhaps, is that this refers to goods trade as being more real than short selling in shares, because concrete objects were involved, as distinct from mere bits of paper and promises. But from a passage in an undated, untitled pamphlet printed in that same collection there comes a stronger sense that it is the way the *windhandel* is carried on that seemed aberrant, not the nature of the transactions themselves. The author refers ironically to the aura of the miraculous that enthusiasts for share dealings managed to convey, setting it above the realm of ordinary trade. For those inclined to believe, (1) it is possible to make in a single night what ordinarily would require a year; (2) there is only gain, not gain *and* loss; and (3) far from the old saying being true that "ready money bargains best," in the "wind trade" pieces of paper count for more than coin (*Extract uyt een Geschrift* n.d., in *Verzameling,* 2:263–66). Here the problem seems to have been excesses in the behavior of those involved, rather than the nature of the short sale of shares as such.

That impression is confirmed by the reasoning in a pamphlet of 1687 (Muys van Holy, *Middelen en motiven*). Share dealings in Amsterdam in the latter part of the 1680s were described as frenzied and chaotic by one active participant, Josseph de la Vega (see Bianchi and De Marchi 1993). Muys van Holy, an Amsterdam lawyer who wanted to see all share transactions taxed, was vigorous in castigating share traders for a whole range of excesses. He seemed to view options as a form of betting on the price, and denounced them ("a snare and bait to those of little capital") along with *windhandel*—mere "smoke," and damaging in all the ways already familiar. Yet he ends by asserting that everything he has said applies, *mutatis mutandis,* to all such transactions in commodities as well.

The nature of short selling, as distinct from the behaviors it seemed to spawn, did trouble one writer. The author of *Den Loosen Handel* (1642) professed amazement that one might trade in something already pledged to another. The reader must be supposed to know already why this is odd, since no explanation is given. To guess at the reasoning: if what is pledged is as good as sold, to resell it would be like selling a mere shadow, or perhaps the wind. Among the texts we have seen, however, this is an isolated instance.

More frequently what one encounters is an indirect affirmation that there are rules that govern any well-modulated trade; *windhandel* in effect plays fast and loose with them. It is these rules which define the "excesses" that troubled many. The notion that there are norms, hence normalcy, in trade, is not stated in so many words, but it clearly lies behind certain remarks made almost in passing. Norms redefine "natural" as routine, and by contrast with routine we find *windhandel* being referred to by some writers as *inventie* (*Discours* 1645, 10; also *Extract* n.d., in *Verzameling* 1721–22, 2:264).

The word *inventie* could mean "fabrication" or "fantasy"; but merchants used it to denote trade practices that were not in accordance with the conventions established by experience as appropriate: the abnormal practices merited being called by the plural form, *inventiën.* Stols (1971, 2:274) records the derogatory comment made in 1637 by a Flemish merchant on the behavior of a pair of brothers who engaged in sometimes rash, sometimes overingenious moves involving currencies: "nowadays, trade is carried on entirely by unusual tricks (*inventiën*)." The brothers' moves, which seem to have involved manipulation of currency rates, simply went against the rules. Similarly, in the first half of the seventeenth century Antwerp merchants who were members of the expatriate colony of traders in Seville applied a special name to interlopers who ignored the conventions of reputation, networks of agents, mutual financing, and so on, by simply bursting in on a line of trade with a one-time load of wares that they carried with them and would sell even below cost, to get a quick return. They called them *cladders,* literally "rough players," "spoilers" (Stols 1:27, 275). *Windhandel* was just such a deformation of the normal, or true and proper, manner of trading.

Why Could Short Selling Not
Be Accommodated?

Was short selling itself after all the problem, or was the problem the sort of behavior often associated with short selling? No absolute separation between these alternatives was made, to judge from the arguments we have surveyed. What does seem to emerge from our survey is that contemporaries were not especially troubled by the fact that short sales of shares meant selling the wind. That is to say, the difficulty—for most, anyway—was not that such transactions were somehow less real than physical exchanges of commodities, or even forward sales of commodities where there was an honest intention to deliver the goods. This is not surprising. Over the course of the century, Dutch traders came to know spot and forward transactions in goods and in shares, as well as secondary transactions involving pieces of paper, such as bills of exchange, promissory notes, deposit slips for specie held in the Amsterdam Exchange Bank, and so on; and all of this seems to have been judged quite ordinary. Even the so-called tulip mania of 1636–37, which caused problems for many when prices collapsed, and was essentially a matter of short selling, did not excite opposition to short selling as a trading technique. While those caught out in the chaos fussed about getting their money back, no voices were raised claiming that short selling in and of itself was somehow odd, unnatural, or evil. The complaints on the whole were about the excesses that accompanied the sharp run-up in prices. Thus, lust for money and easy profit, and the accompanying guile, was condemned; a scale of values that enabled tulip bulbs to sell for 1,400 guilders when they were "truly worth" less than five cents (a *stuiver*) was deemed an obvious distortion; and the redirection of resources by those who staked their wealth, or laid aside their work, to join the speculative rush, was judged regrettable and foolish (see Krelage 1942, 19, 70, 78–79, 111, 190, 192, 240, 295). The problem with short selling of shares was that, like the tulip speculation, it seemed all too often to go along with behaviors and attitudes that could not be approved.

There were two inherent weaknesses. On the one hand, short selling inherently involved a gamble—the gamble, on the part of the short seller, that price would (or could be made to) fall below the agreed forward sales price. This gave sellers an incentive to manipulate price so as to reduce the risk borne by themselves. But even if they refrained from such intervention to shape the market outcome, they had to hope or pray that things would go their way. This created a moral dilemma: how could a Christian pray for a result that would inflict loss on another? The second aspect of the problem was related to this. Christian ethics aside, a problem still remained with short selling in that the contracts made involved no equivalence. All the gain had to be on one side, all the loss on the other. The practice thus had to be accounted either immoral or unfair. The only way around the fairness issue was to argue from uncertainty: just as the uncertainty of exchange rate movements was used to justify interest (profit) on transactions involving foreign currencies (De Roover 1948, 62), so the uncertainty of the outcome for short sellers of shares might justify the otherwise unfair division involved in the outcome. So far as we have been able to discover, this argument was not in fact used.

That suggests that the sellers themselves might not have felt they were exposed to any very substantial risk. Differently expressed, perhaps they took deliberate steps to ensure that the risk they bore was minimal. That indeed was the general perception at the time, implying (to the extent that it was true) that short sellers in general did not resist the temptation to manipulate outcomes in their favor. Fraud (deception), the spreading of false information, and creating situations such that others were "threatened," if only in the sense that they felt obliged to go along with share price movements for fear of missing out if they did not—these were charges repeatedly brought against the short sellers. Insofar as playing false and imposing on others were the invariable accompaniments of short selling, the practice clearly undermined public morality.

Finally, and stemming as an additional consequence from the sly tricks that were deemed de facto inseparable from short selling, *windhandel* simply flew against the conventions governing business behavior. If it was not unnatural in a sense that Aristotle would recognize, it thrived nonetheless on rule-bending and defying the normal. This made it at the very least difficult to fit into the merchant's conventional frame of thinking.

De la Vega offers a description of activity on the *beurs* in the late 1680s, when options and variations on the option had become popular, that illustrates vividly how this might have been received among merchants. He has a share trader try to explain share transactions to two innocents, a philosopher and a merchant, in a series of dialogues. This construct itself implies that a considerable gap had come into existence between ordinary trade and the traffic in shares. But not only that; what the merchant heard, he found extremely disturbing. In the third dialogue, he tells of a restless night he has had following their previous conversation, of a sleep disturbed by nightmares and torments. At one point he dreamed that the devil had invaded his body, at which he experienced spear pricks, imagined persecutions one after the other, felt driven to vain attempts to flee, and found himself ultimately forced into a cave where he was attacked and stripped of food, weapons, and clothing (De la Vega [1688] 1939, 90–91).

For his part, the philosopher tries to relativize this experience by suggesting that, of course, what they have heard about share trading has conveyed only a sense of imbroglio, but perhaps the share trader could tell them when and why share prices move, as a sort of guide. The share trader declines this invitation, on the ground that "shares are enveloped in a veil of almost religious mystery such that the more one reasons the less one grasps, and the more cunning one tries to be the more mistakes one makes." All he can advise is: buy and sell randomly, maintain the pleasure of it, practice patience, pay the "surplus"—the difference between actual and contracted-for price—on losing, and (here speaking of options) simply extend the contract so long as the mood of the exchange does not alter or no important news arrives. All the same, one should understand that the one constant in the market is that it is forever mutating (91).

At this the merchant throws up his hands and asks what then is to be done; to which the share trader replies: flow with the current and ride the waves (93). Finally, to drive home the apparent arbitrariness of it all, he offers this extended dis-analogy to draughts and to chess:

> It is no game of draughts, according to which players may not jump from a black to a white square; for in an instant we see individuals switch from a position in the light to a place in the shadows, while some remain standing on white, some on black, and some in darkness; the squares themselves swirl and mix together, the lines fuse, the very playing board is upended. It is more like a game of chess[; one, however,] in which the pieces may make strange movements, now stately, then hurried, suddenly pell mell, again calm; in which each fixes on the goal, to win, but some walk, others run, these cross diagonally, those leap, and everyone lives hereby. (95)

In Short . . .

Short selling in shares, then, was not problematic because it differed in kind from the familiar trade in goods. It was suspect for four more straightforward reasons. (1) Short sales contracts failed to meet the equivalence standard for fairness, since one party had to lose. (2) Short selling also fell below Christian ethical standards, in that the seller had to wish, or pray, for loss to overcome the other party. (3) The incentive to reduce one's own risk, moreover, in practice meant that short selling was too often accompanied by lies, cheating, and a sort of pressure to follow the crowd that the weak could not withstand, but which too easily drew them in out of their depth. (4) Finally, these attendant practices and implications, ethics aside, simply were at odds with the routines and conventions of merchant practice, making of short sales of shares a thing both apart and unwelcome.

We draw no moral from the story; but it is worth stressing the connections with the larger subject of higgling. One link we see is that our understandings of market outcomes, including the meaning we put into such elemental terms as price, may be challenged when new sorts of transactions arise. In the case of short selling of shares, the basic techniques were already known from, say, the grain trade; yet grain markets had a distinct history, related to the fact that grain is such a basic commodity. Regulators felt comfortable about trying to set up an ideal market in grain, respecting preconditions such as no middlemen, all supplies to be sold on the market at open auction, under official supervision, and so on. The equivalents for producer, final consumer, product, and even supply, in the case of shares which could be sold short, were not obvious; nor, as a consequence, was the connection between market price and fairness or objectivity. The practices which accompanied *windhandel* had therefore to be reexamined to discover their effects on individuals and on public morals, as well to ascertain how they compared to conventional business practices. The effort to negotiate an understanding and accommodation of the new and problematic elements is itself a sort of higgling.

Renegotiation is required every time a problematic innovation occurs. Hence, to the extent that markets are treated *by their participants* as forums for trying out new rules and practices (cf. Loasby 1991), this process of "higgling" toward an understanding and accommodation may be expected to recur, even if irregularly.

References

Anonymous, undated, and otherwise unattributed seventeenth-century sources are cited from collections in Amsterdam: the University of Amsterdam Library and the Economic History Library.

Aristotle. 1988. *The Politics*. Edited by Stephen Everson. Cambridge Texts in the History of Political Thought. Cambridge: Cambridge University Press.

Bianchi, Marina, and Neil De Marchi. 1993. The Emergence and Regulation of Share Trading Practices in Seventeenth-Century Amsterdam. Mimeo in possession of the authors.

Burk, James. 1992. *Values in the Marketplace: The American Stock Market under Federal Securities Law*. New York: Aldine de Gruyter.

Cloppenburgh, Johannes. 1637. *Christelijke Onderwijsinge van woecker, interessen, coop van renten, ende allerleye winste van gelt met gelt*. Amsterdam: Theunis Jacobsz.

[CGO] Committee on Government Operations. 1991. *Short-Selling Activity in the Stock Market: Market Effects and the Need for Regulation (Part 1)*. Eleventh report. House Report 102–414. Washington: U.S. Government Printing Office.

Daston, Lorraine. 1988. *Classical Probability in the Enlightenment*. Princeton: Princeton University Press.

Dillen, Van, J. G. 1927. Termijnhandel te Amsterdam in de 16de en 17de eeuw. *De Economist* 76:503–23.

———. 1930. Isaac Le Maire en de handel in actien der Oost-Indische Compagnie. *Economisch-Historisch Jaarboek* 16:1–165.

Discours op verscheyde voorslaghen rakende d'oost en West-Indische trafijken. 1645. Anonymous. No publisher.

Extract uyt een Geschrift, spreekende van de Loteryen en Actien. N.d. Anonymous. In *Verzameling tot waarsschouwinge* (1721–22), 2:263–66.

Kaplan, Steven L. 1976. *Bread, Politics and Political Economy in the Reign of Louis XV*. 2 vols. The Hague: Nijhoff.

King, Mervyn, and Ailsa Roel. 1988. Insider Trading. *Economic Policy* 6 (April): 165–87. (With comments by John Kay and Charles Wyplosz, 187–93.)

Krelage, E. H. 1942. *De pamfletten van den Tulpenwindhandel 1636–1637*. The Hague: Nijhoff.

Lehmann, Bruce N. 1992. Asset Pricing and Intrinsic Values: A Review Essay. *Journal of Monetary Economics* 28:485–500.

Lessius, Leonard. 1630. *Je justitia et jure ceterisque virtutibus cardinalibus libri quattuor ad 2.2.D*. Lyon.

Loasby, Brian J. 1991. *Equilibrium and Evolution: An Exploration of Connecting Principles in Economics*. Manchester and New York: Manchester University Press.

Den Loosen handel van de actionisten. 1642. Anonymous. No publisher.

Lowry, S. Todd. (This volume). The Market as a Distributive and Allocative System: Its Legal, Ethical, and Analytical Evolution. In *Higgling: Transactors and Their Markets in the History of Economics*, edited by Neil De Marchi and Mary Morgan. *HOPE* 26, special issue. Durham: Duke University Press.

Memorie van hetgene in Oost-Indien is gesuccedert. August 1609. In Van Dillen 1930, 39–45 (document no. 4).

Muys van Holy, Nicolaes. 1687. *Middelen en motiven om het kopen en verkopen van Oost- en West-Indische actien.* Amsterdam: no publisher.

Naerder Aenwysinghe der Bewinthebbers Regieringe. N.d. [ca. 1622]. Anonymous. No publisher.

Noonan, John T. 1957. *The Scholastic Analysis of Usury.* Cambridge: Harvard University Press.

Nootwendich Discours oft Vertooch aan de hooch-mogende heeren Staten Generaal van de Participanten der Oost-Indische Co. tegens Bewinthebbers. 1622. Anonymous. No publisher.

Request van de Bewinthebbers der Oost-Indische Compagnie aan de Staten van Holland en West-Friesland betreffende den verkoop in blanco van de actien der Compagnie. 1609a. In Van Dillen 1930, 31–33 (document no. 2).

Request van eenige actiehandelaren aan de Staten van Holland en West-Friesland waarin zij verzoeken den actiehandel vrij te laten. 1609b. In Van Dillen 1930, 33–39 (document no. 3).

Request van eenige actiehandelaren te Amsterdam aan den Hoogen Raad en aan het Hof van Holland, waarin zij het verzoek van der Bewinthebbers der Oost-Indische Compagnie tot verbod van verkoop van actien in blanco bestrijden. 19 January 1610. In Van Dillen 1930, 50–57 (document no. 9).

Roover, De, Raymond. 1948. *Money, Banking, and Credit in Mediaeval Bruges.* Cambridge, Mass.: Mediaeval Academy of America.

Steensgaard, Niels. 1982. The Dutch East India Company as an Institutional Innovation. In *Dutch Capitalism and World Capitalism*, edited by Maurice Aymard. Cambridge: Cambridge University Press.

Stols, Eddy. 1971. *De Spaanse Brabanders of de Handelsbetrekkingen der Zuidelijke Nederlanden met de Iberische Wereld 1598–1648.* 2 vols. Brussels: Royal Flemish Academy.

Thompson, E. P. 1971. The Moral Economy of the English Crowd in the Eighteenth Century. *Past and Present* 50:76–136.

Udemans, Godefridus. 1637. *Coopmans Jacht, Brenghende goede tijdinge uyt het lant Canaan, voor alle vrome koop-luyden om te verkrijgen ende te behouden eenen gewenschten zegen over hare negotie.* Dordrecht: Boels.

———. 1655. *'T Geestelijck Roer van' t Coopmans Schip.* Dordrecht: Boels.

Vega, De la, Josseph. [1688] 1939. *Confusion de confusiones.* Reprint of the Spanish edition, with a modern translation into Dutch by G. J. Geers. Edited by M. F. J. Smith. The Hague: Nijhoff, for Het Nederlansch Economisch-Historisch Archief.

Verzameling tot waarschouwinge voor de Nakomelinge van alle de Projecten en Conditien van de Campagnien van Assurrantie, Commercie en Navigatie. 1721, 1722. 2 vols. 'sGravenhage: Cornelis Hoffeling.

Higgling:
The Language of Markets in
Economic Discourse

Vivienne Brown

According to the *Oxford English Dictionary*, the word *higgling* refers to the notion of close bargaining, cavilling or disputing about terms in market transactions, and itinerant dealing in provisions and petty commodities.[1] A "higgler" by trade was an itinerant dealer or middleman and in some cases was subject to the popular opprobrium attached to speculation and engrossing which was thought to lead to price increases.[2] In Edgeworth's entry on "higgling" in *Palgrave's Dictionary of Political Economy*, the primary meaning is given as the "higgling of the market," which is distinguished from higgling as the "art of bargaining" in the absence of competition (Edgeworth 1987, 652–53).[3] In the general context of market behavior, therefore, "higgling" is a term that is subject to different nuances. One aspect of higgling, however, is the use of language in order to effect advantageous transactions, including all

---

1. For the purposes of this paper, higgling and haggling are treated as synonymous. *OED* suggests that haggling may signify noisier or more aggressive action; alternatively one quotation suggests that higgling refers to sellers' trying to push up the price, whereas haggling refers to buyers' trying to push it down—but these variations are not standard in the economics literature.

2. The term *huckster* was a near synonym for *higgler,* signifying a retailer of small goods, a pedlar, regrator, engrosser, or one who basely barters his services. Cf. the regulation of middlemen, including "hucksters, higlers, and retailers," in the eighteenth-century English grain trade (Thompson 1991a, 193–95; but see also 1991b, 316, 318, where higglers and jobbers are mentioned without such overtones).

3. It was not until the second edition of the *OED* in 1989 (first edition 1933), that an entry appeared for the *higgle of the market* as "the adjusting of prices so that demand and supply are equal." The quotations for higgling as close bargaining date from the seventeenth to nineteenth centuries, but the single quotation for the higgle of the market is dated 1908.

the means of persuasion that the transactors can command in the circumstances. Seen from this point of view, market processes are located firmly within the domain of the exercise of language and the linguistic and rhetorical strategies that are available to the transactors. Such a notion of higgling might be thought central to all market processes, from the local street market of costermongers shouting their wares, to the sophisticated world of multinational corporate and financial dealings. Despite the intuitive plausibility of this view, the notion of higgling has not been central to discourses on the market, and an account of its place in the history of economic thought inevitably becomes something of an exercise in historical retrieval.

I address this issue here by examining the place of higgling in selected economic texts, and by relating this to theories of language. Discussion below explores the notion of higgling by constructing an account of the interface between theories of markets and theories of language in the history of economic thought. It will be found that the term *higgling* is subject to different constructions in different discursive contexts, and that these differences may be related analogically to different conceptions of language. In studying aspects of the history of a word, therefore, this essay illustrates the importance of discursive context for reading texts in the history of economic thought.[4]

Language and Rhetoric

The expression "the higgling and bargaining of the market" occurs most famously in a passage in Adam Smith's *Wealth of Nations* in the context of measures of value and the distinction between the real and nominal price of commodities. The text argues that when the products of different kinds of labor are exchanged, some allowance is made for the relative hardship and ingenuity involved in the exercise of that labor, but that this adjustment takes place "not by any accurate measure, but by the higgling and bargaining of the market, according to that sort of rough equality which, though not exact, is sufficient for carrying on the business of common life" (*WN*, 1.5:4). In spite of the familiarity which its presence in the opening chapters of *The Wealth of Nations* has conferred upon it, the term *higgling* does not feature prominently in the rest of

---

4. It also suggests that the selected quotations supporting dictionary definitions are themselves but one mode of reading past texts.

the book. Neither does it appear in the later chapter which presents the core account of market dynamics in terms of the relation between natural and market price. As *The Wealth of Nations* is commonly regarded as the first systematic statement of the advantages of a competitive market economy, its cursory reference to and subsequent lack of interest in the process of higgling and bargaining might be thought to denote an important theoretical absence, but it is one which has characterized much of the history of competitive economic theory.

In the second chapter of *The Wealth of Nations* it is argued that the propensity to truck, barter, and exchange is probably "the necessary consequence of the faculties of reason and speech," and here is found the celebrated description of the rhetoric of economic bargaining based on the appeal to self-love. In order for a man to prevail on others "to do for him what he requires of them," it is necessary to "interest their self-love in his favour" rather than mistakenly appeal to their benevolence. The most appropriate rhetoric of the marketplace is therefore an appeal to other people's self-interest: "We address ourselves, not to their humanity but to their self-love, and never talk to them of our own necessities but of their advantages" (*WN*, 1.2:2). The need to prevail on others by appealing to their feelings was recognized in classical rhetoric by *movere*, the need to move the passions of the hearers and so persuade them of the speaker's point of view. In Smith's *Lectures on Jurisprudence*, the importance of persuasion is also recognized. The linguistic aspect of market transactions is tied to a natural inclination to persuade, and the meaning of an economic transaction is interpreted as a form of argument designed to persuade the other party: "The offering of a shilling, which to us appears to have so plain and simple a meaning, is in reality offering an argument to persuade one to do so and so as it is for his interest" (*LJA.*, 6:56).

In terms of the divisions and distinctions of classical rhetoric, such discourse is generically linked to oratory, as that form of discourse which is expressly designed to persuade and to move its audience. And, indeed, in *Lectures on Jurisprudence* this link is formulated directly: "Men always endeavour to persuade others to be of their opinion. . . . And in this manner every one is practising oratory on others thro the whole of his life" (6:56). Although most people are uneasy when others differ from them, and try to persuade them to the contrary, those with a well-developed sense of self-command will desist from this practice: "You are uneasy whenever one differs from you, and you endeavour to persuade [him] to be of your mind; or if you do not it is a certain degree of self command" (6.56). It is significant here that the Stoic virtue of self-command is presented as a counterforce to the natural or instinctive need to practice oratory on others. In *Theory of Moral Sentiments*, self-command is one of the highest virtues and derives from the overwhelming importance of Stoicism for Smith's moral philosophy; its presentation in *Lectures on Jurisprudence* at this point signifies the lack of esteem and even somewhat pejorative connotations attached to oratory as a form of rhetorical discourse.

This is elaborated in Smith's *Lectures on Rhetoric and Belles Lettres,* which commends a clear plain style, unembellished by ornament or flowery effects. A didactic style is one which instructs and persuades only as far as the argument is a convincing one, and which fairly presents both sides of the argument. Oratorical or rhetorical discourse, by contrast, is compared unfavorably with didactic discourse on the grounds that it attempts to persuade at all costs, irrespective of the strength of the case, and to this end presents only one side of the argument, magnifying all the points on one side and diminishing those on the other. To achieve this unscrupulous effect it appeals not to reason and sober conviction, but is "adapted to affect our passions and by that means persuade us at any rate" (*LRBL,* 2:14):

> [The didactick] . . . proposes to put before us the arguments on both sides of the question in their true light, giving each its proper degree of influence, and has it in view to perswade no farther than the arguments themselves appear convincing. The Rhetoricall again endeavours by all means to perswade us; and for this purpose it magnifies all the arguments on the one side and diminishes or conceals those that might be brought on the side conterary to that which it is designed that we should favour. Persuasion which is the primary design in the Rhetoricall is but the secondary design in the Didactick. It endeavours to persuade us only so far as the strength of the arguments is convincing, instruction is the main End. In the other Persuasion is the main design and Instruction is considered only so far as it is subservient to perswasion, and no farther. (*LRBL,* 1:149–50; also 2:13)

The use of oratory on others in order to persuade at all costs is denigrated and constitutes an inferior form of discourse compared with the more authoritative and detached discourses which compel assent by virtue of the objective strength of the argument. Thus, to the extent that higgling as the language of the marketplace also resorts to rhetorical techniques, it is also an inferior and fallen form of discourse. Its characteristics are the inevitable result of the requirements of the market situation which require of transactors, not a detached pursuit after truth or understanding, but the achievement of their commercial objectives. However inevitable or even necessary this characteristic may be, as a form of language it is potentially deceitful and, hence, derogated to some degree.

Here we see an example of the binary oppositions set up between philosophy and rhetoric, reason and passion, necessity and contingency, that have been in play in one form or another since Plato's writing (Kennedy 1963, 1980; Vickers 1982 and 1988, chapters 2, 3). Within the terms of these binary oppositions "one side is right, the other wrong; one side is privileged as authentic, legitimate, true, while the other receives the negatives of those concepts and is dismissed from serious consideration" (Vickers 1982, 249). In Plato's *Gorgias,* for example, rhetoric is compared unfavorably with philosophy; whereas philosophy seeks the truth, rhetoric is concerned only with persuasion and so plays upon its audience in order to achieve its ends. Philosophy's only end is to find the truth, but rhetoric's ends are determined by interests outside the argument, which is then used purely instrumentally to achieve those ends. Other accounts of rhetoric in Plato's *Phaedrus,* Aristotle's *Rhetoric,* and Cicero's *De Oratore,* in various ways modified or challenged this attack on rhetoric, for example, by claiming that as with all skills, rhetoric may be used for good or ill purposes, or by arguing that good rhetoric must be based on sound knowledge. Nevertheless, the power of Plato's attack is still felt in the pejorative concept of "rhetoric" as verbal chicanery that its modern practitioners have to counter. It is also registered in the Aristotelian argument, in defense of a role for rhetoric, that it may properly be regarded as the sphere of probable or contingent truths, whereas philosophy is directed to the pursuit of necessary and absolute truths. It is also to be seen in a long-lasting philosophical distrust of language as a verbal means of communication; ideally, it is held that language should function as the transparent means by which communication takes place, and that the forms of language, its figurative power or inherent ambivalencies, should not be part of this process. Once it is recognized that these linguistic features do have real effects, language is seen as something potentially dangerous and deceitful.

During the Renaissance there was a flowering of interest in classical rhetoric, which was considered as an essential part of a liberal humanist education. Generations were schooled in the ethos of classical rhetoric with its formally structured discourses and its many categories of figures and tropes. During the course of the seventeenth and eighteenth centuries, however, classical rhetoric came to be severely criticized with a move toward a plainer style of language without ornament; Adam Smith's lectures on rhetoric can be seen as part of this general reorientation away from classical presuppositions. Partly this shift may have been related to the movement for a scientific language associated with the Royal Society, but Locke's *Essay Concerning Human Understanding* also contributed importantly toward this.[5] Locke's *Essay* warned against the imperfections of words and the inherently problematic nature of language as a means of communication. Accordingly, it also cautioned against rhetoric insofar as rhetoric functioned as a "powerful instrument of error and deceit," and urged a clear, plain style:

> All the art of rhetoric, besides order and clearness; all the artificial and figurative application of words eloquence hath invented, are for nothing else but to insinuate wrong ideas, move the passions, and thereby mislead the judgment; and so indeed are perfect cheats: and therefore, however laudable or allowable oratory may render them in harangues and popular addresses, they are certainly in all discourses that pretend to inform or instruct, wholly to be avoided; and where truth and knowledge are concerned, cannot but be thought a great fault, either of the language or person that makes use of them. (3.10:34)

Here is a classic statement of the perils of rhetoric, where eloquence may distort a person's judgment by moving the passions. Here, too, is the contrast between a perjured rhetoric and a plain style which is associated with truth and knowledge. In this account oratory belongs to the realm of rhetorical deliveries in the form of harangues and popular addresses, and so is far removed from sober and proper disquisitions relating to truth and knowledge.

Once again rhetoric is counterposed to philosophy in the same binary opposition, but in addition oratory is here associated with public forms of discourse such as "harangues and popular addresses." This relates to yet another inflexion of these oppositions in that rhetoric is seen as the language of public places, but this characterization also includes the marketplace, whose own particular language is therefore also

5. For different accounts see Howell 1967, 1971; Kennedy 1980; Vickers 1985, 1988.

derogated. In cataloguing possible remedies for the imperfections and abuses of words, Locke's *Essay* contrasts the language of the market to that of learned discourse: "But though the market and exchange must be left to their own ways of talking, and gossipings not be robbed of their ancient privilege . . . yet methinks those who pretend seriously to search after or maintain truth, should think themselves obliged to study how they might deliver themselves without obscurity, doubtfulness, or equivocation, to which men's words are naturally liable, if care be not taken" (3.11:3). Here the language of the market is contrasted with that discourse which seriously searches after or maintains truth; as the opposite of such learned discourse, the language of the market is inevitably suspect. And it is not only the public nature of the market that is in play here, but also its ordinariness and its place in the everyday life of things: "Vulgar notions suit vulgar discourses: and both, though confused enough, yet serve pretty well the market and the wake. Merchants and lovers, cooks and tailors, have words wherewithal to dispatch their ordinary affairs" (3.11:10).

Thus, just as rhetoric and oratory are set pejoratively against philosophy, truth, and knowledge, so too is the language of the marketplace. And it is this association of rhetoric and oratory with the language of the market that can be discerned in the comments in Adam Smith's *Wealth of Nations* and *Lectures on Jurisprudence*. In interpreting the meaning of the offer to buy as the attempt to persuade, and in claiming that this is a form of oratory, the texts are keying into a broad swathe of philosophical writings in which both rhetoric and the language of the marketplace were regarded as inferior and devalued forms of discourse.

The "True" Language of the Market

It has been argued so far that the inferior standing attached to the language of the market may be understood as one version of the Platonic opposition of philosophy and rhetoric, reason and interests. This suggests that one way of understanding the treatment of the language of markets as forms of higgling and bargaining is by reference to this larger discursive context. In particular, the classical binary opposition may also be seen at work in the treatment of the process of higgling in economic discourse. There is a kind of true or honest higgling which provides the market with an ideal process by which certain theoretically identifiable results are actually instantiated in the market; market transactors of course try to sell and buy their wares at the most advantageous price, but their efforts, however self-interested, simply formalize the objective conditions of the market. By contrast, there is another kind of higgling involving, to some degree, the classical deceits of rhetoric; here market outcomes may not be entirely desirable or warranted, and so may be placed at some distance from proper market outcomes.

The famous account of higgling in *The Wealth of Nations* referred to above presents it as the process by which the product market makes allowance for the different kinds of labour inputs. In this way it is expected that those commodities produced by labor involving greater hardship and ingenuity would sell at an enhanced price which reflects this difference. Higgling is therefore represented as the process by which these objective characteristics of the labor inputs are somehow incorporated into the final price of the product. This process may result only in a rough approximation of the objective difference in the labor inputs, but such approximations are not likely to be wide of the mark and are sufficiently accurate for most ordinary and everyday dealings. In this case, the process of higgling corresponds to the first type of higgling outlined above and functions as a heuristic device by which the objective and necessary outcome is generated in actual markets. But once it has been established that market outcomes are generated in accordance with the objective or natural characteristics of the system, the actual process of higgling becomes theoretically immaterial, as it does not affect the values of the final outcome.

This may be seen in Smith's later chapter on the relation between the natural and the market price. Here an analysis is presented of the way in which market prices gravitate toward the natural price in competitive markets: if the quantity of any commodity brought to market falls short of/exceeds the effectual demand at that price, then the market price rises above/falls below the natural price; if this happens, laborers and employers are prompted to offer more or less of the good until once again the market price is equal to the natural price (*WN*, 1.7). Although this is one of the most detailed accounts of the dynamics of the competitive market process to be found in *The Wealth of Nations*, the process of higgling and bargaining is not referred to. The divergence of the market price from the natural price is explained simply in terms of the "competition" arising from the imbalance between the effectual demand and the quantity offered for sale, and the output response on the supply side which secures the equality of natural and market price is explained in terms of the individual interests of the landlords, laborers, and employers. Again, there is no reference to higgling and bargaining as such. One reason for this is that the main analytical contribution of the chapter is not to be found in its account of market dynamics, but in its consolidation of the previous chapter's account of the three revenues of rent, profit, and wages, as the component parts of exchangeable value and the annual revenue of society. It was this theoretical contribution that was crucial for the argument in favor of the system of natural liberty, rather than the equilibrating properties of the competitive market as such, because the superiority of natural liberty was to be demonstrated in terms of the growth of these components of the annual revenue.[6] Another reason, however, for the absence of higgling from this chapter (1.7) is that the market process of price adjustment is theoretically irrelevant in establishing the values—the natural prices—of the final outcome. If higgling is the means by which objective solutions are realized in the market by means of the actions of transactors, then the process of higgling cannot affect final values.

In this case, too, higgling reduces to the means by which the inevitable laws of the market are rendered manifest, and the final price is achieved by a market process in which the transactors discover that only one single price outcome had been feasible all along. In such a view of the market, higgling becomes invisible because it has no independent effect on final values. In this sense, the language of the market may be seen as a transparent medium by which the true outcome is realized. This corresponds to the classical view of language as a transparent mechanism by which a person's thoughts may be communicated to another; according to this view, language itself has no independent effects and is simply the vehicle by which arguments may be conducted and truth may be discovered. In this case, the language of the market corresponds with the idealized view of language in that it provides a vehicle of inquiry but cannot itself affect the outcome, as truth is independent of all contingent forms. An implication of this, however, is that the language of the market becomes irrelevant theoretically, and higgling becomes redundant to theoretical inquiry.

Cantillon's *Essay on the Nature of Trade in General* provides a brief description of higgling or "altercation," but here too it results in a market price which must equal the "intrinsic worth" of a commodity. Sellers try

---

6. This argument is developed in Brown 1994, chapters 6 and 7.

to hold out for a high price and buyers for a low price, but eventually the market price must reflect the relation between demand and supply and, ultimately, the good's intrinsic value: "The Butcher keeps up his Price according to the number of Buyers he sees; the Buyers, on their side, offer less according as they think the Butcher will have less sale: the Price set by some is usually followed by others." But this price must reflect the objective conditions in the market: "It is clear that the quantity of Produce or of Merchandise offered for sale, in proportion to the demand or number of Buyers, is the basis on which is fixed or always supposed to be fixed the actual Market Prices; and that in general these prices do not vary much from the intrinsic value" (Cantillon [1755] 1931, 119). This overall result is achieved in spite of differences in bargaining tactics among the transactors; here, in a brief account, traces of the other side of discourse creep in, where some are clearly "more clever in puffing up their wares, others in running them down" (119), while others still make mistakes in assessing the market situation (121). It is acknowledged too that this method of fixing prices "has no exact or geometrical foundation, since it often depends upon the eagerness or easy temperament of a few Buyers or Sellers" (119). But, in spite of this, the process of bargaining results in those market prices which are equal to the intrinsic values of commodities.

Turgot's *Reflections on the Nature of Wealth* also provides an account of higgling or "chaffering" in which the eventual market price, the "current value," is determined by the objective conditions of the market ([1770] 1963, 28–31, 48). The starting point for this account is the model of individual exchange in which two transactors negotiate on the basis of their own individual preferences: "If the parties are not in accord, it will be necessary that they should approach one another by yielding a little on one side and a little on the other, offering more and contenting themselves with less" (28). Once the analysis moves from the isolated exchange of two individuals to the general case of market exchange, the emphasis shifts from bilateral bargaining or chaffering to that of the objective requirements of the market taken as a whole: "The value of corn and of wine is no longer debated between two isolated Individuals in relation to their relative wants and abilities; it is fixed by the balance of the wants and abilities of the whole body of the Sellers of corn with those of the whole body of the Sellers of wine" (30). In this case, the midway price between the extremes of the individual offers will constitute the current price.

In these cases, the language of the marketplace is effectively neutralized and rendered invisible by the requirement that it has no independent effect on the value of market outcomes. This tendency can also be seen at work in the later development of classical political economy, where the process of higgling and bargaining is hardly mentioned. What takes its place is the notion of "competition" as the means by which the law of value is operative in the market, and demand and supply are equalized. Extensive discussion is directed toward the relation between supply and cost of production and/or the quantity of labor, but it is competition which secures the necessary change in price. Thus the focus of debate is directed to the ways in which the objective characteristics of the market, in terms of such supply-side factors as labor, capital, abstinence, or costs of production, are related to the market price, rather than to the ways in which the market price is achieved in the market. Within this unifying framework provided by the workings of competition, all market forms are subsumed within the law of value, including monopoly as a special case where the monopoly price is determined by the relation between demand and a fixed or controlled supply unrelated to costs or labor/capital inputs.

Thus the operation of higgling came to be seen as the process by which the final, true price is discovered in the market, rather than the means by which that price is determined, and this holds whether the true price is thought to be determined by cost of production/labor or by the conditions of demand and supply. In Jenkin's *Time-Labour System,* for example, the "true market price" is discovered by a "tentative process" where "the higgling of the market ascertaining the result of the relative demand and supply in that market does not in the long run determine the price of either eggs or tea; it simply finds out the price which has really been determined by quite different means" (Jenkin 1887, 2:139).[7] Walras's *Elements,* too, contrasts the process of *tâtonnement* or "groping" as a real market process with the mathematical solution on which it must necessarily converge: "What must we do in order to prove that the theoretical solution is identically the solution worked out by the market? Our task is very simple: we need only show that the upward and down-

7. Cf. the following from *The Graphic Representation of the Laws of Supply and Demand:* "If every man were openly to write down beforehand exactly what he would sell or buy at each price, the market price might be computed immediately, and the transactions be then and there closed" (Jenkin 1887, 2:79).

ward movements of prices solve the system of equations of offer and demand by a process of groping (*par tâtonnement*)" (Walras 1954, § 125, p. 170).[8] Edgeworth's "recontracting," presented as a more fundamental conception of higgling than *tâtonnement* could be, also subscribes to this view of higgling as a market process of discovery:

> He [Walras] describes *a* way rather than *the* way by which economic equilibrium is reached. For we have no general *dynamical* theory determining the path of the economic system from any point assigned at random to a position of equilibrium. We know only the statical properties of the position. . . . Walras' laboured description of prices set up or "cried" in the market is calculated to divert attention from a sort of higgling which may be regarded as more fundamental than his conception, the process of *recontract*. . . . It is believed to be a more elementary manifestation of the property to truck than even the effort to buy in the cheapest and sell in the dearest market. (Edgeworth 1925, 2:311–12, original emphasis; also quoted in part in Walras, 1954, editor's n. 5 of Lesson 11, p. 515)

Keynes, as well, in his response to Hawtrey, made the same distinction between higgling as a market process of discovery and the theoretical determination of price:

> It [i.e., entrepreneurs' reactions] corresponds precisely to the higgling of the market by means of which buyers and sellers endeavour to discover the true equilibrium position of supply and demand.
>
> Now Hawtrey, as it seems to me, mistakes this higgling process by which the equilibrium position is discovered for the much more fundamental forces which determine what the equilibrium position is. (Keynes 1973b, 182, also 27; see also 1973a, 602)[9]

In all these instances, higgling is the process of finding out or groping, a technique of trial and error, by means of which the actual market discovers the true or long-term equilibrium solution.

Marshall's *Principles* provides a detailed account of the higgling and

---

8. Cf. the editor's note at Lesson 6, n. 11, p. 501. See also Lesson 12, n. 12, p. 520, and Lesson 20, n. 5, p. 528.

9. See also Lawlor, this volume.

bargaining of the market, but here this process becomes problematic in that it is structured in terms of the requirements of comparative static analysis. The text describes a market day in a local corn exchange, with given stocks of corn, and presents simple supply and demand schedules showing a unique equilibrium price of 36 shillings. The account then turns to the process of higgling and bargaining:

> Of course some of those who are really willing to take 36s. rather than leave the market without selling, will not show at once that they are ready to accept that price. And in like manner buyers will fence, and pretend to be less eager than they really are. So the price may be tossed hither and thither like a shuttlecock, as one side or the other gets the better in the "higgling and bargaining" of the market. But unless they are unequally matched; unless, for instance, one side is very simple or unfortunate in failing to gauge the strength of the other side, the price is likely to be never very far from 36s.; and it is nearly sure to be pretty close to 36s. at the end of the market. (*Principles*, 1961, 333)

The explanation provided, however, is framed in terms of the argument that if buyers and sellers think that the equilibrium price is going to be 36 shillings, their actions will then ensure that it is so. For example, if price should rise above 36s, then buyers will argue that the excess supply implies that price should eventually fall; this means that even those buyers prepared to pay more than 36s will wait until the price does actually fall. Similarly, if price should fall below 36s, even sellers prepared to accept the lower price will wait for the equilibrium price to be established. This means that the process of "higgling and bargaining" referred to in Marshall's account is strictly redundant, as it is not higgling that results in the final price, but a foreknowledge on the part of transactors. This is evident in the explanation provided of the "true equilibrium price" as that which "if it were fixed on at the beginning, and adhered to throughout, it would exactly equate demand and supply . . . and because every dealer who has a perfect knowledge of the circumstances of the market expects that price to be established" (333–34). Having obviated any need for higgling, the text then proceeds to deny that the foregoing analysis has assumed that dealers have a thorough knowledge of the market, on the grounds that disequilibrium trades based on incorrect information will nonetheless "probably" still result in the market actually closing on the equilibrium price.

This claim, however, is undermined in the following paragraph by the acknowledgment that the foregoing analysis is based on the "latent assumption" that the closing trades would not be affected by the earlier disequilibrium trading (334–35). Thus the theoretical requirements of the comparative statics of competitive equilibrium have effectively replaced the notion that there is a market process at work in which market transactors higgle and bargain over price. The apogee of this approach might be thought to be Walras's *Elements of Pure Economics,* in which higgling, although presented as a market process, is effectively displaced by the services of the fictional auctioneer, where transactors respond to exogenous prices, and disequilibrium trading at "false" prices does not occur. Provisional offers to buy and sell (tickets) are elicited in response to prices being cried out, but this means that market transactors buy and sell only at equilibrium prices and do not engage in bargaining with other transactors (Walras 1954, Lessons 5, 12, 20).[10] In Edgeworth's *Mathematical Psychics,* too, despite the emphasis on recontracting as a more fundamental conception of higgling, recontracting performs the same function of disallowing false trading.[11]

In these accounts, the process of higgling corresponds to the classical view of language as the transparent means by which abstract and necessary truths—the "true" equilibrium price—are discovered. But at the same time higgling itself as a process of bargaining becomes redundant to theoretical analysis, either because it is seen simply as the process by which the objective market facts are discovered, or because the formal requirement of exogenous prices in comparative static competitive analysis entirely bypasses the issue of disequilibrium adjustment paths.

The Deceits of the Market

This is not always the case, however, as there are some instances where the language of the marketplace does have real effects but, as the result is an improper distortion of what would or should prevail, such linguistic interventions are subject to derogation and suspicion. Here a moralistic or critical tone intervenes, exemplifying the suspicion that such rhetorical ploys inevitably elicit.

10. Cf. the editor's note at Lesson 20, n. 6, pp. 528–29.

11. Cf. "even if the dispositions of all the parties were known beforehand, there could be predicted only the position of equilibrium, not the particular course by which it is reached" (Edgeworth 1987, 652).

An early example of this is provided in Defoe's *Complete English Tradesman*, published in 1726 as advice to young tradesmen setting up in business. Chapters 2 and 3 advance the standard eighteenth-century argument concerning the need for clear, plain English without ornament in order to convey the intended meaning: "easy, plain, and familiar language is the beauty of speech in general, and is the excellency of all writing, on whatever subject, or to whatever persons they are we write or speak. The end of speech is that men might understand one another's meaning" (Defoe 1987, 23). This advice also includes a recognition of the power of language in that it urges young tradesmen to master the language of their own trade, because without this linguistic competence they will be cheated by other tradesmen brandishing the rhetoric and clamor of their trade (26).[12] Here Defoe's text is marking the same antinomies of language and rhetoric, knowledge and dissimulation, that are found in Locke's *Essay* and Smith's *Lectures on Rhetoric and Belles Lettres*—which involves the text in a tortuous moral assessment of conventional trading practices later on. Chapter 17 and 18 raise the difficult question of "trading lies" and "shop rhetoric," where the tradesman is forced to utter literal lies in haggling over price (159–61) and in extolling the attractions of his merchandise (175–79). The text here excoriates such practices of deception while recognizing that they constitute a daily part of the tradesman's life, and so is poised uneasily between moral condemnation and pragmatic acceptance:

> However, it were to be wished that on both sides buying and selling might be carried on without it [i.e., trading lies]; for the buyer as often says, "I won't give a farthing more," and yet advances, as the seller says, "I can't abate a farthing," and yet complies. These are, as I call them, *trading lies;* and it were to be wished they could be avoided on both sides; and the honest tradesman does avoid them as much as possible, but yet must not, I say, in all cases, be tied up to the strict, literal sense of that expression, *I cannot abate,* as above. (161, original emphasis)[13]

12. The possibility of a universal trading language is also considered, where "every trades-man would study so the terms of art of other trades, that he might be able to speak to every manufacturer or artist in his own language, and understand them when they talked to one another; this would make trade be a kind of universal language, and the particular marks they are obliged to, would be like the notes of music, an universal character, in which all the trades-men in England might write to one another in the language and characters of their several trades" (Defoe 1987, 25). Inevitably, even a text which extols plain language must resort to metaphorical illustrations.

13. At this point the editor of the 1839 edition includes the following note: "The practice

Accepting trading lies as part of the ordinary conduct of trade, the text cannot recommend young traders to abjure them altogether, although it also recommends that buyers should not haggle over the price if they wish tradesmen to be honest in their turn.

In the case of shop rhetoric "composed of a mass of rattling flattery to the buyer, and that filled with hypocrisy, compliment, self-praises, falsehood, and, in short, a complication of wickedness" (175), the text launches into an intense attack on shopkeepers' mendacity.

> The shopkeeper ought, indeed, to have a good tongue, but he should not make a common prostitute of his tongue, and employ it to the wicked purpose of abusing and imposing upon all that come to deal with him. . . . Let them confine themselves to truth, and say what they will. But it cannot be done; a talking rattling mercer, or draper, or milliner, behind his counter, would be worth nothing if he should confine himself to that mean silly thing called *truth*—they must lie; it is in support of their business, and some think they cannot live without it; but I deny that part, and recommend it, I mean to the tradesman I am speaking of, to consider what a scandal it is upon trade, to pretend to say that a tradesman cannot live without lying, the contrary to which may be made appear in almost every article. (175–76, original emphasis)

The best course of action, it is recommended, is a "happy medium" where the shopkeeper truthfully points out the qualities of his goods, and where buyers sensibly appreciate these true qualities without excessive harangues and fawning language. In this case, the goods speak for themselves, and a rattling tongue becomes counterproductive signifying only those cases where "trash" is being sold or where the buyers are taken to be fools. Thus Defoe's text exemplifies the tensions of a discourse on trading language based on the classical antithesis between truth and rhetoric. According to this approach, the language of the marketplace is assessed according to criteria which will always find it wanting. Translated into the plain, homely language which the *Complete English Tradesman* extols, the language of the market is an exchange of lies "wrapped up in silk and satin" (177).

In *The Wealth of Nations* the language of the market is subject to derogation when it involves deceit or secrecy. Instances of this occur where

---

of haggling about prices is now very properly abandoned by all respectable dealers in goods, greatly to the comfort of both buyers and sellers."

the market price is kept artificially above the natural price by the actions of the suppliers. This action incorporates a deceitful use of language: in the absence of natural causes and the regulations of "police," the market price may persist above the natural price only if there is a systematic "concealment" of the market conditions and if the suppliers are able to maintain a veil of "secrecy" over the true situation (*WN*, 1.7:21–22). In this case, the outcome is similar to the natural monopoly outcome in that the market price may persist above the level of the natural price. Similarly in the labor market, the bargaining of the masters and their workmen will have an effect on the final outcome; in this case the market wage will depend on the tactics and bargaining behavior of the two parties. The masters' strategy to sink the wages of labor involves secrecy and "tacit combinations"; masters always enter into their particular combinations "with the utmost silence and secrecy" (1.8:13). The workers, on the other hand, always have recourse to "the loudest clamour" on account of their sense of desperation and powerlessness in their uneven struggle with their masters. On these public occasions, however, the masters are "just as clamorous upon the other side, and never cease to call aloud for the assistance of the civil magistrate" (1.8:13). The text concludes that the workmen very seldom derive any lasting benefit from their collective action, as the power is loaded on the other side of the dispute. Thus, to the extent that masters do collude, their secrecy and silence is ultimately successful in depressing the market wage below the natural wage. Here the outcome depends on the bargaining behavior of the two parties, and so the determination of the market wage is not independent of the process of bargaining, as it is depressed by the silence and secrecy of the masters.

In these cases, the process of higgling and bargaining is inherently deceitful, as the masters and manufacturers attempt to portray the situation not as it truly is, but according to their own interests. Their strategies involve concealment and secrecy in order to misrepresent the true state of affairs and prevent natural outcomes from occurring. Thus, here, the bargaining strategies of market transactors do have independent effects, but their activities result in a number of distortions; market prices are above natural prices for some goods, and wages are below the natural level. Further, repeatedly in *The Wealth of Nations* it is argued that the "clamour and sophistry" and the "interested sophistry" of the merchants and manufacturers have brought about legislative measures that have promoted their own interests over those of other sectors in society and have secured official monopolies where the market price is kept above the natural level. Here the word "sophistry" epitomizes the ancient attack on rhetoric in promoting specious forms of argument as, in categorizing those arguments as fallacious, it is also referring directly to the Sophists who were the target of Plato's attack on rhetoric. As a result of these sophistic interventions, the manufacturing and trading sectors have been boosted artificially above the levels that would have pertained naturally in the absence of those measures. Throughout *The Wealth of Nations* the system of natural liberty is counterposed to the mercantile system by juxtaposing "plain reason" and "common sense" to "vulgar prejudice" and "interested sophistry": "The proposition [i.e., relating to free trade] is so very manifest, that it seems ridiculous to take any pains to prove it; nor could it ever have been called in question, had not the interested sophistry of merchants and manufacturers confounded the common sense of mankind" (4.2: c.10). Here, the language pertaining to markets and market interests is not the transparent means by which the necessary market values are realized in the marketplace, but becomes a dissembling mode of linguistic activity which prevents the proper and natural outcomes from being realized.

In Edgeworth's *Mathematical Psychics,* contract is indeterminate in the case of bilateral monopoly where there is an indefinite number of final settlements marked out by the contract curve. This theoretical indeterminacy would be resolved in any particular market by the process of higgling and bargaining, which would result in a final solution somewhere on the contract curve. In this bilateral monopoly case, then, market transactors do have an influence over the final outcome which will depend on the relative bargaining position of the two agents, but this is seen as an evil. At this point in the text, the arts of higgling are seen as a dissimulating discourse in terms that echo the classical attacks on rhetoric: "An accessory evil of indeterminate contract is the tendency, greater than in a full market, towards dissimulation and objectionable arts of higgling" ([1881] 1932, 29–30). Support is claimed from Jevons's *Theory of Political Economy,* which argues that in the case of bilateral monopoly "such a transaction must be settled upon other than strictly economic grounds. . . . The art of bargaining mainly consists in the buyer ascertaining the lowest price at which the seller is willing to part with his object, without disclosing if possible the highest price which he, the buyer, is willing to give" (quoted in Edgeworth [1881] 1932, 30). Contrasting "this clogged and underground procedure" with "the smooth machinery" of the Walrasian competitive market, where each dealer simply has to write down his demand at each price "without attempting to conceal his requirements; and these data having been furnished to a sort of market-machine, the *price* to be passionlessly evaluated" (30, original emphasis), the text registers its clear preference for a market system devoid of this kind of higgling. Later on, when considering indeterminacy and the imperfections associated with it, reference is again made to the "Art of Bargaining—higgling dodges and designing obstinacy, and other incalculable and often disreputable accidents" (46). The solution proffered is that of utilitarian arbitration, thus proposing a "moral" solution as a means of rectifying the evils of indeterminacy and higgling in a situation where economic solutions are deemed inadequate (51–56, 136).[14]

Thus, such a treatment of the process or "art" of higgling is an inversion of the previous approach. Whereas the first approach sees higgling as an essential truthful activity, this second approach sees it as deceitful and reprehensible. The first approach sees higgling as the process which leads to the enactment of natural or "true" market outcomes, but the latter sees it as the means by which proper outcomes are subverted for the sake of sectional interests. The first type of higgling is benign, the second is malign; the first deals with outcomes that are necessarily implied by the objective market situation, the second refers to outcomes that are contingent upon the skills and tactics of the transactors. Thus these two different treatments of the behavior of market transactors are playing out the same set of binary opposites that are found in the recurring debate between philosophy and rhetoric. With one set are associated characteristics that are highly valued; with the other are associated the derogated terms. Transposed within economic discourse, this treatment means that the positive attributes are attached to a model of the competitive market where individual agents are unable to affect outcomes but simply provide data for a "sort of market-machine," while the negative attributes are imputed to the case where higgling has real effects and individual market transactors may influence final outcomes. The construction of the model of a competitive market within economic discourse is thus worked out within a theoretical space that has already been marked by centuries of debate over the proper place of philosophy and rhetoric, and the role that

14. Cf. the discussion of J. B. Clark in Morgan, this volume.

language plays in human and social relations. Within such a discourse, the place ascribed to higgling and bargaining as a process of persuasion will inevitably be marginal, pushed out to the boundaries of a discourse which valorizes only that form of higgling which has no effect on true market values.

The Rhetoric of the Market

My argument has so far focused on the ways in which the process of higgling and bargaining have been largely eclipsed in discourses on the market. Two different approaches to higgling and bargaining have been examined, and their points of contrast and difference have been discussed analogically with the classical view of language and its criticisms of rhetoric. But this presentation of their differences is sustained on the shared common ground on which the binary oppositions are themselves constructed. The account of these two different versions of higgling is grounded in a discursive field denominated in terms of the classical view of language which makes possible the set of oppositions between philosophy and rhetoric, truth and falsehood, necessity and contingency. Thus the account of higgling as a benign process is the obverse of higgling as a malign process; despite their differences, such accounts are united by a shared view of the proper functions of language and of market exchange. If this common ground is challenged, however, the oppositions themselves become problematic. Now, what becomes striking is not the distinctness and incompatibility of the two sets of juxtaposed terms, but their discursive links and dependencies. For example, once the importance of language for all discourse is taken to be significant, the high wall separating systematic inquiry from rhetoric is seen to be not at all impervious to the flow of influences from one side to the other. Now, instead of seeing rhetoric as the opponent of truthful inquiry, it becomes something which characterizes all discourse, for good or ill. In this sense, all discourse, even reasoned and serious discourse, may be susceptible to readings which are sensitive to the rhetorical power of those works; language is no longer the transparent medium by which thoughts and meanings are ideally communicated from one person to another, but may on occasion appear to have a force of its own. Similarly, the antithesis between truth and falsehood, and between necessity and contingency, may also be seen to be much more problematic in that knowledge is determined discursively as the product of debate and the interplay of argument and ideas, where communication itself and the means of scholarly persuasion are also significant.[15]

Interpreted analogically within economic discourse, such a rejection of the grounds sustaining the set of classical oppositions would result in a different approach to the process of higgling and bargaining in the market. The linguistic transactions of economic agents would not be perceived in terms of the either/or binary oppositions which set truthfulness against chicanery and necessary outcomes against contingent outcomes. Instead, an alternative model of the competitive market process would be developed in which competition is not seen in bipolar terms of the ways in which transactors passively adjust to the competitive requirements of the situation or deceitfully attempt to manipulate market outcomes, but in terms of the ways in which transactors' negotiations and perceptions of market possibilities also contribute towards determining the market outcome itself. In this case the transactors are not posited as something external to the market process, but are conceptualized as an integral element within that process, whose actions and strategies go some way towards constituting the characteristics of the market. According to this view of a competitive market, outcomes are contingent to some degree on the responses of the agents in it, and this is not seen as an aberration of market behavior or a thwarting of natural market outcomes, but as a constitutive element in competitive outcomes.

As public address and rhetoric were important aspects of city life in ancient Greece and Rome, it is not surprising that early manifestations of this approach can be found in ancient conceptions of the market. The market was understood in terms of a public space in which public speaking formed a routine part of life:

> Private transactions, therefore, took place in the setting of a public arena that provided a sense of publicly recognized value combined with an endorsement of individual voluntarism in exchange. The image of a bargaining process was clearly framed in the tradition of public debate and, at the individual level, in the dialectic of argu-

---

15. This emphasis on the power and complexity of language has taken diverse and multiple forms within philosophy, literary theory, and rhetoric, including, as divergent examples, the attempt to reconstitute classical rhetoric and its tropes (Vickers 1988) and deconstruction (e.g., Derrida 1976). The original landmark publication in economics is McCloskey 1986. See Brown 1993 on some implications for reading the history of economic thought.

ment in the law courts, where . . . rhetoric anticipated many modern economic nuances. (Lowry, this volume; see also Lowry 1987, esp. 139–42)

This sense of the public nature of the bargaining process can also be seen in later attempts to regulate trading practices by ensuring that they were conducted in the open marketplace rather than in secret cabals beyond the reach of public scrutiny. In this context, eighteenth-century regulations on the grain trade in England and France, for example, were designed to promote an "open market" (Thompson 1991b, 305) where transactions were required to take place in public view, such that "parties to a prospective deal were expected to show signs of 'bargaining,' that is, proof that they had not prearranged the transaction and that the price agreed upon resulted from genuine haggling" (Kaplan 1976, 1:69). In this case, the normative connotations of haggling are entirely positive in that it is taken as evidence of playing fair under the public gaze.

Within economic discourse, however, markets with face-to-face bargaining are often conceived as imperfectly competitive in some way or another and comprise a heterogeneous collection of discrete market transactions such as bilateral monopoly, auctions, and cases of strategic interdependence. In these instances, the process of higgling is seen as characterizing a varied range of transactions where agents' individual behavior and responses necessarily or properly determine market outcomes. The challenge to supply and demand analysis in Thornton's *On Labour* falls within this approach to conceptualizing the bargaining aspect of competition in that the various examples of Dutch and English auctions, localized imperfect markets, and the labor market were all illustrations of direct bargaining. In each of these cases, the small number of buyers and sellers means that market transactors are engaged in an exploratory process of establishing market price, and here the term *higgling/haggling* denotes this process of price determination without pejorative overtones (Thornton 1869, 51, 82; 1870, 62, 106).[16] The notion of law-governed outcomes is decisively rejected on the grounds that the transactors themselves determine final outcomes and that these outcomes are path-dependent (1870, 80–82). Thornton's (1870) response to a review in the *British Quarterly Review* (50, no. 100 [1869]) points up this difference in the underlying notion of market competition. The

16. Cf. Mill 1869, 510, 690–91.

reviewer's claim that "the theory of price is neither more nor less than a statement of the conditions by which the price of any commodity would be determined if all the facts of the case were accurately known, and towards which it tends in proportion as they are accurately known" (460) elicited the response that such a view "is quite incompatible with any phenomena of commerce, either actual or possible. By no repetition of experiments could it be ascertained beforehand what in retail, and still less in wholesale transactions, would be the daily or otherwise periodical demand for any commodity" (Thornton 1870, 66n.). Without this knowledge, the existence of trade at disequilibrium prices would affect the final outcome.

This point was grudgingly acknowledged in Edgeworth's *Mathematical Psychics* in the context of the contract curve, and also links up with the issue of indeterminacy: "where the field of competition is sensibly imperfect, an indefinite number of *final settlements* are possible; that in such a case *different* final settlements would be reached if the system should run down from different *initial positions* or contracts. The sort of difference which exists between Dutch and English auction, theoretically unimportant in *perfect competition,* does correspond to different results, *different final settlements* in imperfect competition" ([1881] 1932, 47–48, original emphasis).[17] Cournot's analysis of duopoly had produced a determinate market outcome, and this led to critical discussion as to whether such an outcome should be seen as determinate or indeterminate.[18] In time, Cournot's solution was accepted, but it was also recognized that the question whether a determinate solution exists depends on the assumptions made concerning the reaction functions and strategies of the players in the game.

It also came to be recognized that the indeterminacy of Edgeworth's contract curve is of a different kind from that of strategic interdependence. Here the analogy with chess came to be used in order to illustrate the way in which the actions and expectations of the players are constitutive of the outcome of the game and are not seen as obstructing either market or moral outcomes. Pigou, for example, noted that in this case the outcome depends on the judgment of each transactor, "as in a game of chess each player will act on some forecast of the other's reply; but the

17. The footnote at this point in *Mathematical Psychics* reads: "As Thornton suggests. Now we believe, but not because that unmathematical writer has told us" (Edgeworth [1881] 1932, 48).

18. Magnan de Bornier 1992 charts in detail the Cournot-Bertrand debate.

forecast he acts on may, according to his mood and his reading of that opponent's psychology, be one thing or another thing" (1962, 267).[19] From the fifth edition of Marshall's *Principles,* too, in 1907, the discussion of complementary monopoly, where two firms meet in an input market as bilateral monopolists, is presented in terms of a framework of strategic interdependence, and this is directly linked to the process of higgling. But the term here no longer refers to the redundant higgling of the perfectly competitive market, nor to the dissembling arts of higgling in an indeterminate situation, but to "strategical higgling." It is argued that "there is no means of determining where the price of the ultimate product will be fixed," because what is of central importance here in determining that outcome is the policy of bluff and "strategical higgling and bargaining" between the two transactors (Marshall 1961, 493, 494). The final outcome, therefore, will have to be made by the two firms as the product of their bargaining, rather than delivered to them as something external or objective which they must accept.

An early instance of strategic higgling is provided in Mandeville's *Search into the Nature of Society,* first published in 1723 (three years before Defoe's *Complete English Tradesman*), which presents an account of the process of bargaining between a mercer and a lady customer over the price of a piece of silk (Mandeville [1723]1988, 349–52). Whereas Defoe's account of this instance is constructed in terms of a critical moral assessment of the linguistic turpitude of "shop rhetoric" and an attempt to reconstitute the tradesman as a tolerably honest man, Mandeville's encounter is presented in terms of the strategic interdependence of the two transactors and the crucial role played by flattery in this game of words. The context for Mandeville's illustration is the infamous argument that private vices conduce to public benefits, and so his account of the lies and flattery of the shopkeeper is devoid of the moral opprobrium of Defoe's description. The mercer has an advantage over the lady in his greater knowledge of the costs and price of the article, which he "knows to a farthing" (351), but an even greater asset for him is his experience in close bargaining, in which he has "learn'd unobserv'd to slide into the inmost recesses of the soul, sound the capacity of his customers, and find out their blind side unknown to them" (351). In this particular case, the mercer knows full well how to play on the lady's vanity:

19. See also Chamberlin 1962, 46, 55. In the earlier discussion of bilateral monopoly and bargaining, deception is discussed alongside the "brain work" of bargaining (Pigou 1962, 200–3).

> By all of which he is instructed in fifty other stratagems to make her over-value her own judgment as well as the commodity she would purchase . . . tho' here he has the liberty of telling what lies he pleases, as to the prime cost and the money he has refus'd, yet he trusts not to them only; but attacking her vanity makes her believe the most incredible things in the world, concerning his own weakness and her superior abilities. (351–52)

The upshot is that the lady thinks the agreed price is a bargain and accepts it on that basis. It is, however, the one the mercer wanted all along, as it will give him the customary profits of the trade even though he would have accepted less in order to make the transaction. Although this is the mercer's own reference price, the actual outcome depends on the strategic skills of the two transactors.

Thus, in these various instances, the notion of higgling is constituted as central to a view of market exchanges as discrete or imperfectly competitive in some way or another, involving a process of direct higgling which determines the final outcome. Considered analogically with theories of language, this corresponds to the view of language which challenges the classical opposition of philosophy to a deceitful rhetoric, and which recognizes the importance of language, rhetoric, and diverse forms of communication in the production of knowledge.[20] According to this view, to disregard the implications of the constructedness and linguistic complexity of forms of discourse is to ignore a fundamental aspect of the production of knowledge. Analogically for economics, this corresponds to the view that overlooking the constructedness of markets and their place in a broader social and institutional context also results in neglecting important aspects of the operation of markets.

Conclusion

Tracing the term *higgling* in the history of economic thought shows an uneven landscape, as the term is used in different senses in diverse analytical contexts. Partly, the different uses of the term have been the product of fundamental debates about different concepts of the market and different notions of competition. But partly, these different uses may

---

20. Cf. "the proliferation of incommensurate alternative solution concepts in game theory left you back with no *optimum optimorum* . . . but only an infinitely expansible taxonomy of rest positions: it was just as bad as classical rhetoric!" (Mirowski 1990, 247).

also connect with broader debates relating to the role of language and language use within the wide sweep of intellectual history, and this too relates to questions of human and institutional agency in the furtherance of economic and social outcomes.

I would like to thank Neil De Marchi and Mary Morgan for their comments on the conference draft of this paper and for suggesting further references. I am also grateful to the participants at the Higgling Conference, Duke University, and the Hermes Conference, York University, Ontario, for additional comments. The usual disclaimer applies.

References

Aristotle. 1991. *The Art of Rhetoric*. Harmondsworth: Penguin.

Brown, Vivienne. 1993. Decanonizing Discourses: Textual Analysis and the History of Economic Thought. In *Economics and Language*, edited by W. Henderson, T. Dudley-Evans, and R. Backhouse. London: Routledge.

————. 1994. *Adam Smith's Discourse: Canonicity, Commerce and Conscience*. London: Routledge.

Cantillon, Richard. [1755] 1931. *Essay on the Nature of Trade in General*. Edited by Henry Higgs. London: Macmillan.

Chamberlin, E. H. 1962. *The Theory of Monopolistic Competition*. 8th ed. Cambridge: Harvard University Press.

Cicero. 1982, 1988. *De Oratore*. Loeb Classical Library. Cambridge, Mass., and London: Harvard University Press and Heinemann.

Defoe, Daniel. [1726] 1987. *The Complete English Tradesman*. Gloucester, U.K.: Alan Sutton.

Derrida, Jacques. 1976. *Of Grammatology*. Baltimore and London: The Johns Hopkins University Press.

Edgeworth, F. Y. [1881] 1932. *Mathematical Psychics: An Essay on the Application of Mathematics to the Moral Sciences*. London: Kegan Paul.

————. 1925. *Papers Relating to Political Economy*. London: Macmillan.

————. 1987. Higgling. In *The New Palgrave: A Dictionary of Economics*. London: Macmillan. Reprinted from *Palgrave's Dictionary of Political Economy* (1923–26).

Howell, W. S. 1967. John Locke and the New Rhetoric. *Quarterly Journal of Speech* 53.4:319–33.

————. 1971. *Eighteenth Century British Logic and Rhetoric*. Princeton: Princeton University Press.

Jenkin, Fleeming. 1887. *Papers Literary, Scientific, &c.* Edited by S. Colvin and J. A. Ewing. London: Longmans, Green.

Jevons, W. Stanley. [1871] 1965. *The Theory of Political Economy*. New York: Augustus M. Kelley.

Kaplan, Steven L. 1976. *Bread, Politics and Political Economy in the Reign of Louis XV*. The Hague: Nijhoff.

Kennedy, George. 1963. *The Art of Persuasion in Greece*. Princeton: Princeton University Press.

—————. 1980. *Classical Rhetoric and Its Christian and Secular Tradition from Ancient to Modern Times*. London: Croom Helm.

Keynes, J. M. 1973a. *The General Theory and After: Part I, Preparation*. In *The Collected Writings of John Maynard Kenyes*, vol. 13. London: Macmillan.

—————. 1973b. *The General Theory and After: Part II, Defence and Development*. In *Collected Writings*, vol. 14.

Lawlor, Michael Syron. 1994. On the Historical Origin of Keynes's Financial Market Views. In *Higgling: Transactors and Their Markets in the History of Economics*, edited by Neil De Marchi and Mary S. Morgan. *HOPE* 26, special issue. Durham: Duke University Press.

Locke, John. 1959. *An Essay Concerning Human Understanding*. New York: Dover.

Lowry, S. Todd. 1987. *The Archeology of Economic Ideas: The Classical Greek Tradition*. Durham: Duke University Press.

Magnan de Bornier, Jean. 1992. The "Cournot-Bertrand Debate": A Historical Perspective. *HOPE* 24.3:623–56.

Mandeville, Bernard. [1723] 1988. *The Fable of the Bees: Or, Private Vices, Publick Benefits*. Edited by F. B. Kaye. 2 vols. Oxford: Clarendon Press, 1924. Facsimile reprint, Indianapolis: Liberty Press.

Marshall, Alfred. 1961. *Principles of Economics*. 9th variorum ed. London: Macmillan.

McCloskey, Donald N. 1986. *The Rhetoric of Economics*. Brighton: Harvester Press.

Mill, J. S. 1869. Thornton on Labour and Its Claims. *Fortnightly Review* 5.29:505–18, 5.30:680–700.

Mirowski, Philip. 1990. The Rhetoric of Modern Economics. *History of the Human Sciences* 3.2:243–57.

Morgan, Mary S. 1994. Marketplace Morals and the American Economists: The Case of John Bates Clark. In *Higgling: Transactors and Their Markets in the History of Economics*, edited by Neil De Marchi and Mary S. Morgan. *HOPE* 26, special issue. Durham: Duke University Press.

Pigou, A. C. 1962. *The Economics of Welfare*. 4th ed. London: Macmillan.

Plato. 1960. *Gorgias*. Harmondsworth: Penguin.

—————. 1973. *Phaedrus*. Harmondsworth: Penguin.

Smith, Adam. 1976. *An Inquiry into the Nature and Causes of the Wealth of Nations*. Glasgow Edition. Oxford: Oxford University Press. Reprinted, Indianapolis: Liberty Press, 1981.

—————. 1978. *Lectures on Jurisprudence*. Glasgow Edition. Reprinted, Liberty Press, 1982.

—————. 1983. *Lectures on Rhetoric and Belles Lettres*. Glasgow Edition. Reprinted, Liberty Press, 1985.

Thompson, E. P. 1991a. The Moral Economy of the English Crowd in the Eighteenth Century. In *Customs in Common*. London: Merlin.

———. 1991b. The Moral Economy Reviewed. In *Customs in Common*.

Thornton, W. T. 1869. *On Labour, Its Wrongful Claims and Rightful Dues*. London: Macmillan. (2d ed., 1870.)

Turgot, A. J. J. [1770] 1963. *Reflections on the Formation and the Distribution of Riches*. New York: Augustus M. Kelley.

Vickers, Brian. 1982. Territorial Disputes: Philosophy versus Rhetoric. In *Rhetoric Revalued*, edited by B. Vickers. Binghamton, N.Y.: Center for Medieval and Renaissance Texts and Studies.

———. 1985. The Royal Society and English Prose Style: A Reassessment. In *Rhetoric and the Pursuit of Truth: Language Change in the Seventeenth and Eighteenth Centuries*, edited by B. Vickers. Los Angeles: William Andrews Clark Memorial Library, University of California.

———. 1988. *In Defence of Rhetoric*. Oxford: Clarendon Press.

Walras, Léon. 1954. *Elements of Pure Economics: Or, The Theory of Social Wealth*. London: George Allen & Unwin.

Higgling with Money:
German Contributions between 1900 and 1945

Michael Hutter

Higgling in a Money World

The word *higgling* brings to mind images of arguments about prices in oriental bazaars, or sales pitches in old-fashioned fairs, such as the ones investigated by Clark and Pinch (in this volume)—rather quaint and exotic events, so it seems. In fact, the scope of higgling is much wider. Higgling encompasses every mutual determination of prices at which transactions actually take place. Higgling includes auctions, and it includes the negotiations about financial modes of payment. To focus on higgling, then, is neither exotic nor trivial. The noise of higgling is the sound of markets in action.

Yet in modern economic theory higgling is not regarded as a relevant activity. That opinion stems from the assumption that there exists an equilibrium price at which the negotiations between buyers and sellers in a market stabilize. Once that assumption has been accepted, it is only consistent to regard all actions at nonequilibrium prices as transitory and therefore secondary in relevance. In consequence, an economic theory that is able to recognize higgling must work with an alternative to equilibrium as an organizing principle for an economy.

What is it that distinguishes higgling from common talk, or from other forms of argument? Obviously, there is a kind of conflict between the parties involved, and there seems to be a common rule that constrains and, ultimately, resolves the conflict. The rule consists in the agreement that value perceptions can be articulated in money unit terms. Even the most casual look at any but the most primitive economies shows that money is used in virtually all exchanges. Money is not only used in local trade and in consumer good markets, which are the markets that meet the eye most easily. It is even more irreplaceable in markets for investment projects, obligations, and company shares. The volume of these markets dwarfs that of consumer goods. Higgling in such markets is unthinkable without the competence of handling a variety of sophisticated money forms. It may be historically true that early forms of higgling dealt with the reciprocal exchange of objects. But it is just as true that market transactions gained in volume and importance after it had become possible to express the value of single items in money prices.

Higgling, then, is a form of talk that uses reference to a peculiar value indicator, namely, money prices. Of course, higglers use all kinds of references, but it is the reference to a specifically economic value, expressed in measurable units, which distinguishes higgling from arguing. There seems to be good reason, then, to investigate the particular role of money in the higgling process. What do we know about the role of money in making markets possible? How does a value medium for higgling come about, and how does its availability determine to what extent transactions can be carried out?

Money: Scarce Language for Scarce Objects

Negotiations, auctions, financial arrangements—in all the higgling talk, money units serve as communication hardware. The availability of and competence for applying that hardware determines the extent to which a sphere of higgling or, to use a more respectable term, market transactions is able to develop within a society. Given the observation that higgling is a form of communication, we need a theory where language and signs are the central rather than the peripheral categories of an adequate economic theory. But such a theory has been conspicuously lacking in the history of Western thought. As Brown (in this volume) documents, the tradition of neglect for "rhetoric and oratory" goes back to Greek philosophy. There are systematic, logical reasons for that neglect, which will be dealt with below.[1] Only recently has it been possible to develop a social theory of communication that is capable of dealing with the epistemological difficulties involved.[2] That theory can be used to elucidate the role of money in higgling encounters.

1. For an early version see Turgot's 1769 paper "Value and Money." For contemporary attempts see Polanyi 1968 and Crump 1981.
2. The theory of "self-reproducing social systems" has its empirical basis in biology, ac-

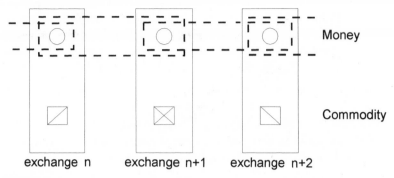

Figure 1

To demonstrate the change in approach, we must investigate briefly the difference between the traditional concept of material exchange and a concept of communication through payment. Consider figure 1. In each of the exchanges n, $n + 1$, and $n + 2$, a different commodity is evaluated not through another commodity, but through a *payment form*. As the identical payment form is used in all three exchanges, the evaluation of $n + 1$ is compared to the evaluation of the previous (remembered) evaluation of exchange n and the subsequent (expected) evaluation of exchange $n + 2$. This means that the money "sequence" (indicated by dotted-line rectangles) is a sequence of events in which the same material or immaterial sign is passed on. In contrast, the commodity "sequence" (indicated by solid-line rectangles) is not a sequence at all. It is a succession of entities whose connection with each other is determined solely by the fact of their consecutive evaluation.

We may conclude: an exchange is not complete in its observation unless we are able to compare it with the previous and the following exchange. A money form is the medium in which the comparison is expressed.

This leads to a change in the understanding of economic value. Every transaction[3] has both a spatial, synchronous dimension of comparing a commodity to a payment form (exchange) and a temporal, diachronous

quired its logical structure through language philosophy and cybernetics, and found its application to social phenomena through an interpretation of society in terms of communication systems. The major author developing the theory is Niklas Luhmann (e.g., 1988, 1990).

3. Exchanges involving money are hereafter called transactions. In the literature, "transactions" is used for exchanges involving time (and cost), and it is also the term for exchanges involving money use. Both uses of the term refer to the same phenomenon: as soon as time is involved, there must be agreed-upon signs to pass on value.

dimension of comparing two comparisons involving the same payment forms (credit). In a transaction sequence, every commodity evaluation is constructed out of a comparison with the previous exchange and with the following exchange: the ratio of at least two ratios determines the "value" of the commodity in question. Value is given a specific meaning in this context: it is a ratio of ratios.[4]

Economic value ratios are expressed with reference to a property called "scarcity." Scarcity, however, is not a natural state, but a complex result of interests and evaluations within a society. It is the peculiarity of money languages to refer to scarcity by operating with a quantitatively limited number of signs. Higgling, then, is a way to exchange observations about the scarcity of items by using a language code that is, in itself, scarce.

After having concentrated on the single event of a transaction, we may now focus on the connection between the events. Figure 1 contains the implication that the continuity of a trade is not to be thought of as a sequence of commodity exchanges. In contrast, a sign-oriented approach distinguishes primarily between the endlessness of payment on one side, and the discontinuity of the objects exchanged, on the other side. The "endlessness of payment" is, in essence, a process of communication. In communication, two messages connect themselves—like a question and an answer, or like one payment and the next payment. Address A sends a message to address B, or, to stay in our field, A passes a coin, a bank note, a bill of credit, or a stock share to B. A observes that B reacts to the message—B accepts the money form. A does not know how B has processed or "understood" A's message, and yet the two addresses are able to continue their dialogue under the supposition that they understand each other. This phenomenon is quite remarkable. It explains why there is such a tremendous continuity in the valuation of specific money forms. The English shilling, for instance, is the contemporary form of a coin that can be traced back to the golden *solidus* of the Eastern Roman Empire, and beyond. It also explains why there is such a thing as change or evolution in the communication hardware called money: change occurs whenever the meaning of a communication form becomes ambiguous, and when the circumstances allow the

---

4. In contemporary terms: value is a difference of differences. The self-referential nature of the process creates a paradox, an inner circle, a class of classes. Reproduction proceeds by differentiation, instead of multiplication. See (apart from Luhmann 1990) Foucault 1973 or, closer to academic logic, Bateson 1979.

temporary coexistence of different interpretations. In both of the major innovations in Western monetary history—the emergence of the coin, and the emergence of the bank note—such ambiguities can be historically documented (Hutter 1993, 1994).

Now we are in a position to reflect upon the logical difficulties in formulating theories about any kind of communication. We, as observers, are in a particular predicament when we observe the particular communication of payment. We all participate in various codes of communication. Among other social skills, we have learned how to use money to communicate economic evaluations. In addition to that, we have made it the object of our scientific observation. In the first case, we are *part of the performance* of a specific payment. We perceive money the way we observe words, or musical sounds. We observe because we know what it means to operate inside the medium. In the second case, we perceive money from the outside, like the *spectator of a performance*. From that perspective, one defines and quantifies money as the total volume of the medium in which economic evaluations are expressed. Observation, therefore, is split into two perspectives. In the first perspective, money appears as a *flow of language*. In the second perspective, money appears as a *stock of signs*. The two perspectives are perspectives of one and the same phenomenon, but they must be kept distinct, lest we confuse the self-evidence of our daily communication with the results of our scientific inquiry.

The endlessness of payment, as it is expressed in figure 1, is not without its distinct limits. All language communities are operationally closed. The signs used within them are only understood in their particular context, just as specific money forms are understood only in a specific "currency community." A common metaphor for such phenomena is the play. The moves in a play contain all the information about the boundary of the play; there can be no outside information. Every move in the play is coded for recognition by other, possible moves in the play. It follows that, in the code of the play, there can be no observation of the play's own boundary, of the unity of the difference between the play and its environment. The play observes its environment (and possibly itself) in the terms of its code—the way in which a style of music observes something about the world around it, and the way a monetary system observes the scarcity relations in the world around it.[5]

---

5. The metaphor of the "economic game" has a long tradition in the literature, without ever making clear the terms of the comparison. For Knight's extensive use of the notion see Emmett, this volume.

To sum up: the proposed theory is a social theory. Society is the play of all observed communication events. The economy, the law, science, arts, and politics are plays within that play. They are totalities of communication events, embedded in the flow of social communication. They are all value-coded through specific media. Plays reproduce themselves in a self-organized process. Maintenance of self-organization replaces maintenance of equilibrium as the core concept in this theory.

The economic play maintains itself by reproducing its own valuation medium. As higgling, in all its sophisticated forms, continues, the money medium is continued and varied through the multitude of transaction sequences which use it to transport value notions into the future. Higgling, then, is the central process by which a money economy comes about. At the same time, the scope and shape of higgling changes as a result of new communication hardware in forms of money and credit.

Criteria for a Theory of Money Higgling

The communication theory of a money economy outlined just above exists today in an embryonic state at best. Still, we can identify several features which characterize its contributions. Thus we should be able to recognize these features when they appear in traditional texts.

A first characteristic feature of a sign/language theory is *self-reference*. Self-reference realizes itself through operations which refer to themselves while referring to something else: signs may signify something objective in the surrounding world, but signs can only be signified by other signs. The signs refer to themselves, and objects cannot enter their sphere. Because of that, self-referential operations are necessarily relational. There is no external grounding. All signs, including money signs, are without beginning and end.

The communication events that constitute a social system or play reproduce themselves, and thus they continue the total system into the future. *Self-reproduction* is characteristic of monetary communication as well. The continuous reestablishment of the participants' ability to pay drives the economy. In traditional theories, the economy's self-reproduction has been captured in the notion of capital accumulation. Usually, capital was interpreted as material capital, not as a money capital stock. A communication-oriented theory offers a way to think about the continuity of economic value without assuming the existence of a value substance.

A third feature is the focus on observation rather than operation. Social science observes the way in which other participants in a society observe; economists observe the way in which participants (including themselves) observe scarcity value. (*Self-observation* was discussed in the previous section with respect to the double existence of participants in economic and scientific observation.) Traditional theory has only vague notions of self-observation. One is the Weberian discussion about implicit value judgments. Another is the notion of "economists' rhetoric" (McCloskey 1985). The observation of "market practices" is a further approach (De Marchi and Harrison, this volume).

Self-reference is a logical property of single events. Self-reproduction is a property of entire plays. Self-observation is a consequence of realizing that one's observation is in the environment of the play observed. All observations, including those of scientists, are self-referential and self-reproductive.

Contributions to an Unknown Paradigm

Given the outlines of a communication-oriented theory of markets with money, the question about earlier contributions to higgling with money can be posed anew. It may well be—and this is the working hypothesis for the second part of this essay—that earlier writings on money contain insights and arguments which made little sense in the light of traditional economic theory, but which make much more sense in the light of a paradigm that interprets higgling as the process of discovering and inventing the actual payments made. The three criteria outlined just above can be applied as a test to determine whether a particular contribution deals with the relevant issues.

What would be the specifications of a subset of texts that promises a relatively high rate of insights about higgling with money? German economics in the early part of this century has several arguments in its favor. The systemic or organic tradition of social science had a particularly strong following among German-speaking authors. One way to pursue that research program was to use the notion of organism (Hutter 1994b); another was to focus on money as the communication medium of the system. Specialized contributions to monetary theory began to appear increasingly after the turn of the present century. These authors were familiar with the English literature, but there was yet no sense of an orthodox opinion in the field. That is why we might be able to identify hitherto neglected insights and arguments.

German Texts on Money Communication, 1900–1945

Historical Situation and Method

The period between 1900 and 1945 covers several distinct phases in the development of economics in the German-speaking countries. The major texts that would dominate discussion after the Great War appeared right at the beginning of the period: Simmel's *Philosophy of Money* in 1900, Knapp's *State Theory of Money* in 1905, and Wieser's *Monetary Value and Its Changes* in 1909. After the war, the number of contributions to the discussion of money increased sharply. Discussion gained an additional dimension when the experience of hyperinflation (1922–23) demonstrated the precariousness of gold as a standard for value communication. After 1930 the contributions dwindled. There came a renewed interest in historical issues, like money emergence, probably as a way of withdrawing from a thoroughly politicized academic context.

Many texts emphasize the sign or language qualities of money.[6] We may now consider their contribution to each of the three criteria proposed earlier. For each selection below, arguments relevant to the three criteria are outlined and supported with quotations. Key words are given in both English and German, to illustrate the difficulties one encounters when shaping thought into communication through metaphor. Truth hides in the cracks of meaning.

Self-Reference

Self-reference is a logical property of signs. Signs take their meaning from previous uses of the sign. But the "connection" between signs in time is different from material connections.

The implications of that difference are touched upon by a number of authors who treat the connection between exchange acts as a valid topic. Texts from Knapp, Moll, Schumpeter, and Simmel serve as examples

6. Secondary sources on the period, place, and topic are rather scant. Döring 1922, Palyi 1924, Rist 1938, and Schumpeter 1970 (ch. 3) are valuable contemporary sources, even though historical account and contemporary theory formulation inevitably intermingle. Wagner (1937) merits special mention; although his history of credit theories only sparsely touches on the subject, his insights are of great precision. The large treatise by Ellis (1934) serves as an exhaustive bibliography, but the treatment is on average dissertation level. Recent sources are Krohn 1986 and Cowen and Kroszner 1992.

here. Since the historical context is probably little known, I have supplied brief introductions.

Georg Friedrich Knapp had already attained a solid reputation as a legal and economic historian when he turned his attention to the theory of money. His *State Theory of Money* was first published in 1903, with later editions over two decades; the new material is contained in the seventy pages of the first chapter. Knapp begins with a distinction between "metalist" and "nominalist" constitutions of money. In the older, metalist constitutions, money forms could be used in a concrete, technical manner. In the new, nominalist constitution, money forms are used in a circulatory manner (*zirkulatorische Verwendung*). Proclaimed money forms work because everyone is, at the same time, both debtor and creditor in many directions. Money units are valuable because they are proclaimed valuable by the "legal order" (*Rechtsordnung*). Thus Knapp shifts the emphasis from exchange goods to payment means and, particularly, to the act of proclaiming, that is, to the actual event of calling something money.[7]

He states three conditions for proclaiming a new means of payment: the legal order has to *describe it* in a recognizable manner, it has to *give a name* to the value unit, and it has to define the relation to the historically prior value unit ([1905] 1921, 17). The "recurrent connection" (*rekurrenter Anschluss*) with a prior value is the property which is of particular interest in our context. Apparently Knapp recognizes that there is a recursive, self-contained connection between valuations even if entire currency systems change.

Bruno Moll's *Logik des Geldes* (1912) is an essay of less than a hundred pages with a much narrower scope than Knapp's treatise. He begins, quite similarly, with a distinction between metal money and "substance-value–less" (*substanzwertlos*) paper money. To prove the point that money cannot be construed without an anchor in substance value, he poses the following question: "How can one think the end of a monetary system?" ([1912] 1922, 26). He discovers an antinomy: "A money without substance value must circulate without end," but at the same time "a money must give the expectation of an eventual conclusion" (27). His argument is straightforward: it is part of economic logic that money

7. A very carefully reasoned definition of money as a means of payment can be found in Moeller 1925, 138. He emphasizes the expectation of future use in accepting money.

leads to material or immaterial satisfaction; infinite validity is a property of ideas, not of historical institutions; therefore, money must contain a sufficient share of substance (57–58). The substance base can be reduced if there is faith (*Glauben*) in the ability of the state to convert its metal currency into commodities (70). The two sides of the antinomy can be "reconciled" (*versöhnt*) if we see that finite satisfaction is necessary; but that satisfaction does not have to consist in metal (96).

Moll arrives at a conclusion that puts him into the traditionalist camp. But his approach is by no means old-fashioned. The logic of self-reference implies endlessness, and Moll addresses the endlessness of payment chains more clearly than any other author. His error lies in a lack of distinction between "eternal" and "endless." Historical institutions are not timeless or infinite, but they may well go on without their end in sight. Moll cannot imagine historical endlessness; therefore he declares "finite satisfaction" an axiomatic truth.

The problem of reference to prior and future value was not unknown to subjectivist authors. The trick suggested by the Austrian School consisted in a distinction between productive and consumptive spheres, which were then engaged in circular validation. Mises (1912, 218) works with the premise of a connection between yesterday's objective value and today's subjective value, which in turn determines tomorrow's objective value. Schumpeter (1917) follows closer in Wieser's tracks by distinguishing between income from production factors and income from consumer goods. Again, two magnitudes determine each other in a circular manner.[8]

Schumpeter gained his initial vision of the economic process through Walrasian general equilibrium. From that perspective, it seemed sufficient to set the circle of validation in motion by proposing an initial, external unit of account, the "critical *chiffre* of the system (*die kritische Ziffer des Systems*)" (Schumpeter 1970, 217).[9] But the linkage of commodities to money, the "money ligament," [10] introduces complications, because the "chosen variety of the money method" (*die gewählte Spielart der Geldmethode*) (1970, 258) has its own laws.

It seems that Schumpeter was increasingly aware of the autonomy of

8. The purchasing power or income approach had a strong influence on the contemporary literature. See Krohn 1986.

9. *Ziffer* means "number" as well as *chiffre* ("cipher").

10. Note that Schumpeter uses a biological analogue.

the process in which money signs[11] were passed on, and of the problems which that autonomy posed to general economic theory. The book on money which he had planned to publish in 1930 was never finished; the manuscript was published posthumously in 1970. The latest version of Schumpeter's view on money can be found in his *History of Economic Analysis* (1954). There he clearly proposes a credit theory of money that depends on a continuity of "differences": "It may be more useful to start from [credit transactions] in the first place, to look upon capitalist finance as a clearing system that cancels claims and debts and carries forward the differences—so that 'money' payments come in only as a special case without any particularly fundamental importance" (1954, 717).

Georg Simmel's *Philosophy of Money* is not the work of an economist. The method he uses is literary rather than scientific. Topics and arguments are presented in a loosely connected manner, without any reference to the existing literature. For Simmel, the consideration of monetary value is a methodological strategy to shift the focus of philosophy from ontological to relational concerns. There is also an empirical concern. Simmel is interested in the effects of money's historical success on all other value relations in modern society. In the course of his argument, he touches on issues that are traditional themes in economists' discourse.[12] But he talks about these themes with the competence of a philosopher skilled in logic. That competence makes his book still relevant to a communication theory of money.

The relevance of money for the philosophical discussion stems from the observation that money expresses social value. Social values are the objective expression of subjective values. Two examples are economic value and aesthetic value. Exchange is a good example to show how things gain their value through each other. Exchange is "the double fact (*Zweimaligkeit der Tatsache*) that a subject has something which it did not have before" (Simmel [1900] 1989, 62). The mutuality or reciprocity of the "double fact" cannot be broken down into individual forces. Exchange is a new, third logical entity. The precursor to the third-entity exchange must be another social activity, like taking by force (*Raub*), but not individual exchange (89).

Both paper and metal money are "a promise" (214). A money form

11. He insisted (Schumpeter 1970, 42) that they were signs, not legal assignments, as proposed by Knapp.

12. In 1980 Laidler and Rowe published an extensive review. Their emphasis, however, was on congruency with existing theory, rather than on a presentation of Simmel's approach.

is able to operate if there is a double faith (*doppelter Glaube*): faith in the issuer of a money form, and trust in the economic circle (*Wirtschafts-kreis*) into which the money form is to be spent. That faith consists in "the feeling that there is a connection (*Zusammenhang*) between our idea of an entity and the entity itself" (216), just as is the case with religious faith. One aspect of promises is their self-binding force: "Money is among those norm-setting imaginations (*normierende Vorstellungen*) which inflect themselves (*beugen sich*) under the norm which they themselves are" (126).[13]

Another recognition of self-reference lies in the observation that the expression of social values, including economic value, can only be articulated in relational terms. There is no final outside reference. Money owes its ability to stabilize and continue value to its property of being "nothing but the relation of economic values embodied in a tangible substance" (130). Money shows more clearly than any other value expression "that things find their meaning *between each other* (*aneinander*) and that the reciprocity of the relationships in which they float constitutes their being and their being-thus (*Sein und Sosein*)" (136).

Because of its self-referential nature, money is outside of exchange as insignificant as priest and temple outside of a common religiosity (212). For the same reason, Simmel comes to the remarkable conclusion that economic value must emerge within the continuity of exchanges, independent of the persons who carry out the exchanges: "The point is that the value of a money does not spring (*quillt*) from its carrier, but that the carrier is altogether secondary" (253).

Self-Reproduction

Self-reproduction refers to the notion that the money play reproduces itself in toto, complete with rules and institutions, into an open future. Thus, the entire "hardware system" for higgling evolves and changes. As the effectiveness of that system increases, new kinds of market transactions become possible.

A system that reproduces itself is a system with a history. Given the historicist tradition, it is not surprising that a number of authors investigated the emergence and development of monetary systems. There were,

---

13. Schabas, in this volume, uses the term "commitment to commitment" with respect to Hume's treatment of property and justice.

however, no attempts to discuss that development from a theoretical perspective. All that we find are general observations on the evolutionary nature of changes in the system (Kaulla 1945) and interesting suggestions about the origin, or rather the precursor, of money valuations: Laum (1924) argues persuasively that all money items receive their trust within the religious sphere before they become usable for exchange or store of value purposes. Gerloff (1940) leaves open the specific source of previous use of a money commodity. He cites examples of decorative use, of treasure, and of ceremonial use. He traces the "need for distinction"[14] to psychological roots. One may also, in the context of communication theory, see money as one of the ways in which human beings are able to delineate social personality. Individuality is by no means something given. It must be constructed by applying signs that can be observed by others who share the same set of values. Gerloff provides a wide array of evidence.

Other sources of potential insight are careful observations of the surrounding, contemporary monetary system. Such observations are, due to a lack of convincing theory, commonplace in the money literature. Practitioners in the money markets have been able to hold their place in academic discussion longer than in any other area of economics.[15] The existence of a Giro accounting system in Germany was an additional reason for the interest with which the system of banking and credit money creation was observed (Cowen and Kroszner 1992). Such knowledge of the process was used to give Knapp's ideas economic plausibility (Bendixen 1907),[16] or to challenge mechanical applications of quantity theory (Liefmann 1916). Hahn (1924, 1925) has been credited with working out a systematic theory that fits the facts of bank credit (Schumpeter 1954, 1116), but his structure is simple and quite familiar. It starts with a distinction between money markets and capital markets. Capital credit appears as a transfer between deposits (*Überweisungsgeld*). This transfer money is the essential form of money. Only banks are able to draw this form of money. For exchange purposes, transfer money has to be transformed into central bank money (*Reichsbankgeld*) for certain periods of time (87–88). The circle works again: the value of credit is determined

14. "The psychological motive of this mass behavior . . . is the need for distinction, authority, acknowledgment, excellence, discrimination according to rank" ([1940] 1947, 27).

15. In Germany, the outstanding examples were two bank directors, Friedrich Bendixen and Albert Hahn.

16. Bendixen suggests a way to introduce the proclaimed state notes into the markets by discounting commodity bills of exchange—a method well known since the days of Adam Smith.

by yesterday's price for bank money, which in turn is determined by the prior value of credit.

It seems quite apparent that theoretical insights into the self-reproduction of money communication were modest. However, it should not be underestimated how strongly the understanding of money was still tied to silver and gold, so that even the description of credit money creation was controversial. Ongoing discussion did have its effects on the convictions of monetary practitioners, and it had a profound effect on the strategy chosen to end hyperinflation in the fall of 1923.[17] The central figure was Karl Helfferich, an economist and member of parliament. Helfferich's book on money (1903), a widely used textbook, shows him as a "practical metalist" with an open ear for nominalist ideas. During the frantic discussions of 1923 he suggested the issue of a type of bank note based on interest-bearing annuities, drawn on agricultural land and industrial property. Simultaneously the bank of issue (*Rentenbank*) was to extend a bridge-the-gap credit to the state. That proposal solved two problems: it gave a new basis for trust in the bank notes issued, and it gave the state a way to stop refinancing itself through discounted treasury bills in paper marks. The proposal shows a clear understanding of the artificial nature of the monetary process. It took several fortunate coincidences to transform it into government action, against the bitter resistance of all those who saw gold currency as the only solid solution.

For more imaginative theoretical contributions we must turn to Simmel. First, he offers some explanation of just what it is that reproduces itself. To Simmel, individuals and society constitute each other. Society is identical with the sum of relationships between individuals, just as life is identical with the sum of the interactions of a body's atoms ([1900] 1989, 210). Within the flow of these relationships, certain types of relationships—like exchange, armed conflict, servitude—develop their own rules and institutions for reaching agreement on value observations. To be able to express the relation between two magnitudes by relating both to a third, abstract, artificial relation "is one of the greatest steps forward which mankind has made, as it is the discovery of a new world out of the material of the old one" (162). As such relations of relation develop—and money is one of them—the immediate tangibility of things is substituted by "secondary symbols" (170). These symbols are constantly reproduced in social interactions.

Simmel applies his approach to social history. The existence of spe-

---

17. See Pfleiderer 1976 for a detailed account.

cific "objectified" relations, like money, must have had a profound effect on the development of a community or society: "The entire life of a community depends on the relationship between culture turned objective and culture of the subjects" (642). In the course of history the emergence of social symbols has tremendously increased the relevance of intellectual abilities for the pursuit of life. But no other such symbol has had such a profound effect as money: "As money, to a degree like no other value perspective (*Wertgesichtspunkt*), lends equality and disequality to things, it activates innumerable efforts, to link them with the rankings of other values in an effort to equalize the unequal, and to find differences in what seems equal" (704). Thus money is, on one hand, the clearest symbol of a world that is constantly in motion. On the other hand, its property of expressing proportions makes it totally stable: "Just like the general notion (*allgemeiner Begriff*), in its logical validity independent of number and modifications of its realization, indicates, as it were, their law (*das Gesetz eben dieser*), so is money—i.e., that inner sense (*Sinn*) [18] through which a single piece of metal or paper becomes money—the general notion of things inasfar as they are economic. They do not need to be economic; but if they are intended to be, then they can only do so by complying to the law of Becoming-Value (*Wert-Werden*) which is condensed in money" (715).

Simmel devotes the second half of his book to demonstrating the effect of money on social development. One chapter shows the influence of money on the notion of individual property, a second one follows the stages of development until—to use our terms—actors were able to higgle about labor services. A third and last chapter argues that money has changed the range, the rhythm, and the speed of modern societies.

To my knowledge, only one of his contemporaries attempted to relate Simmel's framework to economic science.[19] That was Kiichiro Soda, a doctoral student in Tübingen when he wrote *Geld und Wert* (1909). Apparently he was able to apply his knowledge of Japanese thought to Simmel's work. He is close to Simmel in his rigorous use of the object/subject distinction: if money is the "objective expression of economic value," we are able to observe such expressions only to the extent that there is a means of exchange called money through which ratios of sub-

---

18. *Sinn* means "sense" as well as "meaning."

19. Frankel 1977 is an attempt to introduce Simmel into economics by drawing comparisons with the social perspective of classical authors and contrasting it with Keynes's approach.

jective evaluations can be given a numerical magnitude. The first function is "the other side" (31) of the second function. Monetary evaluation takes place within something called society. But what is society?

Soda follows Simmel's suggestion according to which society consists of the "reciprocal action" (*Wechselwirkung*) between individuals. But there is a hitch, and Soda sees it: in Simmel's theory, the term "individual" logically presupposes the term "society." Yet "the individual cannot be grasped as something that exists independently of other individuals" (63). There is, then, no notion of society separate from individuals, and there is no social value unless "several individuals as subjects of individual evaluation create a form of society out of themselves (*aus sich selbst*). We will call such a society an *evaluation society* (*Bewertungsgesellschaft*)" (100). Evaluation societies gain their specific evaluation "intensities" out of the individual contributions. *Intensität*, however, remains an unexplained term. Soda postulates that at a certain stage of historical development, the means of exchange are sufficiently differentiated to allow the formation and maintenance of money circulation communities as a new, distinct form of an evaluation society. Whenever inner evaluations have found an exterior mark (*äusseres Merkmal*), we are in a position to observe a money economy (*Geldwirtschaft*) (152). Money marks are, in the world of objects, equivalent to number marks in the world of experience (150). These marks, and the institutions which process them, are the topic of economic science: "Only at the point where they can be reduced (*zurückgeführt*) to the money relation, do [commodities] begin to be the topic of economic science. In this sense, money is at the center of today's economic science" (153). This observation, of course, coincides with Simmel's statement (cited above) that things become economic by "complying to the law of Becoming-Value which is condensed in money."

Self-Observation

Self-observation, as I remarked in the first part of this essay, "is a consequence of realizing that one's observation is in the environment of the play observed." This sentence has two implications.

The first implication is that the "play observed," namely, the economy, consists of observations. As economic values are discussed and negotiated, observations are made that find their mode in the value relations of money and credit. Higgling comprises the language hull surrounding this process of passing on scarcity value observations. Forms of self-observation within the economic play have to operate in money language as well. They find their expression in the context of money markets, where rates of expected value change are agreed upon. The changes may go in different directions, as we consider currency, credit, or stock markets. But in every case the observation has to be expressed in the units of the system. The regulating function of money rates (interest) has been recognized, and numerous policies by central banks and other actors have been conceived. It remains fundamental to recognize that all the talk, speculation, and collusion around money transactions is strictly part of the play's environment.

The second implication is that scientific observations are observations within a play as well. There must be something, then, that cannot be observed in such operations. Where science operates with language, language itself becomes unobservable (Foerster 1981). We can observe the consequences. Rhetoric and oratory are excluded from the set of phenomena worth observing, higgling is an irrelevant and/or exotic activity. Language and higgling are expected to be transparent, that is, to function without being visible. They are only noticed when they malfunction and thus disturb the normal procedures. The exclusion of higgling from economics is therefore neither a coincidence nor willful intention. It is a consequence of a scientific approach that has not yet reflected upon its own communication process.[20]

The literature under survey has little to contribute to an understanding of self-observation, although there certainly was a keen interest in such issues. All attempts to describe nations and societies as interactive systems led to the question of observability. However, that problem seemed to be solved by using organism as a metaphor for social interaction. Thus the process observed was made distinct from the process of observation, the question disappeared, and so did the possibility of arriving at relevant conclusions (Hutter 1994b).

We do find aspects of concern in the writings of Schumpeter and Simmel. Schumpeter runs into the problem of an autonomous language pro-

---

20. Such a view might help to explain the conversion of a moral economist like J. B. Clark to neoclassical economics: once money price is accepted as a measure for real price, the code has become invisible. Problems of morals and mercantile codes do not disturb normal transactions, and the mutual understanding of the value measure performs smoothly. See Morgan, in this volume.

cess in his discussion of methods used to establish the "critical *chiffre*" and to link the critical *chiffres* of different economic states. The method adapted is the social institution we call money. The methods of monetary practice work in an autonomous fashion "which does not consider changes in the commodity body (*Warenkörper*) and which is meaningless from its perspective." There is a practical impossibility to change the critical *chiffre* continuously without putting the economic process through adaptions that "are based solely on the logic of its accounting process" (Schumpeter 1970, 224).

To Simmel, as we saw above under the heading "self-reference," things find their meaning between each other, in a comparison of descriptions or observations. Money has the "function" of processing the observations. It seems that Simmel can be counted among the first who interpreted market transactions as observation operations in the economic play. However, he does not interpret scientific operations the same way. He mentions the limits of observability in different contexts. A relatively extensive treatment can be found in his discussion of historical materialism, where he argues that even matter is a result of imagination, "determined in its recognizability by the forms and conditions of our mental organization (*geistige Organisation*)" ([1900] 1989, 586).

Conclusions

In the context of a sign/language theory of money, higgling is central: higgling is the talk surrounding exchanges, and money is its code. Traditional theory is about commodities, not about codes. We can talk about higgling if we have a theory that is able to handle communication. The basic structure of such a theory was outlined in the first part of this essay.

The historical survey in the second part of this essay brought several results. First, it is indeed true that money was the topic of a lively, ongoing debate. It is also true that many authors tried to grasp the sign or language aspects of money, emphasizing the process of exchange rather than its material substratum. It is, however, not true that there were many neglected contributions toward a communication theory in German texts on money during the first half of the century. The two exceptions are Schumpeter and Simmel, both "social scientists." Schumpeter is instructive in his slow development toward a position where money and commodity streams are autonomous but mutually dependent processes.[21] Yet he never leaves the orbit of general equilibrium theory. Simmel discusses the very foundations of social science, namely the distinction between subjects and their environment, called the objective world. Despite that distinction he emphasizes differences instead of entities, and he finds a way to discuss value as a relation of relations. Social relations are his topic of observation, even though mental powers of will and imagination are considered necessary premises.

Taken together, the German sources offer a considerable number of comments related to self-reference, fewer to self-reproduction, and even fewer to self-observation. That result mirrors the difficulties for future theory development. But it also indicates that the relevance of higgling to our understanding of the economic process has yet to be fully apprised.

References

Bateson, Gregory. 1979. *Mind and Nature*. New York: Bantam.

Bendixen, Friedrich. [1907] 1926. *Das Wesen des Geldes*. 4th ed. Munich: Duncker & Humblot.

Brown, Vivienne. (This volume). Higgling: The Language of Markets in Economic Discourse. In *Higgling: Transactors and Their Markets in the History of Economics,* edited by Neil De Marchi and Mary Morgan. *HOPE* 26, special issue. Durham: Duke University Press.

Clark, Colin, and Trevor Pinch. (This volume). The Interactional Study of Exchange Relationships: An Analysis of Patter Merchants at Work on Street Markets. In *Higgling: Transactors and Their Markets in the History of Economics,* edited by Neil De Marchi and Mary Morgan. *HOPE* 26, special issue. Durham: Duke University Press.

Cowen, Tyler, and Randall Kroszner. 1992. German-Language Precursors of the New Monetary Economics. *Journal of Institutional and Theoretical Economics* 148.3:387–410.

Crump, Thomas. 1981. *The Phenomenon of Money*. London: Routledge & Kegan Paul.

De Marchi, Neil, and Paul Harrison. 1994. Trading "in the Wind," and with Guile: The Troublesome Matter of the Short Selling of Shares in Seventeenth-Century Holland. In *Higgling: Transactors and Their Markets in the History of Economics,* edited by Neil De Marchi and Mary S. Morgan. *HOPE* 26, special issue. Durham: Duke University Press.

---

21. See the last sentences of *Wesen des Geldes,* just before the manuscript breaks off (1970, 318).

Döring, Herbert. 1922. *Die Geldtheorien seit Knapp*. Bamberg: Griefswald.

Ellis, Howard W. 1934. *German Monetary Theory 1905–1933*. Cambridge: Harvard University Press.

Emmett, Ross B. 1994. Maximizers versus Good Sports: Frank Knight's Curious Understanding of Exchange Behavior. In *Higgling: Transactors and Their Markets in the History of Economics*, edited by Neil De Marchi and Mary S. Morgan. *HOPE* 26, special issue. Durham: Duke University Press.

Foucault, Michel. 1973. *The Order of Things*. New York: Vintage.

Frankel, Herbert. 1977. *Money: Two Philosophies*. Oxford: Blackwell.

Gerloff, Wilhelm. [1940] 1947. *Die Entstehung des Geldes und die Anfänge des Geldwesens*. 3d ed. Frankfurt: Klostermann.

Hahn, Albert. 1924. *Geld und Kredit*. Tübingen: Mohr.

———. 1925. *Volkswirtschaftliche Theorie des Bankkredits*. Tübingen: Mohr.

Helfferich, Karl. [1903] 1916. *Das Geld*. 3d ed. Leipzig: Hirschfeld.

Hutter, Michael. 1993. The Emergence of Bank Notes in Seventeenth-Century England. *Sociologia Internationalis* 31.1:23–40.

———. 1994a. Communication in Economic Evolution: The Case of Money. In *Evolutionary Concepts in Contemporary Economics*, edited by R. England. Ann Arbor: University of Michigan Press.

———. 1994b. Organism as a Metaphor in German Economic Thought. In *Markets Read in Tooth and Claw*, edited by Philip Mirowski. Cambridge: Cambridge University Press.

Kaulla, Rudolf. 1945. *Beiträge zur Entstehungsgeschichte des Geldes*. Bern: Francke.

Knapp, Georg Friedrich. [1905] 1921. *Staatliche Theorie des Geldes*. 3d ed. Munich: Duncker & Humblot.

Krohn, Claus-Dieter. 1986. Geldtheorien in Deutschland während der Inflation 1914 bis 1924. In *Die Anpassung an die Inflation*, edited by G. Feldman, C.-L. Hiltfrerich, G. Ritter, and P.-C. Witt. Berlin: de Gruyter.

Laidler, David, and Nicholas Rowe. 1980. Georg Simmel's Philosophy of Money: A Review Article for Economists. *Journal of Economic Literature* 18.1:97–105.

Laum, Bernhard. 1924. *Heiliges Geld*. Tübingen: Mohr.

Liefmann, Robert. 1916. *Geld und Gold: Ökonomische Theorie des Geldes*. Stuttgart: Deutsche Verlags-Anstalt.

Luhmann, Niklas. 1988. *Die Wirtschaft der Gesellschaft*. Frankfurt: Suhrkamp.

———. 1990. *Essays on Self-Reference*. New York: Columbia University Press.

McCloskey, Donald N. 1985. *The Rhetoric of Economics*. Madison: University of Wisconsin Press.

Mises, Ludwig von. 1912. *Theorie des Geldes und der Umlaufsmittel*. Munich: Duncker & Humblot.

Moeller, Hero. 1925. *Die Lehre vom Gelde*. Leipzig: Quelle & Meyer.

Moll, Bruno. [1912] 1922. *Logik des Geldes*. 2d ed. Munich: Duncker & Humblot.

Morgan, Mary S. 1994. Marketplace Morals and the American Economists: The Case of John Bates Clark. In *Higgling: Transactors and Their Markets in the His-*

tory of Economics, edited by Neil De Marchi and Mary S. Morgan. *HOPE* 26, special issue. Durham: Duke University Press.

Palyi, Melchior. 1924. Ungelöste Fragen der Geldtheorie. In *Die Wirtschaftswissenschaft nach dem Kriege: Festgabe für Lujo Brentano,* edited by M. J. Bonn and M. Palyi. Munich: Duncker & Humblot.

Pfleiderer, Otto. 1976. Die Reichsbank in der Zeit der grossen Inflation, die Stabilisierung der Mark und die Aufwertung von Kapitalforderungen. In *Währung und Wirtschaft in Deutschland 1876–1975,* prepared by the Deutsche Bundesbank, 157–202. Frankfurt: Fritz Knapp.

Polanyi, Karl. 1968. *Primitive, Archaic and Modern Economics.* New York: Doubleday Anchor.

Rist, Charles. 1938. *Histoire des doctrines relatives au crédit et à la monnaie, depuis John Law jusqu'à nos jours.* Paris: Librairie de Receuil Sirey.

Schabas, Margaret. (This volume). Market Contracts in the Age of Hume. In *Higgling: Transactors and Their Markets in the History of Economics,* edited by Neil De Marchi and Mary Morgan. *HOPE* 26, special issue. Durham: Duke University Press.

Schumpeter, Josef. 1917. Das Sozialprodukt und die Rechenpfennige: Glossen und Beiträge zur Geldtheorie. *Archiv für Sozialwissenschaft* 44:627–715.

———. 1954. *History of Economic Analysis.* London: Allen & Unwin.

———. 1970. *Das Wesen des Geldes.* Edited by Fritz Karl Mann. Göttingen: Vandenhoeck & Ruprecht.

Simmel, Georg. [1900] 1989. *Philosophie des Geldes.* Frankfurt: Suhrkamp.

Soda, Kiichiro. [1909] 1924. *Geld und Wert.* Tübingen: Mohr.

von Foerster, Heinz. 1981. *Observing Systems.* Seaside: Intersystems.

Wagner, Valentin F. 1937. *Geschichte der Kredittheorien.* Vienna: Springer.

Wieser, Friedrich von. 1909. Der Geldwert und seine Veränderungen. *Schriften des Vereins für Sozialpolitik,* no. 132.

Part 2 Economic Order Supersedes Market Disorder

Market Contracts in the Age of Hume

Margaret Schabas

> Gentility and Fairlooks buy nothing in the Market.—Eighteenth-century
> Dutch proverb
>
> Why all this higgling with thy friend about such a paultry sum? Does this
> become the generosity of the noble and rich John Bull?—John Arbuthnot,
> from Samuel Johnson's *Dictionary*, 1755

Exchange in the marketplace can be represented as the formation of voluntary and peaceful contracts between two or more interested persons. But what precisely are the motives and accompanying factors which enable these contracts to be reached? The simplistic answer of mutual gain blurs over all of the correlative factors such as trust and perhaps even "gentility and fairlooks," the Dutch proverb given above notwithstanding. Moreover, are these attributes developed in advance, or do they coincide with the formation of markets?

David Hume, in both *A Treatise of Human Nature* (1739–40) and *Political Discourses* (1752), spins out an interesting answer to these (among other) questions. He offers a rich array of insights on the subject of market contracts, provided one takes the trouble to stitch his claims together. But one must keep in mind that Hume's primary problem is that of political instability, which he inherited from Thomas Hobbes and John Locke. Indeed, in many respects even Hume's profound insights into epistemology and metaphysics serve this greater end of "the peace and security of human society" (Hume 1978, 526). For Hume, however, there was no original contract by which political consent was formed: "reason, history, and experience shew us, that all political societies have

had an origin much less accurate and regular; and were one to choose
a period of time, when the people's consent was the least regarded in
public transactions, it would be precisely on the establishment of a new
government" (Hume 1985, 474). Political contracts—if they exist at
all—are relatively unstable (precisely because they are not based on consent), and thus civil society is vulnerable to deterioration. But economic
contracts, which Hume recognized as grounded in consent, both draw
upon and help to foster trust and civility and thereby bring out the best in
humankind. A central question that might have been put to Hume is how
could commercial contracts, which are so tagged to trust and civility,
become widespread in a world of political mistrust and conflict.[1]

Albert O. Hirschman has substantially advanced the view that several Enlightenment philosophers saw political liberty following in the
wake of economic growth. As Sir James Steuart cautioned: "[A] modern oeconomy, therefore, is the most effectual bridle ever was invented
against the folly of despotism" (cited in Hirschman 1977, 85). I shall
extend this line of reasoning in the case of Hume, who certainly kept
one eye directed toward the problem of political instability but who
also recognized that ongoing transformations in the economy had far-
reaching stabilizing effects. For Hume, the critical historical moment
came not as in Locke's account with the advent of money in some ancient unrecorded age, but rather with the arrival of extensive commerce
and money, where "no hand is entirely empty of it" (Hume 1985, 294).
In short, Hume heralded the time when bartering and, I will suggest,
in one sense even higgling becomes a thing of the past. He was a keen
advocate of unimpeded economic contracts (lubricated by money) and
of price uniformity. And he favored these not only because of their service to economic prosperity but because of their civilizing tendencies.
Hume would have shared Arbuthnot's sentiment (cited in the epigraphs
above) that it did not "become the generosity of the noble and rich John
Bull" to higgle.

Hume lived in a time of considerable commercial expansion and
social transformation, particularly between London and the surround-

1. Hume has been much more thoroughly treated as a political philosopher than as an economist (for an outstanding example, see Forbes 1975). The only comprehensive treatment of his
economic papers is Eugene Rotwein's excellent introduction to an edition of Hume's economic
essays and letters, published long ago in 1955. The secondary literature on Hume the philosopher is vast, but only in a few instances has it informed scholarship in the history of economics
(see, for example, Hont 1983; Moss 1991; Teichgraeber 1986).

ing countryside. As E. A. Wrigley has noted, "if it is fair to assume that one adult in six in England in this period had had direct experience of London life, it is probably also fair to assume that this must have acted as a powerful solvent of the customs, prejudices and modes of action of traditional, rural England" (1967, 50). Now Hume was Scottish, not English, and in some respects this made a world of difference. Certainly, he worried out loud to Lord Kames about the welfare of his beloved homeland, at the expense of the English (see Rotwein 1970, 201). Nevertheless, when dealing with other Europeans he deemed himself a "British subject" (Hume 1985, 331). Hume saw the English as the most developed national group and spent considerable effort charting their history. Like Adam Smith, he made it his business to follow the development of England if only to forecast the economic future of Scotland.[2] For the sake of argument here, I focus on the English economy, but make it clear for the record that my description can only be partly extrapolated to the Scottish economy.

The rise of the London market brought with it a marked increase in activities by middlemen. The demand for beef, for example, resulted in a lengthy chain of transactions—breeding, feeding, droving, stocking, and butchering—with a profit exacted at each link in the chain. Presumably each transaction involved some dispute over the price and quantity of the stock. In short, one would assume that the reconfiguration of the English economy into one with a central London market meant that higgling was rife. There is a large grain of truth to this assumption, but of greater significance, I suggest, is the actual decline of higgling during the first half of the eighteenth century, as patterns of markup pricing took hold at both the wholesale and retail levels, and as consumers acquired new habits of shopping. It was this tendency toward price conformity that Hume appreciated. In a virtuous and just society, even transactions with strangers would be conducted with the utmost respect and civility.

What does it mean to *higgle?* The most central meaning, which the word shares with its older synonym *haggle,* is to engage in close bargaining over the terms of an exchange, to dispute a contract.[3] But higgling is

2. A good case for Hume as a keen economic historian and observer, at least in connection to his multivolume *History of England,* can be found in Stockton 1976. His credibility is also borne out in his argument for the recent growth in population (see Hume 1985, 377–464).

3. I am here relying upon three dictionaries, Samuel Johnson's *Dictionary* (1755), Richard Rolt's *A New Dictionary of Trade and Commerce* (1761), and our contemporary *Oxford English Dictionary,* as my source for definitions.

said to be less noisy and less prolonged than haggling. One might higgle for up to half an hour, but haggle for the better part of a day. There is also a word for a higgler, namely one who sells provisions door-to-door or takes them up to London. A higgler is generally bent on raising the price, whereas a haggler (the buyer) is bent on lowering it (as a tourist might be in a Turkish bazaar). In some sense, of course, it always takes two to higgle, or higgle-haggle as the word has been coined. A higgler could either be crooked (*huckster* was a synonym for *higgler*) or an honest trader (Samuel Richardson, 1748, cited in Samuel Johnson's *Dictionary,* 1755). Finally, a higgler might operate by buying livestock, especially poultry or pigs, and fatten them up for market. Hence we have the term "higgling up a pig" and possibly "higgledy-piggledy" (Johnson suggests a link between the two words).

Higgling in shops seems to have been commonplace. Bernard Mandeville (1732) describes a dispute over the price of some silk between a vain woman of means and a prosperous London shopkeeper that has all the formalities of a sarabande (Mandeville 1988, 1:349–53). She does her utmost to appear well bred and knowledgeable about the wares (which she is not), while he skillfully sustains an obsequious and flattering demeanor toward her as a way of conveying his (unfounded) knowledge of her preferences. But provided he makes his customary profit, he is inclined not to overcharge so as to win her long-term business. The end result, therefore, is a price more or less identical to that of every other customer. For Mandeville, it is the ritual that matters. His description of how both parties feign civility, in order to mask their ignorance and pecuniary motives, readily serves his broader theme of the hypocrisy that surrounds commercial transactions.

Higgling in shops has undoubtedly persisted to this day. But there is some reason to believe that it was not as prevalent by the middle or end of the eighteenth century as it was when Mandeville put pen to paper. This was the period during which shops sprang up in rows and clusters. Even Mandeville realized that the proximity of similar dealers resulted in price uniformity, though he believed the reasons the fair sex would prefer one shop to another were "often very whimsical" (1988, 1:352). Some of the reasons, he suspected, were due to the manners and good looks of the shopkeeper, or the way in which he arranged his wares. According to Daniel Defoe, a number of London shopkeepers spent more than five hundred pounds on displays and fixtures such as the bow windows that extend out over a passageway (Westerfield 1968, 343–44). To become apprised of the various goods and their prices, Londoners readily took to the activity of window-shopping.

To reinforce the practice of fixed prices, newspapers started to advertise shop prices as early as 1658. By the mid-eighteenth century, Londoners were inundated with information. The first daily newspaper started in 1702, and by the 1780s London had nine dailies and about fifteen more newspapers that appeared at least once a week (see Trusler 1786, 124–25). In addition to listing the prices of wares in the shops they promoted the policy of fixed prices and explicitly discouraged higgling as an acceptable form of behavior (Westerfield 1968, 344). In Reverend Trusler's manual for the newcomer to London, one finds the firm advice to purchase from proper establishments which extend lines of credit. While the price might be higher, the shopkeeper nonetheless has "a character at stake, and will use you well, in hopes of having your custom in future; but if you buy in general of those who undersell the fair trader, and advertise things at a very low price, depend upon it, unless you are a very good judge of the articles you buy, and take especial care, you will be taken in" (1786, 150). Here we have much the same lesson as Mandeville's: shopping, at least among the well-to-do, was effectively a process of assessing trust and "good character." No doubt negotiations frequently transpired between customers and retailers, probably more than is true today, but markup pricing and price obedience seem to have become the rule.[4]

The more interesting form of higgling at the time, at least for my purposes, was that undertaken by middlemen or higglers. It seems warranted to form the impression that higgling was a commonplace feature of an emerging commercial society. As the guilds and municipal price regulations were dismantled, as shops and daily markets replaced seasonal fairs, and as the links between producer and consumer grew ever more complex, price discrepancies became the norm. Higgling, one might suppose, would tend to occur in cases of asymmetric information, where prices are relatively flexible, and where there is a lack of trust

---

4. Trevor Pinch's interesting study of pitching (see Clark and Pinch, this volume) suggests that the reverse happened in the case of those who were not refined enough to enter shops. They effectively "pay" for the goods in the form of insults to their character. As Trusler would say, they are "taken in." Department stores, which were first set up in the latter part of the nineteenth century, were the great equalizers. Clerks were instructed to stick to the posted prices. Those who were too timid to negotiate in a well-appointed shop could enter the large store and make their purchase without much concern for their social countenance.

between the buyer and seller. And while it is perfectly feasible to higgle over the quantities exchanged, the primary locus for dispute appears to have been the price.[5]

Ray B. Westerfield's classic study *Middlemen in English Business between 1660 and 1760* (1915) provides a number of interesting examples of higgling.[6] As he submits, middlemen were adversely perceived by the public for raising prices for services not rendered, while in actuality they reduced prices for consumers by inducing various economies of scale and efficiencies from the division of labor.[7] One significant feature of this transformation to a commercial society was the rapidity with which middlemen adopted specialized roles not only with respect to a particular good but to a specific stage in the processing or retailing of the good— such as cattle grazier, coal crimper, or corn chandler. Presumably such traders could take advantage of asymmetric information. They made it their business to know the prevailing prices, particularly in London.

According to Westerfield, the activities of middlemen had the ironic result of reducing the practice of higgling, by extending the volume of trade out into the countryside and centralizing transactions. By the early to mid-1700s, for example, it became customary for corn jobbers to purchase corn from the farmer in bulk by bidding on samples.[8] No doubt

5. Many of the goods traded at the time were relatively perishable or difficult to store, such that the producer would be especially desirous to sell all his stock. Moreover, transactions were often carried out in customary units, a trend that increased during the Enlightenment (see Kula 1986, 115). This did not mean that the units were standardized across the British Isles. They were, however, locally regulated and understood. Coal was sold by weight, with some attention paid to its grade. Fish were displayed according to kind and length.

6. I have no particular expertise in eighteenth-century economic history and thus rely heavily on Westerfield. But numerous more recent scholars attest to the excellence of his book and to its singularity. According to Hoppit, "it is a vivid testament to the lack of historical inquiry into the fate of middlemen that the best general study of wholesalers remains R. B. Westerfield" (1987, 6n.). Given the advent of cliometrics since 1958, this neglect is readily explicable. If neoclassical theory has no room for price negotiators, why should economic historians include them in their models?

7. In the Kress Collection at Harvard University one can find a number of short diatribes against middlemen dating from this period. E. P. Thompson also cites an anonymous tract of 1718 that sets out to "prove that Regrators, Engrossers, Forestallers, Hawkers, and Jobbers of Corn, Cattle, and other Marketable Goods are Destructive of Trade, Oppressors to the Poor, and a Common Nuisance to the Kingdom in General" (1971, 85n.).

8. There are different views about the extent to which sampling took over at this time. According to Thompson, the practice met with much more resistance than the descriptions by Daniel Defoe would imply. Thompson cites specific outcries against sampling in 1710 and 1733 and some attempts at enforcement by the magistrates as late as 1801. But he grants that sampling was widely practiced by the large farmers by 1725, and that by the 1760s (particu-

there were still disputes over the terms of trade, but by creating a market for the display of samples (with delivery at a later date), transactions were much simplified. According to Westerfield, farmers much preferred to sell to one buyer than to higgle with several customers. Moreover, the largest purchasers of wholesale corn were the brewers, and insofar as the retail prices of such beverages were regulated by the government (as was the price of bread, for that matter), the whole set of antecedent activities was fairly constrained by the final market. Price information also became more available. By 1750 *Gentleman's Magazine* published the corn prices prevailing in the larger towns, and the pattern that emerged was one of conformity with the London price.[9] All of this suggests that in the trading of corn, higgling declined over the course of Hume's life.

Higgling was more frequent and long-lasting in the market for fish, if only because the sales were on a daily rather than an annual basis. Although London sprouted a fish market as early as 1283, prices were firmly regulated. At the shore, a twelve-hour price was contracted between the first fisherman of the tide and his merchant. All subsequent fishermen of the day sold their catches at the prevailing "tide price." As the market grew, the transactions both at the shore and in the wholesale market were less regulated. In 1699 Billingsgate became a "free and open Market for all Sorts of Fish" (Westerfield 1968, 209). The fishmongers of the early morning were wholesalers, and bent on driving prices up. So their daily activities might rightly be described as higgling, the large level of transactions notwithstanding. By 1760, however, in response to ongoing complaints that the price of fish was too high, the main

---

larly in years of abundant harvests) complaints and convictions were much less frequent. The strict regulations against sale by sample, as well as engrossing, forestalling, and regrating, had been in place since the time of Edward VI (1551) and were only partly repealed in 1772. Nevertheless, as Thompson concludes, "the paternalistic model [to regulate corn prices and markets] had an ideal existence, and also a fragmentary real existence. In years of good harvests and moderate prices, the authorities lapsed into forgetfulness. But if prices rose and the poor became turbulent, it was revived, at least for symbolic effect" (1971, 88). Adam Smith, who praised the corn merchants in his *Digression Concerning the Corn Trade and Corn Laws,* claimed that "the popular fear of engrossing and forestalling may be compared to the popular terrors and suspicions of witchcraft" (Smith 1981, 1:534).

9. Tables of eighteenth-century corn prices in the Kress Collection at Harvard University show that the London price was on the lower end of the scale, but not the lowest. The 1776 per bushel price ranged from 3 shillings 11.5 pence to 6 shillings 4 pence, with the London price, posted at the top, at 4 shillings 5.25 pence. The London price may well have been what Adam Smith had in mind when he referred to the "natural price" or "central price" as the one to which all other prices were "continually gravitating" (1:75).

fishmongers agreed to let a small number of factors (twenty or thirty) control the initial stage of the market (the tidal price). Since factors are paid by commission, this tended to bring prices down and smooth out price discrepancies (214). A similar impression may be gleaned from Trusler's guide (1786, 31–33), which provides information about "average" prices for Billingsgate fish by kind, weight, and season.[10]

Cattle jobbers also higgled with the graziers (those who fatten but do not breed the livestock), since they tended to be better informed of the prevailing market price. By about 1750 jobbers had much greater control over the livestock market than the graziers, due to the improvement of roads into London and through the construction of stockyards. Unlike corn jobbers, who might move from one region to the next and also take advantage of bad harvests, cattle jobbers were much more constrained by the lay of the land. It is reasonable to assume that the benefits of regular and smooth transactions with their graziers outweighed the costs of persistent higgling. According to Westerfield, the jobbers developed various tactics to induce the graziers to sell at a more uniform rate, thereby insuring a regular supply as well as price stability at the wholesale level. One of these tactics was to offer more than the prevailing price, for a brief spell, as a means of inducing loyalty (1968, 191).

Westerfield also discusses higgling in the wholesale coal market, though it was an early morning affair. Once the first few contracts with the coal factors were settled (by considerable higgling), the price was then constant for the rest of the day. A parliamentary act of 1711 required that the price and grade of each transaction be recorded and posted, primarily as a means to reduce swindling. But the availability of such information undoubtedly also helped to level those transactions, as buyer and seller became more symmetrical. There is thus reason to suppose that both in this trade and in the cattle trade, higgling declined during the eighteenth century. Moreover, the shift from periodic to continuous marketing helped to strengthen the efficacy of market forces and thus bring about price uniformity.

Judging from this historical account, David Hume (1711–76) was alive at a time when higgling may have peaked but then declined, as seen, for example, in the intensification and remission of fish higgling from the

---

10. Trusler, for example, informs his readers that an act of Parliament obliged Billingsgate fishmongers (at a penalty of 20 shillings) to sell brill, bret, or turbot up to sixteen inches long for sixpence a pound.

legislature between 1699 and 1760. A man of little means but expensive tastes (purportedly a gourmand), Hume was probably quite sensitive to prices. As a young man he spent four months as a clerk for Bristol sugar merchants, so he may have acquired some firsthand knowledge of business dealings. In his essay "Of Money," however, we find no discussion of incremental price adjustments, let alone the activity of higgling. At one point Hume alludes to the traditional argument that prices are settled by comparing the "overplus" to the demand. But he is much more interested in analyzing the price level overall and noting the role of the supply of money: "It seems a maxim almost self-evident, that the prices of every thing depend on the proportion between commodities and money, and that any considerable alteration on either has the same effect, either of heightening or lowering the price" (Hume 1985, 290).

Hume made some interesting observations about relative prices by region: "There is more difference between the prices of all provisions in Paris and Languedoc, than between those in London and Yorkshire" (1985, 354–55). In his view this was due to the enormous size of London and the fact that it was still growing. Large cities and the concomitant network of trade in the countryside were thus to be encouraged.[11] Hume, however, was more interested in temporal comparisons of prices. With the rise of commerce and the use of money for transactions, real prices had fallen secularly (1985, 292). He based this claim on his belief that the influx of specie since the fifteenth century had much exceeded the approximate fourfold increase in the price level. So he did not share the concerns of many at his time that the middlemen were responsible for raising prices. Indeed, if higgling is to be understood as attempts by middlemen to raise prices, then for Hume, the opposite was the prevailing tendency. Merchants, by spreading money into new regions of the economy, served to bring prices down:

> But after money enters into all contracts and sales, and is every where the measure of exchange, the same national cash has a much greater task to perform; all commodities are then in the market; the sphere of circulation is enlarged; it is the same case as if that individual sum were to serve a larger kingdom; and therefore, the proportion being

11. As Adam Smith was to remark in his celebrated section in *The Wealth of Nations* (1776) on "the natural progress of opulence," trade between town and countryside served to smooth out price discrepancies. Corn will sell in the town for the same price whether it grows a mile away or comes some twenty miles' distance (1981, 1:376–77).

here lessened on the side of the money, every thing must become cheaper, and the prices gradually fall. (1985, 292)

For this reason, merchants are said to be "one of the most useful races of men" (300). The more they can steer the economy away from the landed gentry, who are wont to be prodigal and keep interest rates high, the better for one and all. In Hume's estimation, they are fully entitled to accumulate vast sums of money and vie with the aristocracy for titles. Merchants induce industry and frugality, and thus help spur everyone (both rich and poor) away from indolence. For Hume, excessive idleness is one of the more deplorable vices and the cause of many a sad demise (1978, 587; 1985, 301).

Merchants thus play a critical role in spreading money, which in turn stimulates economic growth. "In every kingdom, into which money begins to flow in greater abundance than formerly, every thing takes a new face: labour and industry gain life; the merchant becomes more enterprising, the manufacturer more diligent and skilful, and even the farmer follows his plough with greater alacrity and attention" (1985, 286). Money, those "little yellow or white pieces" as Hume likes to call them, has almost magical properties in inducing everyone to work harder. And while the end result of an increase in the quantity of money in a region is inflation, this does not concern him.[12] The price level, he grasps, is entirely arbitrary. What matters is that an increase in money "keeps alive a spirit of industry in the nation, and encreases the stock of labour, in which consists all real power and riches" (288).

For Hume, money seems to have vital properties, such as restoring the spirit of industry as it circulates and diffuses. Like the Physiocrats, Hume also embraced the metaphor of money as the blood that nourishes the body politic as it is "digest[ed] into every vein" (294). More often, however, he speaks of money in terms of oil or water, as a fluid that coats the wheels of trade or that spreads itself over the land. He exploits the equilibrating and diffusional properties of fluids.[13] While the discovery

12. As Michael Duke has argued (1979, 576–77), Hume did not treat prices as upwardly flexible. New injections of money result in an increased exertion of extant underutilized labor. Inflation only comes to pass at the end of the day, after inventories have been reduced and production increased.

13. Money is almost like an electric charge that galvanizes the economy. Possibly, Hume's conception of money was influenced by the doctrine of subtle fluids which was prevalent in Enlightenment natural philosophy. Heat, light, and electricity were mysterious phenomena that

of more gold or silver may increase the global stock, it will eventually spread out like the oceans: "It is impossible to heap up money, more than any fluid, beyond its proper level" (312). He also depicts merchants as building (metaphoric) canals on the economic landscape, in order to allow money to flow into more regions: "Merchants . . . beget industry, by serving as canals to convey it through every corner of the state" (301). Dutch merchants, having virtually no more land in which to vent their hard-earned profits, are quintessential figures insofar as they "flourish only by their being the brokers, and factors, and carriers of others" (330).

While Hume often refers to economic exchanges as contracts, he makes, as far as I can tell, no explicit references to higgling. He remarks at one point that in tropical regions there are fewer quarrels because there are fewer goods to be had (267). An implication of this might be that there are more disputes in the richer northern climes, though money would help to reduce such frictions. He also notes that contracts between artisans and peasants reach back to "the infancy of society," but as transactions between neighbors these contracts were "entered into immediately" and thus unproblematically (299). As contracts between more distant places were required because of an uneven distribution of goods (butter one place, bread another), merchants sprang into service to meet those needs. But nowhere does Hume give the impression that higgling might have accompanied the spread of commerce.[14]

---

had vital properties and produced a wide range of effects without apparent mechanical causes. Yet they also seemed connected to one another, as the development of the concept of energy a century later would demonstrate. To make sense of these entities, physicists treated them as fluids endowed with the appropriate set of properties: conservation, condensity, and capacity, as well as rapid diffusion (see Hankins 1985, 50–53). It had long been believed that heat and light were ubiquitous and essential to the natural order. By the 1730s, thanks to Francis Hauksbee's invention of the electrostatic generator, experimental physicists had shown that virtually all substances could be electrified and that electricity was therefore a universal property of matter and possibly even the key to life itself. The emphasis Hume placed on the global diffusion of money is appropriately analogous. The 1730s and 1740s, precisely when Hume was writing his political and economic essays, were a celebrated era for parlor displays of electricity (Hankins, 55).

14. In the *Treatise* Hume describes a dispute over an estate in order to make an argument about the moral neutrality of property claims. As to the two parties in the dispute, "one is rich, a fool, and a batchelor; the other poor, a man of sense, and has a numerous family: The first is my enemy; the second my friend." For Hume, it is obvious that whatever the circumstances, "I would be induc'd to do my utmost to procure the estate to the latter." To act solely on moral considerations, however, "wou'd produce an infinite confusion in human society." It is im-

For Hume, the growth of commerce, of nonbarter exchange, is one of the most important advances of his time. Once one makes the transition from a barter economy to one with extensive commercial networks, a unique form of reciprocity between strangers is established (291, 300). This in itself is a good thing, if only because of the growth of population. More important, however, is the change that comes about in the habits and manners of the people. While there are certain stable features to human nature, by and large "man is a very variable being, and susceptible of many different opinions, principles, and rules of conduct" (255–56). The spread of commerce both reduces indolence and increases knowledge of the arts and sciences. And the cultivation of letters and other refined pursuits brings more honesty (170). Commerce also fosters political order, which in turn brings more "mildness and moderation" (272–73). This in turn induces more refined manners in place of the simpler and cruder ones of ancient times (292–93). A true cosmopolitan, Hume sees that money and trade may be the great palliatives for national rivalries: "Nothing is more favourable to the rise of politeness and learning, than a number of neighbouring and independent states, connected together by commerce and policy" (119). Hence his celebrated prayer for the flourishing commerce of Germany, Spain, Italy, and even France (331).

This transformation to a commercial society depends very much upon the process by which contracts arise out of "mutual confidence and security": "The freedom and extent of human commerce depend entirely on a fidelity with regard to promises" (Hume 1978, 546). This is particularly true of the market for services, which Hume, to his credit, sees as a different process from the distribution of goods. To reap the advantages of others (for to be self-sufficient, he notes, would mean poverty), we make promises and expect reciprocity at a future point in time. We contract the sale of a house, the delivery of corn or wine, the attention of a surgeon. Precisely because the contract to hire a service must transpire over a block of time, it must draw upon already accumulated stocks of trust, on promises made in the past (1978, 520).

Hume discusses the origins of promise-keeping at length in book 3 of the *Treatise*. He grants the existence of actions motivated by passions

---

perative, therefore, to lay down inflexible rules for the transference of property that would not be subject to spite or favoritism even if this results in the property's going to the richer person (Hume 1978, 532).

"implanted in human nature" (1978, 518), such as the protection of a father for his children. There is no natural inclination to keep promises, however, particularly to strangers. Promises are "human inventions, founded on the necessities and interests of society" (519). What sustains this activity of promise-keeping is the realization that any failure would entail losing the trust of others. Such a betrayal is contrary to our own interests, our own desire for gaining goods and services from others. This realization comes to each of us quite readily and takes hold collectively:

> There needs but a very little practice of the world, to make us perceive all these consequences and advantages [to keeping promises]. The shortest experience of society discovers them to every mortal; and when each individual perceives the same sense of interest in all his fellows, he immediately performs his part of any contract, as being assur'd, that they will not be wanting in theirs. All of them, by concert, enter into a scheme of actions, calculated for common benefit, and agree to be true to their word. (522)

In this analysis, Hume has maintained that promise-keeping is deeply ingrained—it readily arises out of an appreciation for simple commerce (perhaps even barter exchange)—and in turn helps to fuel more commerce, especially services that bridge temporal gaps. "The commerce and intercourse of mankind, which are of such mighty advantage, can have no security where men pay no regard to their engagements" (1985, 481). More remarkably, this comes about almost in unison, "by concert." There is thus no need for political order or even an iterative process of learning and negotiation. A breach of one's word quite simply carries the "penalty of never being trusted again" (1978, 522). Nor does the commercial motive for promise-keeping undercut "the more generous and noble intercourse of friendship and good offices," which do not depend on contracting (521). Trust, so to speak, comes in the back door as well as the front.

Having established the depth of our commitment to commitment, Hume then argues that property and justice emerge together, like two sides of the same coin: "the origin of justice explains that of property. The same artifice gives rise to both" (491). As Todd Lowry has shown (this volume), choice is a central component of ancient concepts of justice. Hume echoes those sentiments by underscoring the role of consent in property claims. Moreover, since commerce precedes the formation of property and a judicial system, it has already helped to spread the practice by which men consent to one thing as opposed to another and thereby experience some modicum of liberty. Commerce is for Hume part and parcel of the transition to a more liberal and thus just society.

Hume provides us with his own version of the original state of nature. The obvious fact that we enter the world with parents and siblings suggests to him that there never was a Hobbesian state of war of one against all (1978, 493, 542). For Hume, life was never solitary, and hence it was never really nasty or brutish either. Cooperation between persons, such as the rowing of a boat, can arise naturally, without an explicit contract or even a government (490). Indeed, he maintains, "the state of society without government is one of the most natural states of men, and may subsist with the conjunction of many families, and long after the first generation" (541). As long as three "fundamental laws of nature" are met, "that of stability of possession, of its transference by consent, and of the performance of promises," there is no need for a polity (526). If anything, governments arise only when regions are attacked by foreigners, or so Hume supposed (540).

The original contract as depicted by Locke is for Hume a total myth. "In vain, are we asked in what records this charter of our liberties is registered. It was not written on parchment, nor yet on leaves or barks of trees. It preceded the use of writing and all the other civilized arts of life" (Hume 1985, 468). Nor can we find it in human nature. Political authority came from "violence and submission, not consent or promise." Indeed, "human affairs will never admit of this consent; seldom of the appearance of it" (473). One is not, therefore, obliged to obey one's country because one's ancestors consented to its constitution. Nor, contends Hume, is it feasible to entreat a dissenter simply to migrate elsewhere, as Locke maintained (he argued for the right to emigrate if one did not wish to adopt the ruler of one's birth). Moreover, even the best example we have of a democracy, the government of ancient Athens, only represented some one-tenth of the population: women, slaves and foreigners did not enter into the contract (473). Hume is thus very skeptical about the possibility of forming a constitution by consent.

In sum, economic contracts are more fundamental, both historically and psychologically, than political contracts. The latter only draw upon the essential acts of consent and promise-keeping in the case of property claims. Moreover, economic contracts are much more easily made and dissolved. There are critical differences in the time it takes to see the advantages of economic and political order, or put aside any doubts: "One thinks he acquires a right to a horse, or a suit of cloaths, in a very short time; but a century is scarce sufficient to establish any new government, or remove all scruples in the minds of the subjects concerning it" (Hume 1978, 557). This and many other remarks leave the impression that economic contracting is much less problematic than the formation of political contracts.

While Hume is severe toward the Lockean tale, he is no Hobbesian either.[15] True, he grants that "self-interest, fear, and affection drive government" (1985, 34). He also submits "a just political maxim that every man must be supposed a knave" (42). And it is well known that statesmen can break their word more readily than a private gentleman (1978, 569). Hume also grants that trust is ever vulnerable to betrayal: "No weakness of human nature is more universal and conspicuous than what we commonly call CREDULITY, or a too easy faith in the testimony of others" (112). Nevertheless, political society is but an extension of the family (1985, 37), which for Hume is the locus of generosity and goodwill. One important step that he took away from such thinkers as Hobbes and Mandeville was on the issue of the degree of selfishness of human beings. As he relates in the *Treatise*, "So far from thinking, that men have no affection for any thing beyond themselves, I am of opinion, that tho' it be rare to meet with one, who loves any single person better than himself; yet 'tis as rare to meet with one, in whom all the kind affections, taken together, do not over-balance all the selfish" (1978, 487).

Hume thus believed that we have a genuine capacity for generosity and compassion. Affection between the sexes is the most deeply planted passion, and thus "begets a friendship and mutual sympathy" from which arises marriage and the family. Of the more genuine passions, we have gallantry, which is "as generous as it is natural" (1985, 132). This in turn engenders good manners, particularly the deference of the strong to the weak, as we find in our customary respect for the elderly, the hospitality bestowed upon foreigners, and the kindness of men toward women. For Hume, such good manners are much more widespread in the modern era than in ancient times, as is evident in the current custom of offering one's guests the better bread and wine (132). Trust is also more deeply

---

15. While Laurence Moss (1991) has made a good case for Hume's indebtedness to Hobbes, he fails to acknowledge the serious differences in their views on the extent of peace and goodwill that would once have prevailed in the most original state.

entrenched, as is evident in the increase in the number of cartels (406), not to mention the extensive rise of commerce.

His central thesis, however, is that commerce itself has changed the habits and customs of the time. This happens slowly. Certain passions, such as "ambition, honour and shame . . . are of a very stubborn and intractable nature" (97), while others, such as curiosity and courage, wax and wane according to external conditions (99, 113–14, 212, 255). But Hume is sanguine about social reform due to the growth of commerce. The full benefits from trade—happiness, civility, and political stability—have yet to be reaped: "It is not fully known, what degree of refinement, either in virtue or vice, human nature is susceptible of; nor what may be expected of mankind from any great revolution in their education, custom or principles. . . . Trade was never esteemed an affair of state till the last century; and there scarcely is any ancient writer on politics, who has made mention of it" (87–88).

Hume has thereby extended the temporal framework by which one accounts for economic and political order, rather than settling it *tout court* as did Locke. He unfolds a tale of passions, interests, and human fraility on a global scale. What comes forth loud and clear in Hume, particularly in his treatment of contracts, is that the economic activities stabilize the political—historically, behaviorally, and institutionally. Trust and consent are central ingredients to the rise of commerce and hence the path to a better world. While Hume is known more as a political philosopher than as a political economist, it is fair to say that market contracts figure much more prominently in his thought than has hitherto been acknowledged.

The author expresses her appreciation for the many helpful criticisms and references offered by A. W. Coats, Avi Cohen, Neil De Marchi, and Mary Morgan, and for the preliminary investigations of her research assistant Limor Kaduri. Comments and questions from those present at the Duke Workshop on Higgling and at the first Hermes Conference at York University are also gratefully acknowledged.

References

Allen, William R. 1976. Scarcity and Order: The Hobbesian Problem and the Humean Resolution. *Social Science Quarterly* 57.2:263–75.

Appleby, Joyce Oldham. 1978. *Economic Thought and Ideology in Seventeenth-Century England*. Princeton: Princeton University Press.

Clark, Colin, and Trevor Pinch. 1994. The Interactional Study of Exchange Relationships: An Analysis of Patter Merchants at Work on Street Markets. In *Higgling: Transactors and Their Markets in the History of Economics,* edited by Neil De Marchi and Mary S. Morgan. *HOPE* 26, special issue. Durham: Duke University Press.

Duke, Michael I. 1979. David Hume and Monetary Adjustment. *HOPE* 11.4:572–87.

Forbes, Duncan. 1975. *Hume's Philosophical Politics.* Cambridge: Cambridge University Press.

Gauthier, David. 1979. David Hume, Contractarian. *Philosophical Review* 88.1:3–38.

Haakonssen, Knud. 1981. *The Science of a Legislator: The Natural Jurisprudence of David Hume and Adam Smith.* Cambridge: Cambridge University Press.

Hankins, Thomas L. 1985. *Science and the Enlightenment.* Cambridge: Cambridge University Press.

Hirschman, Albert O. 1977. *The Passions and the Interests.* Princeton: Princeton University Press.

Hont, Istvan. 1983. The "Rich Country–Poor Country" Debate in Scottish Classical Political Economy. In *Wealth and Virtue: The Shaping of Political Economy in the Scottish Enlightenment,* edited by Istvan Hont and Michael Ignatieff. Cambridge: Cambridge University Press.

Hoppit, Julian. 1987. *Risk and Failure in English Business, 1700–1800.* Cambridge: Cambridge University Press.

Hume, David. [1739] 1978. *A Treatise of Human Nature.* 2d ed. Edited by P. H. Nidditch. Oxford: Oxford University Press.

———. [1777] 1985. *Essays: Moral, Political and Literary.* Edited by Eugene F. Miller. Indianapolis: Liberty Classics Reprint.

Hundert, E. J. 1974. The Achievement Motive in Hume's Political Economy. *Journal of the History of Ideas* 35.1:139–43.

Hutchison, Terence. 1988. *Before Adam Smith: The Emergence of Political Economy, 1666–1776.* Oxford: Basil Blackwell.

Ignatieff, Michael. 1984. *The Needs of Strangers.* London: Chatto & Windus.

Kula, Witold. 1986. *Measures and Men.* Princeton: Princeton University Press.

Livingston, Donald W. 1984. *Hume's Philosophy of Common Life.* Chicago: University of Chicago Press.

Lowry, S. Todd. 1994. The Market as a Distributive and Allocative System: Its Legal, Ethical, and Analytical Evolution. In *Higgling: Transactors and Their Markets in the History of Economics,* edited by Neil De Marchi and Mary S. Morgan. *HOPE* 26, special issue. Durham: Duke University Press.

Mandeville, Bernard. [1732] 1988. *The Fable of the Bees.* Edited by F. B. Kaye. Indianapolis: Liberty Classics Reprint.

Mitchell, Neil J. 1986. John Locke and the Rise of Capitalism. *HOPE* 18.2:291–305.

Moss, Laurence S. 1991. Thomas Hobbes's Influence on David Hume: The Emergence of a Public Choice Tradition. *HOPE* 23.4:587–612.

Rosenberg, Nathan. 1990. Adam Smith and the Stock of Moral Capital. *HOPE* 22.1:1–17.

Rotwein, Eugene. 1970. Introduction. In *David Hume: Writings on Economics*. Madison: University of Wisconsin Press.

Skinner, Andrew S. 1990. The Shaping of Political Economy in the Enlightenment. *Scottish Journal of Political Economy* 37.2:145–65.

———. 1992. *David Hume: Economic Writings*. Discussion Papers in Economics, no. 9201. Glasgow: University of Glasgow.

Skinner, Andrew S., and Thomas Wilson, eds. 1975. *Essays on Adam Smith*. London: Oxford University Press.

Smith, Adam. [1776] 1981. *An Inquiry into the Nature and Causes of the Wealth of Nations*. Glasgow Edition. Edited by Roy H. Campbell and Andrew S. Skinner. Indianapolis: Liberty Classics Reprint.

Stockton, Constance Noble. 1976. Economics and the Mechanism of Historical Progress in Hume's *History*. In *Hume: A Reevaluation*, edited by Donald W. Livingston and James T. King. New York: Fordham University Press.

Teichgraeber, Richard F., III. 1986. *"Free Trade" and Moral Philosophy: Rethinking the Sources of Adam Smith's Wealth of Nations*. Durham: Duke University Press.

Thompson, E. P. 1971. The Moral Economy of the English Crowd in the Eighteenth Century. *Past and Present* 50:76–136.

Trusler, Reverend. 1786. *The London Advisor and Guide*. Kress Library Manuscripts, Harvard University.

Vaughn, Karen. 1980. *John Locke, Economist and Social Scientist*. Chicago: University of Chicago Press.

Venning, Corey. 1976. Hume on Property, Commerce, and Empire in the Good Society: The Role of Historical Necessity. *Journal of the History of Ideas* 37.1:74–92.

Wallech, Steven. 1984. The Elements of Social Status in Hume's Treatise. *Journal of the History of Ideas* 45.2:207–18.

Westerfield, Ray B. [1915] 1968. *Middlemen in English Business: Particularly between 1660 and 1760*. New Haven: Yale University Press. Reprinted, New York: Augustus M. Kelley.

Wrigley, E. A. 1967. A Simple Model of London's Importance in Changing English Society and Economy, 1650–1750. *Past and Present* 37:44–70.

Young, Jeffrey T. 1990. David Hume and Adam Smith on Value Premises in Economics. *HOPE* 22.4:643–57.

Disequilibrium Trade as a Metaphor for Social Disorder in the Work of Jean-Baptiste Say

Evelyn Forget

On the day the Bastille fell, the price of bread was at its highest level in sixty years. The vicissitudes of climate in a largely primitive agricultural economy (Le Roy Ladurie 1983), exacerbated by court intrigue (cf. Faure 1961), generated periodic crises. Poor harvests led to annual price variations, but even more onerous a burden for the poor were the seasonal variations in the prices of grain and bread. The public, ignorant of the social good that speculation could bring about, demanded strict prohibitions against hoarding and agitated for price ceilings on grain and bread. The inevitable shortages led to hunger riots, and the alarmed authorities set up a complex system of supply management for Paris, where the situation was particularly explosive, and banned exports, intervened extensively in the markets, and attempted to build stockpiles of grain. Nevertheless, this was not sufficient to supply Paris in the event of poor harvests, and the hardship was extreme.

One can imagine the impact of bread shortages and the rising price of grain on the poor if one remembers that half the income of the Parisian worker was spent on bread in noncrisis periods. Rudé estimates that a Parisian laborer in 1789 earned 20 to 30 sous a day, a mason 40, and a joiner or locksmith 50. A family of two adults and two children consumed eight pounds of bread a day (1959, 33). When the price of a four-pound loaf rose suddenly from 8 sous to 15 or 20 sous, starvation was imminent. The demand for the *maximum* is easy to understand, as are the hunger riots as a response to the inevitable shortages.

It is in this context that one should read Jean-Baptiste Say on *prix courant*, demand and supply, and disequilibrium trade. Most of the classical economists, especially by the time of John Stuart Mill and William Thornton, conceived of disequilibrium trade as a process during which information is made available to the actors and potential actors in a market, and the debates centered around whether or not the information and the behavioral responses it generated would drive the economy toward some equilibrium (market-clearing) position. Even Adam Smith, Say's ultimate authority in matters economic, conceived of out-of-equilibrium trade as a process of equilibration by means of which prices gravitated towards their "natural" levels. In the work of Say, this process of equilibration is so attenuated as to be negligible. The matter of finding and realizing a market price which brings the quantities supplied and demanded into equality under conditions of perfect liberty, according to Say, is almost instantaneous. Individual markets, and, by analogy, the entire economy, are rarely out of equilibrium when laissez-faire rules.

This is not, however, to suggest that Say never described or discussed markets which did not costlessly and quickly clear. Ill-advised attempts on the part of political authorities to intervene in the market inevitably generated such situations. For Say, disequilibrium trade always signified social upheaval, which he described in dramatic terms. Higgling was not, under these circumstances, the means of discovering an equilibrium price, but rather a process by means of which individual buyers and sellers attempted to gain differential advantages when the social ideal implicit in competitive equilibrium was not realized. Higgling would persist until the system of natural liberty was restored.

The next section of this essay outlines Say's analysis of market price without government intervention. It demonstrates the minor role that a process of equilibration plays in such circumstances, and highlights the mechanical analogies and scientific language in terms of which Say casts the story. He even develops demand in geometrical terms, which simply emphasizes the absence of economic agents as people engaged in trade in a real marketplace. Then, I demonstrate the contrast in the language in terms of which Say articulates out-of-equilibrium trade in a market burdened with government intervention. These disparate descriptions of disequilibrium trade suggest that, according to Say, disequilibrium trade is a metaphor for social disorder. Well-functioning markets in a free economy characterize a stable society; disequilibrium trade is the mark of riot and revolution.

Prix Courant under Laissez Faire

Whenever Say discusses market price determination in a free market, three things are clear. First, there are no real people cluttering up the narrative; everything is cast in terms of scientific necessity. Individual trading behavior, in all of its potential irrationality and subjectivity, makes no appearance. Second, "demand" and "supply" are treated almost as physical entities. Say is aware that messy institutions and human psychology are the ultimate determinants of demand and supply and, ultimately, market price, but the story proceeds by means of mechanical analogies which suggest certainty and scientific precision. Finally, the normal state of the economy is one in which all markets clear very quickly. That is, there is little recognition of disequilibrium as a protracted process, or of "false trading" as a usual state of affairs.

Say's fascination with "science," and his Baconian rhetoric, are very apparent in almost everything he wrote. In the introduction to his *Treatise,* for example, he lauds the inductive method:

> In political economy, as in natural philosophy, and in every other study, systems have been formed before facts have been established; the place of the latter being supplied by purely gratuitous assertions. More recently, the inductive method of philosophizing, which, since the time of Bacon, has so much contributed to the advancement of every other science, has been applied to the conduct of our researches in this. The excellence of this method consists in only admitting facts carefully observed, and the consequences rigorously deduced from them; thereby effectually excluding those prejudices and authorities which, in every department of literature and science, have so often been interposed between man and truth. (Say 1880, xvii)

These are the same sentiments he expressed in his early notes on Smith's *Wealth of Nations,* but, as I have argued elsewhere (Forget 1993), Say's rhetorical attachment to the inductive method should not be overstated. Say was quite aware that "there is not an absurd theory, or an extravagant opinion that has not been supported by an appeal to facts; and it is by facts also that public authorities have been so often misled" (1880, xx–xxi). Moreover, he recognized that

> to obtain a knowledge of the truth, it is not then so necessary to be acquainted with a great number of facts, as with such as are essential, and have a direct and immediate influence; and, above all, to

examine them under all their aspects, to be enabled to deduce from them just conclusions and be assured that the consequences ascribed to them do not in reality proceed from other causes. Every other knowledge of facts, like the erudition of an almanac, is a mere compilation from which nothing results. And it may be remarked, that this sort of information is peculiar to men of clear memories and clouded judgments. (xxiii)

Say's crusade was not against "system-building" per se; systems are useful and, indeed, essential. His real concern was no more than to ensure that the initial premises upon which the systems are built do not deviate far from actual experience which, he believed, could be recognized as such by anyone (xxvi).

One direction in which Say was not prepared to push the deductive method was in the application of mathematics to political economy, because he believed the "facts" too numerous and too imprecise for the method to be of any value. Fortunately for us, he illustrated his concern by demonstrating the absurdity of mathematical reasoning in the case of market price determination:

We may, for example, know that for any given year the price of wine will infallibly depend upon the quantity to be sold, compared with the extent of the demand. But if we are desirous of submitting these two data to mathematical calculation, their ultimate elements must be decomposed before we can become thoroughly acquainted with them, or can, with any degree of precision, distinguish the separate influence of each. (xxvi–xxvii)

He went on to enumerate the factors which would determine the quantity supplied: the quantity and quality of the vintage estimated *before* it is harvested, the stock on hand, the financial circumstances of the dealers, expectations of export opportunities which depend upon political factors, "and probably many others besides" (xxvii). Quantity demanded, he noted, would depend upon price, "as the demand for it will increase in proportion to its cheapness" (xxvii), stock on hand, tastes, incomes, the "condition of industry in general, and of their own in particular" (xxvii), and the possibilities for substitution in consumption ("beer, cider, &c."). In both cases, he was aware that he "suppress[ed] an infinite number of less important considerations" (xxvii).

The mathematical method, he claimed, was inappropriate because of

the complexity of the problem and the uncertainty surrounding any numerical estimates of the data required. The only appropriate method for
the political economist is

> the same which would be pursued by him, under circumstances
> equally difficult, which decide the greater part of the actions of his life.
> He will examine the immediate elements of the proposed problem,
> and after having ascertained them with certainty, (which in political
> economy can be effected,) will approximately value their mutual in-
> fluences with the intuitive quickness of an enlightened understanding,
> itself only an instrument by means of which the mean result of a crowd
> of probabilities can be estimated, but never calculated with exactness.
> (xxvii)

That is, mathematics is not useful because of the complexity of the data
requirements, and not because the system itself is not determinate.

This discussion, which occurs in a footnote to the introduction of his
Treatise, appears to recognize the complexity inherent in individual market behavior. There are other places, throughout the body of his work,
where similar insights are articulated: for example, "The want or desire
of any particular object depends upon the physical and moral constitution of man, the climate he may live in, the laws, customs, and manners
of the particular society, in which he may happen to be enrolled" (Say
1880, 285; cf. 1843, 168). But Say never implies that such complexity
might impede the market price of any commodity from being established
very quickly at a level at which markets clear. The uncertainty which he
recognizes might prevent the political economist from forecasting market prices correctly, but it will not prevent markets from working, nor
will it lead to protracted disequilibria.

This distinction is responsible for allowing Say to recognize the complexity of human systems and to point to uncertainty and individual
irrationality in a discussion of *method,* and, simultaneously, to deempha-
size the role of individual market behavior (indeed, of people in general)
in his *theoretical* discussion of supply and demand as the determinants
of market price.

In his theoretical analysis of demand in the *Treatise* Say suppresses all
discussion of expectations and uncertainty and notes only that the "demand for all objects of pleasure, or utility, would be unlimited, did not
the difficulty of attainment, or price, limit and circumscribe the supply"
(1880, 290). Interestingly, as price increases, quantity demanded falls,

both because "the number of consumers [is] diminished" and because "the consumption of each consumer is reduced also" (289). Similarly, all discussion of the financial exigency of dealers and the uncertainty of political situations or climate is suppressed in his discussion of supply, which "would be infinite, were it not restricted by the same circumstance, the price, or difficulty of attainment: for there can be no doubt, that whatever is producible would then be produced in unlimited quantity, so long as it could find purchasers at any price at all" (290). Demand and supply determine market price, and he explains the process by means of a very clear mechanical analogy: "Demand and supply are the opposite extremes of the beam, whence depend the scales of dearness and cheapness; the price is the point of equilibrium, where the momentum of the one ceases, and that of the other begins" (290). The moral of the story is that there is an equilibrium market price which ensures that quantity demanded is just equal to quantity supplied, and that the laws of political economy (just like the laws of physics) will ensure that the equilibrium is established.

The mechanical analogy of Say's *Treatise*—the "beam"—gives way to a geometrical representation of demand in his *Cours complet d'économie politique pratique* (see figure 1). Say's explanation of the diagram is as follows:

> The scale in this picture shows the height of the market price of different commodities, whatever the causes of the price. Beside the scale is a pyramid, which should be imagined as constructed of a multitude of vertical lines, the length of each representing someone's wealth [*sic*]. Now, imagine the pyramid cut horizontally at different heights, according to the price of the product we want to consider; the horizontal section of the pyramid corresponding to the price represents the number of "fortunes" that can afford the product. The number of potential consumers declines as the price increases. In this example, a number of "fortunes" represented by vertical lines which do not exceed AA can afford a price represented by the 4th degree on the scale. Those whose wealth reaches the line BB can afford the price represented by the 19th degree. The 24th degree represents a price no one can afford. The area of the pyramid represents, even more precisely, the total expenditure that consumers are able *and want to* allocate to a particular product. A country where individual fortunes are, in general, very limited can be represented by a low, wide pyramid. One where

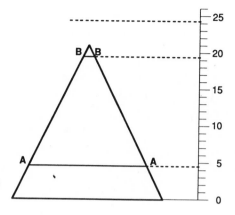

Figure 1

there are many small fortunes and a few large can be represented by a pyramid with concave sides. One where wealth is fairly evenly distributed, and extremes of fortune rare, will generate a pyramid with convex sides. Such countries are the happiest. (1843, 169; translation and emphasis mine)

Before we consider the significance of this metaphor, it is worthwhile to underline some of its features. Say casts this explanation in terms of "fortunes," which represent (presumably) some measure of ability to pay on the part of each potential consumer; he does not consistently consider quantity desired at each price, despite the phrase italicized above, making this diagram quite different from our demand curve. Say has drawn his diagram as if each individual had a perfectly price-inelastic demand curve for each commodity, and the height of each vertical line represents the extent of that individual's resources which he is prepared to devote to the commodity in question. Similarly, the units in terms of which the commodities are to be measured (four-pound loaves per day?) are not specified. These represent limitations of Say's diagram, rather than his understanding of demand, as is clear from an example he gives in the text, where he must torture this diagram a little bit to represent his meaning:

When a commodity increases in price, either because of a tax or for some other reason, a certain number of consumers stop buying it, but others reduce their consumption. Consider a consumer of coffee who, when coffee increases in price, might not be forced to give it up completely. He simply reduces his usual consumption. We must imagine him as two individuals, one disposed to pay the price demanded, and the other (not so disposed) who stops drinking coffee. (1843, 169)

How useful it might be to estimate potential consumption of coffee on the basis of how many people can afford to buy it if they spent their entire fortunes on coffee remains an open question. For the Parisian laborer who did spend virtually his entire income on bread, however, this is a reasonable way to conceptualize demand. This is clearly an instance where Say is in command of the concept of price elasticity of demand for individual consumers (he does, after all, consider the possibility of commodity substitution, 1880, xxvii), but cannot capture the concept diagrammatically.

Say's diagram betrays his tendency to conceive of economic questions in terms of the images of science. This picture is not a geometrical representation of demand, as is a contemporary demand curve; it is not a line in Cartesian space, but rather a picture which resembles a three-dimensional beaker in a chemistry lab. It is conceived in terms of fixed volume measurable, in principle, on a cardinal scale. This is not a metaphor which brings to mind the uncertainty and subjectivity of Say's methodological discussion of demand and supply, where real people with unique (and possibly incorrect) expectations engage in trades in a real marketplace; it is a metaphor which, by contrast, conjures images of measurement and precision and equilibrium.

If these extracts are representative of Say's conception of market-price determination, one would expect that his equilibrium focus would drive the process of equilibration from center stage. There is, in fact, very little "friction" in an economy without government intervention:

A law, that simply fixes the price of commodities at the rate they would naturally obtain, is merely nugatory, or serves only to alarm producers and consumers, and consequently to derange the natural proportion between the production and the demand; which proportion, if left to itself, is invariably established in the manner most favorable to both. (Say 1880, 291)

In fact, the market works so well that anticipated demand and supply drive market prices, and there is no indication that expectations do anything other than clear markets more rapidly:

The prospect of an abundant vintage will lower the price of all the wine on hand, even before a single pipe of the expected vintage has been brought to market; for the supply is brisker, and the sale duller, in consequence of the anticipation. The dealers are anxious to dispose of their stock in hand, in fear of the competition of the new vintage; while the consumers, on the other hand, retard their fresh purchases, in the expectation of gaining in price by the delay. A large arrival and immediate sale of foreign articles all at once, lowers their price, by the relative excess of supply above demand. On the contrary, the expectation of a bad vintage, or the loss of many cargoes on the voyage, will raise prices above the cost of production. (1880, 290)

The analysis of the *Cours complet* is similarly frictionless; Say, for example, extends the analysis of market price to explain how supply accommodates itself to demand in cases of constant and increasing cost industries (1843, 170–71). As in all the previous examples, there is no indication that this process takes any significant period of time, or that there is any risk of protracted disequilibrium. Indeed, Say downplays the importance of the adjustment process and assures us that equilibration will occur rapidly after any disturbance:

Accidental causes, the fear of a poor harvest, the hope of a good one, fashion, often influence for some time the quantities of some commodity that one is prepared to demand or supply; and, as a consequence, the price which represents the mutual influence of these two quantities. But the costs of production on one side, and the usual needs on the other, tend always to draw the price to a level we might call "natural," and at which producers are induced to produce and consumers to consume. (1843, 172)

That is, even in the posthumously published *Cours complet,* the process of equilibration is frictionless; there is no higgling in this description.

To summarize, then, Say's world is one where the market, if left to itself, clears quickly and costlessly. Market price adjusts frictionlessly to ensure that quantity demanded is made equal to quantity supplied. The entire process is conceived in terms of mechanical, or at least scientific, analogies; there are no people in Say's stories.

Administered Prices and Social Disorder

The market, when left to itself, operates as a well-lubricated machine. Contrast the language in which Say describes the operation of the economy operating under the weight of administered prices. In both the

Treatise and *Cours complet,* Say organizes his story of market-price determination in very much the same way as a twentieth-century *Principles* text. First, he discusses demand and quantity demanded, and emphasizes that the latter depends upon price. Then he defines supply. Next he tells us how demand and supply influence market price. And finally he illustrates how price adjustment clears markets, by considering the impact of price ceilings and price floors. He parts company with Samuelson only in the extent to which his language becomes more and more passionate as the story of ill-advised government intervention unfolds. Not only are there people in this story, but there are evil people and starving people and cunning people and dishonest people, all engaging in trickery and false trading in an attempt to profit at the expense of others. Administered prices, Say claimed, prevent the market from clearing. He could not but be aware that they might have other effects, including starvation, riot, and bloody revolution.

Notice the words Say uses in his *Treatise,* when he discusses administered prices, and notice also that the market he has in mind is the corn market:

> When the price of any object is legally fixed below the charges of its production, the production of it is discontinued, because nobody is willing to labor for a loss: those who before earned their livelihood by this branch of production, must die of hunger, if they find no other employment. . . . Even the produce already existing is not so properly consumed as it should be. For, in the first place, the proprietor withholds it as much as possible from the market. In the next, it passes into the hands, not of those who want it most, but of those who have most avidity, cunning, and dishonesty; and often with the most flagrant disregard of natural equity and humanity. A scarcity of corn occurs; the price rises in consequence; yet still it is possible, that the laborer, by redoubling his exertions, or by an increase of wages, may earn wherewithal to buy it at the market price. In the meantime, the magistrate fixes corn at half its natural price: what is the consequence? Another consumer, who had already provided himself, and consequently would have bought no more corn had it remained at its natural price, gets the start of the laborer, and now, from mere superfluous precaution, and to take advantage of the forced cheapness, adds to his own store that portion, which should have gone to the laborer. (1880, 291)

Finally, we have evidence of real people "higgling" in the marketplace, and it is clear that Say does not regard this activity as equilibrating. It occurs only when there is an artificial impediment to the establishment of equilibrium, and the most heinous impediment Say can imagine is the establishment of the *maximum*.

Say's real preoccupation in the discussion appears even more clearly in the next paragraph, where he compares the activity of a national government to that of a producer with a monopoly:

> Neither need we advert to the operation of the causes of a nature purely political, that may operate to raise the price of a product above the degree of its real utility. For these are of the same class with actual robbery and spoliation, which come under the department of criminal jurisprudence, although they may intrude themselves into the business of the distribution of wealth. The functions of national government, which is a class of industry, whose result or product is consumed by the governed as fast as it is produced, may be too dearly paid for, when they get into the hands of usurpation and tyranny, and the people be compelled to contribute a larger sum than is necessary for the mainte-nance of good government. This is a parallel case to that of a producer without competition. (291–92)

Perhaps aware of the mounting passion apparent in his discussion, Say ends the chapter by attempting to regain perspective, noting that "it is impossible to avoid sometimes touching upon the confines of policy and morality, were it only for the purpose of marking out their points of contact" (292).

Cours complet tells the same story in terms of "une autorité abusive"; precisely the same vehement language occurs in this posthumous vol-ume and the *Treatise* (1843, 171), where Say recognizes that a shortage of grain ensures that "la marchandise passe, non pas là ou il y a plus de besoins, mais là ou il y a plus d'avidité, d'adresse et d'improbité; sou-vent même c'est en blessant cruellement les droits les plus communs de l'equité naturelle et de l'humanité."

Again, it is clear enough that it was the hunger riots of the 1780s that motivated Say's impassioned outburst against the *maximum:*

> There are frequent examples [of fixed prices] in the market for bread, especially in large cities. Parisian bakers, when wheat was dear, were forced to sell for 14 sous bread that cost them 16 sous to make, and

for 16 sous that which cost 18. They submitted to this onerous situation, either because they were forced to by the government, or because
their licence, gained by privilege, was still worth more than this enforced loss. At other times, they were authorized to charge 12 sous for
bread that cost them 10 sous. It is as if the government had authorized
the bakers to charge consumers a tax of 2 sous per loaf. This would
never have occurred, except through the agency of a law, and the law
is evil, because it disturbs the interests of buyers and sellers which
would be ameliorated by the market. Under such circumstances, the
unjust profits of the bakers would quickly multiply their numbers, had
not another abuse ensured that the number of bakers was fixed because bakers required a licence from the police to exercise a profession
which, by rights, should be open to all. (1843, 171)

Government intervention in the market leads to disequilibria, to higgling, and to social disorder. Unlike the smoothly functioning market
mechanism which, when left to itself, ensures that all markets virtually
always clear, and usually clear at a price just equal to cost of production,
intervention (especially in the form of the dreaded *maximum*) ensured
prolonged periods of chaos.

Conclusion

The argument of this essay is a simple one: Say was quite aware of how
markets ought to work under perfect liberty, and his exposition of the
demand-supply mechanism was so clear and so much superior to those
of other early nineteenth-century writers that it was called up by John
Stuart Mill in his *Principles* as the authoritative account. Say's analysis, however, was the product of the French Revolution. He underplayed
the role of the equilibration process in a competitive situation, implying
that the economy moved instantaneously to a position of market-clearing
equilibrium by means of market-price adjustment, and very quickly to
an equilibrium where demand just equaled supply at a price equal to
cost of production. There was no higgling to speak of. By contrast, disequilibrium in the form of shortages, surpluses, black markets, and (if
allowed) wide fluctuations of price characterized an economy burdened
by government intervention. Say emphasizes these two distinct portraits
of how markets operate by articulating the analysis in quite different
language. The competitive situation is explained in terms of scientific

language, using mechanical metaphors and demand diagrams and eliminating people, subjectivity, expectations, and disequilibrium from the story. The economy with government intervention is characterized by persistent disequilibria, cunning, and avaricious dealers, stupid bureaucrats, and the clear threat of social upheaval. Disequilibrium trade, I have argued, is a metaphor for social disorder.

The vehemence with which Say rejected higgling in the context of free markets is a bit startling, but it is not inconsistent with his stated desire to consider only "necessary" facts. Except for a brief period in the 1760s, when market prices were anything but orderly and stable, Say had very little recent French experience of free markets to draw upon. The English experience, with which he was familiar, was unlikely to model frictionless adjustment in practice. In the real world higgling did exist. Adam Smith, from whom he borrowed a great deal, does not focus on market clearing as a primary characteristic of equilibrium, and therefore Say could not have just reproduced Smith's analysis. The model is not the result of Say's experience of free markets in the sense of naturally ordered exchange and production, because he had very little such experience to draw upon. Moreover, his criticism of administered prices is limited almost entirely to the very recent French experience of the *maximum*. The grain market was heavily regulated in France, but it had been for some two centuries, excluding a very brief and unstable interlude in the 1760s. Kaplan (1976) recounts the history of the "grain police" during the seventeenth and eighteenth centuries. Moreover, for most of that period, the administered price imposed market clearing. In Paris, for example, during the early eighteenth century grain not sold by the third day could not be withdrawn but was forcibly sold in one way or another by officials. Ironically, then, the administered price in this semiregulated market was probably not very different from Say's market-clearing "natural" price.

It seems clear enough that Say was doing something more than objectively observing and reporting upon how various markets worked. In fact, his analysis is not consistent with what we now know to be the case in the French grain market during the eighteenth century. But Say's political economy is part of a much larger program which attempted to demonstrate the superiority of a system of perfect liberty on rational, scientific grounds. It is not inexplicable that he saw the free market operating without the instability and irrationality that higgling represented, while the regulated market (a manifestation, in Say's eyes, of a system of constraints upon liberty) necessarily exhibited irrationality and instability. Higgling, in this context, is not about discovering an equilibrium price; it is indicative of social disorder caused by the attempts of some individuals to gain at the expense of others, and a legacy of misguided intervention in the marketplace which creates opportunities for such differential gains.

I thank Neil De Marchi, Mary Morgan, and Michael White for helpful advice. The research upon which this paper is based is funded by the Social Science and Humanities Research Council of Canada.

References

Aftalion, Florin. 1990. *The French Revolution: An Economic Interpretation.* Cambridge: Cambridge University Press.

Faure, E. 1961. *La disgrace de Turgot.* Paris.

Forget, Evelyn L. 1993. J.-B. Say and Adam Smith: An Essay in the Transmission of Ideas. *Canadian Journal of Economics* 26.1 (February): 121–33.

Kaplan, Steven L. 1976. *Bread, Politics and Political Economy in the Reign of Louis XV.* 2 vols. The Hague: Nijhoff.

Le Roy Ladurie, E. 1983. *Histoire du climat depuis l'an mil.* Paris: Flammarion.

Rudé, G. 1959. *The Crowd in the French Revolution.* Oxford: Clarendon Press.

Sauvy, A. 1985. *De la rumeur à l'histoire.* Paris: Dunod.

Say, Jean-Baptiste. 1843. *Cours complet d'économie politique pratique.* 6th ed. Edited by Horace Say. Brussels: Société Typographique Belge. Reprinted, Rome: Edizioni Bizzarri, 1968.

———. 1880. *A Treatise on Political Economy, or the Production, Distribution, and Consumption of Wealth.* Translated from the 4th ed. by C. R. Prinsep. New American Edition by Clement C. Biddle. Philadelphia: Claxton, Remsen & Haffelfinger.

"That God-Forgotten Thornton": Exorcising Higgling after *On Labour*

Michael V. White

> I am suffering the torments of the damned from that god-forgotten Thorn-
> ton, who is boring on about supply and demand. . . . He is not a bad
> fellow, but just now I hate him like poison.—Leslie Stephen, at the Political
> Economy Club, December 1866

Between 1866 and 1868 the *Fortnightly Review* published a series of
articles by William Thornton.[1] The articles, Thornton subsequently
noted, "incurred a good deal of criticism, both public and private"
(1869, 57), and the criticism continued when they appeared in 1869 as
chapters in his book, *On Labour*. With the widespread attention which
that text received, indicated by a significant number of reviews, review
articles, and a second edition in 1870, it set off an extensive debate on
the explanation of price determination, the effects of which can be seen
in the early work of Alfred Marshall,[2] H. C. Fleeming Jenkin's exposition of supply and demand diagrams (1870), and W. Stanley Jevons's
Theory of Political Economy (1871). Although *On Labour* used to be remembered principally for the review article by John Stuart Mill which
rejected the notion of a determinate wage fund,[3] the contemporary focus

---

Epigraph: Maitland 1906, 189. Seven years before, Stephen was not quite so bored with supply
and demand, since he had begun a "little treatise" on political economy, adopting "the graphic
method of illustrating supply and demand by means of curves" (75).

1. Following the first two articles (Thornton 1866, 1867), a further six appeared until May
1868, under the general heading "Stray Chapters from a Forthcoming Book on Labour."

2. Bharadwaj 1978; Marshall 1975, 121.

3. "Thornton on Labour and Its Claims," part I, *Fortnightly Review* 29 (1 May): 505–18;
part II, 30 (1 June) 680–700. Reprinted in Mill 1967, 632–68.

should not be surprising, for the nub of Thornton's analysis was not the dismissal of the wage fund per se, which accounted initially for only a page-length footnote in his text.[4] What also attracted much attention at the time was his attack on the coherence of claims made about the "laws of supply and demand."[5] Focusing on a price adjustment process, which he and other commentators referred to as "higgling,"[6] Thornton argued that references to the laws could not explain the determination and existence of a market equilibrium price. Although *On Labour* has sometimes received a disparaging treatment from historians of economics,[7] section 1 below shows how it problematized the mechanical metaphors which contemporary analysts used to "explain" the existence of a "determinate" market equilibrium position. For Thornton, price adjustment was a matter of social calculation necessitating a path-dependent process, so that, even if an equilibrium point did exist, it was analytically irrelevant.[8]

The following sections consider the two principal ways in which various commentators attempted both to defend and rework the meaning and representation of the laws of supply and demand in the years immediately following the publication of *On Labour*. The first was to defuse Thornton's key arguments by reading the text as consisting of a series of anomalies or misunderstandings which could be explained by the laws.

---

4. Thornton 1869, 84n.–85n. In the second edition, however, Thornton moved the criticism of the wage fund to the beginning of his discussion of wage formation and widened the analysis (1870, 84–89).

5. Thornton's replies to the critics of the first edition are in book 2, chapter 1 of the second edition, which consequently grew to 67 pages as compared with 44 in the first edition. As a result of the replies, the argument of that chapter, which contains his critique of supply and demand, became far more difficult to read when compared with the first edition.

6. Thornton 1869, 51. This was changed to "haggling" in the second edition (1870, 62).

7. Stigler (1965, 9) labeled it "absurd"; Uemiya (1981, 52) termed it "bizzare"; Bharadwaj (1978, 260) thought the arguments were "rather confusing and weak"; Breit (1967, 519, 521) referred to Thornton's "fatuous" examples and "flimsy criticism." A more recent account continues in the same vein, referring to the "blatant naiveté of Thornton's assault," which was "totally off the mark," an "unsophisticated stab in the dark" (Ekelund and Thommesen 1989, 577, 582, 588). For good measure, the same authors add some epistemological abuse: While Mill was "ever the scientist," Thornton's "purpose appears not to be a scientific search for truth, but rather to find an argument that will support his preconceived political conclusions" (571n., 572). Alternative assessments of *On Labour* can be found in Schumpeter 1954, 669–70; Dennis 1977, 180–83; Negishi 1986; and Mirowski 1990, 74–81.

8. Thornton further criticized the relevance of the laws by arguing that the process of price formation in labor markets was unlike that for other commodities. Although the discussion of labor markets gave his arguments about supply and demand particular contemporary relevance, they are not considered here, for reasons of space.

As is shown in section 2, Mill's influential review provided the most detailed exposition of that reading, within an account where, at equilibrium, the market price converged on a long-period ("natural") price determined by the cost of production. When read in conjunction with his *Principles of Political Economy,* however, Mill's review produced a confusing explanation of price determination with regard to price adjustment and the properties of market equilibrium positions.

While Mill's review avoided an analysis of market price adjustments by gesturing toward mechanical metaphors, the second way of dealing with Thornton's critique was to reformulate a mechanistic approach where all prices were explained in terms of the laws of supply and demand. For theorists such as Jenkin and Jevons, the economy should be understood and represented as a machine, governed by the "laws" of mechanics.[9] Partly reworking some components of Mill's argument, this approach depicted the laws of supply and demand in strict functional terms, with all transactions occurring at market-clearing equilibrium positions. Jenkin's analysis is outlined in section 3. Section 4 then considers how Jevons broke new ground in explaining such equilibria as the result of a "perfectly competitive" system which was mirrored in "actual" markets.

The determinacy which Jenkins and Jevons claimed to have produced for the laws of supply and demand by the early 1870s was illusory. As section 5 shows, while purporting to account for the determination of prices, they were forced to preclude any explanation of price adjustment by higgling, since this would destabilize the possibility of equilibrium on which their accounts depended. With equilibrium thus assumed rather than explained, Thornton's critique was dissolved by exorcising higgling from the domain of the "science of political economy."

1. Thornton's Heresies

Thornton's objective was to attack the claim that the laws of supply and demand "determine price." While he was particularly concerned with "popular" statements of that doctrine, he also criticized Mill's *Principles of Political Economy,* which had "systematised" the argument that

---

9. Jenkin 1870, 151; Jevons 1871, viii, 24. For reasons of space, I do not consider here the metaphors which Jenkin and Jevons used to produce their "models" of the economy; but see Mirowski 1989; Wise 1992; White 1991b, 1992; and the references cited therein.

"price depends on the equality of supply and demand" and that a market was "always tending" to an equilibrium position (Thornton 1869, 43, 46, 52). Nearly thirty years before *On Labour,* William Whewell had expressed some skepticism as to "the postulate of equilibrium," where this was understood in terms of a market price converging on a long-period natural price which was "determined by the cost of production." [10] Thornton, however, considered the formation of market prices where sellers' commodity stocks were given. He followed the account in Mill's *Principles* [11] by arguing that the price of any "merchantable" commodity depended on its being "at once useful and difficult of attainment" and that the price could settle at one of, or between, two "extreme" points. The upper limit was set by the "utility, real or supposed, of the commodity to the customer," while the lower was set by the utility to the dealer, forming the reserve price which characterized all commodity sales, with the exception of labor (1869, 45, 56, 58). Although the price could vary between the limit points, dealers would aim to maximize revenue by initially setting the price as high as possible and then altering it in a sequence of adjustments, eventually clearing all their stock (50).

In his *Principles* Mill had argued that the explanation of competitive price formation applied in wholesale markets where "the axiom is true, that there cannot be for the same article, of the same quality, two prices in the same market." The axiom of a single price did not, however, prevail in retail sales. Due to accidents, habit, indolence, carelessness, and "ignorance and defect of judgement" on the part of customers, prices differed considerably for the same commodities, so that customers "give much higher prices than necessary for the things they consume" (Mill 1909, 441). This issue of retail price dispersion and, in effect, of unequal exchange had been discussed at the Political Economy Club during the 1850s, and Mill's position was subsequently supported in J. E. Cairnes's *Leading Principles* (Weinberg 1966; Cairnes 1874, 128–34). While Thornton (1869, 60) acknowledged that Mill's argument was possibly correct, he assumed that there was sufficient competition between dealers to overcome the effects of customers' "indolence" or "habit." Hence his rejection of the laws of supply and demand did not require re-

10. Whewell 1831, 12–14. Whewell produced a far less critical account in a subsequent memoir (1850, 22).

11. See Mill 1909, book 3, chapters 1–3. (See also Hearn 1864, chapter 14.) Mill's account owed a good deal to De Quincey's *Logic of Political Economy* (1844) and to J.-B. Say (see E. Forget's contribution to this volume).

jecting the possibility of a single price in a market at any particular time.

For Thornton, prices were governed by dealers' calculations as to "the actual state and future prospects of the market" so far as demand and supply conditions were concerned. Price setting was a process of trial and error, for expectations would differ and dealers would be subject to varying pressures to sell their stock according to their credit positions. The lowest price at which any dealer was prepared to sell would then become the initial "set-up" price. No dealer was prepared to sell below this "if in his judgement customers will readily purchase at the current price all that he has to sell." Since the initiative on pricing lay with the dealers rather than the customers, it was competition between dealers which determined the set-up price and the subsequent sequence of adjustments, the necessity for which was indicated by unsold stocks (1869, 59, 61, 71, 77).

Since prices were the result of a competitive process, the results of which depended on the estimates made by dealers of future supply and demand conditions, of how other dealers would adjust prices and of their own credit position (60–62), calculations could not be made in any precise, uniform, and predictable manner:

> The same probabilities of supply and demand may affect competition very differently at different times. The state and prospects of the market being in other respects the same, competition will be more or less keen according as the dealers, or some of them, are more or less experienced, more or less shrewd, or more or less ready. The estimates of the future formed by individual dealers will thus depend partly on individual necessity and partly on individual discretion; and for discretion, or anything dependent on it, to be subject to law or rule, is not in the nature of things. (63)

Thornton's principal contention was, therefore, that pricing calculations had to be formed in a context of uncertainty, where conditions of credit availability were not uniform and where it was necessary to estimate the competitive price strategy of other dealers. Hence the calculations "need not always be the same in all circumstances . . . and the same estimates may affect different dealers differently" (64). To the argument that dealers would learn to estimate accurately through experience, Thornton replied (in the second edition) that this procedure was "quite incompatible with any phenomena of commerce, either actual or possible. By no repetition of experiments could it be ascertained beforehand what in retail, and still less in wholesale transactions, would be the daily or otherwise periodical demand for any commodity" (1870, 66n.).

While estimated conditions of "supply and demand" were only one element in dealers' calculations, Thornton argued that even if a price did exist where supply equaled demand, most commodities would not be sold at that price. Since traders followed a pattern of price adjustment, most of their stock would be sold before the stock clearing price was reached. In the case of a sequence of price declines, this would mean that most sales would occur where supply was greater than demand, which "compelled" the subsequent changes in price: "when we speak of prices depending on certain causes, we surely refer to the prices at which all goods, or at least the great bulk of them, not that at which merely a small remnant of them, will be sold. How can we say that the equation of supply and demand determines price, if goods are almost always sold at prices at which supply and demand are unequal?" (1869, 54). The notion of equilibrium was virtually irrelevant in a sequence of trading at "intermediate" prices, which was "almost typical of commercial transactions in general, most of which partake more or less of the character of sales by auction" (50, 55, 56).

This argument applied in the case of trading from parametric stocks. In the second edition, Thornton gave a further reason why the notion of an equilibrium point was irrelevant. In his review of On Labour, Mill had argued that with a given level of production, a static equilibrium position would only occur "momentarily," because new "disturbing forces" would appear in a market (see below). Thornton noted that this argument required that production levels would change in response to changes in market price, producing a process where "action and reaction continually succeed each other." Allowing for imperfect knowledge and mistakes, while supply and demand could be "continually gravitating towards equilibrium . . . equilibrium is no sooner reached than overpassed." Hence the notion of a "stable equality" between supply and demand was a "figment of the economic brain" (Thornton 1870, 48n., 66n.). This analysis complemented Sir John Herschel's previous criticism of "statical" analyses in political economy.[12]

---

12. Some months after Whewell had presented his 1850 memoir, in which he muted his qualms about "the postulate of equilibrium" (see above), Herschel argued that the "one great source of error and mistake in political economy consists in persisting to regard its problems as statical rather than dynamical." He protested against "confounding the propagation of an impulse with a step toward equilibrium. . . . Demand may tend to increase supply by stimulat-

The discussion of price formation did not exhaust Thornton's critique. The proponents of the laws of supply and demand claimed that price increased (decreased) when demand (supply) exceeded supply (demand) so that supply and demand would be equal at the stock-clearing price (Thornton 1869, 461).[13] It was possible, however, to think of anomalous cases where those rules would not apply. The price of a commodity could remain unchanged, for instance, even though there were unsatisfied buyers willing to pay the price at which a unit of a commodity was sold. This depended on there being a limited stock and a series of buyers, all of whom were willing to pay the same maximum price. More buyers entering the market on the same conditions would increase demand, but the price would remain unchanged. While it was the case that if supply exceeded demand, the price would fall (provided there was competition and no reserve price set by dealers), it was not "always" the case that price rose if demand exceeded supply (49–52). Using the same example, Thornton argued that at the highest possible price for which a unit of the stock was sold in a market, there could be unsatisfied customers willing to pay that price, so that supply did not equal demand (53).

The point of these examples (describing the sales of hats, gloves, and horses) was primarily epistemological. For Thornton, there were many exceptions to the rule that supply and demand were equilibrated at the ruling market price. But even if there was only one exception, that was enough, because "a scientific law admits of no exceptions whatever; one single exception suffices to deprive it of all legal character" (50). Here, Thornton was turning the dogmatism of supply and demand proponents, such as H. D. Macleod and W. B. Hodgson, against them. For as late as 1870 Hodgson approvingly cited Macleod's earlier statement that "the universal law of Political Economy is . . . that *the relation between demand and supply is the sole regulator of value.* This law, like the law of gravity, holds good in all cases whatever" (Hodgson 1870, 18).[14]

---

ing exertion, but a supply proportionate to the demand, and steadily following its variations, is what no sound political economist will ever expect to see" (Herschel 1850, 40–41).

13. See White 1989, 428, for statements of the laws by Jevons and Mill.

14. Unless otherwise stated, all emphases (italics) in quoted matter appear in the original sources.

The recent statement that Thornton's "no exceptions" argument, "perhaps under the influence of Augustus Comte, was inappropriately applying the methods of the natural sciences to the social sciences" (Ekelund and Thommesen 1989, 571n.) does not explain the contemporary significance of the argument. Lest it be suggested that Hodgson was a "minor" figure at the time, it should be noted that in an 1874 letter to Walras, Jevons (1977, 66) included Hodgson

Thornton used the example of a fish market to illustrate his argument that demand could increase with a given supply but the price could remain unaltered. He also used a fish market to illustrate the possibility of Dutch and English auction systems, where, for the same stock and number of customers, the prices could be different (1869, 47–48).[15] But he was explicit that this particular discussion of auctions with different outcomes was not designed to illustrate his general argument that supply and demand did not determine price. Rather, it was meant to illustrate the "utility" of his definitions of supply (the quantity offered for sale at a price specified by the dealer or the customer) and demand (the quantity the buyer was willing to pay at a specified price). The supply and demand conditions differed in the Dutch and English auctions because the transactors were willing to sell and buy the same quantity of a commodity at different prices (45, 48–49).[16] The illustration, then, simply set the scene for the following analysis by showing how, in a simplified example, prices could differ, in part because of the ways in which buyers and sellers calculated their particular offers (cf. 1870, 56–58).

Thornton acknowledged that his analysis might be regarded as unsatisfactory in the sense that it entailed that no precise explanation of price formation could be produced, as was suggested by references to the laws of supply and demand. But this conclusion was an analytical gain, because it showed why the apparent precision of the laws depended upon a misleading mechanistic approach to the economy:

> Nine-tenths of the confusion and obscurity in which the doctrine of price has hitherto been involved has arisen from . . . straining after precision where to be precise is necessarily to be wrong. Supply and demand are commonly spoken of as if they together formed some nicely-fitting, well-balanced, self-adjusting piece of machinery, whose component parts could not alter their mutual relations without evolving, as the product of every change, a price exactly corresponding with that particular change. . . . [Due, however, to]

in a small group of British analysts who would be interested in Walras's *Elements*. The others were G. H. Darwin, L. H. Courtney (see below), and Jenkin.

15. It was noted in the 1960s that "the Dutch auction method is utilized in the sale of fish in Hull, England, while the English system is employed in Grimsby, just across the Humber River" (Cassady 1967, 60).

16. In *Unto This Last* (1862), Ruskin considered the possibility of fixing wage rates "irrespective of the demand" for labor. He argued that "wages are already so regulated," providing the following example: "We do not sell our prime-ministership by Dutch auction" (1967, 19).

that ever-changing chameleon, human character or disposition, price cannot possibly be subjected to law. (1869, 65)

Thornton thus rejected the mechanistic accounts of price adjustment used by proponents of the laws of supply and demand. Such adjustments were not explained, with reliance placed instead on metaphorical references such as gravitation. By contrast, he posited a path-dependent adjustment process, where the price "evolved" as a "product" of preceding changes. It was the rejection of depicting the economy as a "well-balanced piece of machinery" which most of his contemporaries appeared unable or unwilling to understand.

2. Mill's Review:
With Friends like These

In explaining the significance of his anomalous cases, the weakest component of Thornton's analysis was his use of the epistemological claim that "a scientific law admits of no exceptions whatever." Not surprisingly, it was that claim on which critics were to fasten so as to defend the laws of supply and demand. Thornton's argument may now appear rather odd and was certainly at variance with the explanations of scientific laws by Herschel, Whewell, and Mill. Nevertheless it was recognized at the time that his argument was, as the *Pall Mall Gazette* put it, a "pertinent reply" to the "many smatterers in political economy who talk nonsense about the 'inexorable laws of supply and demand' " (1869, 27). Indeed, in 1867 this aspect of the argument had been applauded by John Stuart Mill, who was reading the chapters of *On Labour* as they appeared in the *Fortnightly Review*. While Mill was critical of Thornton's treatment of "justice" as compared with "utility" when discussing income distribution (a point to which Mill returned in his subsequent review), he wrote Thornton to praise "all the good I find in it":

To mention only one thing, the book will be very serviceable in carrying on what may be called the emancipation of political economy—its liberation from the kind of doctrines of the old school (now taken up by well to do people) which treat what they call economical laws, demand & supply for instance, as if they were laws of inanimate matter, not amenable to the will of human beings. . . . This is one of the queer mental confusions which will be wondered at by & by &

you are helping very much in the good work of clearing it up (Mill 1972a, 1320).[17]

While the *Pall Mall Gazette* (1869) acknowledged the role of Thornton's anomalies in criticizing the "smatterers," it argued also that the criticism did not apply to the "more reasonable" defenders of "the orthodox doctrines." Using an argument similar to that outlined by Whewell (1850, 21), the reviewer noted that no natural science could produce exactly correct results since, in working from "perfect" or ideal constructs, "we make a statement which is only approximately true, though sufficiently true for some purposes, and it may be added, the precise truth is beyond the powers of human calculation. The same may be said of political economy, only that the differences between its hypotheses and the facts is [*sic*] very much greater." Nevertheless, while Thornton may have been strictly incorrect, the more reasonable defenders of orthodoxy were left with a substantial problem:

> [Political economy] deals with an ideal state of things which is never realized and very frequently is not even approximately true. It neglects many social forces which are of immense importance, and supposes a simplicity and uniformity in the motives of action which are never found in practice. Yet, as mathematics are highly useful in spite of the divergence between the ideal and the actual, political economy is sometimes useful in spite of a far greater divergence. . . . It would be worthwhile for the next author of a treatise on the dismal science to explain a little more clearly what are the assumptions which it

17. In April 1869 Mill wrote to Cairnes concerning his forthcoming review of Thornton: "I feel pretty sure you will concur in what I have written on the so-called wages-fund, a subject on which I expressed myself in my Political Economy as inaccurately as other people, and which I have only within the last two or three years seen in its proper light" (1972b, 1587). It has been claimed that because of this 1869 reference to a reassessment within "the last two or three years," Thornton "*may* have influenced Mill's opinion but not by the first edition of *On Labour* (1869)" (Ekelund and Thommesen 1989, 588n.). Any possible influence of Thornton on Mill regarding this matter cannot, however, be disposed of in such a cavalier manner. While it is clear that Mill was expressing doubts about a wage fund doctrine in 1866 (Kurer 1993, 14–15), Thornton's critique of the wage fund (as it was to appear in the first edition of *On Labour*) was published in the *Fortnightly Review* in early 1867 (Thornton 1867, 564n.), and Mill's 1867 letter to Thornton indicates that he was reading Thornton's argument as it appeared in that journal. (Indeed, Kurer suggests that "what Mill may have got from Thornton was the suggestion of an institutional theory of wage determination.") The publication of Thornton's critique of the wage fund in 1867, and the subordinate role which it played in his initial argument, also make irrelevant the charge that Thornton had plagiarized the work of Francis Longe (Wilson 1871; see also Forget 1991).

makes, and upon the approximate realization of which in actual life its conclusions may be assumed to be valid. (1869, 27)

Even the most vulnerable part of Thornton's analysis could, therefore, be turned into a critique that the dismal science was not precise about its assumptions and the conditions in which they were "realised in real life." Given this, one other possible response was simply to assert that Thornton's analysis was irrelevant. This approach was taken by the *Spectator* (1869, 393–94) in a no-nonsense review which, in defending a "cost of production" approach to pricing, claimed that *On Labour* foundered on "an elaborate blunder." The correct approach or "well-known formula," based on the work of Adam Smith and Ricardo, was that the natural price "sets limits to the operation of supply and demand that *affect* market price, but do not determine it." Hence Thornton's discussion of price formation through "competition" was "absurd," because political economy "treats of the general causes affecting the operations of industry, but is hardly concerned with the 'higgling of the market,' which, for scientific purposes, would be quite as exact an expression as competition. The real problem is to express the general laws which affect competition." Since any discussion of market higgling was outside the domain of science, it followed that Thornton's anomalous cases could be ignored.

If this review was consistent with Ricardo's treatment of market prices in his *Principles* (1951, chapter 4), it might also have puzzled readers of Mill's *Principles,* where a supply and demand explanation was used to deal with wages and international trade. Mill himself dismissed it as "most crabbed and cantankerous," observing to J. E. Cairnes that "it is very amusing . . . to see how the tyros in Political Economy think themselves bound to give no quarter to heresies, being afraid to make any of the concessions which their masters make" (1972b, 1588). Nevertheless, as a "master" in the subject, Mill was not prepared to concede that the laws of supply and demand were irrelevant, as Thornton had argued. Using a strategy of rejection by partial incorporation,[18] he reduced all the arguments in *On Labour* to a series of anomalous or "exceptional" cases which the "current theory" had either ignored or failed to explain clearly (Mill 1967, 641). This neutralization of Thornton's analysis can be followed in three steps of Mill's review.

Mill's first tack was to explain the role and significance of the laws of

18. A phrase borrowed from Novick 1988, 410.

supply and demand in producing an equilibrium position within a general theory of price determination. Here, he cited his argument, from book 3, chapter 3 of his *Principles*, regarding the limited role of supply and demand in relation to long-period costs of production. This read in part:

> In all things which admit of indefinite multiplication, demand and supply only determine the perturbations of value, during a period which cannot exceed the length of time necessary for altering the supply. While thus ruling the oscillations of value, they themselves obey a superior force, which makes value gravitate towards Cost of Production, and which would settle it and keep it there, if fresh disturbing influences were not continually arising to make it again deviate. (Mill 1909, 456, as cited in 1967, 635n.)

While the condition of a "*stable* equilibrium" was that the market price would equal the commodity's "Natural Value" (635n.), Mill went on in his review to emphasize the fleeting possibility of such a position—the "point of exact equilibrium may be as momentary, but is nevertheless as real, as the level of the sea" (635–36). This claim for determinate, albeit "momentary" equilibria was to be used subsequently by Jenkin and Jevons (see below). It should be noted, however, that there was no explanation in Mill's *Principles* or in the review for the process of market-price adjustment. Rather than explaining the process of higgling, Mill simply invoked a gravitation metaphor.

Mill's second tack was to explain the significance of Thornton's anomalous cases which the *Spectator* had brushed aside. Here, he drew on the discussion of scientific laws in his *Logic* (Forget 1991, 207–8), arguing that the anomalies simply required an "*addition* to the scientific theory of the subject," that is, a "supplementary law," so as to acknowledge that in certain cases (the Dutch and English auctions; horses and gloves), the conditions necessary for supply to equal demand could not be met. Hence the hats and gloves cases remained exceptions, because they could not apply "in any considerable market—and, far more, in the general market of the world" (Mill 1967, 637; see also 638–39).

While Thornton's discussion of Dutch and English auctions was presented as an anomaly, its significance was construed in a manner different from those of the other exceptional cases. As was noted above, he made clear that his analysis of the auctions was a prelude to the explanation of price formation. However, as Negishi (1986) has shown, Mill read the discussion as an example of indeterminacy where the "same" demand and supply conditions could produce different prices. In such cases, Mill noted, the price depended upon "whether sellers or buyers hold out longest," which in turn depended upon their relative "patience" and ability to withstand "inconvenience" (Mill 1967, 636–37, 642). Mill's concentration on this point might be explained by his focus on wage determination. That is, because wages were an "exceptional case," he sought to link the discussion of auction outcomes with Thornton's argument that wage outcomes were theoretically indeterminate because there was no reserve price for labor (Thornton 1869, 66–87). For Mill, then, although Thornton's discussion of Dutch and English auctions was of "minute" importance for the "common case" of commodities, it was of "great practical importance" for the case of labor (Mill 1967, 642–43).

The third tack in Mill's review was to deal with the basic discussion of price formation in *On Labour*. Here, his approach was to read Thornton's analysis as if it consisted of two quite separate propositions, which were then dismissed by different criteria. The first proposition concerned Thornton's argument that even if sales occurred at a point where supply was equal to demand, an equilibrium position was virtually irrelevant. Mill acknowledged that some "voluntary agents, may resist for a time the force to which they at last succumb." (Note the reference to the gravitational metaphor.) This was, admittedly, a "limitation" of the law, but Thornton's argument amounted to "only saying that the law in question resembles other economical laws in producing its effects not suddenly but gradually"; and Mill went on to reassert that the law "fixes the exact point which the fall of price will reach" (1967, 639). On Mill's reading, Thornton had mistaken a "limitation" of the basic law of supply and demand for a decisive rejection of it. If this claim failed to grasp the point of Thornton's argument, a reader of Mill's *Principles* might also have been puzzled by it. For when Mill closed book 3, chapter 3, by defining "the condition of *stable* equilibrium" as being "when things exchange for each other according to their . . . Natural Value," he claimed that "demand and supply always rush to an equilibrium" (1909, 456).

Mill's second proposition concerned Thornton's analysis of price adjustment involving the use of reserve prices. Here, he argued that Thornton's type of reserve pricing—that is, where "a dealer . . . holds out for a price which he can obtain for part of his supply, but cannot obtain for the whole"—could only occur when there was a lack of competition, so that Thornton had presented an "exceptional" case. The more general situation was that "when supply exceeds the demand, the two may be equalised by subtracting from the supply as well as adding to the demand. Reserving a price is, to all intents and purposes, withdrawing supply." If dealers could not sell all their stocks at the prevailing prices, the inventories could not be considered part of the market supply, so that "the price has been determined without any reference to . . . [the] withheld stock, and determined in such a manner that the demand at that price shall (if possible) be equal to the supply which the dealers are willing to part with at that price" (Mill 1967, 640–41).

As J. E. Cairnes explained in a letter to Mill, this argument was a tautology ("an identical proposition"). In the case of a dealer setting a reserve price, it amounted to claiming that *demand [is] the measure of supply*"; alternatively, for a buyer's reserve price, it meant that "*supply is . . . used to measure demand.*" Moreover, Cairnes noted, since Mill had effectively ignored Thornton's discussion of the factors entering into the calculations of dealers and customers, he had no substantive explanation for the determination of an equilibrium position through "the higgling of the market" (O'Brien 1943, 283–84).[19] While conceding that "I admit almost all that you say," Mill's response was that he had attempted only to explain that the causes of variations in market prices would "operate" to change prices in the requisite direction so as to equate demand with supply (Mill 1972b, 1616). But this was hardly the point at issue. Thornton's general "model" of prices was not concerned with questioning whether prices would necessarily change in the required direction, but rather with obtaining a precise explanation for the causes, process, and analytical significance of the price changes.[20]

Like the *Pall Mall Gazette* and *Spectator* reviewers, who focused on Thornton's anomalous cases, Mill was apparently unable to understand the general model of price formation in *On Labour*. Faced with an argument which destabilized any claims for the precision and hence the relevance of the laws of supply and demand and an equilibrium market

19. See also Cairnes 1874, 101–4.

20. Cf. a recent account which concludes that when responding to Cairnes, Mill's defense was "sound . . . as far as it went." The same author, while failing to report Mill's concession to Cairnes ("I admit almost all that you say"), considers that Cairnes's tautology charge depended on reading Mill as arguing that "at a particular price there may correspond not a single quantity but a range of quantities supplied." Since this "is not accurate," Cairnes "misunderstood Mill" (Hollander 1985, 277, 278). As was explained above, however, Cairnes's criticism was couched in different terms.

position, Mill exhibited cognitive dissonance. It was apparently not possible to think of price determination other than by means of mechanical analogies. In this he was followed by subsequent commentators. Indeed, Mill's review set out the two principal ways in which Thornton's troublesome and difficult text came to be read so as to neutralize its disturbing conclusions.

First, commentators writing soon after the review appeared followed Mill in treating Thornton's arguments as a series of special cases.[21] It might be acknowledged, albeit in a grudging fashion, that Thornton had drawn attention to the necessity to be clearer about the assumptions underlying the laws of supply and demand. (Examples of these were the "existence of an open market" with "unrestricted competition" and continuity in trading which entailed "an infinitely fine gradation of men in respect of their powers and faculties"; Rickards 1869; Courtney 1869.) However, the focus was placed on Thornton's anomalies, which included the Dutch and English auctions, as if his whole case pivoted on them. Hence he had "misunderstood" the meaning of the laws of supply and demand (Courtney; Rickards, 393–94).[22] Since Thornton's general pricing "model" was read as only another example of his misunderstanding of the laws, the effect was to obliterate any serious discussion of it. At best, it might be referred to in Mill's terms. The *Westminster Review* (1869, 86), for example, in repeating the claim that "reserving a price is to all intents and purposes withdrawing supply," declared that Thornton had "been caught tripping by Mr. Mill."[23] The more general approach, however, was to ignore the basic pricing model altogether.[24]

21. A procedure followed by a later commentator: "All of Thornton's strictures, Mill was able to demonstrate, turned on special cases" (Hollander 1985, 275).

22. See also the extended discussion in *British Quarterly Review* 1869, esp. 457–65.

23. For a recent discussion which replicates Mill's tautology see Ekelund and Thommesen 1989, 582.

24. Subsequent commentaries have followed the same pattern. See, for example, Breit 1967, 520; Hollander 1985, 275–279. Ekelund and Thommesen, who claim that the "purpose" of their article is, in part, "to scrutinize Thornton's 'model,'" then fail to discuss it, although the relevant pages from *On Labour* are referred to in a footnote (1989, 568, 584n.). Even more nuanced accounts still focus on Thornton's anomalous cases, with scant attention paid to the basic pricing model (Forget 1992, 213–16). Perhaps surprisingly, Negishi (1986, 573–76), who argues that Thornton "emphasized . . . the possibility of trade carried out at disequilibrium prices," appears also to treat Thornton's "exceptional" cases as the nub of the argument and does not describe Thornton's general analysis of price formation. He does refer to that analysis, however, characterizing it as a "non-Walrasian, non-tâtonnement process," the significance of which is that disequilibrium trades shift the equilibrium positions "eventually established"

The second way to neutralize Thornton was to argue as if any discussion of the problem of higgling could be ignored while asserting that
the laws of supply and demand had determinate results. As was noted
above, Mill was dismissive of the *Spectator* review which argued that
an analysis of higgling was outside the domain of "the science." Yet
Mill had, in effect, only produced a variant of that argument. While
he insisted, for example, that the law of supply and demand "determines that the price of a commodity should fall, and fixes the exact
point which the fall will reach" (1967, 639), he could not explain the
process of market price adjustment and, in the last resort, relied on the
gravitation metaphor in *Principles*. This perplexed Cairnes. In his letter
to Mill regarding the Thornton review, Cairnes noted that while it was
possible to produce a systematic (or "scientific") theory of natural (or
"average") prices, that was not the case for market prices. It might be
possible to identify the relative importance of the "various influences"
which could account for the process of "the higgling of the market,"
in the sense of explaining the different prices which prevailed for different types of commodities. Such an analysis would be based on "the
facts" on a case-by-case basis. However, because the "influences" in
any market period were "too numerous and too indeterminate to admit
of a generalisation which should embody them," it was not possible to
produce a scientific "theory of *market* [as distinct from average] prices."
For this reason Cairnes "doubted" that "the game [would] be worth the
candle" in any search for theoretical determinancy in an account of the
laws of supply and demand (O'Brien 1943, 284).[25] This classical characterization of market prices which underlay the *Spectator* review, was, of
course, hardly new. Mill was quite familiar with it, and Cairnes had provided a detailed account in his *Character and Logical Method of Political
Economy* (White 1989, 434–35). What puzzled Cairnes, however, was
that in his review of Thornton, Mill made no mention of it, while creating the impression that the laws of supply and demand operated in
some mechanical manner which could be expressed in a theoretically
determinate fashion.

---

(575). However, Thornton doubted whether any equilibrium point was relevant (see above),
and it was subsequent commentators who referred to the possibility of shifts in demand with
its effects on equilibria.

25. See also Cairnes 1874, 104–12.

Mill's approach was followed by subsequent reviewers for whom it was an act of faith that if equilibrium prices were the result of market "higgling," "demand and supply are facts. . . . Competition is the *expression* of these facts—the barometer which indicates the fluctuations of the commercial atmosphere. Supply and demand determine price" (Rickards 1869, 393–94). Nevertheless Mill's analysis raised substantial problems. It could be, and was, accepted that any market equilibria were only "momentary." Yet Mill had produced contradictory arguments about the speed of price adjustment: did it take some time, or did prices rush to the equilibrium? Moreover, the argument in the review that unsold stocks were "off the market" could be read as a claim that all market transactions took place at equilibrium positions. Mill had been too clever by half in his review, but the confusing story was reworked by those commentators who argued, contrary to Mill, that all prices were to be explained by reference to the laws of supply and demand. For this reason and also because of the influential reading which it gave of Thornton's text, Mill's review provided one resource which was used in stabilizing the laws of supply and demand in the wake of *On Labour*.

3. Restoring Mechanism: Jenkin's Diagrams

Thornton argued that a mechanical adjustment of prices to a "stable" equilibrium was irrelevant because the adjustment entailed a path-dependent process. One common response from supply and demand proponents was, therefore, simply to deny that that process could occur. This approach was first signaled in a long review of Thornton in the *Times*. Published after Mill's review, it was written by Leonard Courtney, who was to occupy the University College (London) political economy chair in the period between Cairnes and Jevons. Ignoring the reference in Mill's review to a lengthy period of adjustment, Courtney cited the passage from Mill's *Principles* on the "rush" to equilibrium, arguing that in a "free market" there would be "continuity of trading" and a "stability of price" (Courtney 1869).[26] If these assertions simply ignored Thornton's problematization of the price adjustment process, Fleeming

---

26. The article was unsigned, but De Marchi (1973, 184n.) has identified Courtney as the author. As was noted above, in 1874 Courtney was one of the few British analysts whom Jevons thought would be interested in Walras's *Elements*.

Jenkin's article, which was published the next year, indicated that there was a more substantial reason for supply and demand theorists to argue that price adjustment virtually took no time at all.

In the first set of (quantity–form) supply and demand diagrams published in English, Jenkin followed Mill's reading by treating Thornton's argument as a series of anomalous cases. For example, he depicted the Dutch and English auction outcomes by means of a perfectly inelastic segment on a demand schedule. That case, where "the demand at prices in the neighbourhood of the market price is constant at all prices" was of peripheral importance, because it "represents an unusual state of mind" (Jenkin 1870, 160). If this obliterated Mill's link between the auctions and the labor market, Jenkin further departed from Mill in claiming that all prices were to be explained by the laws of supply and demand. While Jenkin identified three different periods in his analysis, the focus here will be on the first, subsequently termed a "market" period, where the total available supply of, and the "purchase fund" or demand for, commodities was fixed (as in *On Labour*).[27] In this period the law of supply and demand was that *"in a given market, at a given time, the market price of the commodity will be that at which the supply and demand curves cut"* (Jenkin 1870, 153).

Jenkin's statement entails that because, at any time, the market price would be an equilibrium one, any adjustment was instantaneous. The reason for this was that if the adjustment took time and there was disequilibrium trading (at Thornton's "intermediate prices"), it was possible that "the market price will . . . be changed by the sales" (154). To preclude this possibility Jenkin used two devices. The first concerned expectations: "The law . . . assumes that each man knows his own mind, that is to say, how much of his commodity he will there and then sell or buy at each price, and that the conditions of his mind will not vary" (153–54). The second device, when referring to "actual" markets, was to introduce specialist traders: "Bargainers all day long will be watching the market, to ascertain whether a given price is above or below that at which the quantity to be bought and sold will be equal" (154). There

---

27. In Jenkin's second period, both demand and supply were allowed to vary; in the third ("long run") period, price was principally determined by the cost of production, and the quantity produced depended on the demand at that price (Jenkin 1870, 157, 163). Cf. Milgate (1987, 181), who attributes the periodization only to Marshall.

was, however, no precise explanation of how the specialists would behave, and it was unclear how they would obtain their information, since it was the commodity sellers who received the appropriate signals: "The excess or defect of the supply over the demand at a price is inferred from the briskness of the sales" (153). The effect of Jenkin's two devices was thus to smuggle in an assumption of perfect knowledge.

Jenkin acknowledged that "in practice, men's minds do not remain constant for five minutes altogether" and, therefore, that even with a parametric commodity supply, "the market price of the commodity may vary immensely, as men's minds vary" (154, 155). This was Mill's notion of momentary equilibria, which Jenkin was able to transform and formalize by depicting it in terms of shifts in the supply and/or demand functions. It was clear, however, that all trades at any moment were to be understood as market-clearing outcomes, since Jenkin reiterated that "at each moment the first law of supply and demand holds good" (156). The key points in Jenkin's stabilization story were thus the given set of expectations at any moment, coupled with the (unexplained) role of specialist traders and momentary shifting equilibria.

While Jenkin discussed all prices in terms of the laws of supply and demand, he did not employ a marginalist theory of behavior. This was not because he was unfamiliar with its broad outline. In 1868, following the publication of an article of his which gave an algebraic formulation of the law of supply and demand (Jenkin 1868, 13n.–14n.), some correspondence ensued with Jevons regarding the latter's marginal utility theory. Jenkin appears, ironically, to have been unconvinced by Jevon's account, because Jevons assumed a given exchange ratio for trading between two actors (Jevons 1977, 168–78). In 1870, despite using the same assumption as Jevons, Jenkin was still unconvinced by the marginal utility theory. His market-period demand function, for example, was explained by a given "purchase fund" (Jenkin 1870, 151), so that the inverse relationship between quantity and price was apparently the result of purchasers' entering or leaving the market as the price changed. For Jenkin, it was simply not possible to explain the behavior underlying the curves in any functional fashion: "The demand in the buyers' minds corresponds to the utility which, in their opinion, attaches to the article; and the causes which help to form that opinion are too numerous for classification" (177). The laws of supply and demand were thus phenomenal; ultimately, their veracity depended on their being understood as statistical laws (166, 169). For this reason, as Jenkin made clear subsequently, it was not possible to represent economic behavior and thus the laws in "algebraic" terms (White 1989, 445).[28]

That other proponents of the laws agreed that human behavior could not be directly represented in functional terms was suggested by John Macdonnell's *Survey of Political Economy*, which was published at the same time as Jevons's *Theory of Political Economy*. Summarizing the recent debate over price formation, Macdonnell argued that the "theory of supply and demand is the general theory." However, since the laws depended on the complex working of the human mind and, therefore, "obey no law capable of being numerically expressed," they could not be represented in mathematical terms (Macdonnell 1871, 253–54, 259). In the last instance, Jenkin's attempt to stabilize the laws depended on the impression of precision conveyed by his diagrams. The economic behavior and the type of market required to explain the apparent precision remained, to all intents and purposes, a black box.

4. Utility and Perfect Competition: Jevons

Since Jevons agreed with Jenkin that the phenomenal laws of supply and demand could only be identified retrospectively and would vary according to the market period and the type of commodity transacted, he had eschewed the use of supply and demand diagrams (White 1989, 1991a). Jevons argued, however, that by reducing behavior to a single-valued function via the marginal utility theory, it was possible to explain the universal "natural" behavioral basis which underlay any set of market transactions, whatever the vagaries of their phenomenal manifestation. This account could be made more precise than Jenkin's because it deployed both geometry and the calculus to show a determinate equilibrium position. Irritated by Jenkin's failure in 1870 to refer to his "Brief Account" of the marginalist theory (Jevons 1866), Jevons then wrote up his *Theory of Political Economy* (*TPE*) for publication.

Jevons concluded in *TPE* that "no one is ever required to give what he more desires for what he less desires, so that perfect freedom of exchange must be to the advantage of all" (1871, 134). This claim was made in the analysis of exchange with parametric market stocks in chap-

---

28. Cf. Brownlie and Prichard (1963, 209), who suggest that as early as 1868 "some notion of diminishing marginal utility would seem to be implied" in Jenkin's analysis.

ter 4. It was reiterated in the next chapter, when Jevons introduced cost of production into the analysis of price determination where labor was the only cost. He argued that there would be an equalization across the economy of "the amount of utility which can be obtained by producing a little more" of a commodity—that is, an equalization of the product of the marginal productivity of labor and the marginal utility of the output. In equilibrium, there could "be no motive for altering or regretting the distribution of labour [between employments], and the utility produced is at a maximum" (179–80).

Given these material welfare properties of an equilibrium position, the principal difficulty which Thornton raised for Jevons was clear in the "Brief Account." Written in 1862 but first published in 1866, the "Account" argued that the ratio of the final degrees of utility would be "indeterminate but for the existence of a law that all quantities of the same commodity, being uniform in kind, must be exchanged at the same rate. The last increments, then, must be exchanged in the same ratios of the whole quantities exchanged" (Jevons 1866, section 14). The importance of this law, which simultaneously imposed a uniform price and a market-clearing equilibrium condition, was further emphasized in *TPE*. Characterized as a "self-evident principle," it was first called the "principle of uniformity" and then, in the second edition, the "*law of indifference*" (Jevons 1871, 94, 99; 1970, 137, 141). However, because the law was "one of the central pivots of the [marginalist] theory" and thus was "of the utmost importance" (1970, 137), there was a substantial lacuna in the theory. Even with the exchange ratio given, Jevons acknowledged in his "Brief Account," to "explain in ordinary words how the adjustment [to equilibrium] takes place under this condition is almost impossible" (1866, section 14). As Thornton's first article on price formation was published a few months later, the timing of this acknowledgment was most unfortunate. The problem, however, remained in *TPE*. Since Jevons claimed that "the ordinary laws of supply and demand . . . are the practical manifestation of the [utility exchange] theory" which assumed "perfect competition" and that it was "not difficult" to show how the theory "is verified in the actual working of a great market," he responded to Thornton's arguments by insisting that the "theoretical conception of a perfect market is more or less completely carried out in practice" (1970, 86, 105).

Apart from the standard device of focusing on the "anomalous" cases, Jevons used two strands of argument to dismiss Thornton's analysis in chapter 4. The first was to argue that all markets closely approximated the conditions in the "public exchanges" of London and Manchester which produced perfectly competitive results. Here, brokers ensured a uniform price "at any moment," so that if a given commodity stock was sold in successive lots at different prices, all transactions occurred at equilibrium positions. The second strand was to introduce speculators, so that market traders behaved, on average, in a determinate independent fashion. Thornton's argument concerning dealers' competitive strategies was then reduced to a special case which was outside the domain of "scientific political economy." While apparently drawing on Jenkin's account, the effect of this strategy was to provide more detailed information on the market structure and the means of disseminating information which were necessary to produce an equilibrium point for each set of market transactions. For, by using a notion of market-clearing perfect competition, Jevons introduced a highly restrictive concept of competition which was quite different from that of the classical political economists.[29]

In *TPE* a market was defined, after the manner of "commercial men," as "any body of persons who are in intimate business relations and carry on extensive transactions in any commodity." Although the term could refer to "two or more persons dealing in two or more commodities," "perfectly free competition" required large numbers of traders whose actions were independent and who had "perfect knowledge" of market demand and supply conditions. The ratio of exchange "between any two persons should be known to all the others," and there could be no "secret or unknown stocks," no conspiracies manipulating supplies so as "to produce unnatural ratios of exchange." It was further assumed that all commodities in a market were "perfectly homogeneous" and infinitely divisible to enable "continuity of variation" (Jevons 1871, 22–23, 84–87, 106, 116).[30]

While it "may or may not be localised," the "central point of a market is the public exchange,—mart or auction rooms, where the traders agree

29. For discussion of the differences between these concepts of competition see Eatwell 1982; Duménil and Levy 1987; Ciccone 1991.

30. Jevons's treatment of utility as a single-valued function depended on making economic behavior analogous to a "force" such as gravity and then depicting exchange as a balance of forces in equilibrium. It was this mechanical model, where an equilibrium condition could be given a concise formulation with the "language" of the calculus, which imposed many of the assumptions necessary for Jevons's specification of perfect competition: infinite divisibility and continuity, homogeneity, and the independent actions of large numbers. The equilibrium condition then imposed the assumption of a uniform price.

to meet and transact business." Examples of such "central points" were the Stock Exchange, the corn, sugar, coal, and Consolidated Funds markets in London, and those for cotton and cotton waste in Manchester. In these cases, unlike the money market,[31] trading took place in a confined or localized space, enabling direct and "close communication." The relevance of this point was that a trader who did not know the prevailing price at any moment "must not be considered part of the market" (84, 85, 108). The role of brokers was essential in communicating between traders: "a complete consensus is established, and the stocks of every seller or the demands of every buyer are brought into the market," so that "every purchase shall be made with the most thorough acquaintance with the conditions of the trade." With continuous trading, brokers ensured that the market price "must be uniform at any one moment" and that all trades occurred at equilibrium positions (86–87, 91–92).

In considering Jevons's argument it is useful to distinguish between two types of auction systems. In a Call system, with listings of approved stocks, there is discrete trading because no transactions are allowed until the market-clearing price is settled for a particular stock. This requires trading in a "single location" at a "single point in time," the "Call of the official exchange list," and a limited number of brokers. "The market is perfectly competitive only because it is highly regulated" (Kregel 1988, 369). While Call trading was abandoned on the New York Stock Exchange in 1871, it still prevailed on the Continent, with the Bourse providing the "model" for Walras's discussion of *tâtonnement* with parametric commodity stocks (Walker 1987, 760). It was the type of market required for Jenkin's suggestion as to how any destabilizing effects, due to trading at disequilibrium prices, could be effaced.[32]

By contrast, in an open-outcry auction system, which Jevons discussed, trading is "two-sided" and continuous, with nearly simultaneous trading of all stocks. In a large market, however, two problems become apparent. The first is that of communication. For Jevons, as noted above, this was "solved" by brokers' establishing a uniform price. The second

---

31. The "common expression *Money Market* denotes no locality: it is applied to the aggregate of those bankers, capitalists, and other traders who lend or borrow money, and who constantly exchange information concerning the course of business" (Jevons 1871, 85).

32. "If every man were openly to write down beforehand exactly what he would sell or buy at each price, the market price might be computed immediately, and the transactions be then and there closed" (Jenkin 1870, 154). For a recent proposal of a "single-price" market which would prevent continuous trading and market volatility see Grundfest 1991, 78.

problem is to establish price continuity. This could be explained by the presence of arbitrageurs. For example, if, with large trades distributed randomly throughout a trading day by brokers, there is a "mismatch" between buyers and sellers, floor traders arbitrage, buying from and selling to different brokers in sequences as brokers enter and leave the trading floor. At any one "moment," competition is supposed to keep the market price near to (or randomly distributed around) the hypothetical equilibrium price (Kregel 1988, 371–72).

At the time *TPE* was written, jobbers (or "dealers") acted as arbitrageurs working between the brokers on the London Stock Exchange, and they were also active in the Consolidated Funds market, at least so far as Consols were concerned (Jenkins 1973, 91). It has been suggested that while *TPE* presented a "statical" exchange theory, "there must be a dynamical view of trading" which "lay" behind it and that Jevons "had in mind a piecemeal exchange process" of recontracting and arbitrage (Negishi 1982, 220, 222, 225–26). However, there was no discussion of arbitrage and no possibility of recontracting in *TPE*. This point can be shown by considering a footnote which Jevons introduced in the second edition, arguing that on the New York Stock Exchange, stocks were auctioned in successive lots "without disclosing the total amount to be put up." The result was that depending on whether the total stocks were greater or less than market expectations at the beginning of the day, early buyers would "suffer" or gain an "advantage" when compared with those buying subsequent lots. It was concluded that this auction system "only exhibits in miniature what is constantly going on in the markets generally on a large scale" (Jevons 1970, 137n.).

Jevons's argument appears peculiar if only because it seems to violate the condition, imposed in *TPE*, that all transactors knew the amount of stocks to be traded. What Jevons had done, however, was to define the "requisite" knowledge as applying to trading at any particular "moment" so that all trades occurred at equilibrium. Acknowledgment that trading took place in successive lots could have opened the door to Thornton's disequilibrium trading process. That door was closed by claiming, like Jenkin, that while a specific equilibrium price would prevail only momentarily, all trading took place at market-clearing positions.[33] There was, therefore, no careful examination or critique in *TPE*

---

33. Cf. the subsequent commentary, which in dismissing Thornton's argument on the irrelevance of a final stock-clearing price as *obiter dicta*, asserts: "What Thornton seems to be

of Thornton's argument that any explanation for market price formation had to account for dealers' interdependent calculations, and that most transactions occurred before the final stock-clearing price prevailed. Moreover, Jevons failed to explain precisely how brokers solved the coordination problem, something which is not self-evident (Nell 1980; Kregel 1991). Nor did he explain who played the role of broker outside of specialized commodity markets.

If brokers were to establish the market price at any moment, speculators were also required to deal with the problem of uncertainty. When he introduced the "law" that "*in the same open market, at any moment, there cannot be two prices for the same kind of article,*" Jevons added that in "practice" some differences might occur due to "the effective credit of the purchasers, their imperfect knowledge of the market, and so on." But these differences were brushed aside as resulting from "extraneous circumstances" (1871, 92). This apparent reference to Thornton's discussion of calculation under uncertainty was simply an assertion, although it had some theoretical rationale in the way Jevons had argued in the "Brief Account" that uncertainty could be reduced to calculable risk and that, on average, transactors would behave in a predictable and determinate fashion (1866, sections 16, 18). In *TPE* this argument was amplified by the introduction of speculators' actions and a critique of *On Labour*.

While acknowledging that Thornton had shown "that the action of the laws of supply and demand was inadequately explained by previous economists," Jevons insisted that most of his arguments were "beside the question" (1871, 107). The anomalous cases, which assumed there to be no "regular" or continuous variation in supply and demand, could not "touch" the laws:

> Because, in retail trade, in English or Dutch auction, or other particular instances, we cannot at once observe the operation of the laws of supply and demand, it is not in the least to be supposed that those laws are false. In fact, Mr. Thornton seems to allow that, if prospective demand and supply are taken into account, they become substantially true. But, in the actual working of any market, the influence of future

---

saying is what no economist has ever denied: equilibrium takes time to work itself out since it is a process that works through the higgling of the market" (Breit 1967, 520). On the difficulties which a lengthy adjustment creates for subsequent accounts of supply and demand see Dore 1984–85.

events would never be neglected whether by a merchant or an economist. (106)

Given the way in which Thornton had described the formation of expectations in pricing strategies, Jevons's argument was "beside the question" unless it could be shown that uncertainty was reduced to calculable
risk and that accurate calculations would prevail on average across a
market. Such conditions were effectively acknowledged to be necessary
when Jevons closed his critique of Thornton by noting that "in practice"
equilibrium points were always shifting:

> From the various accidents of life and business, there are sure to be
> many people every day compelled to sell or having sudden strong
> inducements to buy. There is nearly always, again, the influence of
> prospective supply or demand depending upon the political intelli-
> gence of the moment. (Speculation complicates the action of the laws
> of supply and demand in a high degree, but does not in the least de-
> gree arrest their action or alter their nature.) But we shall never have a
> Science of Political Economy unless we learn to discern the operation
> of law even among the most perplexing accidents and interruptions.
> (1871, 109; 1970, 150)[34]

Speculators thus had a crucial role to play in Jevons's depiction of
market trading. His general argument was that by anticipating future
price changes, speculators would tend to "equalise prices" over a series
of trading periods so that speculation was "advantageous to the public" (1871, 87). Although it was not explained clearly, the argument
involved two distinct points which can be considered using Jevons's reference to corn sales (88). The first concerned corn prices in the period
between "normal" harvests, where prices rose toward the end of the
period. Here, the role of speculators (merchants) was to buy early in the
period and then gradually release their stocks as prices began to rise. If
every harvest was "normal" and total sales changed gradually, speculators would learn to predict the general movement and timing of price

---

34. The sentence in parentheses was added in the second edition. In citing this passage
Ekelund and Thommesen (1989, 583, 584, 588) conclude that Jevons "applied considerable
insight to the auction problem Thornton had posed." This claim for Jevons's "uncanny accuracy" depends on reading *TPE* as maintaining a careful distinction between the "theoretical
fiction" of market equilibrium and "actual market functioning." The claim is only possible,
however, because no mention is made of Jevons's statements that the "theoretical conception"
of a perfect market was "more or less completely carried out in practice" (see above).

movements. The second point referred to the role of speculators in a consecutive series of harvest failures (scarcities) as depicted, for example, in the King-D'Avenant Price-Quantity Table which Jevons discussed in the same chapter of *TPE*. (The argument could also have been relevant for the "cotton famine" of the 1860s.) Here the role of speculators was even more important in initially raising prices, reducing consumption, and preventing the scarcity from becoming a famine, while reducing the amplitude of price increases. The argument was well known and could be traced to the eighteenth century, but Jevons introduced a new twist to the explanation with the explicit introduction of probabilistic decision-making under conditions of risk, so that he presented a stochastic analogue for perfect knowledge in discussing the effects of speculation. Since Jevons argued that unexpected events would produce only mild fluctuations in all markets, he was assuming and claiming that, on average, speculators could make no systematic mistakes in their calculations (White 1989, 439–40).

In referring to specialized commodity markets to deny the relevance of Thornton's argument about the effects of uncertainty, Jevons simply assumed a different and highly restrictive mode of decision-making so that the type of calculations which Thornton had identified could not occur. Jevons was, however, prepared to acknowledge a case in which Thornton's argument was correct. But this was characterized as having no relevance for a "scientific" analysis. This discussion occurred when Jevons dealt with some "failures of the equations of exchange" due to indivisibilities in commodities (1871, 118–27). In the "Brief Account" it was acknowledged that with an indivisibility the exchange equations "may prove without solutions" (1866, 284–85). In *TPE*, however, Jevons used a number of rhetorical devices to downgrade the importance of the problem. One of these was to exclude cases of a small number of transactors from the analysis. Using the example of two transactors bargaining over a house price, and citing the passage from *On Labour* where Thornton argued that the market price could vary between the consumers' maximum and dealers' minimum (Thornton 1869, 58; Jevons 1871, 123), Jevons acknowledged that the outcome was analytically indeterminate. However:

I conceive that such a transaction must be settled on other than economical grounds. The disposition and force of character of the parties, their comparative persistency, their adroitness and experience in business, or it may be a feeling of justice or of kindliness really influences the decision. These are motives altogether extraneous to a theory of Economy, and yet they appear necessary considerations in this problem. It may be, that indeterminate bargains of this kind are best arranged by an arbitrator or third party. (1871, 124).

Actions based on bargaining (higgling) were thus to stand on the same footing as those founded on motives of "justice or kindliness": they were extraneous to the domain of the science of political economy.[35] By restricting economic behavior to price-taking actions, Jevons thus created the impression that insofar as Thornton's analysis had any validity, it was outside the domain of a "scientific" analysis.

5. The Fragility of Equilibrium

Jevons's discussion of perfectly competitive markets in chapter 4 of *TPE* turned on a distinction between a static and a dynamic analysis. He acknowledged that the "real condition of industry" was "dynamic" in that commodities were "continually being manufactured and exchanged and consumed." Because he was unable to produce such an account of economic activity, he was restricted to a static exposition, where holders of parametric commodity stocks would "exchange until they come to equilibrium" (Jevons 1871, 93–94). With this distinction, which is reminiscent of that made in Mill's *Principles* or Richard Jennings's *Natural Elements of Political Economy* (1855),[36] Jevons argued that the treatment of exchange could be represented as a position of rest (as compared with motion produced by a force) in a mechanical system.

Jevons acknowledged in his "Brief Account" that he had no substantive explanation for how such a static equilibrium point would be reached (see above). No such acknowledgment was made in chapter 4 of *TPE*, although the problem was referred to in chapter 5, where Jevons considered the role of production costs in determining relative prices. With labor as the only production cost, in the "long run," the market exchange ratio would be "determined by a kind of struggle between the conditions of production and consumption" at the margin. Jevons noted, however, with words similar to those used in his "Brief Account" in reference to

35. For discussion of the way in which Jevons identified this domain see White 1993a.
36. For the importance of Jennings in the formulation of Jevons's marginalist theory see White 1992.

parametric stock trading, that it "is not easy to express in words how the ratios of exchange are finally determined" (1871, 181, 189), and no explanation was actually given. A number of subsequent comments indicate that this long-run analysis incorporated the possibility of disequilibrium trading before equilibrium was reached.[37] No explanation was given as to how such trading was to be reconciled with the previous claims about market equilibrium and the role of speculators.[38] Given that discrepancy, it remains a task for the historian to explain why Jevons was so insistent in chapter 4 that all trades took place at market-clearing positions. Space limitations necessitate that this be reserved for another occasion.

6. A Final Insult

In late 1871 one reviewer argued that *On Labour* "was so . . . revolutionary in its effects that it rendered obsolete all existing economical works. . . . [Consequently,] it is time that political economists put their house in order" (*Examiner* 1871, 1095). Today the process of producing "order in the house" could be understood in terms of the argument that economists are continually "negotiating" the "meaning of the economy," which means that their activities

> are concerned with stabilizing the meanings of propositions that express ideas about inflation, say, or equilibration of the balance-of-payments deficit. Models and theorems and evidence of various natures, empirical and formal and definitional, are adduced to convince other members of the concerned community that some meanings are preferable for the agreed purposes, where those purposes themselves must be renegotiated from time to time. (Weintraub 1991, 127)

The debate immediately following the publication of Thornton's text provides an illustration of such "negotiation" with a series of attempts

37. In chapter 5 of *TPE* Jevons noted that there could be overproduction or a glut of commodities in particular markets, so that "our equations [of exchange] will not hold true." Much the same point was made in chapter 8: "we often observe that there is an abundance of capital to be had at low rates of interest, while there are also large numbers of artisans starving for want of employment" (1871, 257, 191).

38. Given the importance of chapter 4 in *TPE*, it is misleading to claim that the "primary theoretical object" of the text was to explain a "long run" equilibrium position "characterised by a uniform rate of profit" (Milgate 1987, 180).

to stabilize *the* meaning of the laws of supply and demand and a concomitant notion of equilibrium. The possibility of stabilization turned on the resolution of five major issues. First, what was the role of the laws in explaining prices? Did they provide a general explanatory principle, or could they play only a subordinate role relative to another principle, such as "natural price"? Second, under what conditions or assumptions did the laws take effect, and what type of market was necessary to explain their existence? Third, what results would follow if trading took place at "intermediate" (or nonequilibrium) prices, and what was the status and meaning of equilibrium in that case? Fourth, what was the epistemological status of the laws? Did they provide precise statements about "actual" market prices, or could they refer only to "tendencies," the precise effects of which might not actually prevail in a market? In either case, how could these claims be established? Fifth, what instruments should be used to represent the laws? Could they be described only in words, or could they be given a more "precise" representation by means of mathematics? If the latter approach was adopted, what did this entail about the representation of human behavior which underpinned the laws?

By the mid-1870s, however, there was precious little stabilization with regard to these matters. Indeed, there seems to have been general agreement concerning only two issues: that all prices should be explained by reference to the laws, and that any exploration of Thornton's discussion of indeterminacy had no place in subsequent work. The proponents of supply and demand might have been divided as to the explanation, meaning, and means of representation of the laws. However, the arguments in *On Labour* had been marginalized by reducing them to a series of anomalous cases, while the problem of the coherence of the notion of market equilibrium had been secured by assumptions which effaced the possibility of higgling.

If this was a curious analytical victory, the at times acerbic debates over value and price determination, which included sustained attacks upon the authority of Mill, had also helped to create a general public impression of instability about "the science." It was that impression which Alfred Marshall attempted to neutralize in 1876 when he defended Mill's "Theory of Value" with a reassuring account for the cognoscenti of the *Fortnightly Review*. In the most favorable verdict of *On Labour* able to be delivered by a marginalist, Marshall folded Thornton into a smooth historical narrative of progress in economic thought. Suggesting that Mill's *Principles* was quite compatible with Jevons's *Theory of Political Economy,* since Mill was an "implicit" marginal utility theorist, Marshall observed that while *On Labour* was not "free from faults," Thornton "has not received his due meed of gratitude" for having "led" economists to explain "the" theory of market "values" which they had previously ignored. He had, for example, led Mill "to give an exposition of his views" on that subject, which had not been "explained carefully" in the *Principles.* It could now be accepted that *the* theory of market prices was that the "higgling and the bargaining of the market tend to force the exchange value to that position which will just equate supply and demand" (Pigou 1925, 128n., 131–32).

Quite apart from the extraordinary suggestion that Mill had explained anything about the formation of market values which was not in the *Principles,* this was a classic Marshallian smoke screen. The whole point of Thornton's analysis, as he himself reiterated in 1876 (830–31), had been to question the possibility and relevance of a point where supply was equal to demand, even when prices changed in the requisite direction. The problem which faced supply and demand proponents such as Jevons and Jenkin was that if there was market higgling, any tendency to equilibrium could be thwarted by the concomitant changes in the underlying parameters if trading took place at Thornton's intermediate prices. The only clear published result which had emerged by 1876 was that an equilibrium resulting from the laws of supply and demand depended on the introduction of highly restrictive assumptions so that there was no "higgling and bargaining of the market."

The stage was now set for the publication of the next series of attempts to explain the determination of market prices. However, when Marshall came to consider the problem of the "temporary equilibrium" of a market period in his *Principles* (Marshall 1959, book 5, chapters 1–2), his discussion of the possibility of higgling rested on the same assumptions made by Jevons: small price changes, no effects from changes in the marginal utility of money, and dealers with, in effect, perfect knowledge (Kregel 1991). Clearly dissatisfied with his own results, as well as those obtained by Edgeworth, Marshall told the latter in 1902 that "I never apply curves or mathematics to market values. For I don't think they help much. And market values are . . . either absolutely abstract or terribly concrete and full of ever-varying (though individually vital) side-issues" (Pigou 1925, 435). Despite the confident statement of 1876, so far as the later Marshall was concerned, the discussion of market price determination remained essentially at the impasse which it had reached at the time of the debates over *On Labour*.

I thank Peter Groenewegen, Geoff Harcourt, and John King for helpful comments. The usual disclaimer applies.

References

Bharadwaj, Krishna. 1978. The Subversion of Classical Analysis: Alfred Marshall's Early Writing on Value. *Cambridge Journal of Economics* 2.3:253–71.

Breit, William. 1967. The Wages Fund Controversy Revisited. *Canadian Journal of Economics and Political Science* 23.4 (November): 509–28.

British Quarterly Review. 1869. On Labour. 50 (October): 448–74.

Brownlie, A. D., and M. P. Lloyd Prichard. 1963. Professor Fleeming Jenkin 1833–1885: Pioneer in Engineering and Political Economy. *Oxford Economic Papers* 15.3 (November): 204–16.

Cairnes, J. E. 1874. *Some Leading Principles of Political Economy Newly Expounded.* London: Macmillan.

Cassady, R. 1967. *Auctions and Auctioneering.* Berkeley and Los Angeles: University of California Press.

Ciccone, Roberto. 1991. Classical Natural and Market Prices versus Walrasian Temporary Equilibrium Prices. *Economic Notes* 20.3:545–60.

[Courtney, L. H.] 1869. Mr. Thornton on Labour. *The Times,* 16 October, 4.

Davidson, L. S., and R. E. Meiners. 1976. A Note on the Microfoundations of Macroeconomics: The Contribution of Philip H. Wicksteed. *Rivista Internazionale di Scienze Economiche e Commerciale* 23.9:888–99.

Davidson, P. 1972. *Money and the Real World.* London: Macmillan.

De Marchi, Neil B. 1973. The Noxious Influence of Authority: A Correction of Jevons' Charge. *Journal of Law and Economics* 16.1:179–89.

Dennis, Kenneth G. 1977. *Competition in the History of Economic Thought.* New York: Arno.

Dore, M. H. I. 1984–85. On the Concept of Equilibrium. *Journal of Post-Keynesian Economics* 7.2:193–206.

Duménil, G., and D. Levy. 1987. The Dynamics of Competition: A Restoration of Classical Analysis. *Cambridge Journal of Economics* 11.2:133–64.

Eatwell, John. 1982. Competition. In *Classical and Marxian Political Economy: Essays in Honour of Ronald L. Meek,* edited by Ian Bradley and Michael Howard. London: Macmillan.

Ekelund, R. B., and Thommesen, S. 1989. Disequilibrium Theory and Thornton's Assault on the Laws of Supply and Demand. *HOPE* 21.4:567–92.

Examiner. 1871. Mr. Macdonnell's Political Economy. No. 3327 (4 November): 1095–97.

Forget, Evelyn L. 1991. John Stuart Mill, Francis Longe and William Thornton on Demand and Supply. *Journal of the History of Economic Thought* 13.2 (Fall): 205–21.

———. 1992. J. S. Mill and the Tory School: The Rhetorical Value of the Recantation. *HOPE* 24.1:31–59.

———. 1994. Disequilibrium Trade as a Metaphor for Social Disorder in the Work of Jean-Baptiste Say. In *Higgling: Transactors and Their Markets in the History of Economics*, edited by Neil De Marchi and Mary S. Morgan. *HOPE* 26, special issue. Durham: Duke University Press.

Fusfeld, Daniel. 1990. The Single Price Theorem. In *Research in the History of Economic Thought and Methodology*, edited by Warren Samuels, vol. 7. Greenwich, Conn.: JAI Press.

Grundfest, Joseph A. 1991. When Markets Crash: The Consequences of Information Failure in the Market for Liquidity. In *The Risk of Economic Crisis*, edited by Martin Feldstein. Chicago: University of Chicago Press.

Hearn, William Edward. 1864. *Plutology: Or, The Theory of the Efforts to Satisfy Human Wants*. London: Macmillan; Melbourne: Robertson.

[Herschel, J.] 1850. Quetelet on Probabilities. *Edinburgh Review* 92.185 (July): 1–57.

Hodgson, W. B. 1870. *Competition*. London: Head.

Hollander, Samuel. 1985. *The Economics of John Stuart Mill*. Vol. 1. Oxford: Blackwell.

Jenkin, H. C. Fleeming. 1868. Trade Unions: How Far Legitimate? *North British Review* 48.95 (March): 1–62.

———. 1870. The Graphic Representation of the Laws of Supply and Demand. In *Recess Studies*, 151–85. Edinburgh: Edmonston & Douglas.

Jenkins, A. 1973. *The Stock Exchange Story*. London: Heinemann.

Jevons, W. Stanley. 1866. Brief Account of a General Mathematical Theory of Political Economy. *Journal of the Statistical Society* 29:282–87.

———. 1870. An Oversight by Faraday. *Nature* 1 (10 February): 384.

———. 1871. *The Theory of Political Economy*. London: Macmillan.

———. 1970. *The Theory of Political Economy*. Edited by R. D. Collison Black. Harmondsworth: Pelican.

———. 1977. *The Papers and Correspondence of William Stanley Jevons*. Vol. 4. Edited by R. D. Collison Black. London: Macmillan.

Kregel, J. A. 1988. Financial Innovation and the Organization of Stock Market Trading. *Banca Nazionale del Lavoro Quarterly*, no. 167:367–86.

———. 1991. Walras' Auctioneer and Marshall's Well-Informed Dealers: Time, Market Prices and Normal Supply Prices. In *Alfred Marshall's "Principles of Economics" 1890–1990: International Centenary Conference*, edited by G. Becattini et al. Florence: Università di Firenze, Facoltà di Economia e Commercio.

Kurer, Oskar. 1993. An Institutional Approach to Mill's Recantation of the Wage Fund Doctrine: Was Mill Right After All? Paper presented to the seventh conference of the History of Economic Thought Society of Australia, Wollogong.

Macdonnell, J. 1871. *A Survey of Political Economy*. Edinburgh: Edmonston & Douglas.

Maitland, F. W. 1906. *The Life and Letters of Leslie Stephen*. London: Duckworth.

Marshall, Alfred. [1920] 1959. *Principles of Economics*. 8th ed. London: Macmillan.

——. 1975. *The Early Economic Writings of Alfred Marshall, 1867–1890*. Edited by J. K. Whitaker. Vol. 1. London: Macmillan.

Milgate, Murray. 1987. Equilibrium: Development of the Concept. In *The New Palgrave: A Dictionary of Economics*, edited by John Eatwell, Murray Milgate, and Peter Newman. London: Macmillan.

Mill, J. S. 1909. *Principles of Political Economy*. Edited by W. J. Ashley. London: Longmans, Green.

——. 1967. *Collected Works of John Stuart Mill*. Edited by J. M. Robson. Vol. 5. Toronto: University of Toronto Press.

——. 1972a. *Collected Works*, ed. Robson, vol. 16.

——. 1972b. *Collected Works*, vol. 17.

Mirowski, Philip. 1989. *More Heat than Light*. Cambridge: Cambridge University Press.

——. 1990. Smooth Operator: How Marshall's Demand and Supply Curves Made Neoclassicism Safe for Public Consumption, but Unfit for Science. In *Alfred Marshall in Retrospect*, edited by Rita McWilliams Tullberg. Aldershot: Edward Elgar.

Negishi, T. 1982. A Note on Jevons's Law of Indifference and Competitive Equilibrium. *The Manchester School* 50.3:220–30.

——. 1986. Thornton's Criticism of Equilibrium Theory and Mill. *HOPE* 18.4: 567–77.

Nell, E. J. 1980. Competition and Price-taking Behaviour. In *Growth, Profits and Property*, edited by E. J. Nell. Cambridge: Cambridge University Press.

Novick, Peter. 1988. *That Noble Dream: The "Objectivity Question" and the American Historical Profession*. New York: Cambridge University Press.

O'Brien, G. 1943. J. S. Mill and J. E. Cairnes. *Economica* 10.40:273–85.

Pall Mall Budget. 1869. On Labour. 1, no. 23 (5 March): 27–28.

Pigou, A. C., ed. 1925. *Memorials of Alfred Marshall*. London: Macmillan.

Ricardo, David. 1951. *The Works and Correspondence of David Ricardo*. Vol. 1, *On the Principles of Political Economy and Taxation*. Edited by Piero Sraffa with the collaboration of M. H. Dobb. Cambridge: Cambridge University Press.

[Rickards, G. K.] 1869. Thornton on Labour. *Edinburgh Review* 130.266 (October): 390–417.

Ruskin, J. [1862] 1967. *Four Essays on the First Principles of Political Economy*. Lincoln: University of Nebraska Press.

Schumpeter, J. A. 1954. *History of Economic Analysis*. London: George Allen & Unwin.

Spectator. 1869. New Political Economy. 27 March, 393–94.

Stigler, G. J. 1965. *Essays in the History of Economics*. Chicago: University of Chicago Press.

Thornton, W. T. 1866. A New Theory of Supply and Demand. *Fortnightly Review* 6.34:420–34.

———. 1867. What Determines the Price of Labour or Rate of Wages. *Fortnightly Review* 7.5 (May): 551–66.

———. 1869. *On Labour: Its Wrongful Claims and Rightful Duties, Its Actual Present and Possible Future.* London: Macmillan.

———. 1870. *On Labour.* 2d ed. London: Macmillan.

———. 1876. Professor Cairnes on Value. *Contemporary Review* 28 (October): 813–35.

Uemiya, S. 1981. Jevons and Fleeming Jenkin. *Kobe University Economic Review,* no. 27:45–57.

Walker, D. A. 1987. Walras's Theories of Tâtonnement. *Journal of Political Economy* 95.4:758–74.

Weinberg, A. 1966. A Meeting of the Political Economy Club on 7 May, 1857: From John Eliot Cairnes's Notebook. *The Mill Newsletter* 1.2:12–16.

Weintraub, E. Roy. 1991. *Stabilizing Dynamics: Constructing Economic Knowledge.* New York: Cambridge University Press.

Westminster Review. 1869. Labour and Capital. 36, no. 1 (July): 80–122.

Whewell, William. 1831. Mathematical Exposition of Some of the Leading Doctrines in Mr. Ricardo's "Principles of Political Economy and Taxation." *Transactions of the Cambridge Philosophical Society.* Reprinted in Whewell 1971.

———. 1850. Mathematical Exposition of Some Doctrines of Political Economy. *Transactions of the Cambridge Philosophical Society,* Second Memoir. Reprinted in Whewell 1971.

———. 1971. *Mathematical Exposition of Some Doctrines of Political Economy (1829, 1831 and 1850).* New York: Augustus M. Kelley.

White, Michael V. 1989. Why Are There No Supply and Demand Curves in Jevons? *HOPE* 21.3:425–56.

———. 1991a. Jevons on Utility, Exchange, and Demand: Comment. *The Manchester School* 59.1 (March): 80–83.

———. 1991b. Where Did Jevons' Energy Come From? *History of Economics Review,* no. 15 (Winter): 60–72.

———. 1992. The Moment of Richard Jennings: The Production of the Marginalist Economic Agent. Typescript for publication.

———. 1993a. The Natural and the Social: Science and Character in Jevons's Political Economy. Typescript for publication.

———. 1993b. Multiple Equilibria and Jevons's Trade Diagrams: A Note. Typescript.

[Wilson, John.] 1871. Economic Fallacies and Labour Utopias. *Quarterly Review* 131.261 (July): 229–63.

Wise, M. Norton. 1992. Exchange-Value: Fleeming Jenkin and Measures of Energy and Utility. Typescript.

On the Historical Origin of
Keynes's Financial Market Views

Michael Syron Lawlor

> Another reason for directing attention to speculation is the question as to
> what place shall be given to the study of it in the theory of economics.
> Speculation has become an increasingly important factor in the economic
> world without receiving a corresponding place in economic science.—
> H. C. Emery (1896, 8)

This essay attempts to set the context for Keynes's understanding of
financial markets. My object is to identify the earliest background and
setting of what is distinctive about Keynes's views on financial markets
in his *General Theory*. It is assumed that the reader is familiar with the
broad outlines of Keynes's basic theme, whereby investment drives output under the influence of financial market behavior.[1] Two specific issues
that emerge from his treatment in the *General Theory* are traced backward into the literature and history of Keynes's early career. First, where
did Keynes get his deep institutional understanding of asset market activity? Of the purchase and sale of securities and financial instruments
of all kinds? In this regard his views on *speculation* and its relationship
to the motives of investors is the crucial theme. Second, whence came
Keynes's theoretical treatment of asset market activity presented in the
General Theory—particularly, the most developed expression of it found
in chapter 17? In this regard we need to delve into the influences on his

---

1. For the analysis of his macroeconomic viewpoint that is lurking behind this essay see
Cottrell and Lawlor 1991 and Lawlor 1994a. This paper is part of a larger project on the his-
torical context of Keynes's thought. See Lawlor 1993 for a similar attempt to set the context for
Keynes's labor market analysis.

views of what constituted the subject of chapter 17, "The Essential Properties of Interest and Money." In a sense, I hold out these aspects of the *General Theory* as the touchstone to which our retrospective excursions will be referred back. My aim here, though, is not to characterize the text of the *General Theory* but to shed new light on the larger historical context in which it was written.

Looking Backward from the *General Theory*

To guide our search backward from the *General Theory,* I draw upon two sorts of evidence. First there is the record of Keynes's own statements about his work, much of it emanating from his participation in what the editors of his collected works have aptly dubbed the "Defence and Development" of the *General Theory* (*CW* 14:xxix). Second, there is the wider set of evidence relating to Keynes's theoretical milieu, his contemporaries, predecessors, and teachers, his noneconomic activities, and his own former writings. In this section I concentrate on the first sort of evidence, which sets up the themes to be followed into the second. We shall see that Keynes's own pronouncements on his views offer tantalizing hints, but hints that are difficult to interpret without the aid of the wider historical record.

Keynes regarded the theory of interest as the part of the *General Theory* that was most commonly misunderstood. Almost his entire published corpus of immediate post–*General Theory* writings on the book (1937a, 1937b, 1937c) is dominated by attempts to correct this misunderstanding. Two of these items are particularly relevant to our theme.

In the first, contributed to a festschrift for Irving Fisher, Keynes (1937a) provides a nicely schematized version of his position in relation to what he sees as orthodox theory. Here he asserts an asset-holding, general-equilibrium view, as a sort of financial market metatheory, into which a number of particular theories of interest could potentially be fit.[2]

The metatheory setup is explicitly a *stock equilibrium,* where wealth owners and arbitragers trade existing assets (including money) until expected rates of return are equalized (that is, he is describing "second-hand" markets).[3] But there are, nevertheless, flow-output effects of this

2. An earlier essay (Cottrell and Lawlor 1991) uses a version of this own-rates framework to illustrate the Wicksellian versus the Keynesian views of the dynamic relation of interest and output.

3. A more complete analysis of this framework may be found in Lawlor 1994a.

stock equilibrium. If the asset market equilibrium involves a price for some existing capital goods higher than replacement costs, new (flow) production of those capital goods will result. As this investment goes forward, rates of return fall as profitable production of each type of investment good reaches the limits of the market, given existing cost and demand conditions. The market for assets to hold is thus assumed to operate in such a manner that given differences of opinion about expectations of future changes in asset prices, trading occurs between investors until all traders are satisfied. Given their individual preferences and understanding of the state of the news, in equilibrium, each investor's portfolio exhibits *equalized expected rates of return.*

Notice that since money is one of the assets, its spot and future price (implied by bond prices) determines its rate of interest, just like all other tradable assets. Money may, but need not, by the logic of the equilibrium construct alone, have a predominant influence on all rates of return in this framework. Here, then, is the peculiar two-stage reasoning exhibited both in chapter 17 and in the festschrift article. First there is Keynes's general metatheory by which arbitrage equilibrium is defined. Any theory of interest must be subject to this arbitragers' equilibrium. Second, the question is posed as to the level at which this equalized rate of return will settle:

> These propositions are not, I think, inconsistent with the orthodox theory, or in any way open to doubt. They establish that relative prices (and under the influence of prices, the scale of output) move until the marginal efficiencies of all kinds of assets are equal when measured in a common unit; and consequently the marginal efficiency of capital is equal to the rate of interest. But they tell us nothing as to the forces which determine what this common level of marginal efficiency will tend to be. It is when we proceed to this further discussion that my argument diverges from the orthodox theory. (1937a, 102–3)

This is the juncture at which we can connect Keynes's financial market views to "higgling," the topic of this volume. One must say that the record shows Keynes to have been explicitly uninterested in the higgling process—at least conceived narrowly, as the process by which markets are assumed to work themselves out. In private correspondence in 1937 he criticized Hawtrey, whom he accused of mistaking "higgling"—the process of reaching equilibrium—for the more fundamental forces determining equilibrium:

Now Hawtrey, it seems to me, mistakes this higgling process by which the equilibrium position is discovered for the much more fundamental forces which determine what the equilibrium position is. . . . The main point is to distinguish the forces determining the position of equilibrium from the trial and error means by which the entrepreneur discovers where the position of equilibrium is. (*CW* 14:182)

The distinction is clear in his conception of the process by which asset market equilibrium is brought about. Keynes is assuming that the informational efficiency and speed of trading that characterizes modern asset markets will result in a higgling process by which returns on assets are equalized: that is, expected rates of return for all existing assets, measured in a common unit (money), will be equalized. For him, this higgling process is not the place to look for the fundamental forces characterizing the dynamic changes that establish the common level of expected rates of return at which the equilibrium will settle. Those forces are discovered on another plane of reasoning, the one upon which Keynes claims to be staking the novelty of his own position in the *General Theory*.[4]

But if we take the wider and more interesting view of higgling suggested by this volume, as the "processes" by which transactors are presumed to operate in markets, Keynes in fact had much to say about higgling. What follows should be interpreted as a contribution to the understanding of this concept of higgling—the interaction of transactors and their markets—in the specific case of asset markets.

What is Keynes's theory as to the level of interest rates? Here the peculiarities of money as an asset, the complex psychology of the liquidity premium, and even its characteristics of production and substitution in use play a role, as in the argument of chapter 17. At this point, however, we need only note that all of this is preceded by the general view

---

4. The attitude Keynes expresses here is in conformity with a continuing theme of his post–*General Theory* correspondence: that he should have written the book under the assumption that *short-period expectations*, those concerning forecasts of required short-period output levels, were always, by definition, met—"for the theory of effective demand is substantially the same if we assume that the short-period expectations are always fulfilled" (*CW* 14:181). This, it is worth emphasizing, leaves "long-period expectations"—those relating to forecasts of the real return to investment projects—in an entirely different analytical category. By necessity in an uncertain world, they are liable to disappointment. But also, as (unlike short-period expectations) they are rarely checked by reality, they can assume a life of their own. Long-period expectations thus become one of the three "ultimate independent variables" of his system (*CW* 7:246–47).

of asset market processes outlined above. This view is both more general and more commonsensical. In fact one can find many places where Keynes expresses dismay and dissatisfaction over his readers' failure to understand what he thus saw as the obvious and noncontroversial "essential properties" of all asset market behavior. Consider, for instance, the following:

> To speak of the "liquidity-preference theory" of the rate of interest is, indeed, to dignify it too much. It is like speaking of the "professorship theory" of Ohlin or the "civil servant theory" of Hawtrey. I am simply stating what it is, the significant theories on the subject being subsequent. And in stating what it is, I follow the books on arithmetic and accept the accuracy of what is taught in preparatory schools. (1937b, 215; see also *CW* 7:222 and 1937a, 215)

For present purposes let us file away this "metatheory" conception of asset market equilibrium and note simply that Keynes considered it both fundamental and obvious. Farther along we shall see whence he might have derived such a view and why he would consider it so obvious. The next task, however, is to set up the second issue noted above. Given that Keynes considered all asset markets to be subject to the logic of his equi-expectational equilibrium construct, what is the source of his own specific view of this topic—his theory of where assets prices will settle in relation to expected returns on newly produced capital goods? In the festschrift article he emphasizes his views on uncertainty, expectations, confidence, and the functions of money in this context (1937a, 105–8). But a more complete discussion of all three issues is gained from his second post–*General Theory* article, "The General Theory of Employment" in the *Quarterly Journal of Economics* (1937b).

For our purposes three points about that article are important. First, Keynes claims to be interested in trying to reexpress "the comparatively simple fundamental ideas which underlie my theory" (1937b, 111), and in doing so fills almost all of his space with a discussion of his views on money and financial markets. Second, in pursuing those simple ideas he is very explicit in emphasizing the roles of uncertainty and incalculable expectations, and the consequent conventional nature of market psychology that underlies his view of investment behavior. Thus, as has often been remarked, he is here on the terrain of his analysis of long-term expectations in chapter 12 of the *General Theory*. This is important because it alerts us that what he sees as unique in his own view is tied up with what he saw as the nature of financial market expectations and speculation. As is well known, these topics dominate the discussion in chapter 12. Finally, underlying the whole argument is an application of the asset market equilibrium just outlined, where the importance of these characteristics of asset trading in an uncertain world is illustrated (116–19).

With this evidence from Keynes's own hand before us, I wish to make the following claims that will serve as sufficient reason for the direction of the rest of my argument on the roots of Keynes's *General Theory* views. We must look for the sources of two distinct sets of beliefs. First it is necessary to look for the source of what Keynes saw as obvious and necessary, that asset markets settle towards a (stock) equilibrium where market trading drives prices to positions characterized by equalized expected rates of return among assets at the margin, given market opinions. Second, we must understand his view of what determines the level this equilibrium will seek. This, to Keynes, is what is unique to the *General Theory* view of financial markets and rates of interest. We must therefore seek out the origin of his view of the economic relevance of market psychology, the behavior of traders in a context of uncertainty and how these affect his view of the meaning, function, and consequences of asset market *speculation*. I argue that this view emanates from Keynes's grapplings with a largely forgotten turn-of-century literature on organized exchange speculation, as well as from his practical observations of and participation in actual financial market processes. Part and parcel of his unique viewpoint on these matters, though, from the beginning of his career to the end, was an attempt to classify the rationality of financial market transactors within the terms of his early philosophical work on probability.

At this stage, I can support these claims by noting that in pursuing the main question of chapter 12 in the *General Theory*—the circumstances governing the "prospective yields of capital assets" and so the determining factors governing the influence of the equilibrium rate of interest on new investment—Keynes ends up analyzing the "market psychology" which guides economic actions under uncertain expectations, and he stresses the crucial influence of the degree of "confidence" with which anticipations are held. In this context, he notes the special importance of observation of market processes:

> There is, however, not much to be said about the state of confidence *a priori*. Our conclusions must mainly depend upon the actual observation of markets and business psychology. This is the reason why the

ensuing digression is on a different level of abstraction from most of
this book. (*CW* 7:149)

My conclusions about the sources of Keynes's views on market psychology also rest on two distinct bases. First, I trace a doctrinal history of
the economic treatment of asset markets as he would have known it;
second, a history of what Keynes could have known and may have accepted as the "facts of observation" concerning asset markets. Despite
what he himself may have thought, these "facts" and theories are more
intertwined than distinct.

Stock Equilibrium in Asset Markets
and "The Folly of Amateur Speculators":
The Marshallian Setting

In seeking a source for Keynes's theoretical views one is on firm
ground in starting from the source of economics as he knew it, Alfred
Marshall. In another place (Lawlor 1993) I have analyzed in detail the
extent and nature of Marshall's influence on Keynes with regard to his
labor market analysis. Some claims more fully supported in that essay
relate to his financial market views. First, early in his career, particularly
before World War I, Keynes was almost slavish in following Marshall's
economics. This is borne out by the surviving lecture notes from the
courses he taught in Cambridge at the time. The same can be said of
his monetary work. Second, immediately after the war and increasingly
over the course of his involvement in England's economic travails in
the 1920s, Keynes came to abandon what he saw as an illusory faith
in economic stability characteristic of Victorian ideals and Marshallian
economics. In his financial market views, this first emerges as a response
to the breakdown of the gold standard and his attempts to develop an
analysis appropriate to a world of floating exchange rates. Third, through
all of this Keynes clung tenaciously to a personal Marshallianism that
was in equal parts doctrinal and methodological, essentially relying upon
the Marshallian organon as an organizing framework, but never letting it
shackle him or blind him to contemporary reality—as it did blind Pigou,
for instance. Documentation for this in his monetary work, though, is
more difficult to detect, in that Marshall's monetary work is notorious
for having exerted its influence by "oral tradition" through unpublished
testimony and memoranda (Laidler 1991).

Fortunately, two remarkable documents, never published in Marshall's lifetime and only recently entered into the public domain, can help characterize the extent to which Marshall's monetary and financial market views provided the analytical bedrock for Keynes's own way of doing financial market analysis, up to and including that in the *General Theory*. The first is Marshall's essay "Money" (1871); the second is "The Folly of Amateur Speculators Makes the Fortunes of Professionals: The Wiles of Some Professionals" (1899). The first relates directly to Keynes's preferred metatheoretical approach to monetary theory. The second, as noted by those who have brought it to light (Dardi and Gallegati 1992, 581–86), reinforces the point that Keynes's ideas on stock market speculation, while ultimately radical when considered next to Marshall's, are still firmly within the Marshallian tradition. What Dardi and Gallegati do not pursue, and which we shall, is the light this essay sheds on the full context for Keynes's developing views on speculation. For there is a fascinating commonality between this later essay of Marshall's, Keynes's own work, and a once influential but now largely forgotten book published in 1896: H. C. Emery's *Speculation on the Stock and Produce Exchanges in the United States*. This book was the text on which all turn-of-the-century academic discussion of speculation centered. Furthermore, it is to Emery's book, not Marshall, that Keynes's original attempt to apply his theory of probability to financial market speculation can be traced. Since it was his attempt to merge his theory of rationality under uncertainty with speculative behavior that marked Keynes's views as unique in this field, Emery may be even more important to his thinking in this regard than was Marshall.

To begin with the basis of Keynes's later (metatheoretical) approach to asset market activity, it is interesting to note that it originates in a surprisingly early attempt by Marshall (1871) to achieve just what Keynes claimed to be doing—for the first time—sixty years later in the *General Theory*. Marshall begins his essay with the common lament of monetary theorists that the value of money is never subjected to the same theoretical treatment—"supply and demand"—as is the determination of the exchange value of all other commodities. Thus in the treatment of money "we do not find a clear statement of that balancing of advantages which in the ultimate analysis must be found to determine the magnitude of every quantity which rests upon the will of man. If we seek for this we shall find that 'the rapidity of circulation' is not the most convenient thing to be made the basis of our investigations" (1871, 166).

Instead of the traditional quantity theory approach ("the rapidity of circulation") or the old classical reliance on cost of production, Marshall is here proposing (as Whitaker notes in his 1975 introduction to the collected early essays) to integrate the two approaches under a supply and demand framework. In the case of money the question to be answered is "why does a man keep on hand a large stock of money?" (166). Importantly, he emphasizes that this is not a decision that is made in isolation from one's "total position of wealth" and the various opportunities for employing it—either in productive use or in the prior provision of transaction services ("the ready command over commodities") of otherwise barren money stocks. In Marshall's world, in 1871, these opportunities are conceived of as the choice between owning a horse or a stock of non-interest-bearing coin. But the general view of how the demand for the various opportunities for holding wealth apportions itself among the available stocks of all assets outstanding is—absent the crucial liquidity motive for holding money and the role of expectations of appreciation— exactly that of Keynes in 1936. Asset holders "balance" at the margin the advantages of each and position their wealth portfolio accordingly:

> This then is the balancing of advantages which each individual has to adjust for himself. If he retains but a very small ready command over commodities he is likely to be put occasionally to considerable inconvenience; if he retains a very large one he receives no adequate compensation for the inaction to which so much of his wealth is doomed. He has thus to settle what is the exact amount which on the average it will answer his purpose to keep in this ready form. Each individual settles this and therefore the whole amount retained in this form by the community is determined by this process on the part of each individual member of it balancing opposing advantages. (1871, 167–68)

Note especially in Marshall's treatment the outline of a general theoretical treatment of asset markets—what I have called "asset market metatheory" above, in referring to Keynes. In one way it might be described as perhaps the earliest instance in which Marshall's preoccupation with the economic effects of the passage of time bears theoretical fruit via the application of his marginalist method. For him asset markets are to be treated as elaborate examples of the market day phenomenon, where the existence of stocks becomes an all-important force in establishing equilibrium prices. Beginning here and carrying all the way through to the complex analysis in chapter 17 of the *General Theory*, the application of the marginalist method to such a situation involved a conception of an asset market general equilibrium forming out of the balancing at the margin of two sets of differences. On the one hand, assets themselves have different qualities and social functions, determined by both "natural" properties (such as productiveness) and social practices (such as general acceptability). On the other, individuals have different tastes and preferences over the desired characteristics of their portfolios. In Marshall's simple world of convenient money and productive capital goods, preferences vary only over relative degrees of transaction convenience and return. Thus speculation has no role to play. In Keynes's eventual fullblown version of this framework in the *General Theory*,[5] the assets vary by return, carrying cost and liquidity; and individuals' demands for these assets depend on their preferences for return and convenience (now transformed as liquidity preference), but also on their "speculative" expectations of the likely "appreciation" of each asset.[6] Thus in Keynes's world the influence of opinion can become paramount via the activity of the bulls and bears operating on the exchanges. Nevertheless, in bare essentials Keynes's approach is the same as Marshall's balancing of the advantages of a hoard of coin and a horse.

Previously commentators (see Laidler 1991, 49–64) have noted the extent to which this set the standard for later expressions, by Pigou (1917) particularly, of the Cambridge approach to the demand for money and the micro-foundations approach to the quantity theory. That it may also be seen as the basis of Keynes's later asset market analysis is not widely recognized. But the evidence for this view can be traced all through Keynes's work, as I show below. For now it is sufficient to note that when Keynes wrote his memorial essay on Marshall in 1925, in a period in which he was already working on what was to become the *Treatise on Money*, he singled out the 1871 essay for praise and, after quoting from it, went on to claim:

5. Below I recount his use of this framework in the *Tract*. In another paper (Lawlor 1994b) I compare his uses of the same framework in the *Treatise*, and how it compares to the *General Theory*.

6. I had intended, but due to limitation of space was unable, to show at this point that the influence of Irving Fisher on Keynes can be understood by analyzing the development of this metatheoretical framework between Marshall and the later Keynes of the *General Theory*. There is much evidence in this regard that will have to await a fullblown treatment elsewhere. In essence, one can argue that it was due to Fisher that Keynes came to interpret the asset market equilibrium in expectational terms.

We must regret still more Marshall's postponement of the publication of his *Theory of Money* until extreme old age, when time had deprived his ideas of freshness and his exposition of sting and strength. There is no part of Economics where Marshall's originality and priority of thought are more marked than here, or where his superiority of insight and knowledge over his contemporaries was greater. There is hardly any leading feature in the modern theory of Money which was not known to Marshall forty years ago. (1925, 27)

Even allowing for hyperbole, this is a strong statement—the more so when we recall the denigration of Marshall's theory of interest that Keynes would write less than ten years later. A problem, then, is exactly what features of Marshall's treatment survived in Keynes's esteem over that decade, and which fell from grace? I propose that the metatheory survived, while the full-employment (classical) theory of the "normal" rate of interest did not.

For now, though, let us stay with Marshall and offer some evidence of the attitudes toward stock market activity in general and speculation in particular that he might have bequeathed to Keynes.[7] Here we return to Marshall's 1899 essay. In their excellent introduction to the essay Dardi and Gallegati (1992, 573–81) note that it stands as a sort of halfway house between the traditional view of speculators in English economics (exemplified by Mill 1871, 541–43) and Keynes's later views. In the traditional view speculators had a transient role to play as a class of agents specializing in market arbitrage, whose prominent function was to generate and extend "contagious" buying and selling among the less informed mass of amateur agents who comprised their customers. In doing so they were liable to cause "some accident which excites expectation of rising prices" to result in "a generally reckless and adventurous feeling" (Mill, 542), and this was seen to be a factor in commercial panics and price instability. Dardi and Gallegati emphasize that prior to the 1899 essay Marshall had considered this negative view of speculation appropriate to the analysis of general price instability and the cycle, but was reluctant to admit it as a factor capable of upsetting the tranquil movement from short- to long-period normal values envisioned in the *Principles*. In the 1899 essay, though, he takes more seriously the possibility that speculation might be more than a passing cyclical factor, and

7. See note 9 below.

could even upset the establishment of long-period normal positions—
and thus (though Marshall himself does not mention it, but important
for later comparison with Keynes) the establishment of the "normal"
rate of interest. As Dardi and Gallegati put it: "The main interest in
these pages lies, in our opinion, in clearly highlighting Marshall's shift
of position from a typically nineteenth-century vision of speculation as a
picturesque and sometimes objectionable, but essentially marginal phenomenon, to a modern view which places speculation at the very center
of the capitalistic engine, as an inseparable component of the working
of financial markets" (1992, 572).[8]

The difference in outlook between the old view and the modern view
essentially revolved around the theme of the "informational" context for
speculation and its consequent reinforcement (or not) of the more fundamental forces of "enterprise." For the earlier Marshall, it was incon-
ceivable that speculators could forever forestall the movement of prices
toward those consistent with long-period normal values, that is, consistent with equalized rates of return to all factors including capital. In the
1899 essay, however, he raises the possibility that it may be in the interest
of professional speculators to keep the amateurs misinformed about the
true nature of the fundamentals (say, the future expected earning capacity
of a publicly traded firm). Thus (and analogously to Keynes's "beauty
contest" metaphor) "the first of the valid charges that may be brought
against the general economic influence of stock exchange speculation"
is that "the shrewdest and most far seeing speculators often govern their
action not by their own forecast of the distant future but by their forecasts of the forecasts that will be made by less competent people" (589).
Even worse, attesting to the vast manipulations witnessed in the 1880s
and 1890s, when he comes to consider the "special [role] played in the
stock exchange arena by powerful financiers and [the] great operators,
who belong to High Finance (la Haute Finance, la Haute Banque, die
hohe Bank)" (550) Marshall finds that they may also have reason to use
duplicity and misinformation. Thus on the whole the possibility emerges
that the operation of the exchanges, when speculation dominates, may
hide the true (fundamental) values more than reinforce them.

Now racy as this sounds, coming from Marshall, there are clear signs
that he would have been unwilling to go all the way with Keynes's later
views. As Dardi and Gallegati comment, Marshall's whole argument

8. As we are about to see, Emery had already provided such a "modern" view in 1896.

still presupposes that the "fundamentals" are out there to be found. As we shall discover, this is one crucial point at which the later Keynes diverges from Marshall's most radical view of speculation. For Keynes the fundamentals eventually lost the attractive value that Marshall's term "normal" was meant to convey.

H. C. Emery: *Speculation on the Stock and Produce Exchanges of the United States*

The analysis put forward by Marshall in 1899 was not entirely original. In his theorizing about the nature and role of speculation he apparently relied heavily upon Emery's *Speculation in the Stock and Produce Exchanges in the United States* (1896). In fact in almost all the essentials, he is merely seconding Emery's work. Dardi and Gallegati, for instance, note that Marshall refers to Emery in his 1899 essay, that his personal copy of Emery's book is highly annotated, and that he recorded extensive notes on the book. The reason this is particularly interesting in our context is that Emery's book appears to have served as the standard reference work for the whole profession, up until the 1920s at least, on just exactly what was going on in the most "speculating" country then known:

> The American people are regarded by foreigners as the greatest of all speculators. . . . Speculation proper, as well as the speculative spirit of vast industrial enterprise, has had its most striking development perhaps in the United States. The greatest speculation in produce which the world has ever seen has grown up recently in Chicago, while a speculative market of almost unequaled magnitude is found in the Stock Exchange of New York. [But] . . . little has been written in the country either to describe the details of exchange methods, or to estimate the function of these exchanges in the economic order. (Emery 1896, 7)

Emery saw it as his task to fill this gap. In the process he left a document of amazing detail about the then standard practices on the commodity and stock markets. Almost all major writers on the subject of speculation after him seem to refer to this book. In particular, Keynes, who as we shall see relied heavily upon Emery early in his career, used it as the text in his prewar Cambridge lectures on the stock exchange. Irving Fisher, Emery's Yale colleague, thanks him for his criticisms and quotes him in *The Rate of Interest* (1907). And Thorstein Veblen seems to have relied upon Emery's description of the exchanges as part of the raw material that went into the crafting of his *Theory of Business Enterprise* (1904). Thus it will be very useful to review the highlights of Emery's book, to situate Keynes's later use of its contents. The goal of this rehearsal is to convince the reader that much of what is now thought of as the distinctively Keynesian view of speculation was in fact well known to monetary economists of the early part of this century.[9]

In opposition to what he saw as a one-sided literature on speculation that tended to emphasize the "evils," with no account given of the positive functions, Emery consciously set out to provide a descriptive account of the exchanges, emphasizing that "speculation in the last half century has developed as a natural economic institution in response to the new conditions of industry and commerce" (10). This goal, pursued with great attention to detail and history, clearly sets his work within the American "institutionalist" tradition. Yet in a comment that offers some insight into the subsequent development of the theory of speculation, Emery notes with reluctance that this approach has forced him to forgo an extensive analysis of the "evils of speculation." [10] Interestingly, his excuse for this lack of balance rests on what he saw as the greater difficulties attaching to that subject:

9. Marshall's unpublished essay of 1899, with its striking resemblance to Emery's and Keynes's later views, raises the question of the path of transmission of these ideas. Dardi and Gallegati (1992) offer no direct evidence that Keynes actually ever saw this essay. Neither can I, but the larger view of the context of the then contemporary state of discussion on speculation offered here opens up some indirectly supported hypotheses. First, as so much of Marshall's essay is in fact contained in Emery's book—and, as I shall show for the first time below, Keynes was quite well versed in Emery's work as early as 1909—it is possible that Keynes and Marshall could both be seen as developing Emery independently. Partial support for this view comes from the fact that Marshall in 1899 was actually much more critical of speculation than Keynes ever was before the mid-1920s. But an alternative hypothesis is just as likely on current evidence. It is probable that if Keynes ever did see Marshall's essay, it would have been in 1924. It was then that he wrote the memorial essay on Marshall (Keynes 1925) in which the glowing tribute to his theory of money is contained. I mention this because in the preparation of that essay Keynes utilized a number of Marshall's unpublished papers, provided by Mary Marshall (*CW* 10:161); 1924 was also the year that he started working in earnest on his *Treatise on Money*, which contains the first extended discussions of the type of analysis of the stock market Marshall had made in his essay. One last piece of this puzzle is Keynes's contention in the memorial essay (1925, 34–35) that Marshall's failure to produce his later works was partly due to his insecurity over his grasp of "the progress of events in the 'seventies and 'eighties, particularly in America." It was, of course, just these developments which Emery first analyzed and with which Marshall was grappling in 1899.

10. He confines his discussion of these aspects to a short afterthought in chapter 5.

The evils of speculation, though more widely appreciated by the public, are by no means so simple of comprehension or so easy of description as its benefits. An adequate study of this part of the subject would require not only a careful historical study of the deals and manipulations of the speculative market, but a mind trained by wide experience of business life to weigh justly the influences for harm and good. (11–12)

I suggest that Keynes eventually overcame these difficulties, after his own "wide experience" put him in a position to analyze speculation's influence for harm and good. But first there was Emery.

Emery offers clear descriptions in chapters 2 and 3 of the various instruments and practices found on the stock and produce exchanges, and the economic rationale of their organizational rules. He also provides (chapter 2) a detailed analysis of forward trading, futures contracts, straddles, options, and short selling. Further, he shows how the rules of the various exchanges, and the development of clearinghouses, evolved to provide a framework of self-policing that would create the fiduciary trust on the part of participants necessary to maintain public confidence in the dealings of the exchanges and so allow them to serve as the central markets they did become. For the student of financial institutions this analysis of what today would be called the "theory of clubs" aspects of the exchanges seems amazingly modern.[11]

More important for our purposes is his historical and theoretical treatment of the economic function of speculation, in chapters 3 and 4. He defines speculation by reference to the development of "trading over time." The oldest examples are found in the purchase of actual goods to hold in anticipation of a rise; later this was extended to prior payment for goods in transit, via bills of exchange. Emery notes that the origins of such trades lie in forward trading—a practice that has existed since antiquity, and in organized form since the seventeenth century. In its most general form speculation is just buying or selling though time, in hopes of better terms at the end of the period considered. But evidence of "futures" dealing of the modern kind only arises in the last few centuries.

The mark of this form of trading is to be found in a move toward more

---

11. Though the same sort of notions with regard to banking institutions were also clearly laid out by Bagehot in the nineteenth century and by Vera Smith in the 1930s. See Goodhart 1988 for a discussion of this literature.

abstract trading of standardized products or instruments. Real futures began to occur only with the development of the warrant and grading systems, by which various products—first metals and then various grains—were standardized into grades. It is at this point that the legal rights of ownership were transformed by the issuance of warrants (or receipts) representing generalized claims to a specific quantity of a standardized product, deliverable at a specified future date.[12] Emery notes that the development of such trading also depended on the centralized concentration of trading and information, epitomized by grain markets in the American Midwest and particularly Chicago in the period from 1850 to 1870. There, through the combined influence of the Chicago Board of Trade, the western expansion of the railroads, the development of the grain elevator system, and the invention of the telegraph, a new and massive organization of trading activity could take place: "The development of the system of grading and of elevator receipts is the most important step in the history of the grain trade. It is only with such a machinery that an extension of forward sales in the modern sense is possible, that is of forward sales of goods having no definite existence until the moment of delivery" (38).

Emery makes it clear that although older forms of "trading over time"—such as the trade in receipts of actual specific lots of grain prior to the establishment of generalized "futures"—also offered opportunities for holding for a speculative gain, the modern exchanges greatly altered the scope of speculation. No longer was speculation tied to actual quantities of goods traded, and it became just as easy to speculate for a fall as for a rise in price (38–46). Here we see the development of two crucial distinctions that would later mark both Keynes's and Marshall's analyses of speculation: (1) that the exchanges are first and foremost a method of locking in terms over time by both *producers* and *end users*—a form of price hedging—in which regard, their primary economic function was to be defined in terms of "risk-bearing"; and (2) that such primary activity also creates secondary opportunities for "speculative" time-dealing by a separate class, *speculators*. "All time-dealings arise from a desire to provide in the present for the events of the future. Speculative time-dealings arise when an anticipated difference in the present

12. In this as in other respects, Emery is in concurrence with the most astute modern historian of the Chicago grain trade, William Cronon, whose *Nature's Metropolis* (1992, 97–147) contains a fascinating account of the development of futures trading in grain between 1800 and 1870.

and future prices of a commodity in question leaves room for a possible profit" (33). As we have already seen in the case of Marshall, and as is well known from chapter 12 of the *General Theory,* criticisms of speculation by economists after Emery would turn on the judgment of the role these "insiders" play in fulfilling the primary function of the exchanges.

Emery takes as his paradigm case of speculative trading the grain future. This is important, because it will be seen that the theory of the economic function of speculation that he puts forward—and that I argue was so influential in economic circles in the beginning of the twentieth century—is also based on an analogy to the commodities exchanges. Yet even in Emery's discussion, and later increasingly also in Keynes's discussion, this theory makes only an uneasy transition to the "stock" exchange. The reason for this is already in sight: it is very difficult to establish exactly what, in the stock market setting, constitutes the counterpart to the hedging of intertemporal risk by primary producers and users of commodities that forms the raison d'être of the produce exchanges. Emery does a remarkable job of making the mechanical analogy to "futures" for the stock exchange by detailing the extensive practice of "borrowing and lending" stocks and margin sales which accompanies stock speculation (74–94).[13] This practice, combined with the fact that "stocks and bonds possess in themselves that quality of representativeness which is secured for commodities only by means of classified grades and a warrant system," means that in "the conduct of business on the stock exchanges, the same general principle is found as prevails on the produce exchanges, with some marked differences in the actual methods employed" (74). Yet, having laid out a fine description of these methods, he is nevertheless forced to admit a difference:

> There is not the same economic reason for future dealings in stocks as in produce, for while any kind of produce is something the supply of which is itself a future thing, and so often cannot be contracted for except for future delivery, a particular stock on the other hand is, in the main, fixed in amount. The stock to be delivered is all in existence at the time of sale, and there seems to be no reason, except for speculation, for postponing its delivery. (77)

13. The practice is in many ways unchanged today. See Wood and Wood 1985, 353–61.

Proceeding on to Emery's theory proper, as presented in chapter 4, "The Economic Function of Speculation," it is worth repeating that it is grounded in an attempt to show speculation as a "normal" business practice, exemplified by the activity on the produce exchanges. His previous historical analysis of the development of these exchanges is crucial here, because he essentially argues that the modern speculators—those who secondarily trade in "futures," as opposed to the end users and producers—represent a modern extension of the division of labor among factors of production. In this case the element of risk bearing that had previously been part of the return to the occupations of farmers, grain merchants, and grain users, for instance, could now be seen as the specialized function of the grain exchange speculators.[14] The speculators, engaged in both buying and selling futures that are never intended to result in the actual delivery of grain, make their profit (or loss) by forecasting future price movements and taking positions. The social impact of this development is the creation of *worldwide* markets which channel all information affecting the supply and demand everywhere into the formation of a single world price for staple commodities.

Two passages in Emery's discussion will serve to illustrate his view and to set the context for Keynes's own attempt to define the historical epoch of speculative capitalism in the *General Theory* (*CW* 7: 150–53):

> With this change [to worldwide markets after 1850] the market for all the great staples became a world market, and the total demand and total supply began to determine a single price for all places. The chances of local fluctuations in price became greatly lessened, for the local scarcity or abundance might be offset by opposite conditions elsewhere. At the same time the fluctuations possible because of these distant conditions became of much more importance. Formerly the merchant, from a thorough knowledge of his own market, was well-prepared to assume its speculative risks. Now he was called on to face a wider *Konjunktur,* and to assume the risk of changing values dependent on world-wide conditions. . . . With the advance in knowledge, the trading element and the speculative element in their business had

14. He also notes an intermediate step in this historical evolution, in which the "trading" risks were taken over from the producers by merchants. In the later evolution the strictly trading risks associated with the profitability of any line of commerce are separated off from speculative risks of price fluctuations over time.

come to be more sharply distinguished, and the more important the speculative element became, the greater was the burden on those who pursued their business for its trading profit. (107–8)

What was now needed by the trader was a distinct body of men pre-pared to relieve him of the speculative element of his business, that is of the risks of distant and future changes, just as he had formerly relieved the producer of his distinctive trading risks. A new body was wanted to cope with the *Konjunktur*. And as the need grew, the speculative class became differentiated from the trading body as the latter had been differentiated from the producing body. . . . Now they became a third class, distinct from both producers and exchangers. Whereas formerly each man bore his own risks, the new class has arisen to relieve him of these risks; instead of all traders speculating a little, a special class speculates much. (108–9)

Now we have before us Emery's basic theory, which will already bear testament to the early date at which economists engaged in discussion of such notions as the role of market insiders and the positive function of risk bearing by organized exchange speculation.[15] How did Emery extend this reasoning to the stock exchange? He notes that the history of this exchange in the United States owes much to the "enormous increase in private securities which came with the building of the railroads" (112). Thus, though not directly the result of the commercial revolution in world trade responsible for the produce exchanges, the stock exchange was derivative from this revolution. Again scale was a factor, as the size of the public and private investments required to build large-scale railroad and telegraph systems created risks beyond the means of even the largest individual investors: "The small investor, like the merchant, could hardly take such chances; and, like the merchant, he found a class ready to assume all the risk of buying or selling his security, and a market that fixed prices by which he could intelligently invest."

But instead of focusing on risk-hedging opportunities as the primary social function of speculation on the stock exchange, Emery picks up on what had been a subsidiary theme in his discussion of the produce exchanges in their putative powers of "direction." For the produce ex-

---

15. But which is not really so new at all in the historical time frame considered by De Marchi and Harrison, this volume. They show, for instance, that seventeenth-century Dutch traders had a clear idea of many of these issues. Both De Marchi and John Wood have suggested to me that De la Vega should be considered the real originator in this literature.

changes he had emphasized the influence that speculative prices exerted on consumption: "Speculation, then, tends to equalize consumption over a long period by causing economy in anticipation of a shortage, and free use in anticipation of bountiful crops" (145). In stock market speculation this "directive" influence becomes the now commonplace [16] one of simultaneously providing the liquidity necessary to make large-scale investment palatable to individual investors and, through channeling information into prices fixed on the exchange, ensuring the best distribution of resources among these investments (148–50).

Interestingly, at this point, Emery conducts a running argument against much of the then existing literature, most of it German, in an attempt to establish something very much like the market efficiency view so well known from recent finance literature. For the most part this concerns various refutations of attacks on the social beneficence of stock-exchange-directed investment. More interesting than his arguments, which are not very convincing, are the topics he is thus committed to examine. These include trading under the influence of market insiders ("manipulators") as opposed to trading on "the best information" that is yielded by "expert investigation" (151); the question whether stock prices fluctuate because of speculative activity, or stocks are speculated in because of fluctuating value (152–53); the accuracy of the market's opinion concerning the economic impact of political changes in the news (154–55); and the influence (and its extent) of the opinions of the nonspeculative classes (the "artisan," the "professional man of small income," and "banks, trust companies, insurance companies and the like") on stock exchange prices.

Thus once again we are reminded that there is nothing new under the sun. Many of the issues that concerned Keynes, and which still concern some modern writers about exchange market speculation (Shiller 1991), were well known to Emery in 1896. To conclude this section, let us review the distinctive aspects of Emery's view that will later show up in Keynes's writings, albeit altered and transformed. First, he asserts a positive function for the exchanges, which grew out of the circumstances of the development of the industrial and commercial world over the latter half of the nineteenth century, particularly in the United States. But the primary function of each type of exchange—either for risk bearing and/

16. Again, this is a view usually traced to Keynes's elegant rendering of this view in chapter 12 of the *General Theory*.

or for directing resources—also created secondary opportunities for the accumulation of wealth for certain classes of economic actors; though unintended, these became inseparable from the primary function. Thus speculators are part of the machinery of the modern economy. In fact a guiding theme in Emery's discourse is a self-conscious attempt to attack as misguided the then prevalent opprobrium attached to the role of speculators. He stresses that speculators were merely the messengers of a new, more risky commercial environment. Killing them off by legislative decree would not alter the message: that by the turn of the century Western economies had come to depend upon these exchanges both to engage in large-scale investment and to transact commodity exchange on a world scale. A question remained, in the course of answering which both Keynes and Veblen (1904) would eventually take their distinctive tacks on Emery. Could the casino-like aspect of this system—admittedly ancillary from a social-evolutionary standpoint—ever come to doom the productive process on which it feeds?

A Historical Approach to Keynes on Speculation

It is now time to tie up some of the threads of this argument by bringing the evidence on Marshall's work and on Emery's views on speculation to bear on an evaluation of Keynes's analysis of financial markets. I emphasize that one must recognize the change and development of Keynes's own ideas in this (and other) contexts. Unfortunately space does not allow full documentation of these developments here.[17] In this section I can only offer a brief outline of the influences on his views and how they evolved between 1910 and 1936. We may then closely trace the origins of these views in Keynes's pre–World War I writings and teaching. This essay then closes with an analysis of Keynes's writings on financial markets through 1923. But first the outline of the larger story.

Until the 1920s, Keynes's views of the economic function of speculation were quite orthodox and based largely on Emery. For the most part he defended speculation as economically beneficial, though even at this early stage he introduced some interesting theoretical nuances which emanate from his views on probability. In fact one might say that what

17. The whole story is part of a larger ongoing project. A continuation of the history of Keynes's asset market analysis appears in Lawlor 1994b.

today is usually seen as the "Keynesian" theory of stock markets and long-term expectations based on uncertainty and convention, grew from a seed planted when the young Keynes, fresh from his struggle with the logic of probability in relation to conduct, came upon Emery's work in preparing his early lectures at Cambridge. This is visible in his changing views of the informational context in which speculative decisions are made. Thus, beginning in the 1920s and increasingly over the course of the 1930s, he came to appreciate that in certain contexts speculation might be capable of independently exercising an adverse effect on economic activity. Much of this change of view concerned his evaluation of world economic events in those turbulent decades. But his personal experiences as an investor played a role as well. By the time of the *General Theory,* his critique of the deleterious effects of the "casino" aspects of modern capitalism had hardened into a stance virtually indistinguishable from Veblen's view in 1904. In all of this analysis, though, he remained firmly wedded to the framework set down by Emery and investigated by the later Marshall. That is to say, the question of the economic impact of speculation always turned on the question whether or not it was mere reaction to and possible exaggeration of underlying "real" economic forces, as the traditional benign view supposed. Also constant throughout this development was a staunch unwillingness, more adamant than Emery's own attitude, to blame the speculating class itself for the troubles of speculation. For Keynes, blame should lie with the organization of a system in which the instability of events and the consequent precariousness of confidence could give rise to the predominance of speculation over enterprise. Not surprisingly, this also came down to an issue closely related to his early work on probability and its relation to practical reasoning.

Recognizing the links to probability and to Keynes's practical experience forces us to touch base with many points of the now complex interdisciplinary literature on Keynes. Starting with Skidelsky (1983) and O'Donnell (1989), many writers have suggested that Keynes's philosophical views are at the base of his economics. Without entering into the disputatious secondary literature this claim has spawned, we may nevertheless recognize a continual influence from this philosophical side in Keynes's evolving views on speculation. I am not suggesting a simple one-to-one mapping of Keynes's philosophical views into a theory of speculation: that would depend crucially on the knowledge context one assigns to speculative activity, and the theoretical "whole" in which the effect of speculation is judged to be operative. I simply point out that it was precisely on these issues that Keynes changed his mind over the course of his career.

In the matter of Keynes's own speculative activity, Donald Moggridge, in his role as editor of Keynes's *Collected Writings*, has performed an invaluable service in recording the essential facts and documents concerning Keynes as an investor. These materials plus Moggridge's own editorial comments (*CW* 12) are essential reading for anyone wishing to understand this little investigated side of the many-sided Keynes. The main facts—that he traded both on his own account and with capital provided by friends and relatives; that this often took the form of highly leveraged speculative positions; and that he also engaged in giving investment advice both to his college, King's, and to insurance companies—are well known. Less well known, and more important for our story, are the detailed ups and downs of Keynes's own investments and the mostly internal supporting documents he wrote for insurance companies and bursar meetings, which Moggridge has collected together. What these materials indicate is that Keynes showed as much verve, but not always as much success, at investing as he did at doing economics; and that, also similar to his economics, he changed his investment "philosophy" over his career. Both Moggridge (1992, 586) and Skidelsky (1992, 24–30, 41–46, 340–43, 557–58) attribute to Keynes's personal financial experiences a large degree of influence over his more theoretical interests in speculation.[18] Moggridge in fact describes chapter 12 of the *General Theory* as "largely autobiographical." I happily give limited support to this view, although the topic is more complicated and less clear-cut than either of the two biographers had space to investigate. Most important, Keynes's theoretical views on speculation must be placed in the wider intellectual context we are here investigating. Keynes's discussion in chapter 12, for instance, owes at least as much to Emery and *Probability* as it does to his investment experience.

Finally there is the issue of chronology. What periodization best captures the evolution of Keynes's views on speculation? It is customary for economists to tell this story as one of successive sheddings—or, in less sophisticated versions, one tremendous wrenching molt—of Keynes's many-layered classical skin, eventually emerging as the fullblown "Keynesian" suggested by each particular author's interpretation of the *Gen-*

---

18. This theme had earlier been investigated by Harcourt (1983).

eral Theory. For his evolving views on speculation this analogy, while not entirely inappropriate, is difficult to maintain. Some of the patterning of his previous skins remained intact, while some elements were merely rearranged into a larger, more complex pattern. Thus, as Skidelsky has surely convinced us by now, Keynes's history contains at least as much continuity as change. The challenge is to reconstruct an evolution that played itself out against the backdrop of Keynes's many lives. What follows is an attempt at such a reconstruction.

Keynes I, 1909–1914:
The Young Don as Philosopher of Speculation

For the earliest evidence on Keynes and speculation we turn to the lectures he gave in Cambridge before World War I. Complete notes, in his own hand, for many of these courses are in the Keynes papers at Kings College (KCKP). Two sets of these are particularly relevant to our concerns. The first is a series of lecture notes, dated 1910, entitled "Modern Business Methods II." [19] The second is a collection of notes for lectures Keynes gave over the years 1909 to 1914, titled "The Stock Exchange and the Money Market." [20] There is some overlap between these treatments, but the general impression is that when it came to discussing the organization of the exchanges and speculation, Keynes relied heavily on Emery's discussion in both, sometimes lifting whole passages from his book (with attribution) and for much of the rest paraphrasing him. In one

19. The complete notes from this set of lectures are in KCKP MM/26.1. This material was most likely part of a course, "Modern Business Methods," that had two parts: (1) "Trusts and Railways" and (2) "Company Finance and the Stock Exchange." Moggridge (*CW* 12:689) lists "Company Finance and the Stock Exchange" as having been given in the years 1910–13. In the text of these notes Keynes indicates that the stock exchange lectures are to follow from the lectures on trusts and railways.

The titles themselves are interesting evidence of turn-of-the-century preoccupations. Then current attitudes naturally considered the cutting edge of "modern business methods" to be the practices on the stock exchange and the management of trusts and railways. As Emery makes clear, the beginning of the modern developments on the U.S. stock exchange grew out of the creative financing arrangements used to cover the United States with railroads after the Civil War. It is also worth noting that, besides Emery's *Speculation,* Keynes assigned Veblen's *Theory of Business Enterprise* in this course. The heart of Veblen's theory was that stock market speculation had come to dominate the activities of the large industrial enterprises of the day, beginning with the railroads. I had hoped to show here, but was unable to for lack of space, that Veblen's analysis of financial markets bears some very striking resemblances to Keynes's in the *General Theory.*

20. These are contained in the unpaginated file KCKP UA/4.5.

sense Emery is taken as a source of the "facts" about the machinery of the exchanges. For example, consider the following (characteristically cocksure) remark by Keynes:

> These lectures will be extremely elementary, and only occasionally will any questions of intellectual difficulty arise. The greater part of them will be concerned with simple statements of fact, and to quite an appreciable extent with the explanation of the meaning of terms. A good deal of the apparent difficulty of stock exchange questions arises out of the unaccustomed terminology in which they are expressed. When once the meaning of the words is clearly understood, nothing more is required than a common share of general intelligence. (KCKP UA/4.5)

Keynes also advises that the student will learn much more by "contracting the habit, which every economist, however theoretical his tastes should have, of reading regularly one of the financial weeklies." That this was not just idle advice is attested to by the superb illustrations from current financial events with which Keynes interleaves the lectures. But in a telling remark, considering the course his career would take after 1914, the young don also notes that the stock market is "essentially a practical subject, which cannot properly be taught by book or lecture. *Further, I have myself no practical experience of the questions involved*" (KCKP UA/4.5, emphasis added). No practical experience yet, that is.

Rather than repeat Keynes's version of Emery, it will be helpful to show the context in which the discussion of speculation was situated, and then discuss his sole departure from Emery's book. The context is best conveyed by the section headings of the courses as Keynes outlined them in this notes.

Company Finance and the Stock Exchange[21]
1. Types of shares
2. The flotation of a company
3. Management of a company
4. The Balance Sheet
5. The Stock Exchange
6. Speculation

21. This is a direct quotation of Keynes's own outline in KCKP UA/4.5.

—definition, economic function, methods

—bears, bulls, options, the account, carry over, contango

7. The Different Classes of Securities

—Aggregate value, consols and their history, trustee stock, fluctuations of capital value

8. The current rate of interest

—determining factors

—risk, ease of sale, likelihood of future increases, 'lock up'

9. Foreign Investment

—geographical distribution

Modern Business Methods II [22]

1. The organization of the Exchanges
2. Dealing in Futures
3. Speculation in Stocks and Bonds
4. The Economic Function of Speculation
5. The Effect of Speculation on Price
6. The Regulative Influence of Speculation
7. The Assumption of Risk by the Speculative Market
8. The Evils of Speculation
9. Questions to be Answered [23]

A familiarity with and borrowing from Emery's book is apparent in almost all (sections 1–8) of the "Modern Business Methods" course. Furthermore, part of the same material appears under sections 5 and 6 in the course on the stock exchange. Perhaps the most interesting of these lectures addressed the "economic function of speculation" (Modern Business Methods, item 4). The extent of its dependence on Emery can clearly be seen in Keynes's summary:

Thus the function of an organized speculation is limited to certain classes of goods. Its object is to relieve trade of the risks of the fluctuating values by providing a class always ready to take or deliver a property at the market price; and, in so doing, to direct commodities to their more advantageous uses, and the investment of capital into the most profitable channels. (KCKP MM/26.1, 13–14)

22. This outline is extracted from the headings Keynes gives to his lecture notes in KCKP MM/26.1.

23. These "questions" turn out to be ones that Marshall had set for Keynes on 9 November 1905, when Keynes was his student.

Keynes disagrees with Emery, however, in his evaluation of the proper *definition* of speculation, a subject that arises in Emery's attempt to differentiate it from gambling. Two interesting threads of intellectual history intersect at this point. One is the common turn-of-the-century suspicion of speculators as mere gamblers.[24] The other is the now well-known fact that early in his career Keynes was as much, if not more, involved in the philosophy of probability as he was in economics. Emery (1896, 98–101) had set out to defend organized exchange speculation from this "gambling" charge. It is at this point in his lecture on Emery that Keynes steps in, having in 1910 completed his fellowship dissertation on probability, in which he explicitly deals with both the nature of chance and gambling and the relation of notions of probability to the conduct of everyday life, as well as the very issue of the morality of gambling.[25]

To analyze Keynes's very interesting discussion of the distinction between gambling and speculation, it is useful briefly to recall the account in his *Treatise on Probability* of "practical reason and ethics" (see *CW* 8: chapter 26; O'Donnell 1989, chapter 6). What marks off Keynes's analysis of speculation as different from those by contemporaries is its strong grounding in his own particular theory of probability. In applying his theory of probabilities as rational degrees of belief relative to the knowledge in the possession of the individual, Keynes wanted to show that conduct could be moral and rational if based on a probabilistic estimate of the good consequences that would follow from action. But he insisted that such conduct must give due regard to the "weight" attached to the evidence one possessed in formulating these probable consequences, and the relative "moral risk" of the probable outcomes. The issues of probability in relation to knowledge and the confidence with which we hold that probability (summed up by his term "weight") are perhaps sufficiently well known to Keynes scholars by now to pass over without comment. But the attendant concept of "moral risk" is worth examining

24. "Few things have called forth greater extremes of praise and blame than modern organized speculation. On one side it is strongly denounced, either as being morally wrong in itself, or as being in addition to this a disastrous influence in business. This view is, perhaps that of a large majority of respectable persons outside of business life, and of the greater part of the newspaper press" (Emery 1896, 96). Contemporary fiction was also full of villains who made their living by speculation. Frank Norris's *The Pit* is an interesting example.

25. On the *Treatise on Probability* see O'Donnell 1989 and Davis 1994.

in the present context for the light it sheds on Keynes's evolving views on speculation.

Moral risk is essentially a device for breaking out of a strict reliance on mathematical probabilities in assessing the morality of actions. It is a way of distinguishing between courses of action which might have equal probable goodness (that is, the actions are equal in expected value: the projected goodness multiplied by its probability) but have unequal probabilities of occurring. Keynes asks:

> Is it certain that a larger good, which is extremely improbable, is precisely equivalent ethically to a smaller good which is proportionately more probable? We may doubt whether the moral value of speculative and cautious action respectively can be weighed against one another in a simple arithmetical way, just as we have already doubted whether a good whose probability can only be determined on a slight basis of evidence can be compared by means merely of the magnitude of this probability with another good whose likelihood is based on completer knowledge. (*CW* 8:347)

As O'Donnell's excellent discussion of this issue (1989, 122–33) makes clear, there is a connection between this concept and Keynes's views on the evils of gambling. As he puts it, Keynes "suggested that in some situations there was a greater rationality in playing safe (the more probable smaller good), than in living dangerously and risking much for the larger but more uncertain gain" (123). In the case of gambling—"at poker, for instance, or on the Stock Exchange"—Keynes applies this framework in combination with a strong belief in the declining marginal utility of money to argue that the gambling is only immoral when the players vary widely in initial wealth (*CW* 8:352–53). For though, on average, a fair gamble will result in zero return for long-term players, wealthier players will be able to outlast the poorer and so easily beat a succession of them, as each lacks the resources to play for as long as the wealthy players. Thus

> the true moral is this, that poor men should not gamble and that millionaires should do nothing else. But millionaires gain nothing by gambling with one another, and until the poor man departs from the path of prudence the millionaire does not find his opportunity. (353)

He adds in a footnote a sentiment that will be repeated, both in his official testimony on gambling laws (*CW* 28:395–97) and in the *General Theory* (*CW* 7:159–61) discussion of the stock market:

> From the social point of view, however, this moral against gambling may be drawn—that those who start with the largest fortunes are most likely to win, and that a given increment to the wealth of these benefits them, on the assumption of a diminishing marginal utility of money, less than it injures those from whom it is taken. (*CW* 8:353n.)

The reason for rehearsing these elements of Keynes's philosophical work becomes clear when we read his first attempts, in the lecture notes, to define the essential nature of speculation:

The Nature of Speculation
(1) Where the risk is incalculable
   e.g. some political insurance at Lloyds
(2) Where the risk is more or less calculable
   (a) the risks not averaged
      e.g. roulette at Monte Carlo
   (b) the risks averaged + commission
      life insurance
      fire insurance
(3) Where the speculator's knowledge or judgement is superior to that of the market

1 and 2a—Gambling
2b—Insurance
3—Speculation—Not identical with "taking risks"
Perhaps bookmaking partakes of all these.

The essential characteristic of speculation is, it seems to me, the possession of superior knowledge. We do not mean by the risk of an investment its actual future yield—we mean the degree of probability of the yield we expect. *The probability depends upon the degree of knowledge.* In a sense, therefore, it is subjective. What would be gambling for one man, would be sound speculation for another.

. . . If we regard speculation as a reasoned attempt to gauge the future from present known data, it may be said to form the basis of all intelligent investment. *But it is better, I think, to regard the speculator as a person who endeavors to make a profit by means of a power of forecasting the future superior to the ordinary.* (KCKP UA/4.5, emphasis added)

Notice that Keynes's analysis of the relation of speculation to gambling runs, just like his theory of probability, in terms of judgments relative to the knowledge in one's possession. Also note that he is already attaching importance to the distinction between financial risks which are calculable and those which are incalculable (what he would later call "uncertain" risks). Since the pure chance attached to speculative positions on the part of the small, casual investor means that investor should attribute little *weight* to his judgment, his activity *is* simply gambling. By 1910 Keynes is arguing that the position of market insiders, having due regard to the constant flow of information that Emery stressed is centralized on the exchanges, and to their superior ability, defines professional speculation as rational action.

Now the question arises, how does speculation on the exchanges fit with the ethical view which Keynes expressed with regard to gambling in the *Treatise on Probability*? For much as the millionaire may attain an immoral advantage over the poor gambler, market insiders would have clear advantages over the more ignorant investors on the exchanges. That is, they might, if two things were true according to Keynes's own theory of probability. First, it would have to be possible to secure the knowledge that made for the insiders' superior judgment (that is, such knowledge could in principle *exist*). This follows directly from his definition of probability as a logical relation between a proposition (the price of U.S. Steel will rise) and the evidence related to it ("fundamentals," or market psychology?). Second, it would require the exchanges to be organized in such a way that it is relatively easy for the insiders to prey on the outsiders. Notice that both of these topics were considered by Marshall in his essay on the folly of amateur speculators, and by Emery in his defense of the stock exchange.

What is remarkable about Keynes as of 1910, especially considering what he would say in the *General Theory* twenty-five years later, is that with regard to the first question, at that stage he clearly believed in what we would now call calculable fundamental values: "I shall regard the possession of superior knowledge as the vital distinction, and the only vital distinction between the speculator and the gambler" (KCKP MM/ 26.1) Given this conviction it is not surprising that at this juncture he did not even raise the possibility that speculation could derail the beneficial risk bearing and directive influences of the exchanges on economic activity. This is reflected in that despite his disagreement with Emery over the proper *definition* of speculation, he immediately follows this discussion by repeating Emery's view of the "economic functions of speculation." It is contained too in the praise he clearly expresses for professional speculators. At one point in the lectures he equates the morals of professional speculators to those of bookmakers, quoting approvingly the following passage from the *Economist* (25 September 1909):

> Take professional bookmakers or betting men, for example; they work as hard at their business as human beings can do, and their earnestness is remarkable. Thoughtful men of few words, they are as grave as judges, as reflective as metaphysicians, and as serious as bishops; whatever their faults may be, they cannot be accused of frivolity or of not working for their living. (KCKP MM/26.1)

This is a far cry from the words of the excoriator of casino capitalism who would later compare the activities of professional speculators with "a game of Snap, of Old Maid, of Musical Chairs" and whose perhaps most widely remembered passage would be the famous "beauty contest" metaphor for stock market speculation. Or is it? I prefer to argue that one can rationally reconstruct the development of the Keynes of uncertainty, gloom, and the "dark forces of time and ignorance which envelope our future," the Keynes who appears in chapter 12 of the *General Theory*, from the cocksure, inexperienced, young philosopher lecturing about speculation he had never engaged in or witnessed at close hand, while still maintaining the framework of rationality and probability he had laid out in what Skidelsky (1983, 119) calls "the most important book in his life." Keynes's theory of probability was grounded in relevant knowledge. His own knowledge of speculation and his opinion of the amount of knowledge embodied in speculative activity, however, is something that changed dramatically over his career.

Consider the issue of speculation from his overall philosophical standpoint. In 1910 Keynes judged the risks undertaken by speculators to be subject to more or less calculable probability estimation by those who had the knowledge and skill to forecast prices.[26] Following Emery, he judged the "goodness" of their activity to consist in the beneficial func-

---

26. To repeat from above: "We do not mean by the risk of an investment its actual future yield—we mean the degree of probability of the yield we expect" (KCKP UA/4.5).

tions of risk bearing and directive influence. Moreover, he also agreed with Emery that this probable goodness of the speculators' activity led "on the whole" to the favorable functioning of the economic system—indeed it was an organic outgrowth of the form of commerce grown up in capitalism since the 1850s, a social organization about which Keynes had no doubts in 1910. Now given that he also followed Emery in reporting the possibility of abuses by insiders—what Emery called "the evils of speculation" (1896, chapter 5)—Keynes's estimate of the weight of evidence in favor of the above positive judgments must have been high. Or conversely, in 1910 he evidently attached little weight to the proposition that the moral risk of speculative activity could lead to abuses that would outweigh its positive benefits.

From this perspective Keynes's own theory of practical reason and probability in relation to conduct serves as a guide by which to chart the changes in his attitude toward speculation over the quarter-century between his first optimistic writings on speculation and his eventual critique of it in the *General Theory*. We can expect that his confidence in the "goodness" of speculation on the whole might be upset either by a reevaluation of the basis in knowledge according to which speculators speculate, and/or by an upward revision of his judgment of the moral risk attached to allowing speculation free rein. His later writings show evidence that he changed his mind on both of these issues.

Keynes II, 1919–1923:
The Philosopher Starts Speculating

The 1920s mark a major period of change in Keynes's way of thinking and living. In the latest volume of his excellent biography of Keynes, Skidelsky dates this change quite precisely:

> The years 1924 and 1925 were more obviously watershed years than 1923. He broke decisively with *laissez-faire*; by attacking the return to the gold standard, he burnt his boats with the Treasury and the Bank of England; and he married Lydia Lopokova. Events and the processes of his own thought radicalised him, so that he emerged the self-conscious champion of a new economic and political order. (1992, 173)

In this section I try to chart one current of this sea change in Keynes's outlook by canvassing his radicalization with regard to the issue of speculation. Our story depends on the seemingly odd fact that Keynes became an intellectual radical at the same time that he was amassing a financial fortune through his own speculative activity. I thus want to interweave the story his writings reveal with some evidence of his own experience as an investor. Adopting Skidelsky's dating, this analysis divides the 1920s into two phases, each corresponding to a basic change in Keynes's thinking and a change in his investment activity. The first period extends from his return from the Paris peace talks to the publication of his *Tract on Monetary Reform* in 1923. It was during this period—in August 1919 to be precise—that he first began speculating on a large scale, on the foreign exchange market (Moggridge 1992, 348). It was also in this period that he began to write professionally about speculation.

The foreign currency market is an exchange we have not seen discussed by any of the writers up to this point, for the obvious reason that currency speculation was impossible under the prewar fixed exchange rate system. Keynes, first with his partner Oswald T. ("Foxy") Falk, a colleague from the Treasury during the war, and then on his own, used his early understanding of the machinery of the forward market, what he thought of as his superior insight into the likely course of monetary policy and the exchanges, and the resources of friends and relatives, to take highly leveraged[27] speculative positions in the various European currencies, the dollar, and the rupee. Early in 1920 he was short on marks, lire, and francs and long on dollars. According to Skidelsky (1992, 41) this strategy was founded on the belief that "as British prices rose faster than American ones, sterling would go down against the dollar; whereas with the inflation rate in France, Germany and Italy higher than in Britain, sterling could be expected to appreciate against their currencies." But in late May things went wrong. Francs, lire, and marks appreciated against sterling, exacerbating the effects of an already depreciating dollar. As Skidelsky describes the situation: "finally on 27 May Keynes was forced to liquidate his positions. He lost all his group's capital, and owed his broker nearly £5,000. His debt, that is—including his 'moral debts' to his family and friends—came to just under £20,000" (1992, 43). After this date he rather quickly erased these debts by borrowing heavily and jumping back into the market. And for the rest of the 1920s he steadily

---

27. Moggridge notes: "At the time margin requirements were 10 per cent. Thus the fund could take up forward positions up to an amount equal to ten times their capital and realized capital gains" (*CW* 11:5 n. 5).

accumulated wealth, not without setbacks, by further speculations in currency, commodities, and stocks (*CW* 4:8–9).

The main point is that Keynes's record in the 1920s seems to place him closer to the "gamblers" than the "speculators" as he defined them in his notes in 1910. "The first thing that strikes one . . . is that he was not uniformly successful as an investor. In the 1920s, for example, in five of the seven years between 1922 and 1929 Keynes did worse than the *Bankers' Magazine* index" (Moggridge, *CW* 4:9). It is important for our story that these early setbacks were reflected in a changing attitude toward speculation in his economic writings. He starts out the 1920s mostly praising and defending currency speculation. Later, beginning in 1923, he began to doubt his own earlier characterization of speculators as necessarily superior forecasters or holders of privileged information. But this did not mean that in this period he came to see speculation as an independent economic force, much less a social problem in need of remedy.

Keynes's confident attitude of the early 1920s is reflected in his descriptions both of the currency exchanges, including the all-important forward market, and of the commodity exchanges. He was one of the first monetary economists to write about the mechanism of forward exchange markets. In particular his analysis of the determinants of the forward-spot premium in the *Tract* are an instance of the Marshallian stock equilibrium approach to asset markets—here extended to "hot" short-term money chasing the highest return internationally in a fluctuating exchange world.[28] But while describing the "machinery" of the foreign exchanges, he was also defending speculation from the charges then being leveled against it by government officials and the press. In fact much of what he wrote was for the press,[29] and it is to that literature that we now turn.

For the *Nation and Athenaeum* in 1923 Keynes wrote an article titled "The Foreign Exchanges and the Seasons" that is reflective of much of his writing at the time. He opposes the usefulness of the purchasing-power parity doctrine in explaining short-run exchange rate movements

28. In fact the resulting relationship between spot currency exchange rates, forward prices, and the relative rates of interest in two countries is still part of the basic lore of international finance literature, under the heading of the "covered interest parity theorem."

29. Skidelsky (1992, 27) argues that Keynes's extensive journalistic efforts in the early 1920s, at least partly fueled by the desire to make money, largely explain why he produced no major work of theory until 1930.

(*CW* 19:87–88). He suggests rather that the exchange rate is much more sensitive to "seasonal" trade demands imposed by worldwide commodity production and distribution, and the influence of "speculation." Because of the strong influence of speculative expectations, "a country's exchange is more sensitive than its price level to what the world thinks is going to happen but has not happened yet." But the expectations of speculators are not independent of what actually happens. As Keynes now knew from painful experience, they cannot afford to run contrary to events for long:

> Speculators can only cause the exchange to rise or fall at an earlier date than it would have done otherwise. For they have to reverse their transaction in due course, buying back or selling out as the case may be; so that, whether the thing which they anticipated has happened or not, their influence washes out sooner or later. Generally sooner rather than later, because the mass of speculators take short views and lose heart very quickly if there is any delay in what they had anticipated. . . . Most people vastly exaggerate the effect of speculation on the course of the exchanges. . . . It is only really important on the very rare occasions on which it precipitates a panic—that is to say, imitative action on a large scale by numbers of people who are not speculators at all, but just terror stricken. (*CW* 19:87–88)

This sentiment also shows up in what was Keynes's most extensive foray into journalism, editing and partly writing the *Manchester Guardian Commercial*'s special "Reconstruction Supplements" in 1922. Much of the currency exchange discussion from these supplements eventually ended up in *A Tract on Monetary Reform*.

In the preface to the 1923 French edition of the *Tract*, we get a very clear and colorful view of Keynes defending currency speculation as he excoriates the French minister of finance's opinion concerning the "mysterious and malignant influences of speculation":

> This is not far removed intellectually, from an African witch doctor's ascription of cattle disease to the "evil eye" of a bystander or bad weather to the unsatisfied appetites of an idol.
>
> In the first place, the volume of speculation, properly so called, is always extremely small in proportion to the volume of normal business. In the second place the successful speculator makes his profit by anticipating, not by modifying, existing economic tendencies. In

the third place, most speculation, especially "bear" speculation, is for very short periods of time, so that the closing of the transaction soon exerts an influence equal and opposite to its initial effect. (*CW* 4:xvi–xvii)

In the body of the *Tract*, as in Emery's treatment, speculative markets are viewed as a productive aspect of the modern commercial system. But now Keynes's eye is on the influence of rapid changes in money values on the overall activity level in this commercial system: "Whether one likes it or not, the technique of production under a regime of money contract forces the business world always to carry a big speculative position; and if it is reluctant to carry that position, the productive process must be slackened" (*CW* 4:33). In the case of changes in the value of money, even Emery's specialized risk-bearing class cannot remove all of this risk. Thus the speculator, as Keynes emphasized in the preface just quoted, is not the cause of, though he also cannot prevent, the main social evil confronted in the *Tract*: volatility in the price level.

Another angle on speculation is found in the sole theoretical chapter of the *Tract,* chapter 3, "The Theory of Money and of Foreign Exchanges," where Keynes analyzes the role of forward markets in currency. His general theme is very Emery-like again, emphasizing the risk-bearing factor.[30] It is at this point that his equilibrium asset holding model, the stock equilibrium approach he had learned from Marshall, reappears. Speculators drive the premium or discount between the spot and forward rate to the point where "opinion" is balanced as to the "preferences of the money and exchange market for holding funds in one international center rather than another" (*CW* 4:103).

It may happen that there is so much speculative activity on one side or the other of the market that the existing resources prepared to move money from one center to another are exhausted. This may temporarily drive the difference between spot and forward rates to a level "which represents an altogether abnormal profit to anyone who is in a position to buy these currencies forward and sell them spot." Only when enough new money is drawn into the exchanges will the normal relationship between spot and forward resume. Keynes contends, however, that these

---

30. In fact he repeats (*CW* 4:103) a line that can be found in his 1910 lecture notes and in other places in his writings, which is actually almost a verbatim quote from Emery (1896, 162), to the effect that among large dealers and millers, *not* to hedge in the futures market is considered the most dangerous kind of speculation.

episodes reveal the sagacity of the market opinion in predicting future changes: "when the differences between forward and spot rates have become temporarily abnormal, thus indicating an exceptional pressure of speculative activity, the speculators have often turned out to be right." He then repeats a claim made by Emery, who had gone to the trouble of using data on commodity prices to illustrate the stabilizing effect of speculation on prices: "When the type of professional speculation which makes use of the forward market is exceptionally active and united in its opinion, it has proved roughly correct, and has, therefore, been a useful factor in moderating the extreme fluctuations which would have occurred otherwise" (*CW* 4:109). Thus in the *Tract* Keynes supports Emery's positive view of the "economic function of speculation," extending it to the foreign exchanges:

> Where risk is unavoidably present, it is much better that it should be carried by those who are qualified or are desirous to bear it, than by traders, who have neither the qualifications nor the desire to do so, and whose minds it distracts from their own business. The wide fluctuations in the leading exchanges over the past three years . . . have been due, not to the presence of speculation, but to the absence of a sufficient volume of it relative to trade. (*CW* 4:113)

What then is new in Keynes's account in the early 1920s? Two issues do begin to surface that presage his later views on speculation. First, he begins to differentiate his analysis among the various speculative exchanges. Second, he begins to rethink the philosophical basis of speculative expectations. Yet it is important to distinguish among the various exchanges when evaluating Keynes's developing views on speculation. In the remainder of this essay I argue that from the mid-1920s on, he focused such doubts and criticisms as he held toward speculation almost entirely on stock market speculation. Moreover, this critique of stock market speculation, while it may have had some basis perhaps in his own experiences as a speculator, was also bound up with his changing views about the knowledge context appropriate to each market.

The beginning of his rethinking of this matter emerges in another of the *Manchester Guardian* articles, one that did not make it into the *Tract*. The article appeared in the *Guardian* in 1923 under the title "Some Aspects of Commodity Markets." Here Keynes provides a lucid and concise discussion of the functioning of commodity markets and their rationale. Moreover, it was at this date that he first conducted a serious empirical analysis to complement his interests in commodity markets.[31] Annually, from 1923 to 1930, he compiled his own data series from disparate industry and government sources into his memoranda on "stocks of staple commodities" written for the London and Cambridge Economic Service (*CW* 12:267–647). Reading these memoranda is an important reminder of the depth of his knowledge of the details of the markets he was both engaged in and writing about.

It is no surprise to find that the theoretical treatment in the *Guardian* article is essentially that of Emery. The role of the exchange is to bear the risk of price fluctuations in standardized traded commodities (*CW* 12:259–62). But there arises here an interesting change from his 1910 discussion. Whereas in 1910 speculation was defined by "access to superior knowledge and forecasting ability," now Keynes appears to doubt this view—at least so far as commodity markets are concerned. He describes thus the standard view he now objects to:

> In most writing on this subject great stress is laid on the service performed by the professional speculator in bringing about a harmony between short-period and long-period demand and supply, through his action in stimulating or retarding *in good time* the one or the other. (*CW* 12:260)

To this he objects,

> This may be the case, but it presumes that the speculator is better informed on the average than the producers and the consumers themselves, which speaking generally, is a rather dubious proposition. The most important function of the speculator in the great organized "futures" markets is, I think, somewhat different. He is not so much a prophet (though it may be a belief in his own gifts of prophesy that tempts him into the business), as a *risk bearer*. If he happens to be a prophet also, he will become extremely, indeed preposterously, rich. But without any such pretensions, indeed without paying the slightest

31. That is, both his professional interests and his personal interests. By this period Keynes had begun to speculate in commodities as well as currencies on quite a large scale. In fact in 1923 and 1924 profits on commodity speculation of £13,702 and £15,245 dominated his investment income (see Moggridge's table 4, *CW* 2:12). In 1928 large losses in commodities, particularly rubber, cut his net assets from £44,000 to £13,060 (*CW* 12:11, table 3; 15).

attention to the prospects of the commodity he deals in or giving a thought to it, he may, one decade with another earn substantial re-muneration *merely* by running risks and allowing the results of one season to average with those of others; just as an insurance company [32] makes profits without pretending to know more about an individual's prospects of life or the chances of his house taking fire than he knows himself. (261)

Notice the almost complete reversal here of his discussion of the dis-tinction between gambling and speculation in the lecture notes of 1910. There gambling and speculation were different from each other and from insurance. In gambling, either the risks were unknown, or individual risks could not be "averaged" across instances (that is, they constituted uninsurable risk). Fire and life insurance, then, was a case of ascertain-able average risk plus commission over the expected value. Speculation, though, Keynes had defined in 1910 as betting on price changes by refer-ence to superior knowledge and ability. Now, in 1923, the speculator is no longer a prophet but just a functionary, depending on the law of aver-ages and the fact that producers and sellers of commodities are willing to pay a risk premium for the security of sure future prices. Perhaps the shock of actually turning out to have been wrong with regard to some of his own market prophecies convinced Keynes that the activity was not one which would yield to superior ability. In any event, in the case of commodity markets specifically, this view never changed in Keynes's later writings, though he continued to be actively involved in these mar-kets for the rest of his life, both as a trader and a reformer (see *CW* 12: chapter 3, 21:456–70, 27: chapter 3).

To summarize, then, after the experience of the war had increased his confidence in his own financial judgment and, crucially, introduced him to the world of City finance, Keynes became more deeply involved in speculation—as an investment advisor, financial journalist, and policy analyst, and as a speculator on a large scale. His writings of this period from 1919 to 1923 consist essentially in extending Emery to the analysis of foreign currency exchanges, and defending speculation from contem-porary criticisms. He was still, in all respects save one, less like the Keynes of the *General Theory* than was Marshall in his essay of 1899. The difference was Keynes's unique combination of practical experience

32. By this date Keynes had become a director of the National Mutual Life Insurance Company.

of financial markets and his ability to weave insights from this experience into a philosophical analysis of the rationality of speculation. This gift would finally allow him to outpace his master by the end of the 1920s, when he seriously turned his efforts toward economic theory. It also provided him with a two-part framework of analysis that would be applied in both the *Treatise* and the *General Theory*. One part was his continual use of the Marshallian asset market equilibrium construct. This is explicitly used in much of the *Treatise* and in chapter 17 of the *General Theory*. The other part was his own unique recasting of Emery's speculators into the mold of his theory of probability. This also would be used to telling effect in both the *Treatise* and the *General Theory*. But that story will have to be told in another place.

For their useful comments and suggestions I thank, without implicating, Allin Cottrell, Neil De Marchi, Mary Morgan, and John Wood. T. K. Rymes alerted me to Marshall's 1871 essay "Money." Rod O'Donnell first brought to my attention the possible value of Keynes's early lecture notes on speculation. Jacky Cox of the King's College Modern Archive was of great service during my research in the Keynes Papers. Permission to quote the Keynes Papers has been provided by the Provost and Fellows of King's College, Cambridge. Financial support from the Wake Forest Archie Fund is gratefully acknowledged.

References

Bagehot, Walter. 1873. *Lombard Street: A Description of the Money Market*. London: P. S. King.

Bridel, P. 1987. *Cambridge Monetary Thought: Development of Saving-Investment Analysis from Marshall to Keynes*. New York: St. Martin's.

Clarke, P. 1988. *The Keynesian Revolution in the Making*. Oxford: Clarendon Press.

Cottrell, A., and M. Lawlor. 1991. "Natural Rate" Mutations: Keynes, Leijonhufvud and the Wicksell Connection. *HOPE* 23.4:625–43.

Cronon, W. 1992. *Nature's Metropolis: Chicago and the Great West*. New York: Norton.

Dardi, M., and M. Gallegati. 1992. Marshall on Speculation. *HOPE* 24.3:571–93.

Davis, J. 1994. *Keynes's Philosophical Development*. Cambridge: Cambridge University Press.

De Marchi, Neil, and Paul Harrison. 1994. Trading "in the Wind" and with Guile: The Troublesome Matter of the Short Selling of Shares in Seventeenth-Century Holland. In *Higgling: Transactors and Their Markets in the History of Economics*, edited by Neil De Marchi and Mary S. Morgan. HOPE 26, special issue. Durham: Duke University Press.

Emery, H. C. 1896. *Speculation on the Stock and Produce Exchanges of the United States*. New York: Columbia University Press.

Fisher, I. 1907. *The Rate of Interest*. New York: Macmillan.

——. 1930. *The Theory of Interest*. New York: Macmillan.

Goodhart, C. A. E. 1988. *The Evolution of Central Banks*. Cambridge: MIT Press.

Harcourt, G. C. 1983. Keynes's College Bursar View of Investment. In *Distribution, Effective Demand and International Economic Relations*, edited by J. A. Kregel. New York: St. Martin's.

Horwich, G. 1964. *Money, Capital and Prices*. Homewood, Ill.: Richard D. Irwin.

Kahn, R. F. 1954. Some Notes on Liquidity Preference. *Manchester School of Economics and Social Studies* 22.3:229–57.

Keynes, J. M. 1911. Review of *The Purchasing Power of Money*, by Irving Fisher. *Economic Journal* 21.3:393–98.

——. 1925. Alfred Marshall. In *Memorials of Alfred Marshall*, edited by A. C. Pigou. London: Macmillan.

——. 1937a. The Theory of the Rate of Interest. In *The Lessons of Monetary Experience: Essays in Honour of Irving Fisher*. Reprinted in *Collected Writings*, 14:101–8 (1973).

——. 1937b. Alternative Theories of the Rate of Interest. *Economic Journal* 47:241–52. Reprinted in *Collected Writings*, 14:201–15 (1973).

——. 1937c. The General Theory of Employment. *Quarterly Journal of Economics* 51:209–23. Reprinted in *Collected Writings*, 14:109–23 (1973).

——. 1971–89. *The Collected Writings of John Maynard Keynes* [*CW*]. 30 vols. London: Macmillan for the Royal Economic Society.

Laidler, D. 1991. *The Golden Age of the Quantity Theory*. Princeton: Princeton University Press.

Lawlor, M. S. 1993. Keynes, Cambridge and the New Keynesian Economics. In *Labor Economics: Problems in Analyzing Labor Markets*, edited by W. A. Darity. Boston: Kluwer Academic.

——. 1994a. The Own-Rates Framework as an Interpretation of the *General Theory:* A Suggestion for Complicating the Keynesian Theory of Money. In *Keynes: The State of the Debate*, edited by J. Davis. Boston: Kluwer Academic.

——. 1994b. Keynes and Financial Market Processes: From the *Treatise* to the *General Theory*. Department of Economics Working Papers, Wake Forest University.

Leijonhufvud, A. 1981. The Wicksell Connection: Variations on a Theme. In *Information and Coordination*. Oxford: Oxford University Press.

Marshall, A. 1871. Money. In *The Early Writings of Alfred Marshall*, 2 vols., edited by J. Whittaker, 164–77. London: Macmillan, 1975.

——. 1899. The Folly of Amateur Speculators Makes the Fortunes of Professionals. The Wiles of Some Professionals. Reprinted in Dardi and Gallegati 1992, 586–93.

Meltzer, A. H. 1988. *Keynes's Monetary Theory: A Different Interpretation*. Cambridge: Cambridge University Press.

Mill, J. S. 1871. *The Principles of Political Economy, with Some of Their Applications to Social Philosophy.* 2d ed. Reprinted, edited by J. M. Robson, Toronto: University of Toronto Press, 1965.

Moggridge, D. E. 1992. *Maynard Keynes: An Economist's Biography.* London and New York: Routledge.

O'Donnell, R. M. 1989. *Keynes: Philosophy, Economics and Politics: The Philosophical Foundations of Keynes's Thought and Their Influence on His Economics and Politics.* New York: St. Martin's.

Pigou, A. C. 1917. The Value of Money. *Quarterly Journal of Economics* 37 (November): 38–65.

Shiller, R. J. 1991. *Market Volatility.* Cambridge: MIT Press.

Skidelsky, R. 1983. *John Maynard Keynes.* Vol. 1, *Hopes Betrayed, 1883–1920.* London: Macmillan.

———. 1992. *John Maynard Keynes.* Vol. 2, *The Economist as Saviour, 1920–1937.* London: Macmillan.

Veblen, T. B. 1904. *The Theory of Business Enterprise.* New York: Scribner's. Reprinted, New Brunswick, N.J.: Transaction Books, 1978.

Wood, J. H., and N. L. Wood. 1985. *Financial Markets.* New York: Harcourt Brace Jovanovich.

Part 3   American Economists Recover Fairness and Market Process

Marketplace Morals and the American Economists: The Case of John Bates Clark

Mary S. Morgan

> Do you believe and will you teach, with all the power that God shall give you, that bargains must be mutually advantageous to be morally justifiable?
> —John Bates Clark (1879a, 161)

Thus would John Bates Clark have catechized every potential economics teacher and preacher of his day. Even leaving God to one side, it still seems a strange question to a twentieth-century economist, for whom exchange can only occur if there is mutual advantage. Not so for Clark, and for many of his late nineteenth-century American contemporaries for whom it was a matter of common observation that exchange was often not mutually beneficial. Indeed, matters of exchange economics formed some of the most important political-economic problems of the day. Americans lived in an age of rapid economic change marked by the growth of monopolistic elements across the economy in services, in industry, and even into the agricultural sector. Workers combined to try and wrest fair wages from increasingly concentrated capitalists; farmers railed against monopolistic middlemen; and small firms lost their livelihood, driven out by the predatory pricing of large firms. There was little in the way of institutional or legal support for fair trade or fair prices. Antimonopoly legislation was yet to come, and trade unions had yet to win full legality for their operations, so that suppliers of labor, small farmers, and other weaker parties had little protection to fall back upon.

The economic laws of pricing also seemed to work in a new way, a way which no longer guaranteed a fair price to both buyer and seller. For the late nineteenth-century American economists, the free and benign competition envisaged by classical economists, where buyers and sellers were perceived to be on a common footing, was a thing of the past (see Morgan 1993). They were also a long way from Mill's world, where prices were determined as much by custom as by competition (1848, book 2, chapter 4), for the dynamics of economic change and the Civil War monetary dislocations must have done much to destroy customary pricing. Thus traditional economic exchange relations, where prices were fixed by custom or by competitive behavior in the open market with many buyers and sellers, appeared to have broken down. Instead Americans of their day often experienced monopoly, monopsony, or a variety of sharp practices, which made for a loss or no advantage from exchange, relative, that is, to the ideal outcomes of mutual advantage expected under classical economic predictions.

The problems of exchange relations in nonmarket situations (those involving monopolies, or any individual isolated exchange away from the marketplace) formed one of the dominant economic problems for American economists of the day. Clark's English contemporaries, Jevons and Edgeworth, regarded such cases as difficult problems with indeterminate solutions and spent comparatively little time on them. By contrast, Clark wrote extensively about them in his various early papers which culminated in his first book, *The Philosophy of Wealth* (1886a). He was passionately committed to understanding and trying to solve these problems as part of his lifelong analysis of the distribution of wealth.

With Clark's commentaries, our gaze is directed not to the problem of monopoly pricing itself, but to the higgling or bargaining in individual exchange relations, and to the contexts in which economic laws of exchange based on self-interest might have to be buttressed with moral codes or more formal institutions (laws) to ensure mutual advantage. In his early years Clark believed that the practices of exchange, and thus exchange outcomes, were governed by an amalgam of behavioral, conventional, and ethical elements. It was also his view that these behavioral and ethical elements changed over time with the changing forms of economic exchange; thus each new period had its institutional habits of thought and ways of economic behavior, which played a role in determining exchange outcomes. As we shall see, these behavioral conventions were seen as a prelude to the formation of more recognizable economic institutions, namely laws restricting behavior in exchange.

Clark's methods of analysis of exchange higgling hold particular peculiarities for the twentieth-century economist. He looks both backward with nostalgia to the exchange economies of the earlier age and forward with utopian idealism to that of the future. He regarded his own economy with the eyes of a Christian of socialist leanings and thought that nothing could be worse than the modern predatory behavior of his own society, except perhaps the intertribal trade behavior he reported from the anthropologists. All were grist to his mill, and since he avoided formal mathematical analysis in favor of a multidisciplinary approach drawing on sociology, anthropology, and history, as well as economics, it is sometimes difficult to separate out the true grains of his descriptive analysis from the idealistic chaff.

It is also impossible to abstract the economics from the important moral or ethical arguments involved in his discussion of the exchange process and its outcome. These arguments lie at the center of many late nineteenth-century analyses of higgling by American economists who discussed competitive and exchange behavior between firms, between individuals, and between employers and employees. In all of these discussions of exchange, moral or ethical elements were likely to enter. Rather than sitting alongside, but apart from, the economic analysis, they formed an integral part of the economic commentary.

1. Legitimate Economic Exchange versus the Modern Bargain

To separate off legitimate exchange, in which there is mutual advantage, from illegitimate exchange, Clark used a historical account of the development of exchange relations. For example, in retail trade, strong social or moral conventions in exchange behavior ensuring legitimate exchange were clearly evident. Retail exchange retained some elements of old-fashioned conservative market relations, hangovers from an earlier period in which the artisan was also the retailer. In this earlier period, as Clark recounted,

> the spirit of the time regarded with distrust an attempt of one dealer to injure his rivals by selling for less than a normal profit. The "good will" of a business was then no misnomer, but signified the personal confidence and kindly feeling existing between a dealer and his local constituency. He, perhaps, lived and worked where his ancestors had lived and worked before him, and appeared to inherit a prescriptive right to his customers' patronage. . . . Custom, based on good will

and a sense of prescriptive right, governed, to a large extent, the sales
which took place across the horizontal lines separating one producing
class from another. (1886a, 122)

With the Industrial Revolution, and machine technologies, these small
artisan-retailers began to disappear and plain shopkeepers appeared.
This changed the attitude of the local buyers to the retailer, who no longer
had the same "prescriptive right to patronage" because he appeared to be
merely a middleman between producer and consumer. Thence, "mere
interest comes more and more to determine where the public will buy its
goods" (124). Consequently the retailer began to adopt the competitive
behavior endemic in other market exchange relations.

A similar historical change, Clark argued, could be found in the matter
of pricing, where moral and social conventions, supported by the church
or other authorities, prevailed back to ancient times (for example, the
"just price" of the medieval era). Out of these had developed the impersonal "mercantile code" guiding exchange in open markets, in which
"those who desire an article of value must seek to outdo each other in
offering to its possessor inducements to part with it. Rivalry in giving is,
therefore, the essence of legitimate competition. . . . Within the theatre
of general exchanges the standard is set by the undisguised efforts of
many persons to outdo each other in offering products to society as the
general consumer" (155, 159). The standards of price and service established by general and legitimate competition in the marketplace (that is,
according to the mercantile code) and on offer to the general consumer
were then applied in separate individual dealings away from the market.[1]
The "mercantile code" is a phrase denoting both the way of establishing
a standard price for a given quality and quantity in the marketplace and
then the offering of that same standard in individual exchanges outside
the marketplace. The term therefore incorporates both a behavioral code
and a set of outcomes.

Gradually, Clark claimed, this mercantile code had been abandoned
for individual exchanges, so that in his own era (the 1870s and 1880s)
such exchanges were no longer carried out at values determined by
market higgling, but at values determined by predatory relations which
verged on outright theft: "The system becomes as undisguisedly predatory as one can be without violating the rights of property in actual pos-

---

1. See Lowry, this volume, for some discussion of isolated versus market exchange in the
seventeenth-century literature.

session" (159). In an extended passage, he characterized the "modern bargain" of his day (as he called the predatory outcome) as epitomizing the latent brutality of medieval life in which the greater force prevails. His attack on the "bargain" involved an implicit moral or ethical judgment:

> The theory of the modern bargain appears to be that of the mediaeval judicial combat; let each do his worst, and God will protect the right. As in Mediaeval times, it has too frequently happened that providence has protected the wrong. There is a standard that determines the justice or injustice of bargains, and the so-called "higgling of the market" is utterly inadequate to secure conformity to that standard. (1879a, 161)

Clark's attack may appear an old-fashioned argument that "money-making by exchange is virtual robbery." But this is by no means the case, for his analysis of utility had already recognized that the merchant creates "form utility," "place utility," and "time utility" (162). Merchanting was acceptable, for it created value for others; even some forms of speculation had their uses. Rather, it was the manipulation of prices by traders without the creation of wealth or utility for the other party in the exchange which Clark found problematic: there were "shrewd trading men who create no wealth [no utility], but deal in stocks and real estates, horses and general merchandise, in a manner that benefits no one but themselves. . . . Market prices are nothing to such men; it is their aim to get more value than they give, both in buying and in selling" (162). Market prices on the other hand were presented as the outcome of "legitimate" competition which embodies "rivalry in giving"; in other words, market exchange at market prices creates value for both parties.

In Clark's analysis, the "bargain" is an exchange at some price other than market price, in which one party makes no gain, or gets less value than he gives, thus sustaining a loss relative to the exchange in the open market at the market price. Clark suggested that although such bargains occurred in other countries, in no other country was this form of exchange regarded as something socially acceptable.

> What is ordinarily termed a good bargain is, morally, a bad bargain; it is unequal, and good for one party only. Whenever such a transaction takes place some one is plundered. It is the sufferer, in such cases, who usually regrets the occurrence; in an ideal society it would

be the gainer who would mourn. . . . Sack-cloth and ashes are the proper covering of the man who has made a "good bargain." What is the fact in the case? Do persons who have made such bargains, even by questionable means, don the garments of humiliation, or do they show something of complacency? . . . The whole process is bad; it is odious, and the worst feature of it is that it is characteristically American. The sharp bargaining spirit, which seeks, not to create wealth, but to get it away from other persons by all methods tolerated by law, may exist, in individual cases, in other civilized countries besides our own; but it does not, in most countries, so pervade the entire community as to make it respectable. . . . To seek to buy for less than the market price is considered mean, in those countries; and to seek to sell for more than the market price is considered knavish. (162–63)

We see here that market prices involved an ethical element in the division from exchange, which seemed to be missing from the Americans' "good bargain" of the later nineteenth century. For Clark, social codes of behavior in the market always had moral elements bound up in them: legitimate market exchange was ethically sound because both parties gained; the "good bargain" was in fact "bad" because only one party gained.

2. Moral Economy and the Context of Exchange

As we have found, Clark did not believe that the force of economic laws ensured mutual advantage in exchange away from the marketplace. Rather, if mutual benefit occurred, it must derive from a moral economy[2] of exchange: that exchange should never be a bargain (exploitative) but always create value for both parties. In Clark's analysis, the problem lay in the fact that the *behavior* appropriate to the marketplace in which each is out for all he can get ("the bargaining spirit") carries over into the individual trade away from the market. In such cases the bargaining behavior is the source of evil, because the person who gets exploited is often in a defenseless position. For example, he might be "a borrower

2. The term "moral economy" is usually associated with the economic rights and duties of the economic classes in the precapitalist economy (see Thompson 1971). Here I adapt it to apply to American economists' notions of the moral duties which operate at the individual level in exchange relations. More recently the term has been used by Daston (1992) in connection with the values of scientific investigators. In my particular case of the American attempt to reconstruct economics (see section 6 below) this latter sense may also be relevant.

at the mercy of a single lender" or a merchant who is "compelled to accept the offer of a single customer."[3] By inference, then, what is presented as reasonable behavior (and legally allowable), according to the mercantile code for unrestricted competition in the general market, is in fact a license to rob in individual cases of exchange. Whereas such behavior may be acceptable in the one situation (marketplace bargaining and higgling), it will not be in the other. The conventions of exchange behavior turn out to be context-dependent. The economic context of the marketplace in conjunction with bargaining behavior is consistent with the moral economy of mutual advantage. When that situation changes, the rules of economic behavior ought to change too. If they do not, the moral economy of exchange will not be safeguarded.

This moral economy is well recognized, as Clark pointed out, in certain extreme situations, where moral rules supported by law clearly take precedence over market codes of self-interest. For example, "a boatman does not stop to make terms with a [sinking] man in the water, before taking him on board. . . . Society demands the prompt rendering of the service; the refusal to render it is a crime, and the making of conditions is a temporary refusal" (165).[4] Clark wanted to bring those moral rules to bear in all situations where there is any possibility of exploitation in exchange: "Financial drowning brings ruin to families, and is often as much worse, in its effects, than literal drowning. . . . The moral and legal principle is the same in both cases, and should be equally recognized and obeyed" (165). The constant comparison of situations in respect of their moral elements was what Clark hoped would ensure the mutual advantage required in exchange.

3. An element of monopoly power is involved in any isolated exchange (that is, a "single" buyer or seller). Notice also the hint that an isolated exchange is often not an entirely "voluntary" exchange—the principle that Lowry suggests (this volume) was earlier thought to ensure the justice of any exchange.

4. Seminar reactions to this passage have been extraordinarily varied. Some have argued if the boatman stops to argue, the man will have drowned, and the boatman will get nothing; but one might equally argue that, having been rescued, the man has no economic reason to reward the boatman, only a moral duty. Others have said, on the contrary, that the boatman goes to the sinking man, who then hangs onto the side of the boat, where he is unable to get in unaided; there is thus certainly time to bargain, but the man in the water lacks all power in the higgling relation. Ross Emmett has pointed out another example: in many parts of the world you must bargain with a taxi driver *before* you set out; otherwise you are at his mercy to charge a high price at your destination. Yet one obvious reaction would be to interpret this situation as one in which, *after* taking you to your destination, the taxi driver no longer has any bargaining power over the price, but must accept the minimum you are prepared to pay.

Clark's hopes appear idealistic, but the moral elements were an essential part of his analysis of economic behavior. To understand the basis of these moral elements in his arguments, we need to look at his notion of economic man. Like many of his nationality and generation, Clark reacted against the narrow vision held by classical economists, of economic man driven by nothing but self-interest. Safely under the umbrella of the economic harmonies, such economists had argued that individual greed checked the greed of others and that intervention by agencies of state or church were misconceived. Such "laissez-faire thinking" apparently ruled in the American economics community well into the 1870s (see Fine 1957; and Lerner 1963). Clark rejected this basic assumption about man as purely self-seeking on the grounds that it was patently unrealistic. Man did not always behave in a self-seeking way, not because of the influence of outside factors disturbing him from the true path of selfishness, but because his selfishness was compounded with a complex mixture of all sorts of other inbuilt characteristics.

No doubt, as a Christian, Clark had views about virtues and vices. But he neither denied nor condemned the important role of self-interest in economic outcomes. Rather than considering the outcomes from man's selfish behavior as it was narrowly assumed to be by the classical authors, he appealed, as did others of the period, for an explicitly anthropological study of economic behavior as it actually was (see especially Clark 1877b). It was in this context that he developed his version of marginal utility theory, with its all-important social twist (see 1877a, 1877b). Clark's economic man has ideals and ethical sense, spiritual wants and aesthetic desires, in addition to physical needs and motivations. Man cannot be subdivided into an individual, self-seeking economic man and a separate, noneconomic man; nor can the whole man be separated out from society.

Of particular import here is that Clark's whole man was moral, and that moral qualities informed all his economic actions. In certain fields of economic activity, particularly in *exchange,* morals were often difficult to live with. Remember, the morals were in the individual, but so was self-interest: "Individual conduct is the resultant of two opposing forces, selfishness on the one hand, and the sense of right, on the other" (1878, 536). Clark thus envisaged exchange behavior as the outcome of these two forces in individuals' conduct.

In Clark's account, it was the role of this moral element, "the sense of right," to provoke a constant comparison in which each person measured and assessed his own self-interested behavior against the ideal moral behavior. So, in the context of economic exchange, persuasion and bargaining activity had limits that were based partly on legal injunctions and social customs, and partly on this form of moral reasoning:

> We may still do that to our competitors which ideal morality condemns, and which positive law may, at some time, interdict. We may not lie unrestrainedly; the statutes against obtaining property by false pretences will see to it that mercantile falsehood has limits; but, by avoiding the statute, we may still deceive. We may not place our competitor in the river, and by frequent submergings, compel him to sell his homestead for half its value; but we may place him in commercial exigencies, and extort a portion of his property. We may do much that, in an ideal state, we could not do; and it is not only competent to compare both the methods and the results of the present system with a perfect standard, but our hope lies in the fact that the comparison is constantly made, and that the existing order is compelled into increasing conformity with the best that human reason can conceive. (1883, 362)

It seems, then, that for Clark's individual, moral sense is not so much driven by human sympathy (as it is for Adam Smith, or perhaps for Edgeworth),[5] nor is it an absolute "right and wrong" notion (as offered by Herbert Spencer in his attempt to develop a scientific ethics based on individual learning); rather, it is activated by a sense of justice and fairness in given contexts.[6]

This notion and principle of just division is also the central element in the most convincing solution to the famous "J. B. Clark problem": the problem of how to reconcile the later neoclassical Clark with the earlier Clark, whose work I discuss here.[7] Clark was already a marginalist in his

5. Suppose, Edgeworth argued in a footnote, "our contractors to be in a sensible degree *not* 'economic' agents, but actuated in effective moments by a sympathy with each other's interests" (1881, 53); then the contract could be characterized as settled according to an "ethical" method.

6. For a recent discussion of economic justice in given contexts, with some rather neat historical commentary, see Zajac 1985.

7. One view is to take the early work as anticapitalist and the later as procapitalist. This position can only be upheld by ignoring the ethical elements in the later work and concentrating on the apparently "value-free" neoclassical elements. A recent attempt to reconcile the two Clarks (Henry 1982) does it by portraying the early Clark as pro–capital and competition but antimonopoly. Henry's 1983 paper is not inconsistent with Everett's earlier (1946) analysis,

thinking about utility and prices in his early work (discussed here), but it was only the full marginal analysis of distribution, adopted in his book *The Distribution of Wealth* (1899) and partially in an intermediary paper (1894), which freed him from all these worrying institutional and moral codes of behavior. He had not changed his mind about the importance of just or fair division; he had merely found what seemed to him a better answer, an answer in economic theory, which dealt with all those difficulties of what the laborer should be paid, and what share the employer should take.[8]

I make no claim of originality for this solution to the "Clark problem." It follows naturally from the conclusion reached by Everett (1946), who analyzed Clark's religious views in relation to his economic beliefs. Everett argues that we should interpret Clark's moral concerns throughout his work as a concern with economic justice, a concern which informs his moral outlook and motivates his interest in the economics of distribution in its many different aspects. This, for Everett, provides the crucial element of consistency between the earlier and later Clark. Economic analyses are acceptable to Clark if they contain answers to the problems of just distribution, and not otherwise.

The moral economy that I have identified in Clark's account of legitimate exchange is that individuals recognize, and act upon, principles of justice in recognizing that the division of gains from exchange should always be one of mutual advantage. Its location is in the sphere of individuals and their exchange behavior, very different from Clark's later idea that just distribution flowed from the laws of marginal or neoclassical economics. Nevertheless, his early views should not be lightly dismissed. It might well be just this same sort of individually located moral sense, or sense of innate justice, which seems to be true of the individuals (except economics students) who took part in the recent experiments discussed by Robert Leonard (this volume). These people, in many circumstances, preferred the justice of a "fifty–fifty" outcome

---

though it tells a different story. See Henry 1982 for discussion of the earlier arguments and various positions on the problem.

8. Despite the marginal solutions to just division, the problem of monopoly industry, and its exploitation of customers and suppliers, remained as great a theoretical and policy problem as ever (as Edgeworth and others noted too). Clark continued to worry about the problem and to write about its evils and moral/legal solutions, even after his conversion to the marginal distribution theories (see, for example, Clark 1901, 1904).

to the unequal outcome from self-interested behavior as predicted by the neoclassical economists running the experiments (see also Frank, Gilovich, and Regan 1993).

3. Changing Exchange Behavior and Changing Laws of Exchange

The moral sense of individuals was one restriction on exploitative exchange behavior; legal restrictions were another. Both incorporated notions of the moral economy of exchange, but the legal restrictions lagged behind the socially acceptable conventions. The next questions, then, for Clark, were how did these acceptable codes of higgling behavior arise, and how did they evolve into laws? He believed that the conventional views about exchange behavior and the economic realities of exchange interacted, each mutually constructing the other. Since economic exchange relations and their contexts change over time, Clark argued, exchange behavior could not remain stable or absolute. Rather, exchange behavior evolved in socially acceptable forms over time, and these conventions (incorporating moral elements) gradually became incorporated into formal laws.

To support his interpretation, Clark (like others of his period) looked for inspiration to the anthropological writings of Henry Maine, and to Maine's historical discussion of the development of such codes of behavior. In "Business Ethics, Past and Present" (1879a) Clark suggests that morals first originated in man in response to interaction within a personal relationship (along the lines indicated in the book of Genesis, which was treated as an analogy for how moral codes of behavior develop). This form of moral behavior then came to hold sway in dealings with all family members. Different moral codes applied inside the family than those toward people outside the family. Gradually the circle within which familial moral codes applied widened to the tribe, the community, and the nation, and as these codes became socially acceptable over the wider sphere, they became enshrined into laws.

Exchange behavior is the arena within which Clark most explicitly discussed the evolution of these codes. In Maine's analysis, as interpreted by Clark, the exchange dealings within the family system or village and those outside the family/community were subject to mutually exclusive moral codes: competitive bargaining behavior was restricted to dealings with the outsiders.[9] Gradually the modern market (of Clark's time and place) developed out of these two different sorts of dealings, incorporating elements of each.

> The modern market is a fusion of village and mark [the place where insiders and outsiders met]; the circle within which competition is excluded has been reduced to a zero; but, in compensation, much of the humanity which characterized the dealings of villages with each other has extended itself to the entire operations of trade . . . and though the mark, as such, is extinct, its influence also survives in the latent brutality that characterizes much of customary business intercourse. (1879a, 160)

Thus modern market trading involved elements both of the competitive bargaining spirit and of family morality, in a shared behavioral and moral code.

These culturally shared codes were influenced by economic conditions. What was considered acceptable behavior depended on the character of the prevailing economic circumstances: "When men are united in an organized society, there necessarily exist common ethical ideas, and a national code of right and wrong is the result. . . . The national code of right and wrong is influenced by economic conditions; what is necessary, under the circumstances, is regarded as right" (Clark, 1878, 536). The early nineteenth century, characterized as it was by small-scale competition, had been dominated by a culture of laissez faire appropriate for the economy of that time. But the changing behavior of firms as the structure of industries became more centralized had led most Americans, by the end of the nineteenth century, to change their beliefs about what was acceptable economic behavior. There was widespread demand for effective legislation against the evils of monopolistic practices to restrain predatory pricing behavior of firms and to prevent the lowering of wages by big business. The position of laissez faire was abandoned as no longer the correct policy for the realities of the period, and instead moral and legal restraints on competitive practices were advocated to prevent exploitation in exchange.

As public sentiments about acceptable behavior (and the associated

---

9. Anthropologists still find it convenient to distinguish exchange relations as being between insiders or between insiders/outsiders, and associate different sorts of behavior with each (see, for example, Parry and Bloch 1989).

development of moral injunctions) changed, economic behavior would change and, Clark foresaw, legal changes would follow to put the changed behavioral codes into force.[10] In turn these altered laws would affect economic behavior to produce new economic circumstances in a mutually reconstructing circle: "On the other hand, prevailing economic practices are largely determined by the national code. National ideas of right and wrong thus, regularly produce economic effects, the most important of which is a restraint on unlimited competition" (536).

Clark's analysis of the evolution of socially acceptable forms of exchange behavior can be found echoed in the work of other American economists, for example Hadley (1906), a contemporary, more conservative, but still morally committed economist, as well as (in some respects) Veblen (1904) (see Morgan 1993, section 2). Both, like Clark, portrayed the contemporary policy difficulties associated with predatory higgling behavior as being due to lags between the changes in economic realities, the evolution of socially acceptable (nonexploitative or "fair") ways of behavior for the new economic situation, and the final culmination in legal changes.

4. Just Division and Its Evolution in the Wage-Work Exchange

We notice now another outcome of the changing economic realities: it was not only the population who changed their views about socially acceptable forms of exchange, but also the economists commenting on and analyzing the economy. Nowhere, in this period when Clark was developing his views, were these changing moral codes, changing economic realities, and changing views of economists more evident than in their discussions of the labor market and its dramatic upheavals during the 1870s and 1880s.

To young economists of the day, the old economics and ethics of laissez faire appeared to lead to violent disorder rather than benign order. Clark wrote a historical commentary on the labor market, which was published just after the terrible Haymarket riot of 1886. First, he characterized the old situation, before the growth of large-scale capital and labor unions, when competition was an effective agency for deciding

---

10. Clark recognized that laws were sometimes developed by particular economic interests to defend their own group (see 1879b, 1890).

wage contracts. In those days of high wages caused by the endemic American labor shortage, competition in the labor market acted to provide a reasonably just exchange contract. It was seen as a "social agency for dividing the rewards of industry. It was not blindly adopted. As it came gradually into existence it demonstrated its capacity for dividing products with a certain approach to justice. It commended itself to men's sense of right, and was established as every social institution must be established, on a moral basis" (1886b, 533). The growth of large-scale industry following the Civil War reduced the power of individual laborers to get a fair wage. Thus competition no longer divided justly, so it no longer had claim to a moral basis. Why not? Because the balance of bargaining power had shifted toward the firms and employers: "To divide anything by the process which bids every man get what he can is to give the lion's share to the strongest. In a bargaining process the strongest is he who has no rivals to bid against him, and who is not obliged to trade at all; the weakest is he who has rivals and who must trade" (533).

Notice that Clark made two comments about the distribution of bargaining power: the bargaining power of each party depends on both the presence of rivals *and* need to trade. In explaining why competition no longer divided justly, he extended this discussion of the nature of free contracts and compulsion and its effect on the higgling positions of the parties to exchange:

> A free contract is one that is made between parties who are not under any compulsion to deal with each other. If A makes a bargain with B, knowing that C and D are equally ready to treat with him, A at least, is free; and if B has a similar alternative open to him, the contract is clear from all compulsion. The wage contract was once made under conditions like these, but it is so no longer. When a corporation deals with a multitude of independent workmen, the corporation is free, but the workmen are, practically, not so. The open alternative is the test of economic liberty. (1887, 58)

This commentary hints at Commons's later analysis of transactions and the compulsion or power elements in various contracting relationships (discussed by Rutherford, this volume).

Following the success of combinations of employers (into monopolists, trusts, and the like), labor had also continued its movement into combinations (trade unions). In circumstances where both labor and capital consisted of pooled or organized parties, conditions began to become more equal between the two parties. In this case it appeared to some that the wage contract became merely a "process of crude force" between two giants. Not quite so, Clark argued; the higgling of crude force was also a crude appeal to equity:

> Every great strike or lockout is, in modern times, an appeal to public opinion. The old rule for strikes was that those made on a rising market sometimes succeed; while those against a falling market always fail. It is now necessary to add that great strikes, sustained by a public sense of right, often succeed; while those condemned by that sentiment usually fail. (1887, 58)

As Clark envisaged, the process of crude force accompanied by appeals to the public for justice were gradually replaced by legal codes to ensure the just division of the gains from employer/employee exchange. After further concentration of capital and labor, Clark predicted, the higgling of crude force would be replaced with an alternative method of division of the fruits of industry, namely arbitration:

> If the aggregation of each [capital and labour] were complete there would be no competition. There would be a bargain-making process on a vast scale; the "higgling of the market" would take the form of strikes and lockouts; production would be checked, and social relations would become chaotic. From this condition arbitration would be the natural and inevitable outcome. (1886b, 534)

Arbitration would replace the unjust outcome which resulted from any situation where force prevailed, with a just outcome based on an outside mediator or judge.

The usefulness of arbitration was also discussed by contemporary British economists. Edgeworth advocated arbitration as an "ethical method," an appeal to justice replacing either force or custom, to deal with the division of gains in situations of individual, or monopolistic, exchange.[11] Jevons too made room for arbitration as the solution to the indeterminacy of such situations, when individuals' relative bargaining skills or feelings of justice failed to bring them to a solution.[12] Neither

---

11. "For the required basis of arbitration between economical contractors is evidently *some* settlement; and the utilitarian settlement may be selected, in the absence of any other principle of selection, in virtue of its moral peculiarities: its satisfying the sympathy (such as it is) of each with all, the sense of justice and utilitarian equity" (Edgeworth 1881, 53–54).

12. Although Jevons's treatment of exchange is largely mechanical, and his two parties in exchange are generally to be regarded as two typical individuals in the market situation, he does briefly address the same ground as Clark in a passage on "failure of the equations of exchange," where the "transaction must be settled upon other than strictly economic grounds. The result

of these economists gave much room to discussing the general problem of individual behavioral codes in dealing with exchange outcomes. Edgeworth's discussion remained tied to utilitarian outcomes; Jevons's individuals were hardly individuals at all: as Edgeworth expressed it, they were "individuals clothed with the properties of a market" ([1881] 1932, 31). Unlike Clark, Edgeworth and Jevons were not particularly concerned with the morals of their economic actors.

5. The Rescue of Moral Economic Man

The development of laws of exchange behavior to provide justice in exchange was for the good of both the economy and society. It was also important for employers' moral health. To see why this is so, we need to return to the essential tension between self-interest and moral sense that I pointed out in Clark's account of economic man. This tension seemed to him to be reflected in the behavior of many businessmen who operated under two different codes: one in their business life, in which they were heartless and exploitative and cut the corners of the law; and one in their private life, in which they were morally upright, kind, and good family men. The personal consequences for the modern businessman were stern: "the inexorable law [of competition] that developed in him a dual morality, and made it harder than for a camel to pass through the needle's eye, for a man of the market to obey therein the laws of Christ's kingdom" (Clark 1887, 56).

The terms of the debate on this question were set by Henry Carter Adams in an influential paper in 1887, where he argued that competition and self-interest created a dangerous tendency to level downwards (a sort of lowest common denominator problem). Employers would be driven to pay the lowest wages and operate at the worst conditions for employees, because any employer who set better conditions would find himself taking losses and go out of business. Thus the businessman in the situation of "unguarded competition tends to lower the moral sense of a business community," for it is the "men of the lowest character"

---

of the bargain will greatly depend upon the comparative amount of knowledge of each other's position and needs which either bargainer may possess . . . the art of bargaining. . . . The disposition and force of character of the parties, their comparative persistency, their adroitness and experience in business, or it may be feelings of justice or of kindliness, will also influence the decision. These are motives more or less extraneous to a theory of economics, and yet they appear necessary considerations in this problem. It may be that indeterminate bargains of this kind are best arranged by an arbitrator or third party" ([1871] 1970, 159).

who end up setting the "moral tone to the entire business community" (Adams [1887] 1954, 90, 93). Adams advocated that the state should intervene with legislation to set the "plane of competitive action" so that competition could be continued at some level above that which exploited the workforce or customers.[13]

Clark quoted Adams but did not go along with this analysis. For Clark, men's moral elements vying with their self-interest must necessarily affect their business principles. These moral elements were as much a part of producing as of exchanging: "The human activity which produces wealth is an activity of the entire man, physical, mental, and moral, and there is no industrial product so simple and so purely material that these three elements of the human agency are not represented in it" (Clark 1877a, 178). The "moral" element, as he interpreted it, comes out for example in the truthfulness of a writer's work or in the reliability of a laborer's product. Just like other characteristics, he argued, the "moral" qualities which produce such attributes in products are rewarded in the value in exchange: for example, products which have greater reliability command a premium in the market.[14]

Clark further believed that in the same way that "moral qualities" add to the worth of goods produced, employers who did not exploit their workforce gained from their moral behavior; hence less moral employers in the same market were forced to adopt the same behavior by competition, whether they wanted to or not:[15]

There is a certain grade of honesty, and a certain degree of humanity which are good commercial policy. The man who gauges his business

13. Adams's arguments have a twentieth-century equivalent in "level playing-fields" discussion in international trade negotiations, where a rhetoric of fairness and justice is used directly.

14. Of course, as twentieth-century economists we would no longer interpret product reliability as the outcome of a moral quality in the makers. When a product seems extra reliable—for example, as with Japanese versus American cars—we attribute it to a rational production decision or a success of management (although we recognize, with Clark, that such products may command a premium). The "lemon" has a more recognizable place in the history of economics, and the analysis of its frequency owes something to moral arguments, or at least to the chances of being caught for wrongdoing. A consumer finding rotten peaches hidden at the bottom of a basket makes, on the other hand, judgments on the moral character of the seller, perhaps because such an exchange is still a personal one.

15. This too might strike the twentieth-century economist as strange. Yet there have been employers in both the nineteenth and twentieth centuries who have found it profitable to be "good" to their workforce (such experience is explored in the management literature). And in Clark's day, we find advertisements of the time proclaiming moral superiority of a business on the basis of employment conditions in the workshops.

morality by exactly this standard will get, thereby, a certain advantage over competitors. He can undersell them by being good enough and not too good to win the maximum success. (1886b, 535)

He envisaged there would be a leveling up and down; the profitable moral level for the marketplace was neither rock bottom nor sky high:

> The man who dilutes his moral character with exactly the right proportion of commercial shrewdness will cause his rivals, be they worse or better than he, to strive to attain the same condition. The market has its moral level, and competition presses men from both directions towards it. (535)

Nevertheless the "moral level of the market" was still "far below the standard fixed by nearly every conscience" (535).

So, Clark's preferred route to ensure the moral health of employers was from the process of arbitration. He looked forward to the time when tribunals would provide for justice in exchange, releasing men from the essential tension between self-interest and moral worth which beset them under free-for-all competition, and even under modified competition in the new regime of monopolies: "The arbitrative system, when fully developed, will place no man where he can say that he is compelled to sink either his fortune or his character. Business life will level men morally upward." (536). In other words, under arbitration there would be no excuse at all for immorality in employers. While Adams argued for the paternalistic state to set the standards for the conduct of business as a way of leveling men upwards, Clark argued that arbitration would free employers to level themselves upwards above the market level.

6. Changing Exchange, Changing Economics

Although they diverged on detail, Clark and Adams shared much the same approach to economic problems of the day. Along with a group of like-minded colleagues, they were concerned with a wholesale reform of economic science. The story of how these young turks founded the American Economic Association (AEA) in the 1880s is already well told (see Coats 1960; Dorfman 1949), though the central role of the moral/ethical element in their economic program is sometimes overlooked.[16]

---

16. The best study on this front still seems to be that by Everett (1946), who makes a determined and rather successful effort to interrelate the religious and social ideas of three

But there is another point which has not so much been overlooked, as that its significance has not been fully understood, and which should be integrated into that story.

My analysis of Clark's views on higgling have shown us a rather modern thinker in his understanding of the interrelations between science (both its methods and ideas), the social values of scientists, and the object of their study. Clark's view that changing economies interact with changing conventions of economic behavior suggests that these mutually construct each other as they change. Economics must therefore also be reconstructed anew to understand and explain these changes. We saw how this reconstruction worked in the discussion of work-wage exchange and the changing views of economists (in section 4). So, although we can interpret the AEA as the outcome of various contingencies—such as the German historicist training of a number of the younger generation, or as a Kuhnian-type revolution of the younger ideas against the older conservatism, or as a reflection of the Christian socialist views of the younger group, or as a watershed in the professionalization process—we can also see the total package of ideas, methods, and beliefs which lay behind the founding of the AEA as the outcome of that ongoing mutual reconstruction between economic reality, economic behavior, and economic science. Clark understood this mutual constructivism and played his part in it.[17]

Here, too, moral and social commitments cannot be neglected. The reconstruction of economics involved not only theory and methods but also the social values of the scientists. This can be seen in the following passage, which outlines Clark's attitude toward the laissez-faire economics appropriate to the past, but no longer suitable for the present-day economy:

> Economic science is changing because practical methods of industry are doing so; theory waits upon practice. The change involves a scien-

---

economists: Clark, Ely, and Patten. The extent of the link between church institutions and economics is discussed in May's *Protestant Churches and Industrial America* (1949), where he went so far as to assert that "the movement represented by the Association [AEA] was at once an effect and a cause of the new social tendencies in Christianity" (138).

17. For further discussion of the way the changing environment of this period led to changes in ideas within economics see Morgan 1993 and Parrini and Sklar 1983. For an account of how these realities interacted with the professionalization of economics see Furner 1975. For a more conventional but much more comprehensive account of the changing economic views of this period see Ross 1991.

tific recognition of moral forces in business life because the industrial revolution is calling those forces into active exercise; . . . at a time when such interference was working mischief the doctrine of laissez faire originated; and economic science spent its energy in warning philanthropic agencies, public and private, to keep wholly out of the industrial field. Now that moral agencies are clearly needed and are actively at work in this domain, the science is obliged to change its attitude and to formulate, if it can, the principles that should govern their action. A divorcement of ethics and economics characterized the theories of the past; and it was based on apparent separation between them in practical life. The present movement is restoring the union in theory and practice. (1887, 50)

Here we see, most clearly, Clark's understanding of the interrelationships between the economy, economics, and the values of the economic scientists.

Perhaps no group in the history of economics has ever been so ambitious as to aim at a reconstruction, at one and the same time, of the methods of economic analysis, the characterization of economic man, the main constructs of economic theory, and the policy responses of economists, together with the reintegration of ethics into economics (see Ely 1884). But these economists lived in momentous times. This was, after all, the time and place of drastic economic change known to economic historians as the "second industrial revolution." In the event, it was not the group that formed AEA who seemed, to later scholars, to have succeeded in breaking the mold of conventional economics, but the more eccentric group of scholars who made up the American Institutionalists. The "early Clark" (1870s and 1880s) whose work I have discussed here is usually portrayed as a confused young man, a mixture of socially minded Christian and socialistically minded, German-trained, historical economist. But if we abstract just a little from the constraints of language and expression imposed by those two positions,[18] what we are left with looks remarkably like an early American institutionalist.[19]

Clark's work on higgling and exchange, both in and out of the market,

18. This is, I believe, an admissible abstraction, since God figures as an inspiration rather than an essential element in his economic analysis, and the socialism is reformist and statist rather than radical. See, for example, Clark 1879b, on his socialism; 1887, on his Christianity.

19. Though the early Clark may not have all the characteristics that Mayhew (1987) demands of a budding "old" institutionalist, he seems to have some version of all four of the requirements.

was concerned with the economic behavior patterns of his day, the habits of thought and action, how they had arisen, how they evolved, and the legal structures which finally developed from them. His detailed concern for the development of the codes of behavior appropriate for exchange, and the interrelations between economic change and habitual behavior in exchange, bears the classic hallmarks of American institutionalist economics. He appears to be a forerunner of Veblen and Commons both in approach and in his views on exchange and treatment of it. Veblen took Clark's commentary on predatory relations much further in his work on business ethics and behavior in exchange. Commons, analyzing the power relations of exchange in the unit of transaction, took this aspect of Clark's analysis to much greater length and depth. Both these directions can be followed up in Malcolm Rutherford's essay, this volume. Interestingly, Clark might also be linked in his thinking on ethical elements to the somewhat later commentaries of Knight's alternative (nonscientific, non-neoclassical) economics, as discussed in Ross Emmett's paper, this volume.[20]

Conclusion

The analysis above suggests that Clark's concern in analyzing exchange behavior centered on the justice of division in exchange (following up an ancient tradition discussed by Lowry, this volume). Clark's moral element came into play not to brand behavior right or wrong, or to exhort sympathy and charity for the underdog, but to understand how mutual advantage in exchange might be maintained whatever the context. When economic conditions failed to ensure justice, the moral economy of exchange was safeguarded by institutions that evolved out of individual, and thence shared, moral codes of behavior.

I thank participants at the Duke "higgling" conference (March 1993) and at the York "Hermes" conference (April 1993, in Toronto), for their comments and critical questions during initial presentations of this paper. Bob Coats, Neil De Marchi, and Ross Emmett were kind enough to comment on the written draft, and I thank them especially, without, of course, holding them responsible for the final outcome. The research was funded by a grant from the Suntory-Toyota Centre for Economics and

20. Both Veblen and Knight had personal connections with Clark. Veblen was taught by Clark, and Knight credited the influence of Clark in the development of his thesis. (Knight studied Veblen's works in a study group in Chicago in the later part of the 1910s; an interesting account of this appears in Neill 1972.)

Related Disciplines (STICERD) at the London School of Economics and by further help from the LSE Staff Research Fund.

References

Adams, Henry Carter. [1887] 1954. The Relation of the State to Industrial Action *and Economics and Jurisprudence: Two Essays by Henry Carter Adams, edited and with an introductory essay and notes by Joseph Dorfman.* New York: Columbia University Press.

Clark, John Bates. 1877a. The New Philosophy of Wealth. *The New Englander* 138 (January): 170–86.

———. 1877b. Unrecognized Forces in Political Economy. *The New Englander* 141 (October): 710–24.

———. 1878. How to Deal with Communism. *The New Englander* 145 (July): 533–42.

———. 1879a. Business Ethics, Past and Present. *The New Englander* 149 (March): 157–68.

———. 1879b. The Nature and Progress of True Socialism. *The New Englander* 151 (July): 565–81.

———. 1883. Recent Theories of Wages. *The New Englander* 174 (May): 354–64.

———. 1886a. *The Philosophy of Wealth.* New York: Macmillan.

———. 1886b. The Moral Outcome of Labor Troubles. *The New Englander and Yale Review* 195 (June): 533–36.

———. 1887. Christianity and Modern Economics. *The New Englander and Yale Review* 198 (July): 50–59.

———. 1890. The Trust: A New Agent for Doing Old Work: Or, Freedom Doing the Work of Monopoly. *The New Englander and Yale Review* 240 (March): 223–30.

———. 1894. The Modern Appeal to Legal Forces in Economic Life. *Publications of the American Economic Association* (papers read at the seventh annual meeting), 9:9–30.

———. 1899. *The Distribution of Wealth.* New York: Macmillan.

———. 1901. *The Control of Trusts.* New York: Macmillan. 2d ed., with J. M. Clark, 1912.

———. 1904. *The Problem of Monopoly.* New York: Macmillan.

Coats, A. W. 1960. The First Two Decades of the American Economic Association. *American Economic Review* 50:555–74.

———. n.d. Henry Carter Adams. Unpublished manuscript.

Daston, Lorraine J. 1992. The Moral Economy of Science. Working paper (forthcoming, *Osiris*).

Dorfman, Joseph. 1949. *The Economic Mind in American Civilization, 1865–1918.* Vol. 3. New York: Viking.

Edgeworth, Francis Y. 1881. *Mathematical Psychics.* London: Kegan Paul.

Ely, Richard T. 1884. *The Past and Present of Political Economy.* Johns Hopkins University Studies in History and Political Science, ser. 2, 3. Baltimore: The Johns Hopkins University.

Emmett, Ross B. 1994. Maximizers versus Good Sports: Frank Knight's Curious Understanding of Exchange Behavior. In *Higgling: Transactors and Their Markets in the History of Economics,* edited by Neil De Marchi and Mary S. Morgan. *HOPE* 26, special issue. Durham: Duke University Press.

Everett, John Rutherford. 1946. *Religion in Economics: A Study of John Bates Clark, Richard T. Ely, Simon N. Patten.* New York: King's Crown Press.

Fine, Sidney. 1957. *Laissez Faire and the General-Welfare State.* Ann Arbor: University of Michigan Press.

Frank, Robert, Thomas Gilovich, and Dennis Regan. 1993. Does Studying Economics Inhibit Co-operation? *Journal of Economic Perspectives* 7.2 (Spring): 159–71.

Furner, Mary O. 1975. *Advocacy and Objectivity.* Lexington: University Press of Kentucky.

Hadley, Arthur Twining. 1906. *Standards of Public Morality.* John S. Kennedy Lectures for 1906. New York: Macmillan, 1907.

Henry, John F. 1982. The Transformation of John Bates Clark: An Essay in Interpretation. *HOPE* 14.2:166–77.

———. 1983. John Bates Clark and the Marginal Product: An Historical Inquiry into the Origins of Value-Free Economic Theory. *HOPE* 15.3:375–89.

Jevons, William Stanley. [1871] 1970. *The Theory of Political Economy.* Edited by R. D. Collison Black. Harmondsworth: Penguin.

Knight, Frank H. 1923. The Ethics of Competition. *Quarterly Journal of Economics* 37:579–624.

Leonard, Robert. 1994. Laboratory Strife: Higgling as Experimental Science in Economics and Social Psychology In *Higgling: Transactors and Their Markets in the History of Economics,* edited by Neil De Marchi and Mary S. Morgan. *HOPE* 26, special issue. Durham: Duke University Press.

Lerner, Max. 1963. The Triumph of Laissez-Faire. In *Paths of American Thought,* edited by A. M. Schlesinger, Jr., and M. White. Boston: Houghton Mifflin.

Lowry, S. Todd. 1994. The Market as a Distributive and Allocative System: Its Legal, Ethical, and Analytical Evolution. In *Higgling: Transactors and Their Markets in the History of Economics,* edited by Neil De Marchi and Mary S. Morgan. *HOPE* 26, special issue. Durham: Duke University Press.

May, Henry F. 1949. *Protestant Churches and Industrial America.* New York: Harper Torchbooks.

Mayhew, Anne. 1987. The Beginnings of Institutionalism. *Journal of Economic Issues* 21:971–98.

Mill, John Stuart. 1848. *Principles of Political Economy.* London: John W. Parker.

Morgan, Mary S. 1993. Competing Views of "Competition" in Late Nineteenth-Century American Economics. *HOPE* 25.4:563–604.

Neill, Robin. 1972. *A New Theory of Value: The Canadian Economics of H. A. Innis.* Toronto: University of Toronto Press.

Parrini, C. P., and M. J. Sklar. 1983. New Thinking about the Market, 1896–1904: Some American Economists on Investment and the Theory of Surplus Capital. *Journal of Economic History* 42:559–78.

Parry, Jonathan P., and Maurice Bloch. 1989. *Money and the Morality of Exchange*. Cambridge: Cambridge University Pres.

Ross, Dorothy. 1991. *The Origins of American Social Science*. New York: Cambridge University Press.

Rutherford, Malcolm. 1994. Predatory Practices or Reasonable Values? American Institutionalists on the Nature of Market Transactions. In *Higgling: Transactors and Their Markets in the History of Economics*, edited by Neil De Marchi and Mary S. Morgan. *HOPE* 26, special issue. Durham: Duke University Press.

Thompson, E. P. 1971. The Moral Economy of the English Crowd in the Eighteenth Century. *Past and Present* 50 (February): 76–136.

Veblen, Thorstein Bunde. 1904. *The Theory of Business Enterprise*. New York: Scribner's. Reprinted, New York: Augustus M. Kelley, 1965.

Zajac, Edward E. 1985. Perceived Economic Justice: The Example of Public Utility Regulation. In *Cost Allocation*, edited by H. Peyton Young. New York: Elsevier Science.

Predatory Practices or Reasonable Values? American Institutionalists on the Nature of Market Transactions

Malcolm Rutherford

With only slight exaggeration, the orthodox conceptualization of market transactions can be characterized as one that visualizes informed and rational individuals, possessed of exogenously determined tastes, preferences, and endowments, willingly engaging in mutually beneficial exchanges.[1] This conception of the transaction is crucial to the usual welfare conclusions concerning market exchange, but despite this neither the institutional environment within which markets operate nor the way in which agreements to transact are actually reached is given close attention. Traditional neoclassical analysis disregards the broader institutional context, assumes the existence of an (unanalyzed) market, concentrates on equilibrium states at the level of this market, and slides over the difficulties involved in dealing with how the equilibrium is reached. Although various market adjustment stories are told, these are commonly admitted to be highly artificial. The obvious example is the Walrasian story of the auctioneer, but even more recent search theory stories leave much to be desired. In both cases, the real institutions that pattern market interactions are notable only by their absence.

In contrast, American institutionalists have always been concerned exactly with the institutions of a market economy, particularly with the links between markets and other economic and social institutions, the manner in which the growth of markets and associated institutions have

---

1. It might be complained that this comment ignores recent work that assumes asymmetric information. It is, however, the case that such work still assumes that all parties are aware of the asymmetries and that the market price will reflect the risks and uncertainties involved.

brought about alterations in the nature of the economic activity under-taken, and the extent to which market transactions are subject to manipu-lation and the exercise of power. In some cases this has led to a focus on criticizing what are seen as the socially undesirable aspects of mar-ket exchange, but in others it has resulted in attempts to analyze more closely the process of transacting and the ways in which legal, economic, and persuasive power is both used and constrained. The best examples of these different approaches are to be found in the work of Thorstein Veblen and John R. Commons respectively.[2] Commons provides by far the more detailed analysis of the processes that define and control the higgling of transactors, but important aspects of his thinking were de-veloped from (and in some instances in reaction to) Veblen's arguments. I discuss the work of each writer in turn.

Before proceeding to this it is, however, worth briefly outlining some of the intellectual background to the institutionalism of Veblen and Com-mons. Both men began to develop their thinking in the 1890s, a time when the beneficence of the market was being widely questioned. The so-called New School group, including R. T. Ely, H. C. Adams, and J. B. Clark, generated an array of criticisms of the market and mar-ket outcomes. Of most concern were labor problems, the formation of monopolies and trusts, resource depletion, poor health and safety stan-dards, and a variety of sharp business practices. Many of these issues were expressed in terms of the "ethical level of competition," Adams in particular arguing that competition tends to force all competitors down to the ethical level of the least scrupulous. The remedial action proposed often involved both moral and legal elements, a commitment to Social Christianity being a feature common to many of these writers (Everett 1946). The influence of this group is most obvious in the case of Com-mons: he was something of a protégé of Ely's; early in his career he also displayed interest in the Social Gospel movement; and he continued to use the language of the "plane of competition" (Ramstad 1992). Veblen's work shows less in the way of any direct imprint, his approach being built around evolutionary ideas derived from other sources and his rhetoric much more cynical in nature, but the similarities in the general areas of concern, and occasionally in more specific points as well, are too close to ignore.[3]

2. Other institutionalists could also be discussed, but are omitted due to space constraints. Perhaps the most notable omission is that of G. Means and his administered price concept.

3. See Mary Morgan's paper on J. B. Clark, this volume.

Thorstein Veblen

Veblen's discussion of markets proceeds at several levels. At the most general level, he provides a critique of classical and neoclassical notions of market prices tending toward a "natural" or "normal" equilibrium state. According to Veblen, such notions are based on an ultimate theoretical postulate that may be stated as "in some sort a law of the conservation of energy," implying "an equivalence of expenditure and returns, an equilibrium of flux and reflux," so that it is assumed that "the product that results from any given industrial process or operation is, in some sense or in some unspecified respect, the equivalent of the expenditure of forces, or of the effort, or what not, that has gone into the process out of which the product emerges" (1901, 281). In contrast, Veblen's own basic postulate was that markets do not reflect a balancing of natural forces, but rather the operation of accepted business principles and practices. Conventional factors, in his analysis, determine the operation of markets, including the valuations placed on goods by consumers, the manner in which firms are operated, and the distribution of income, and call into question the usual connotations of efficiency. Social convention and salesmanship impact on consumption decisions, the utility function of consumers being far from a natural given, while the fact of intangible property (usually ignored in classical and neoclassical discussions of capital) and the possibilities of gain through financial manipulation and other forms of disruption remove any necessary equivalence between physical and financial capital and between productive effort and pecuniary reward (1899, 1901, 1908). Veblen also links business principles to business cycles and the formation of monopolies (1904). In his system these phenomena are not the result of disturbing causes, causes that disturb a natural or normal market equilibrium that would otherwise exist, but are an integral part of the functioning of a business system.

Veblen also provides a historical discussion involving a distinction between the circumstances prior to the introduction of "modern" machine technologies that gave rise to large-scale production and those that have come to exist since. With larger scales of production came a vast extension and integration of markets, and with the growth of markets came greater freedom of contract, the emancipation of property rights from "restrictions of a non-pecuniary character" (1904, 69), and the spread of pecuniary habits of thought. These developments also resulted in production and sale being seen as a source of profit on investment instead of a direct (occupational) source of livelihood, an increasing division of labor between industrial and purely pecuniary occupations, and the loss of personal contact between the producer and his customers.

These factors Veblen regarded as of the utmost importance in understanding the nature of markets and market transactions. First, the impersonalization of markets had resulted in a weakening of moral constraints:

> In the older days, when handicraft was the rule of the industrial system, the personal contact between the producer and his customer was somewhat close and lasting. Under these circumstances the factor of personal esteem and disesteem had a considerable play in controlling the purveyors of goods and services. . . . Under modern circumstances, where industry is carried on on a large scale, the discretionary head of an industrial enterprise is commonly removed from all personal contact with the body of customers. . . . The mitigating effect which personal contact may have in dealings between man and man is therefore in great measure eliminated. (1904, 51–53)

According to Veblen, this left business enterprise free to pursue its goals largely untroubled by ethical considerations of equity or honesty: "One can with an easier conscience and with less of a sense of meanness take advantage of the necessities of people whom one knows only as an indiscriminate aggregate of consumers" (53)—a point very close to that made by New School writers.

Secondly, the specialization of occupations had resulted in those in control of business enterprise becoming focused exclusively on matters of financial gain. Their attention therefore centers on "the main chance," and their activities "begin and end within what may broadly be called 'the higgling of the market' " (1901, 294). Thus, just as Lester Ward described business strategy as a highly advanced form of cunning in which the "victim is outwitted" (Ward 1892, 84),[4] so Veblen used the term "predation" and thought of the arts of business as those of "bargaining, effrontery, salesmanship, [and] make-believe" (Veblen 1923, 107). Modern business is a competitive strategic game played against other businesspeople (and consumers),[5] the sole object of which is pecuniary

---

4. Veblen quotes this passage from Ward in a footnote dealing with advertising. See Veblen 1904, 55–57.

5. Veblen also used the language of "sportsmanship" to describe aspects of predatory behavior. Veblen's notion of sportsmanship, however, is limited to the desire to win a competitive

gain. These gains are often related more to the manipulation of markets than to productive effort. Much business activity involves "obstructing, retarding or dislocating" the smooth operation of the system in order to get the better of some rival. Business success means "getting the best of the bargain," and the "highest achievement in business is the nearest approach to getting something for nothing" (1919, 92–93).

The detailed implications of this view of business are to be found in Veblen's discussions of advertising, the operation of financial markets, and the creation of monopoly. These issues relate to what he saw as the "waste" and "sabotage" created by the system and the generation of intangible assets (goodwill); they represent the division between making money and making goods that he thought was a particular characteristic of developed business institutions.

In his analysis of advertising and salesmanship Veblen observed that, originally, the concept of goodwill referred to business or market advantages that arose spontaneously out of a concern's reputation for upright dealing with its customers (1919, 363, 366). Modern businesses, however, sought to *create* similar market advantages through systematic advertising and the creation of monopoly power. He argued that the "great end of consistent advertising is to establish such differential monopolies resting on popular conviction" (1904, 55). However, the conviction in question may be based more on appearance than on actual performance. Veblen did not deny that some advertising carried useful information, but for the most part he thought of advertising as the "organized fabrication of popular convictions," a point he illustrated with the example of medically worthless patent medicines (1904, 56–57; see also Black 1992).[6] Furthermore, he noted that almost all advertising was competitive in nature, aiming either to divert customers "from one channel to another channel of the same general class" or to divert expenditure from one class to another (57–58). Its necessity, then, is not due to any social benefit that is generated, or even to any benefit that accrues to all advertisers, but to the fact that any concern that does not advertise will lose custom to those that do. From a social point of view, sales effort is not productive, although it is paid for, but constitutes waste.

---

game and does not appear to contain the concept of the "good sport" as used by Frank Knight. See Veblen 1899 and Ross Emmett's paper, this volume.

6. Veblen also discussed the extensive use of packaging, particularly in the selling of health and beauty aids (1923, 300–302).

Veblen found even more serious consequences of the extension of markets and the domination of pecuniary modes of thought in the case of financial markets.[7] The development of loan credit and markets in "vendible capital" gave rise to business cycles, excess capacity, the possibility of financial gain purely through the buying and selling of corporation securities, and ultimately monopoly. He argues that the competitive profit seeking of businessmen together with the ability of firms to borrow or sell securities on the basis of expected future earnings leads to periodic bouts of inflation followed by periods of deflation (1904, 186–209). When combined with technological change of a type that provides for profitable investment opportunities even when older plants are still suffering from weak earnings, the result can be persistently low profits for most firms, combined with excess capacity (254–58).

On top of this, incentives are created for the manipulation of stock prices. Firms capitalize on the basis of their earning capacity, and the "nucleus" of this capitalization "is not the cost of the plant, but the concern's good-will" (1904, 138). The total capitalization will consist of some mix of common stock and preferred stock, but voting rights are limited to the common stockholders, and effective control only to the larger of these. Thus "preferred stock is, practically, a device for placing the property it represents in perpetual trust with the holders of the common stock" (146). The holders of debentures are in a similar position. The crucial points here are that the value of a corporation's stock fluctuates in the market on the basis of how outsiders appraise the firm's future earning potential, and that such fluctuations in value fall most heavily on the common stock. The result is to give those who control the firm an interest that may diverge from that of other stockholders, or from that of the firm as a going concern. This interest in stock market gains expresses itself in insider dealing, and in the deliberate creation of misleading impressions and dissemination of false information (156). Insiders gain at the expense of outsiders and, on occasion, of the longer-term viability of the firm that is the subject of the manipulation:

> The ready vendibility of corporate capital has in great measure dissociated the business interest of the directorate from that of the corporation whose affairs they direct and whose business policy they

7. His thinking on financial markets and the way his arguments undermine the conception of competition leading to a long-period equilibrium in which firms are making normal returns were discussed in the conference version of Michael Lawlor's paper.

dictate, and has led them to centre their endeavors upon the discrepancy between the actual and the putative earning-capacity rather than upon the permanent efficiency of the concern. (159)

However, the object of these manipulations lies not only in short-term capital gains but also in "making or marring various movements of coalition or reorganization" (161). In Veblen's work, the attempt to create monopolies is encouraged by the low profits and excess capacity that emerge under competitive conditions. To overcome these problems stock prices are manipulated with "a view to buying and selling in such a manner as to gain control of certain lines of securities" (161). The ultimate aim of this activity is to gain market power relative to one's rivals, and to raise prices to more profitable levels. This involves not only the restriction of output in a conventional sense but the use of market position to damage competitors and, if possible, to exercise control over the pace of new technological innovation. Nevertheless, "in all bargaining, in all transactions of merchandising and price-making, the limitation of merchantable supply is of the essence of the case" (1923, 293). Once well established, the additional earning capacity generated by monopoly power is also treated as a form of goodwill and will normally be capitalized in the reorganized concern's issue of securities to produce a flow of "free income" (1919, 63–84).

Veblen called this restriction of output and general "dislocation" of the system by business strategy "sabotage," thereby indicating the sacrificing of industrial possibilities to pecuniary opportunities. He did not restrict the concept to business enterprises but also applied the term to the withdrawal of effort practiced by labor unions in pursuit of higher wages. This he saw as an attempt to generate a flow of free income through the exercise of monopoly power, similar in nature to business monopoly. Thus "the A. F. of L. is a business organization with a vested interest of its own; for keeping up prices and keeping down the supply, quite after the fashion of management by the other Vested Interests" (1921, 89–90).

Veblen's discussions of sales promotion, financial manipulation, dislocation, and monopoly power all indicate that he saw market transactions as being far from the orthodox conception of exchange outlined above. Instead of performing a balancing of natural forces, markets are dynamic social institutions and a matter of higgling and business practice. The predatory competition between businesses produced the manipulation of consumer preferences by advertising, cycles, and excess capacity; the making of financial gains on the basis of inside, or even deliberately misleading, information; and the creation of market power with the intention of damaging rivals, restricting supply, and controlling prices. With all of this the concept of goodwill had gradually been transformed from something based on a reputation for honesty and fair dealing to something covering a wide range of monopoly and other advantages, regardless of origin or social consequence. Nevertheless, and despite his frequent use of terms such as "higgling," "bargaining," "negotiating," and "transacting," Veblen did not supply any detailed treatment of how transactions take place. That task was taken on by J. R. Commons, at least in part to subject Veblen's highly cynical view of markets to a more critical examination.

John R. Commons

One of the most novel aspects of Commons's approach to economics was his decision to make the transaction his basic unit of analysis, in place of the more orthodox units of individuals and commodities. He rejected both mechanical (equilibrium) and natural selection analogies, stressing the particular importance of the human will in shaping social and economic outcomes. In line with this he argued that the basic unit of analysis should be a "unit of activity." It must also "correlate" economics with law and ethics, and incorporate three salient characteristics of economic activity: conflict of interest, mutual dependence of interest, and the expectation of future activity of a similar type.[8] All of this he found to be possible by using the unit of the transaction. The transaction embodies the activity of negotiation and places that activity explicitly within the surrounding context of what he called working rules, or the set of laws, social conventions, and ethical norms (Commons 1934, 57–58). He rejected the usual notion of an "exchange" on the grounds that the orthodox use of the term tended to indicate an unproblematic physical exchange of goods, whereas economic transactions were more complex in nature:

8. He called these the "principles" of conflict, dependence, and order. For him a "principle" was a "similarity of cause, effect, or purpose," or similarity of actions, and more complex than a "concept" or similarity of attributes. The transaction he also classified as a "formula," defined as a construction designed to investigate a relation between the parts and the whole. See Commons 1934, 94–97.

Transactions . . . are not the "exchange of commodities," in the physical sense of "delivery," they are the alienation and acquisition, between individuals, of the *rights* of future ownership of physical things, as determined by the collective working rules of society. The *transfer of these rights* must therefore be negotiated between the parties concerned, according to the working rules of society, before labor can produce, or consumers can consume, or commodities be physically delivered to other persons. (58)

In approaching the analysis of transactions, Commons defines three basic types: bargaining, rationing, and managerial transactions. Bargaining transactions come closest to what is usually understood as market exchange, involving individuals of equal legal standing negotiating the transfer of rights of ownership by voluntary agreement, but all three types interrelate closely. For example, an agreement to sell arrived at through a bargaining transaction implies the production of goods or services through managerial transactions, and requires enforceable rules of exchange and collective agreements established through rationing transactions.

The details of Commons's discussion of bargaining transactions are best presented in terms of his own "formula" (1934, 59), displayed here in figure 1. His explanation of this formula runs as follows: B1 and S1 are negotiating, B2 and S2 are other competitors. Still other buyers and sellers may exist, but they are potential only. The total number of participants in the market is not defined, and the formula can apply to both competitive and imperfectly competitive conditions. B1 would like to buy at a price of $100 but might be persuaded to pay more; similarly S1 would like to sell at a price of $110 but might be persuaded to accept less. Each has an alternative in the form of the best offer received from other participants in the market. S1 knows B2 has offered $90, and B1 knows that S2 would sell at $120.[9] These alternatives provide the boundaries for their bargaining, what Commons called the "limits of coercion" (331). The transaction, if concluded, will settle somewhere within these limits, but exactly where will depend on the bargaining and persuasive powers of the two parties as well as on the legal and other rules that distinguish the point at which legitimate bargaining and persuasion be-

---

9. Commons set the prices in his formula wide apart for illustrative purposes. He was quite aware that the opening bid and offer prices may be closer together.

B1 $100   B2 $90

S1 $110   S2 $120

Figure 1 Formula of Bargaining Transaction—Legal Equals

comes illegitimate coercion. It should be noted that there is both the potential for mutual gain and a conflict of interest over the division of the gains. Moreover, Commons thought of markets as involving a sequence of transactions between different pairs of transactors, and he does not present the agreement between B1 and S1 (if achieved) as setting a market price. Once any bargain is concluded, the parties involved leave the market. Other parties will continue to negotiate, but on the basis of the alternatives now available to them and according to their own bargaining and persuasive powers.

In some of his presentations of bargaining transactions, Commons explicitly included a fifth party to the transaction in the form of the state (or the supreme court) that lays down and enforces the legal rules (1924, 68; 1950, 51). Even where this fifth party is not explicitly included, Commons makes it clear that the state is always present in the background, both as an enforcer of the rules of bargaining and in the very notion of the transaction as a transfer of *rights*. Thus, "the *individual* does not transfer ownership"; only the state "by operation of law as interpreted by the courts" transfers ownership (1934, 60).

In contrast to the above, rationing and managerial transactions both involve parties of unequal legal standing. These types of transaction take Commons's analysis beyond simple market exchange; but as indicated above, they are by no means unrelated to market activity. They may also include an area for bargaining and negotiation, something that is particularly true of certain types of rationing transaction.

Managerial transactions involve a legal superior issuing orders to an inferior with respect to the carrying out of a task. Commons generally used this concept in connection with the relationship between the manager and the workman, and the issuing of commands with respect to the carrying out of productive activity, but it has extensions to the functioning of hierarchical organizations generally. Within this managerial relationship (once established by whatever means), the role of negotiation is limited, but not necessarily absent. Commons talks of the managerial transaction involving a "certain amount of negotiation," arising "mainly from the modern freedom of labor," particularly the freedom of labor to quit without giving reason (1934, 67). There is also, and particularly in the case of labor, a close relationship between bargaining transactions and managerial transactions, and it is easy to muddle the boundaries between the two. Nevertheless the distinction can be kept clear if the "bargaining terms of employer and employee, or rather of owner and wage-earner, and the managerial terms of foreman or superintendent, and workman" are carefully distinguished (65).

Commons defines rationing transactions as a collective legal superior making decisions that dictate the distribution of costs and benefits among legal inferiors. They are "the negotiations of reaching an agreement among several participants who have the authority to apportion the benefits and burdens to members of a joint enterprise" (67–68). The decisions of a court concerning liability rules, or those of a legislature imposing taxes or tariffs, or those of a corporate board setting budgets, or collective agreements negotiated between the representatives of union and management, are all examples. One of the key roles for rationing transactions is the setting of the rules that surround transactions of a bargaining or managerial type. In transactions such as these, bargaining can occur in the form of bargaining between those authorized to make the decision or reach the agreement. Commons gives the examples of vote trading among legislators, and collective bargaining between the representatives of a union and an association of employers (68).[10] On the other hand, negotiation between the legally inferior parties and those that are legally superior is usually limited to the former representing their cases to the latter, as in the cases of "litigants before a judge or lobbyists meeting with a legislator" (Biddle 1990, 8). More than that may be bribery.

Transactions and Working Rules

As should be obvious from the above, the nature and content of each type of transaction (and the extent of the negotiating and bargaining involved) will depend critically on the set of working rules. At the most

10. It is tempting to classify collective bargaining as a bargaining transaction, but Commons's classification highlights the fact that collective bargaining involves the authorized representatives of each group negotiating terms on behalf of their group. As can be seen from his formula of bargaining transactions, collective bargaining differs from the bargaining transaction in a number of key respects. Nevertheless, problematic aspects remain.

general level the working rules "determine what each party to a transaction can, cannot, may, must or must not do" (Commons 1934, 81). These terms translate into the legal relations of rights, no-rights, privileges, and duties, and into the economic positions of security, exposure, liberty, and conformity (1932, 15). To have a legal right means that the party with that right can call on the power of the state "for security of expectations by imposing a duty of conformity" on others. On the other hand, to have no-right means that the party in question cannot call on the state for security of expectations and is therefore exposed to the economic consequences of the other parties having the liberty to do as they please. Not all working rules are laws; many are conventions and norms. Although these operate on individual behavior in a broadly similar way (defining what individuals can, cannot, may, must, or must not do), they lack the same degree of precision, are more open to variation in interpretation, and are not backed by the power of the state or a formal process of dispute resolution. Legal rules (and the courts that interpret the rules) thus have a special role in generating what Commons called the "correlation" of rights and duties, where each party has the same understanding of what is involved, and the rights (and no-rights) of one party exactly match the duties (and privileges) of the other (1924, 86–87).[11]

Working rules are, of course, variable over time. Changes to the working rules are prompted by changing economic circumstances and the new problems and conflicts that are provoked. They may emerge from acts of legislation or court decisions, or from the evolution of social conventions and norms, and such changes may have profound effects on transactions. A shift in working rules can increase or diminish the scope of managerial authority and alter the definition of what is a reasonable command, change the areas over which rationing authority can be exercised, or even the nature of the rationing process itself, or alter the way in which market power can be used in bargaining transactions. Of most interest here are Commons's discussions of bargaining and rationing transactions.

Concerning bargaining transactions, he discusses a number of interrelated issues that arise out of the conflicts of interest "latent in every

11. In *Legal Foundations* Commons uses a distinction between "unauthorized transactions" based on ethical norms and "authorized transactions" based on legal norms. In the case of the former, "the ethical concepts of rights and duty are there, and it is admitted that the resulting behavior is limited at points beyond which there is no-right and no-duty, but where those limits shall be placed is undecided" (1924, 86).

bargaining transaction," and the working rules that have been established in each case to "bring expectation of mutality and order out of the conflicts of interest" (1934, 62). These issues are those of equal or unequal opportunity, fair or unfair competition, and reasonable or unreasonable price.[12] In all of these cases the key point concerns the distinction between persuasion and coercion and the exercise of economic power in the form of bargaining power. In each case working rules have evolved that define the reasonable limits to the use of such power.

Commons illustrates the issue of equal or unequal opportunity utilizing his formula of bargaining transactions. The question arises if, for example, a seller discriminates between buyers by selling to B1 at $100 and to B2 at $90. Commons outlines the court decisions that between 1897 and 1901 resulted in the expansion of the common law meaning of discrimination. In the earlier view discrimination was associated only with the charging of some customer(s) a higher price than others without reasonable justification in terms of cost of service (extortion). The later view also included the charging of some customers a lower price, thereby giving them a competitive advantage. Thus the Supreme Court

> changed its view of the common law meaning of discrimination from what had evidently been the early meaning, which made no distinction between extortion and discrimination, to the more modern view which makes discrimination in itself illegal, regardless of whether there is extortion or not. . . . The evil sought to be corrected, under the later view, is the partiality or favoritism that gives a competitor free service or services at a *lower* price. The evil sought to be corrected under the earlier view was only that of charging an unreasonably *high* price, and the lower price charged to a competitor was not looked upon as discrimination in itself, but was admitted only as evidence tending to show that the higher price complained of was extortionate. (1934, 785)

This change in viewpoint Commons found to be related to changing business conditions, particularly the reduction in the numbers of competitors in many markets. Where "every person has an available alternative," discrimination is not an evil; but with the "stabilization" of markets,

---

12. He also discusses the issue of due process of law, the point in question being the lawful taking of property. The Supreme Court can overrule state legislatures, the federal Congress, and all executives in cases where these have deprived individuals or corporations of property or liberty without due process of law (1934, 63).

alternatives are few and discrimination becomes a problem for those discriminated against (787–88).

In a similar fashion Commons illustrates the issue of fair or unfair competition. A seller, S2, wants $120 for his product but claims that S1 is unfairly cutting prices to $110; or a buyer, B2, wants to pay only $90 and complains of a competitor, B1, offering $100 and bidding away supply. The issue is whether free competition in these cases is also fair competition, or whether one competitor is engaging in cutthroat or predatory pricing. Here the courts must decide which prices represent reasonable cost or reasonable value. The issue of reasonable value is one that resolves into that of determining the "reasonable limits to coercion" (1934, 332), and this, in turn, is largely a matter of the historical development of bargaining power.

Commons defines bargaining power as the ability to withhold. Bargaining power had gained significance with the development of collective organizations such as corporations and labor unions and with the concentration of markets. Again, in terms of the formula for bargaining transactions, one party may be able, through the exercise of bargaining power, to force the other to the limit of coercion. If S1 has much more bargaining power than B1, B1 may be coerced into paying $120. Obviously, the smaller the number of substitutes for S1, the greater the bargaining power S1 will possess relative to the buyers in the market. According to Commons, the initial reaction to this development was the introduction of antitrust laws, applied to both corporations and unions, in the attempt to eliminate bargaining power altogether. However, the prosecution of these laws was found to strike "at the very base of liberty and property—the right to withhold from others what they need but do not own" (343)—the ultimate result being the recognition by the courts of "reasonable restraint of trade" or the reasonable exercise of bargaining power.

> Thus, with the legal power to withhold commodities and services finally recognized in law, reasonable restraint of trade, according to the court's ideas of reasonableness but contrary to the anti-trust laws, comes to have a standing in law; and its equivalent bargaining power, or intangible property, comes to have a standing in economics. For restraint of trade *is* bargaining power, and reasonable restraint of trade is reasonable bargaining power. (344)

As this passage indicates, Commons linked bargaining power with the development of the concept of intangible property. In this, there are strong similarities with Veblen's idea of intangible property as "the present value of the future bargaining power of capitalists" (Commons 1934, 651), but important differences also. In particular, Commons saw the decisions of the courts as limiting bargaining power to levels considered reasonable. Thus, while in some cases the court's doctrine of reasonable value "sustained the contentions of the capitalists," in others it "greatly reduced the values contended for by the capitalists" (651).

Commons traced the development of property from corporeal property, to incorporeal property (debts), and finally to intangible property. Notions of intangible property grew from the concept of goodwill. Like Veblen, he argued that the original conception of goodwill was one of a business advantage based on good reputation and on the willingness of consumers to pay more for the outputs of a particular concern. Its particular characteristic is that it is measured by "the willing patronage of those who are free to choose" (1924, 273). Unlike Veblen, he argued that the courts had *not* subsequently extended the concept to market advantages based on monopoly power. Thus, although "monopolies, special privileges and economic oppressions" tried to "hide their transactions under the name of good-will" (273), the courts maintained the ideal of the willing buyer and willing seller in determining reasonable values.[13] In this they did not deny the right to withhold, but limited it to reasonable levels.

> The historical explanation of Veblen's cynical antithesis of business and industry is in the failure to trace out the evolution of business customs under the decisions of courts, as he had traced the technological customs. Such an investigation reveals the evolution of his "intangible property" which has consisted in making the distinction, not allowed by Veblen, between good-will and privilege, good-will being the reasonable exercise of the power to withhold, and privilege being the unreasonable exercise of that power. It is only in the analysis of a bargaining transaction that the economic foundation for this evolution can be found. (1934, 673)

What all of this implies is that bargaining transactions take place within an evolving context of law. The courts define and redefine the rights, no-rights, liberties, and exposures of the parties to transactions, and in so doing they define the agreements they will enforce and those

---

13. For further discussion of the differences between Veblen and Commons on the issue of goodwill see Endres 1985 and Black 1992.

that they will not. Not all agreements of purchase or sale will be approved by the courts, not if they involve discrimination, unfair competition, or the unreasonable (coercive) exercise of bargaining power. Although Commons's emphasis on the ideal of the willing buyer and willing seller in determining reasonable value might appear to make reasonable value equivalent to the outcome of free (unregulated) competition, such is not the case. For Commons, free competition could produce unreasonable outcomes due to the effects of discrimination, predation, or economic coercion. As interpreted by the courts, the ideal of the willing buyer and willing seller involved competition (in the form of alternatives, not monopoly), but *fair* competition, not free competition.[14] The courts adjust the law as new problems and conflicts arise and do so with social purposes and ethical standards in mind; it is the courts that through their judgments set the plane of competition.

On rationing transactions, Commons takes a broadly similar view. He wrote at length about the conflicts between monarch and nobles in English history that eventually resulted in the restriction of the power of the monarchy and the beginnings of a parliamentary system (1924, 100–104). He was also very much aware of the growth of private collective organizations and of the substitution of collective bargaining (a rationing transaction) for the individual-level bargaining of orthodox theory. Similar issues of conflict of interest and of reasonable equality of bargaining power arise, as with bargaining transactions. Again, according to Commons, the initial reaction of the courts was to attempt to eliminate the phenomenon by regarding unions as a conspiracy in restraint of trade. He studied the gradual movement of the law toward the recognition of the right of collective organizations such as labor unions to bargain on behalf of their members, the evolution of working rules that constrained the arbitrary power over the job of both unions and management, and saw as the outcome the creation of a new form of industrial government based on equality of collective bargaining power (1924, 283–312; 1950, 261–84). Indeed, Commons was himself intimately concerned with developing many of the working rules used to control collective bargaining and, in particular, the design of systems of labor mediation and arbitration.

In both types of transaction the courts define the area within which the

---

14. Commons's notions concerning the importance of concepts of fairness and reasonableness pick up themes also discussed in Todd Lowry's paper, this volume.

parties to a transaction can legitimately bargain, but the exact outcome of any particular negotiation will depend on the bargaining and persuasive power of the parties concerned. In other words, the working rules define the area for higgling.

Transactions and Negotiational Psychology

Commons coined the term "negotiational psychology" to describe the various factors that affect the outcome of particular negotiations between particular individuals. Each participant in a transaction is attempting to influence or modify the behavior of the other, and each "endeavors to change the dimensions of the economic values to be transferred" to their own advantage (1934, 91). This resolves itself into the "persuasions or coercions, the advertising and propaganda, of bargaining transactions; the commands and obedience of managerial transactions; or the arguments and pleadings of rationing transactions" (91). Negotiational psychologies vary with the circumstances, the objectives, and the role occupied by the transactor, but can also be affected by matters of personality.

Clearly, working rules and changes to the working rules will affect the exact nature of the negotiational psychology that can be brought to bear in any transaction. The evolution of the working rules surrounding bargaining transactions described above altered the ability to use certain types of economic coercion and bargaining power. Other rules have since come to surround the use of advertisements and persuasive power quite generally. Regulations concerning misleading advertising and high-pressure sales tactics are cases in point. In the case of rationing transactions, rules concerning lobbying and contributions to political campaigns, or rules of evidence or court procedure, or rules concerning collective bargaining have obvious importance in affecting the arguments and pleadings employed and the decisions or agreements reached. In the case of managerial transactions the ability of employees to quit without cause had affected the psychology of command and obedience. The "possibility that the worker might exercise his liberty was in the mind of the foreman or manager," and the "worker was aware of both his and his employer's liberty as he considered how to respond to commands" (Biddle 1990, 9).

The outcome of a transaction will, however, also depend on the specifics of the circumstances involved and not just on the working rules that apply generally to that class of transaction. The outcome of a bargaining transaction will depend on the alternatives available to each party (and hence their relative bargaining power) on that particular occasion. Furthermore, all transactions are based on expectations about the future, about other transactors, and about the consequences of various courses of action, and these expectations may vary from time to time. Commons does suggest, however, that if a transaction is of a routine and familiar nature, expectations will be based on a set of "habitual assumptions" derived from past experiences, and may be quite stable. On the other hand, a significant change in circumstances may cause a reassessment, particularly if the individual is of a sagacious type and perceives a strategic opportunity. Finally, what he called the "limiting factor," the key factor in bringing about the result desired in a particular transaction, may change from transaction to transaction (Commons 1934, 91, 683). Thus "it is not a rational state of society that determines action, it is a marvellously irrational and complex set of expectations that confronts the participants in transactions. And it is a situation that changes from day to day and century to century. Within this changing complexity and uncertain futurity they must act *now*" (683).

This picture is further complicated by Commons's argument that identical negotiating circumstances do not necessarily imply identical outcomes. Different negotiators may reach different solutions; the outcome of a transaction is not completely determined by the goals and circumstances of the actors but is also affected by personality and differential negotiational ability. His refusal to abstract too much from the complexities of real transactions is nowhere better displayed than in his rejection of the assumption of homogeneous agents: "Instead of enjoying the assumed equality of economic theory, the participants enjoy or suffer all the differences found among human beings, in their powers of inducing, and their responses to inducements and sanctions" (1934, 91). Commons often talks of the "passions and stupidities" of people and of the ability of others to act upon and manipulate them for their own purposes (752). This talent often expresses itself in the ability to identify correctly, and act upon in a timely way, the limiting factor in any transaction. Successful negotiators, salesmen, managers, union leaders, lawyers, and politicians all share the ability to control the limiting factor at the strategic moment and "determine the outcome of the complementary factors in the immediate or remote future" (91).

All of this detail means that Commons's discussion of transactions, while providing a conceptual framework and an outline of the various factors that might affect the outcome in any particular case, is far from being deterministic in nature. As Biddle has pointed out, "Commons never himself produced a theory of negotiational psychology, or a body of general propositions that answered the difficult questions of how humans would behave in transactional settings" (1990, 24). Nevertheless, Commons saw his formula of transactions as a vitally important investigative tool, capable of guiding the investigator to an understanding of the circumstances that shaped a given transaction or series of transactions in the past, and also to the understanding necessary for active involvement in those processes of institutional reform bearing on transactions.[15] He describes his own investigations of collective bargaining and his use of negotiational psychology in the following terms:

> I formulate certain "psychologies," the business man's psychology, the socialistic psychology, the trade union psychology. What do they want to do? Why do they differ in their psychologies? How can they negotiate an agreement under the circumstances? It is a "technique" of negotiational psychology which I investigate in successful arbitrators, mediators, business managers, executives, and in politicians. . . . Negotiational psychology can be seen actively at work and can be investigated in any bargaining, managerial, or rationing transaction. . . . I name it *objective* psychology instead of the subjective psychology of pleasure and pain. It is the psychology of language, of duress, coercion, persuasion, command, obedience, propaganda. It is the psychology of physical, economic, and moral "power," the truly "behavioristic" psychology of economics in preparing for the unknown future. (1950, 108–9)

Conclusion

Both Veblen and Commons rejected the standard conception of market transactions. Veblen directly attacked the physical analogy of a natural or normal equilibrium; Commons substituted his own basic unit of activity, the transaction, for the individuals and physical commodities of orthodox analysis. Both were concerned to emphasize the institutional character

---

15. Examples of the former use can be found in Commons et al., *Documentary History* (1910–11), and many chapters in *Legal Foundations* (1924). Descriptions of the latter use can be found especially in *Institutional Economics* (1934, 840–73), and part 4 of *Collective Action* (1950).

of markets, and the role of law, convention, and common practice in shaping market interactions. Both conceptualized markets as consisting of a process of higgling within certain rules of the game. Both were concerned with the way in which markets had been evolving, with the decay of traditional moral constraints on economic activity, the development of large and powerful organizations in the form of corporations and unions, and the broadening of the concept of intangible property. Nevertheless each provided a different vision.

Veblen's analysis concentrated on the impact of impersonal pecuniary motives and the predatory nature of business competition, specifically in terms of meretricious publicity, obstruction of traffic, and limitation of supply (1919, 100). These items produce a free income for businesses, an income unrelated to tangible productive performance and at the considerable expense of the community at large. Countervailing power, as in the case of unions, represented no improvement, and as, in Veblen's view, courts and governments tended to support prevailing vested interests, they could not be counted upon to undertake corrective action. Later institutionalists adopted a more reformist position, with government most often being seen as the principal agent of change, but other aspects of Veblen's thinking on market transactions have been retained and elaborated. Wesley Mitchell (1916) took over the distinction between making goods and making money, also related the profit seeking of business to instability and cycles, and expanded on Veblen's discussion of the impact of the extension of markets by arguing that the growth of markets and the use of money were major factors in *creating* that type of pecuniary calculation that lies at the heart of economic rationality. Echoes of Veblen can also be found in Galbraith's "revised sequence" (1971), and in recent work dealing with "corporate hegemony" (Dugger 1989).

Commons recognized many of the problems mentioned by Veblen and attached particular significance to Veblen's discussion of intangible property. Nevertheless, although he admitted that many of the abuses mentioned by Veblen had existed, he saw such problems and conflicts resulting in a gradual adaptation of the rules surrounding transactions. In the case of bargaining transactions, the courts had moved to adjust the rules concerning the use of coercive power in such a way as to retain the ideal of the willing buyer and willing seller. In this, economic power was not eliminated but rather was restricted to reasonable levels. The growth of collective organizations also meant the substitution of collective bargaining for individual bargaining, and Commons concerned himself with the rules relating to collective bargaining and the "thousands of decisions of disputes" that are "continually drawing the line between lawful and unlawful practices of associations" (1934, 770). As noted above, in Commons's system it is the courts that act to constrain the tactics used by businesses and other organizations to those they regard as reasonable.

Commons sought to replace what he saw as Veblen's "exploitation theory" of intangible property with his own vision of a "reasonable capitalism" (1934, 649), based on a rough equality of bargaining power in both individual and collective negotiations. In so doing he produced a discussion of economic transactions that in its understanding of the interrelationship between legal rules and economic activity, and awareness of the multiplicity of factors that combine to produce specific transactional outcomes, has no competitor within the American institutionalist tradition. Commons hoped that others would continue his work and that with the accumulation of case studies, practical experiments, and the continued refinement of his conceptual and theoretical apparatus, generalizations concerning behavior in transactional settings might be obtained. These generalizations would be provisional, based more on a "comparative study of cases" than on deductive inference, but could be used as guides to practical action (Biddle 1990, 24). Although most later institutionalists share Commons's pragmatic reformism, they have devoted little attention or developmental effort to his program of research. The high degree of particularity and lack of determinism may be partly responsible for this outcome, but Commons's research method also makes unusual demands, requiring a knowledge of economic theory and of economic and legal history, a willingness to undertake painstaking investigations and case studies, a deep interest in practical action, and considerable ability as a negotiator and conciliator. This is not a combination of attributes that many possess or are even encouraged to acquire.

References

Biddle, Jeff E. 1990. The Role of Negotiational Psychology in J. R. Commons's Proposed Reconstruction of Political Economy. *Review of Political Economy* 2 (March): 1–25.

Black, Robert A. 1992. Henry Sidgwick and the Institutionalists on Goodwill of the Firm. *HOPE* 24.1 (Spring): 79–116.

Commons, John R. 1924. *The Legal Foundations of Capitalism.* New York: Macmillan.

———. 1932. The Problem of Correlating Law, Economics and Ethics. *Wisconsin Law Review* 8 (December): 3–26.

———. 1934. *Institutional Economics.* New York: Macmillan.

———. 1950. *The Economics of Collective Action.* New York: Macmillan.

Commons, John R., et al., eds. 1910–11. *A Documentary History of American Industrial Society.* Cleveland: Arthur C. Clark.

Dugger, William M. 1989. *Corporate Hegemony.* Westport, Conn.: Greenwood Press.

Emmett, Ross B. 1994. Maximizers versus Good Sports: Frank Knight's Curious Understanding of Exchange Behavior. In *Higgling: Transactors and Their Markets in the History of Economics,* edited by Neil De Marchi and Mary S. Morgan. *HOPE* 26, special issue. Durham: Duke University Press.

Endres, A. M. 1985. Veblen and Commons on Goodwill: A Case of Theoretical Divergence. *HOPE* 17.4 (Winter): 637–49.

Everett, John R. 1946. *Religion in Economics: A Study of John Bates Clark, Richard T. Ely, Simon N. Patten.* New York: King's Crown Press.

Galbraith, John Kenneth. 1971. *The New Industrial State.* 2d ed. Boston: Houghton Mifflin.

Lawlor, Michael Syron. 1994. On the Historical Origin of Keynes's Financial Market Views. In *Higgling: Transactors and Their Markets in the History of Economics,* edited by Neil De Marchi and Mary S. Morgan. *HOPE* 26, special issue. Durham: Duke University Press.

Lowry, S. Todd. 1994. The Market as a Distributive and Allocative System: Its Legal, Ethical, and Analytical Evolution. In *Higgling: Transactors and Their Markets in the History of Economics,* edited by Neil De Marchi and Mary S. Morgan. *HOPE* 26, special issue. Durham: Duke University Press.

Mitchell, Wesley C. 1916. The Role of Money in Economic Theory. Reprinted in *The Backward Art of Spending Money,* 149–76. New York: Augustus M. Kelley, 1950.

Morgan, Mary S. 1994. Marketplace Morals and the American Economists: The Case of John Bates Clark. In *Higgling: Transactors and Their Markets in the History of Economics,* edited by Neil De Marchi and Mary S. Morgan. *HOPE* 26, special issue. Durham: Duke University Press.

Ramstad, Yngve. 1992. Commons, John Rogers (1862–1945). In *A Biographical Dictionary of Dissenting Economists,* edited by Philip Arestis and Malcolm Sawyer. Aldershot: Edward Elgar.

Veblen, Thorstein B. 1899. *The Theory of the Leisure Class.* New York: Macmillan.

———. 1901. Industrial and Pecuniary Employments. Reprinted in *The Place of Science in Modern Civilization,* 279–323. New York: Russell & Russell, 1961.

———. 1904. *The Theory of Business Enterprise.* New York: Scribner's.

————. 1908. Professor Clark's Economics. Reprinted in *The Place of Science in Modern Civilization*, 180–230. New York: Russell & Russell, 1961.

————. 1919. *The Vested Interests and the Common Man*, New York: B. W. Huebsch.

————. 1921. *The Engineers and the Price System*, New York: B. W. Huebsch.

————. 1923. *Absentee Ownership*, New York: B. W. Huebsch.

Ward, Lester F. 1892. The Psychologic Basis of Social Economics. *Annals of the American Academy of Political and Social Science* 3 (November): 72–90.

Maximizers versus Good Sports: Frank Knight's Curious Understanding of Exchange Behavior

Ross B. Emmett

> The Economic Man neither competes nor higgles . . . he treats other human beings as if they were slot machines.—Frank Knight (1947b, 80)

The notion of "economic man" [1] central to neoclassical economics was a troubling one for many late nineteenth- and early twentieth-century U.S. economists. Despite the emergence of marginalism as a theoretical tool during the 1870s, an established neoclassical tradition did not appear in the United States until well into the 1920s, after the publication of Frank Knight's *Risk, Uncertainty, and Profit*. [2] In between, criticisms of neo-classicism—in particular, criticisms of the assumption that markets are actually peopled by individuals who can realistically be characterized as rational utility-maximizers—seem to mark U.S. economic thought (the contributions of the later J. B. Clark and A. T. Hadley aside). Thorstein Veblen's work is the best known of these criticisms, but the ruminations

---

1. Despite my own preference for gender-balanced language, I believe it is appropriate to describe the maximizing individual constructed by neoclassical theory as "rational economic man" because, as Knight says in the passage from "The Ethics of Competition" quoted later on, the real person who comes closest to the ideal type of the maximizing individual is "the unencumbered male in the prime of life" ([1923] 1935b, 49). Although I have generally sought to use passages from Knight's work which do not use male-oriented language, when such language appears I have not changed it because of the close connection Knight sees between males and the ideal maximizer, and because male-oriented language was common in his time.

2. Two different accounts exist of U.S. economic thought between the introduction of marginalism in the 1870s and the 1920s. The first, most recently surveyed by Ross (1991), assumes that the rise of neoclassical economics happened simultaneously with the marginal revolution. The other, which I have followed here, separates the two events. For a fuller account of the second version see Goodwin 1973.

of the early J. B. Clark and others who sought an ethical economics, and the development of an institutionalist tradition in the work of John Commons and Clarence Ayres, cannot be overlooked (see the papers, this volume, by Mary S. Morgan and Malcolm Rutherford).

At first glance Knight's contributions to the debate over economic man appear straightforward. Called the "philosopher of the counter-revolution" (Breit and Ransom 1982, 193), Knight spearheaded a newly emerging American neoclassicism, paying attention, in particular, to providing a defense for the neoclassical assumption of rational, utility-maximizing individuals that was consistent with economics' status as a science. But first appearances can be deceiving, and in Knight's case they definitely are, for his "defense" of the maximizing assumption simultaneously entailed a delineation of the weaknesses of any social analysis based on that assumption—weaknesses based in part on many of the points raised by the critics. Furthermore, these weaknesses, in his view, set sweeping limitations on the social usefulness of any "scientific" economics.[3] His discussion of economic rationality, therefore, is characterized by the tension he sustains between a strong statement of the scientific validity of the neoclassical maximizing assumption and an equally strong statement of the assumption's inadequacy, both empirically and ethically, as a description of actual exchange behavior.

One of Knight's favorite ways of sustaining the tension between the strengths of an economic science and its limited range of applicability was by contrasting the neoclassical metaphor of the market as a mechanical maximization process with the metaphor of the market as a *game*. In contrast with Veblen (esp. 1899, 1904), who spoke of the interplay between rivals in the market as a game of prowess and predation exhibiting the arrested moral development of capitalist society, Knight used the notion of gaming behavior in the market to highlight the exploratory and essentially moral nature of exchange behavior. As we shall see, for Knight the fact that the market as a form of social organization enabled playful behavior had both positive and negative effects on society.

Knight first introduced the metaphor of the market as a game in the revised version of his dissertation, published in 1921 as *Risk, Uncertainty, and Profit*.[4] The notion reappeared in essays he wrote throughout the

---

3. Perhaps the strongest published version of the critical side of his argument can be found by reading (consecutively) Knight 1922, 1923, and 1935a.

4. The metaphor does *not* appear in Knight's dissertation (1916), upon which *Risk, Uncertainty, and Profit* is based. Because the metaphor appears during the process of revision, during

1920s and 1930s (most prominently 1923, 1935a), and in many of his later critiques of market society (e.g., 1956, 1960; several essays, 1947). In contrast with the neoclassical metaphor of the rational economic man, a character whose actions epitomize mechanical maximization, Knight's description of the market as a game introduced the metaphor of the "good sport," a character whose actions cannot be described in purely maximizing language and, therefore, invokes moral categories. While the object of the game may be to win, good sports are distinguished from other players by the moral quality of their play, which balances the personal interest in winning the game with the social interest in continuing it.

> Unless people are more interested in having the game go on than they are in winning it, no game is possible. And the social interest, . . . is precisely the interest in keeping up the game, preventing it from deteriorating, and beyond that in making it a still better game. (1935a, 302)

If the moral quality of play is sacrificed for the sake of winning, something essential is lost from the game itself.

The contrast Knight draws between *maximizers* and *good sports* presents us with a paradoxical tension in his work. Here we have someone who has had a formative influence on the neoclassical tradition in the United States, criticizing the tradition's description of exchange behavior by attacking its strongest assumption. Does this tension between participation in, and criticism of, the neoclassical tradition represent an inconsistency in Knight's work? Is it, perhaps, as James Buchanan has suggested (1987, 74), a "methodological ambiguity" that Knight never resolved, but which, nonetheless, increases his appeal to us? Or does Knight refuse to resolve the tension for a particular reason?

The answers to these questions provided in the following pages will center, in the end, on Knight's attempt to strengthen the neoclassical tradition by limiting its range of application. The tension in his work is neither an inconsistency nor an ambiguity, but a strategy he employed for a particular reason. Paradox is essential to his work, because ultimately he was less interested in mapping out the territory economic theory

---

which time Knight was involved in a discussion group on Veblen's work at the University of Chicago, it is likely that he picked up the metaphor from Veblen. As was common for Knight, however, he adapted the borrowed concept to his own purposes.

explained well, than in exploring the uncharted, and often disputed, regions where economics came into contact with other ways of thinking about social organization. To ensure that those uncharted regions were not simply claimed by economists for their own before society could discuss the competing claims and reach consensus, he set very narrow boundaries for "scientific" economics.[5]

Before we describe the strategy Knight employed and examine the role that he gave the notion of the market as a game, however, we need to look first at his understanding of economics as a science and the role he assigned the maximizing assumption within the theoretical core of neoclassical economics.

Transactors as Maximizers

> . . . There is a science of economics, a true, and even exact science, which reaches laws as universal as those of mathematics and mechanics. The greatest need for the development of economics as a growing body of thought and practice is an adequate appreciation of the meaning, and the limitations, of this body of accurate premises and rigorously established conclusions. ([1924] 1935b, 135)

Knight's understanding of economics' claim to be a science, and of the role the maximizing assumption plays in establishing that claim, constitute one of the distinguishing features of his framework. For Knight, economic theory studies the abstract, idealized world of perfect competition, in which rational individuals with perfect knowledge efficiently satisfy their preferences through exchanges in markets that work perfectly. The theorist's task as a scientist is to isolate the assumptions about human behavior and the market which ensure that such exchanges are reduced to a purely mechanical process. Only when those assumptions

---

5. Knight's employment of paradox as a rhetorical strategy lies behind the frequent references by his commentators to his constant questioning; for example, by Patinkin, who identifies Knight as "the eternal asker of questions" ([1973] 1981, 46). Warner Wick identifies the connection between Knight's questioning mode and the more positive quality I describe here when he observes that the old difference between moving *from* first principles and moving *toward* them could be applied to Knight. After pointing out that Knight was good at moving from first principles (as his theoretical contributions show), Wick goes on to say: "But no man of my acquaintance has been more concerned with movement in the opposite direction, asking questions of . . . relatively established principles, noting in turn their presuppositions and their limitations, in the attempt to discern more clearly how they might fit together in some order according to principles more comprehensive and, of course, more elusive" (1973, 513–14).

are well specified can the theorist determine the critical distance between the perfect markets of economic theory and the imperfect markets of actual human practice.[6]

According to Knight, the central assumption for a scientific economics was the maximizing assumption: the notion that the individuals engaging in exchange relations are rational, utility-maximizing agents. Placed second in most of his lists of the central assumptions of economic theory (behind a general statement regarding the nature of market society), the maximizing assumption was central to his formulation of neoclassical economics, for three reasons. First, it identified the nature of human activity in the market as the deliberate, knowledgeable, and calculated accommodation of known means to given ends. Secondly, it distinguished the morally neutral notion of economic rationality from the morally charged nature of social discussion about what is "good" in human action. And finally, as he formulated it, the maximizing assumption explicitly connected maximization with the assumption of perfect knowledge—a connection which was fertile theoretical ground for Knight himself (1921b) and many others. All three of these reasons for the centrality of the maximizing assumption to the neoclassical tradition can be seen in his statement of the assumption in *Risk, Uncertainty, and Profit:*

> We assume that the members of society act with complete "rationality." By this we do not mean that they are to be "as angels, knowing good from evil"; we assume ordinary human motives . . .; but they are supposed to "know what they want" and to seek it "intelligently." Their behavior, that is, is all "conduct" as we have previously defined the term [i.e., efficient adaptation of known means to given ends]; all their acts take place in response to real, conscious, and stable and consistent motives, dispositions, or desires; nothing is capricious or experimental, everything deliberate. They are supposed to know absolutely the consequences of their acts when they are performed, and to perform them in the light of the consequences. ([1921b] 1971, 76–77)

6. Knight sets out the basic framework of his understanding of economic method in the first half of *Risk, Uncertainty, and Profit* (Knight 1921b). Subsequent restatements of his methodological framework (e.g., Knight 1924, 1940, 1930) are probably best understood as attempts to strengthen the economist's awareness of the critical distance between theory and practice (see Emmett 1990, 212–20).

The theoretical conclusions Knight draws from the maximizing assumption need not detain us here, for they are familiar to anyone schooled in neoclassical economics. There are, however, a couple of unique features of his formulation of the maximizing assumption that deserve special mention. The first, which has already been mentioned, is the special relation he draws between the maximizing assumption and the assumption of perfect knowledge. With the exception of his discussion of risk in *Risk, Uncertainty, and Profit* (see below), he tends to conflate the two assumptions: people maximize want-satisfaction through actions based upon complete knowledge of the consequences. "In acts looking to the future," he tells us, "intelligent action requires perfect foreknowledge" ([1935a] 1935b, 283 n). The question we might ask is, why did he think it necessary to conflate the two assumptions?

The answer will emerge from a look at the other unique feature of Knight's formulation of the maximizing assumption, namely, his belief that, properly formulated, the assumption enables economic exchange to be reduced to an impersonal, mechanical process.

The social organization dealt with in economic theory is best pictured as a number of Crusoes interacting through the markets exclusively. To the economic individual, exchange is a detail in production, a mode of using private resources to realize private ends. The "second party" has a shadowy existence, as a detail in the individual's use of his own resources to satisfy his own wants. It is the market, the exchange opportunity, which is functionally real, not the other human beings; these are not even means to action. The relation is neither one of cooperation nor one of mutual exploitation, but is completely non-moral, non-human. ([1935a] 1935b, 282)

Conceptualized in this fashion, economic exchange is simply a "mechanical sequence" of want-satisfaction ([1935a] 1935b, 280; see also [1923] 1935b, 50). Blessed with perfect foresight, the individuals in the perfectly competitive economy know what equilibrium prices are and can proceed automatically to fulfill their wants and desires within the constraints of their resources. There is no competition, higgling, co-operation, rivalry, or any other kind of human interaction between the two parties to an exchange in the neoclassical model. The market, which provides the context for want-satisfaction to be fulfilled, is what is real to each person; the individuals with whom exchange occurs are mere details—they might as well be "vending machines" (1960, 73). "The Economic Man," Knight says, "neither competes nor higgles . . . he treats other human beings as if they were slot machines" ([1939] 1947, 80; see also 1923, 1935a, 1930).

Reduction of all exchange relations to mechanical processes brings us full circle and illustrates the close relation for Knight between the maximizing assumption and the scientific status of economics. If people can maximize perfectly, exchange is reduced to a mechanical process and economics can claim to be a scientific study of social organization. "The statement that economics describes the way the economic order works," Knight tells us, "refers to its working as a mechanism; *that is the meaning of being scientific*" (1960, 72, emphasis mine). From this perspective, then, "the first question in regard to scientific economics is this question of how far life is rational, how far its problems reduce to the form of using given means to achieve given ends" ([1924] 1935b, 105).

Knight's Criticism of the Maximizing Assumption

Given his participation in the neoclassical tradition and the significance he attached to the maximizing assumption, unsuspecting readers of Knight's writing may be surprised when they discover passages in which he rejects the maximizing assumption as a valid guide to either personal action or the understanding of human action. And the reader *will* encounter them, because they appear over and over again.

For example, one finds a criticism of the maximizing assumption in *Risk, Uncertainty, and Profit,* where Knight suggests that uncertainty is the fundamental context of many (perhaps most) economic activities, and that when uncertainty is present, the judgment required for good behavior departs from the rational calculation required for maximization. For him, the essential differences between certainty, risk, and uncertainty are related to the limits of human knowledge and, hence, the possibility for maximization. In a *certain* universe all outcomes are known perfectly, and maximization is guaranteed. In a *risky* universe the probability of all outcomes can be known perfectly, and maximization is also guaranteed. Hence maximization works equally well in a fully determined, or a fully stochastic, universe. However, maximization is rendered sterile by *uncertainty,* which exists whenever we lack any objective basis—either deterministic or stochastic—upon which to base our knowledge of the consequences of possible actions: "It is a world of change in which we live, and a world of uncertainty. We live only by knowing *something* about the future; while the problems of life, or of conduct at least, arise from the fact that we know so little" ([1921b] 1971, 199). When neither the outcomes of our actions nor their probabilities are known, wise choices must be characterized by *critical judgment* (a nonmechanistic notion for Knight), rather than maximization (197–232).[7]

The criticism of the maximizing assumption first advanced in *Risk, Uncertainty, and Profit* is expanded upon in Knight's methodological and philosophical writings, where he argues that exchange behavior is fundamentally experimental—"an exploration in the field of values" ([1924] 1935b, 105) in which individuals seek, through cooperation with others, to discover what they really want (e.g., 1922, 1923). In this literature Knight's criticism focuses on the fundamental instability of preferences rather than the problem of imperfect knowledge. Human wants are unstable, he suggests, for three reasons. First, our actions are often impulsive, "a relatively unthinking and undetermined response to stimulus and suggestion" ([1923] 1935b, 50). Also, because our wants are informed and shaped by the economic system itself (through advertising, for example, but also through education and social relations), the ends we pursue are not as independent as the maximizing assumption presumes (1923). Third, there is an inherent dynamism to human preferences that is related to the basic drive to improve: "The chief thing which the common-sense individual actually wants is not satisfactions for the wants he has, but more, and *better* wants" ([1922] 1935b, 22, emphasis his). Unfortunately, deception and deceit in the marketplace often undermine our desire to improve, so that the wants we actually pursue do not lead us to become good people.

Knight's understanding of the instability of preferences and its moral implications are summarized in "The Ethics of Competition," his moral critique of the market system:

7. Those familiar with *Risk, Uncertainty, and Profit* may want to argue that Knight's theory of uncertainty does not represent an attack on the maximizing assumption; rather, it is either a (largely mistaken) attempt to identify the need for subjective probability theory (Friedman 1976, 282), or simply a recognition of the distinction between what is insurable and what is not (LeRoy and Singell 1987). Earlier (Emmett 1990, 182–93) I argued, in a manner similar to my presentation in this essay, that these interpretations of Knight's theory of uncertainty are flawed because they fail to pay attention to how Knight employed the notion of uncertainty in his campaign to delineate the strengths and limitations of neoclassical theory.

[Even] the freest individual, the unencumbered male in the prime of life, is in no real sense an ultimate unit or social datum. He is in large measure a product of the economic system, which is a fundamental part of the cultural environment that has formed his desires and needs, given him whatever marketable productive capacities he has, and which largely controls his opportunities. Social organization through free contract implies that the contracting units know what they want and are guided by their desires, that is, that they are "perfectly rational," which would be equivalent to saying that they are accurate mechanisms of desire-satisfaction. In fact, human activity is largely impulsive, a relatively unthinking and undetermined response to stimulus and suggestion. Moreover, there is truth in the allegation that unregulated competition places a premium on deceit and corruption. . . . It is plainly contrary to fact to treat the individual as a *datum*, and it must be conceded that the lines along which a competitive economic order tends to form character are often far from being ethically ideal. ([1923] 1935b, 49–50)

One way of summarizing Knight's criticisms of the maximizing assumption is to say that they focus our attention on the problems associated with the impersonal nature of a market operating under the maximizing assumption. This is not surprising, given discussion in the previous section, where we saw that the impersonal and mechanistic nature of exchange was central to his understanding of the role of the assumption in neoclassical theory. When people know what they want and how to get it, their exchanges become impersonal and the process by which they exchange becomes mechanical. The discipline which studies the mechanical process of exchange, therefore, can aspire to the scientific status given to classical mechanics. Knight's criticisms remind economists, however, that achieving the status of a science has a cost, because reference to the mechanical nature of the price system obscures as much as it reveals. And one of the things it obscures is that mechanical maximizers are neither human, nor do they interact with each other as humans: "The *view* of human behaviour as a mechanical sequence . . . is *impossible* to human beings. . . . This is one of the main differences between the economic man and the real human being" ([1935a] 1935b, 280, 282, emphasis his).

Because human action, for Knight, is ultimately a discussion about the kind of people we want to become, the impersonal nature of market exchange undermines our ability to become good people. Thus the answer to the "first" question of economic science—how far is life rational?—is "not very far; the scientific view of life is a limited and partial view," and this "sets a first and most sweeping limitation to the conception of economics as a science" ([1924] 1935b, 105).

The Market as a Game

The reader who peruses any significant amount of Knight's work will realize that his criticisms of the maximizing assumption are frequently accompanied by reference to the market as a *game*. He seems to have employed the notion of "playing," or "gaming," because it provided a particularly effective way of highlighting two aspects of his criticisms of neoclassicism. First, describing exchange behavior as playful gave him a way of suggesting that decision making is as much a choice of ends as it is a choice of means. Two characterizations of this aspect of play can be found in his work, and they are not necessarily compatible. In *Risk, Uncertainty, and Profit* he began his first criticism of the notion of economic rationality with the statement "Most human motives tend on scrutiny to assimilate themselves to the game spirit" [1921b] 1971, 53), where the concrete objective is a matter of accident and the primary purpose is simply to play.

> It is little matter, if any, what we set ourselves to do; it is imperative to have some objective in view, and we seize upon and set up for ourselves objectives more or less at random—getting an education, acquiring skill at some art, making money, or what-not. But once having set ourselves to achieve some goal it becomes an absolute value, weaving itself into and absorbing life itself. It is just as in a game where the concrete objective—capturing our opponents' pieces, carrying a ball across a mark, or whatever it may be—is a matter of accident, but to achieve it is for the moment the end and aim of being. (53)

In his later philosophical work, however, Knight replaced the notion of an arbitrary selection of ends with a formulation of playful activity which fit more comfortably with his understanding of the explorative nature of human behavior. While it may be sufficient to allow the objective of the game to be simply a matter of accident for the purpose of pointing out the empirical inadequacy of the maximizing assumption, the arbitrariness this implies did not provide him an adequate basis to argue that gaming behavior is explorative and experimental. In particular, it did not allow him to suggest that we keep trying different games until we find a *good* one. Some games call out the best in us; others leave us dissatisfied. The only way to discover the games we most enjoy and play the best is to experiment with different games.

But this, of course, raises the question of what constitutes a good game, which brings us to the second reason why Knight employed the notion of the market as a game, namely, the opportunity it provided him to communicate the moral nature of all action: "The ethical character of competition is not decided by the fact that it stimulates a greater amount of activity; this merely raises the question of the ethical quality of what is done or of the motive itself" [1923] 1935b, 71, 74)

Two things are important for Knight in regard to the connection between the notion of the market as a game and ethics. The first is the way playful behavior points toward the ethical and aesthetic aspect of explorative activity. If the choice of games is not simply a matter of accident, that necessarily raises the question of the standards of value we use to judge games. For Knight, decisions regarding the norms by which we choose are one aspect of ethics and aesthetics: "The actual ranking of games would raise the same problems of value standards which beset the path to objectivity in all fields of artistic criticism" (64).

What, then, constitutes a *good* game? Knight saw four elements as essential to any good game. First, it must involve some level of skill. Knight believed that while people like games of chance, most would agree "that games of skill are 'superior' to games of chance" (63), because the outcome of a game of skill can be influenced by the effort one applies to it. Thus effort is the second element of a good game: it "must test the capacity of the players, and to do this it must compel them to exert effort" (63). At the same time, however, effort by itself (perhaps measured on some objective scale) is not sufficient to make a good game interesting; there must be some measure of uncertainty regarding the outcome: "The result must be unpredictable: if there is no element of luck in it there is no game" (63). Finally, there are the moral qualities that the good game calls out in those who play: "Some games are 'higher class' than others, depending presumably on the human qualities necessary to play them successfully and to enjoy them" (63–64).

How did Knight think the market rated as a game? If a good game calls out the best in people while balancing the elements of skill, effort, and luck, then, he argued, the market was probably *not* a good game, for four reasons. First, the outcome of the market game is not an accurate reflection of business skill:

> [The] differences in the capacity to play the business game are inordinately great from one person to another. But as the game is organized, the weak contestants are thrown into competition with the strong in one grand mêlée; there is no classification of the participants or distribution of the handicaps such as is always recognized to be necessary to sportsmanship where unevenly matched contestants are to meet. In fact the situation is worse still; there are handicaps, but . . . they are distributed to the advantage of the strong rather than the weak. (64–65)

Second, while luck plays a large role in the market game, its effect compounds the problems associated with the differences in skill. Success in the first few rounds of the game (through skill, inheritance, or luck) confers a differential advantage upon the initial leader. Anyone may be eliminated after the first round, or may be "placed in a position where it is extraordinarily difficult to get back into the game" (64). Hence the game, while fascinating for the leaders, reduces the participation of the rest to mechanical drudgery (67).

The third reason Knight provided in support of his argument that the market did not meet the requirements of a good game takes us to his second concern for the ethical quality of playful behavior: his concern for the impact of the market game on the formation of virtue, or good character. Even if the market did balance skill, effort, and luck in a pleasing proportion, it would still not rate as a good game, because it does not cultivate the highest human ideals or a "very high order of sportsmanship" (65). Quoting John Ruskin, he pointed out that the winners in the market game are usually " 'industrious, resolute, proud, covetous, prompt, methodical, sensible, unimaginative, insensitive, and ignorant,' " while the game's losers include " 'the entirely foolish, the entirely wise, the idle, the reckless, the humble, the thoughtful, the dull, the imaginative, the sensitive, the well-informed, the improvident, the irregularly and impulsively wicked, the clumsy knave, the open thief, the entirely merciful, just, and godly person' " (66).

The moral qualities which the market did develop, then, were not the kind of qualities that Knight believed were essential to the improvement of society. While they might foster winning, they did not encourage the kind of social cooperation that would keep the game going and keep it open to participation by all. In such a society, the "good sport" becomes a twisted reflection of the ideal player described earlier—separated from any notion of virtue or good character.

> To "play the game" is the current version of accepting the universe, and protest is blasphemy; the Good Man has given place to the "good sport." In America particularly, where . . . the sporting view of life [has] reached [its] fullest development, there have come to be two sorts of virtue. The greater virtue is to win; and meticulous questions about the methods are not in the best form, provided the methods bring victory. The lesser virtue is to go out and die gracefully after having lost. (67)

Knight took the question of the moral qualities developed in the market a step further in his final criticism of the market as a game, asking whether "success in any sort of *contest,* as such, is a noble objective" (66). Contrasting "the predominance of the institution of sport" (75) and its spirit of rivalry in modern market societies with the pagan ethical ideal of perfect beauty and the Christian ethical ideal of spirituality, he concluded that we "search in vain for any really ethical basis of approval for competition as a basis for an ideal type of human relations, or as a motive to action" (74). Maybe even being a good sport is not enough to preserve society—a thought Knight returned to often in his work.

Maximizers versus Good Sports: Paradox as Rhetorical Strategy

In the previous sections we have seen that Knight's criticisms of neoclassicism closely followed the key features of his formulation of the tradition's central assumption about human behavior—the maximizing assumption. We have also seen that he employed the notion of the market as a game as a means of drawing attention to the exploratory, nonmechanical nature of actual exchange behavior in contrast to the predetermined, mechanical nature of the exchange process in the world of perfect competition. What remains to be seen is why he refused to resolve the paradoxical tension between his participation in the neoclassical tradition and his rejection of the tradition's central assumption as a reliable guide to either human action or social inquiry.

To answer that question we need to look briefly at the intellectual context in which he worked. As indicated in my opening remarks, the context in which most of the work considered here was written was the early twentieth-century debate over the relevance of economic theory to the most important social problems facing the United States. Marginalism, and the scientific status it apparently conveyed, had been essential to the establishment of an independent economics profession earlier (Church 1974; Ross 1991, 172–86). However, a full-blown body of neoclassical economic thought had not emerged in the United States, in part because of concern over neoclassicism's portrayal of people as lightning calculators of utility maximization (to use Veblen's phrase) and the concomitant rejection of laissez-faire economics, which neoclassicism was viewed as supporting. Early twentieth-century social scientists therefore often rejected neoclassical economics both as a theoretical framework and as a viable means of social control. They set out in search of new models of social inquiry which would place a greater degree of social control in the hands of social scientists and policy makers (see, e.g., Barber 1985).

At least during the period in which most of his essays on the market as a game were written, Knight shared social scientists' dream of a social science which would enable the realization of liberal values within the context of modern society. However, he believed that many of the assumptions others made about human beings and the nature of society were mistaken and, therefore, that the means by which they pursued their goal were flawed. In particular, he argued that the extension of the methods of the natural sciences into the social sciences was inappropriate, for both epistemological and ethical reasons, and that the increasing scientism of the social sciences was actually at odds with the liberal values social scientists sought to promote.

As I have argued in more detail elsewhere (Emmett 1990), the paradoxes and tensions in Knight's work emerge from his effort to delineate clearly the senses in which it was appropriate to speak of economics as science which had something to contribute to social policy-making in a liberal democracy. In contrast to most other social scientists of his time, he believed that the very things that made his discipline a science also rendered it inappropriate as a direct guide to democratic social action. The theoretical neoclassical tradition could not tell you what to do; but if specified completely it could sharpen the focus of those participating in the social discussion about what goals to pursue.

One of the ways Knight emphasized the limited range of the economist's vision was by limiting the "scientific" realm of economics to an area as small as possible, in order to highlight the nonscientific nature of social inquiry outside that small realm. In this context the paradox of the conflicting roles of the "maximizer" and the "good sport" in his understanding of exchange behavior makes more sense. Both sides of the paradox were essential to the tension he sought to sustain between economic theory and social practice in a liberal democracy. A sharply delineated characterization of the individuals who populate the world of perfect competition was needed to sustain the scientific nature of economic theory: for this the metaphor of the mechanical maximizer worked well.

But science could only go so far in helping us to understand action in a liberal society. In the language of games, science played a role "only in connection with the interest of the individual in *winning* the game; it play[ed] none in having the game go on, still less in 'improving' it" [1935a] 1935b, 301). To talk about the explorative, experimental, and ultimately moral nature of the social interest in keeping the game going, Knight needed the metaphor of the good sport, the quality of whose actions would help prevent society from degenerating into a war of all against all. In his typical fashion, however, he suspected that in the end the market game would be incapable of creating more good sports, and would therefore undermine its own existence.

References

Barber, William J. 1985. *From New Era to New Deal: Herbert Hoover, the Economists, and American Economic Policy, 1921–1933*. Historical Perspectives on Modern Economics. Cambridge: Cambridge University Press.

Breit, William, and Roger L. Ransom. 1982. *The Academic Scribblers*. Rev. ed. Chicago: Dryden Press.

Buchanan, James M. 1987. The Economizing Element in Knight's Ethical Critique of Capitalist Order. *Ethics* 98 (October): 61–75.

Church, Robert L. 1974. Economists as Experts: The Rise of an Academic Profession in America, 1870–1920. In *The University in Society*, vol. 2, *Europe, Scotland, and the United States from the Sixteenth to the Twentieth Century*, edited by Lawrence Stone. Princeton: Princeton University Press.

Emmett, Ross B. 1990. "The Economist as Philosopher": Frank H. Knight and American Social Science during the Twenties and Early Thirties. Ph.D. dissertation, University of Manitoba.

Friedman, Milton. 1976. *Price Theory: A Provisional Text*. Chicago: Aldine.

Goodwin, Craufurd D. 1973. Marginalism Moves to the New World. In *The Mar-*

ginal Revolution in Economics, edited by R. D. Collison Black, A. W. Coats, and Craufurd D. Goodwin. Durham: Duke University Press.

Grundberg, Emile. 1957. Review of *On the History and Method of Economics: Selected Essays,* by Frank H. Knight. *Journal of Economic History* 17:276–79.

Hayek, F. A. 1967. The Transmission of the Ideals of Economic Freedom. In *Studies in Philosophy, Politics, and Economics,* 195–200. Chicago: University of Chicago Press.

Knight, Frank H. 1916. A Theory of Business Profit. Ph.D. dissertation, Cornell University.

———. 1917. Neglected Factors in the Problem of Normal Interest. *Quarterly Journal of Economics* 32 (November): 66–100.

———. 1921a. Cost of Production and Price over Long and Short Periods. Reprinted in Knight 1935b, 186–216.

———. 1921b. *Risk, Uncertainty, and Profit.* Reprinted Chicago: University of Chicago Press, 1971.

———. 1922. Ethics and the Economic Interpretation. Reprinted in Knight 1935b, 19–40.

———. 1923. The Ethics of Competition. Reprinted in Knight 1935b, 41–75.

———. 1924. The Limitations of Scientific Method in Economics. Reprinted in Knight 1935b, 105–47.

———. 1930. Statics and Dynamics: Some Queries Regarding the Mechanical Analogy in Economics. Reprinted in Knight 1956, 179–201.

———. 1931. Professor Fisher's Interest Theory: A Case in Point. *Journal of Political Economy* 39 (April): 176–212.

———. 1934a. Capital, Time and the Interest Rate. *Economica,* n.s. 1 (August): 257–86.

———. 1934b. Some Fallacies in the Interpretation of Social Cost. Reprinted in Knight 1935b, 217–36.

———. 1935a. Economic Theory and Nationalism. In Knight 1935b, 277–359.

———. 1935b. *The Ethics of Competition and Other Essays.* New York: Harper.

———. 1936. The Quantity of Capital and the Rate of Interest, Parts I–II. *Journal of Political Economy* 44 (August, October): 433–63, 612–42.

———. 1939. Ethics and Economic Reform. Reprinted in Knight 1947, 55–153.

———. 1940. "What Is Truth" in Economics? Reprinted in Knight 1956, 151–78.

———. 1944. Diminishing Returns from Investment. *Journal of Political Economy* 52 (March): 26–47.

———. 1947. *Freedom and Reform: Essays in Economics and Social Philosophy.* New York: Harper.

———. 1956. *On the History and Method of Economics: Selected Essays.* Chicago: University of Chicago Press.

———. 1960. *Intelligence and Democratic Action.* Cambridge: Harvard University Press.

LeRoy, Stephen F., and Larry D. Singell, Jr. 1987. Knight on Risk and Uncertainty. *Journal of Political Economy* 95 (April): 394–406.

Morgan, Mary S. 1994. Marketplace Morals and the American Economists: The Case of John Bates Clark. In *Higgling: Transactors and Their Markets in the History of Economics*, edited by Neil De Marchi and Mary S. Morgan. *HOPE* 26, special issue. Durham: Duke University Press.

Patinkin, Don. 1973. Frank Knight as Teacher. Reprinted in *Essays on and in the Chicago Tradition*, 23–51. Durham: Duke University Press, 1981.

Ross, Dorothy. 1991. *The Origins of American Social Science*. Ideas in Context. Cambridge: Cambridge University Press.

Rutherford, Malcolm. 1994. Predatory Practices or Reasonable Values? American Institutionalists on the Nature of Market Transactions. In *Higgling: Transactors and Their Markets in the History of Economics*, edited by Neil De Marchi and Mary S. Morgan. *HOPE* 26, special issue. Durham: Duke University Press.

Seligman, Benjamin. 1962. *Main Currents on Modern Economics*. Vol. 3, *The Thrust toward Technique*. Glencoe, Ill.: Free Press.

Stigler, George J. 1973. Frank Knight as Teacher. *Journal of Political Economy* 81 (May–June): 518–20.

———. 1987. Frank Hyneman Knight. In *The New Palgrave: A Dictionary of Economics*, edited by John Eatwell, Murray Milgate, and Peter Newman. New York: Stockton Press.

Veblen, Thorstein. 1899. *The Theory of the Leisure Class*. New York: Macmillan.

———. 1904. *The Theory of Business Enterprise*. New York: Scribner's.

Wick, Warner. 1973. Frank Knight, Philosopher at Large. *Journal of Political Economy* 81 (May–June): 513–15.

Part 4 The Nature of Exchange: In the Wild and in the Laboratory

Transactors and Their Markets in Two Disciplines

Anne Mayhew

The treatment—and nontreatment—of higgling by anthropologists and economists serves to illustrate the markedly different ways in which markets and market participation have been understood in the two disciplines. The differences are partly a matter of style; they are to a much greater extent the consequence of the questions asked and of the standards used in assessing adequacy of answers. These differences in questions and standards exist quite independently of the fact that anthropologists and economists often consider different kinds of markets and transactions. In this essay I consider some aspects of the history both of economics and of anthropology in order to explore these disciplinary differences and to suggest why cross-disciplinary hybridization, which might produce superior questions and standards, may be difficult to achieve.

Transactors in Two Disciplines: An Overview

Consider this passage:

> The Redside Market site is on the major north-south interstate in the region, with a large billboard to announce its presence. . . . In the winter well over 100 booths line the aisles of the marketplace in neat rows. . . . Most of the vendors know one another, visiting between booths is the rule and the major mechanism for gathering information about business in Redside Market, as well as in the other intermediate and minor markets. . . . By noon the indoor marketplace is in full

swing with hundreds of patrons and sellers milling through the aisles, arguing over prices and visiting with friends and kin. . . . Flexibility and a constant eye for the good bargain are probably the two most distinctive characteristics of the successful market vendor. Seasoned buyers know how to talk a seller down, an activity that seems to be enjoyed by seller and buyer alike. People who are tied into the system know how to bargain; strangers do not. More important, bargaining is one tool for obtaining items cheaply to resell. (Halperin 1990, 93–94)

Now, rewrite the passage as an economist might:

Easy entry results in competition among sellers. Among both buyers and sellers there is asymmetric information, where asymmetry results from first-comer advantage and varying investments of time in acquisition of knowledge. Psychic income may result from this investment, making the net cost of knowledge acquisition difficult to calculate. Advantage accrues through resale.

Differences in approach are obvious: economists use fewer words, and many fewer modifiers; anthropologists provide colorful detail, economists do not. Economists use general categories to describe the specific as an example of the general and seek formality in doing so. In the pages that follow I describe other differences, both as they are illustrated by treatment of higgling and as they cause that treatment to differ.

Different Markets, Different Transactions

Clarity of subsequent argument will be served by explicit recognition that the markets described by anthropologists are in fact different from the markets described by economists. Anthropologists have usually described market*places* (not market systems)[1] in nonindustrialized parts of the world or, as in the case cited above, peripheral marketing in industrial nations. In such markets higgling—which I define here as open and extended discussion of the terms and conditions of exchange—occurs for two important and fairly obvious reasons.

In marketplaces in nonindustrialized parts of the world higgling often occurs where there is variation in the quality and quantity of units sold

---

1. For the importance of this distinction see Bohannan and Dalton 1965.

(Uchendu, 1967, 37). This description of trade in northeastern Nepal explains why:

> Accepting the going rate [of the place where trade takes place] also means using the weights and measures of the locality. The Tibetans use different ones from the Lhomi, and the Lhomi different ones from the people further south. Now the expression "weights and measures" may convey the wrong impression. It is true that people do talk in terms of rates for barter. People will say: "This year in our village two *kathis* (a round wood pot) of maize exchange for three of potato seed, but last year it was three *kathis* of maize for two of potato seed, and yes, we give four *dokos* (baskets) of manure for one *kathi* of salt," and so on for many, many different items. The whole thing is quite extraordinarily complicated. What they do not bother to say is that all these *kathis* and *dokos* are home-made, and that my *doko* may be really much bigger than yours. (Humphrey 1992, 119)

In his study of Guatemalan peasants Tax similarly noted that haggling occurred over goods for which there were no standard measures of quantity and quality (1953, 137).

Other papers in the present volume suggest that higgling and a lack of standardization of product go together. Forget suggests that disequilibrium trade occurs where information must be exchanged. Lowry speaks of the requirement of "uniformity, or at least ease of comparison of merchandise" for self-regulating market processes. Schabas describes the world of Hume as one in which change in relatively fixed and known patterns of distribution—"As the guild and municipal price regulations were dismantled, . . . price discrepancies became the norm"—led at least initially to an extension of higgling.

In his review of haggling in peasant markets Uchendu also makes the important observation that "haggling characterized the economic behavior of the United States and Western Europe as recently as seventy years ago" (1967, 43), that is, at the end of the nineteenth century. It was precisely of that period that Veblen said:

> Modern industry has little use for, and can make little use of, what does not conform to the standard. What is not competently standardized calls for too much of craftsmanlike skill, reflection, and individual elaboration, and is therefore not available for economical use

in the processes. . . . The materials and moving forces of industry are undergoing a like reduction to staple kinds, styles, grades and gauge. Even such forces as would seem at first sight not to lend themselves to standardization, either in their production or their use, are subjected to uniform scales of measurement; as, e.g., water-power, steam, electricity, and human labor. (1975, 10–11)

In parallel with the better-known struggles of the robber barons, captains of industry, and antitrusters of the turn of the century, the engineers and managers were devising the standards that are today just that.[2]

Standardization of weights, measures, and qualities reduces the need and opportunity for discussion of transactions. The importance, not only of higgling, but of markets as places, is reduced, a point to which I return below. However, anthropologists have continued to describe places where standardization is not so common; little wonder, then, that they talk more of higgling than economists do.

Further, when anthropologists study people in industrial nations they tend to describe peripheral activity, such as flea markets. Halperin describes flea markets such as that at Redside as important parts of the strategy for gaining livelihood among the poor of Appalachia, but flea markets are peripheral to the major distribution networks in this economy. In such peripheral markets goods are often not standardized, and the very process of buying and selling can become part of the consumption package. The buying and selling are—at least for some of the participants—entertainment paid for by largely irrelevant purchases. Economists rarely describe markets where this is true.

Those differences noted, there are others that require further discussion. These are the differences that are independent of the difference in markets and transactions.

2. For one example of how this occurred see the description of development of specifications for steel given in Knoedler 1993. Veblen recognized that commercial activity creates a need for some standardization but observed that the "unprecedented uniformity and precise equivalence in legally adopted weights and measures" of his day had gone beyond that which "would be brought about by the needs of commerce" (1975, 9). As he saw it, the needs of industry were for standardization above and beyond that required for trade over time and distance; he, like Alfred D. Chandler (1977), saw industrially driven standardization as a cause of change in commercial practice.

Process in Economics and in Anthropology

Higgling (or haggling) can be described as what happens when two people or two groups disagree vocally on the terms of an apparently commonly desired goal. It is interesting to note that analyses of disagreements over terms of commonly desired goals and their resolutions are commonplace in economic analysis. These include Edgeworth's demonstration of the gains to trade, the bargaining models of labor economics, and the many demonstrations of the advantages of trade where there is comparative advantage. What these analyses have in common is that they describe the conditions that will lead to higgling and the conditions (or range of possible conditions, if assumptions sufficient to determine a precise outcome have not been made) that will prevail at the end of the higgle. They do not focus on process, and they are not in fact analyses of the vocal disagreement of higgling.[3] As is said in many a text: the gains from trade are available and will depend upon the relative bargaining power of the parties involved. But that is all that is said.

The point is well illustrated in a chapter on "haggling" in a recent book of "microeconomic vignettes" "designed to provide stimulating supplementary readings for introductory or intermediate theory classes" (Hemenway 1993). The chapter begins with the observation that haggling is the exception and not the rule in most modern markets. Haggling is said to occur when there is "personal preference" for it, where it can lead to advantage in subsequent transactions, or where it makes price discrimination possible. Institutional control, high value placed on time, and low cost of items involved militate against haggling. The consequences of haggling are then evaluated—the likely consequences are judged to have mixed impact on welfare—and current laissez-faire policy toward the practice is applauded.

The "questions for discussion" that follow the chapter (reproduced here in the Appendix) reveal the same emphasis on conditions precedent and consequent, or upon evaluation of the existence of haggling.

---

3. Even in economic history where individuals can play a major role and "stories" are told, the *process* of bargaining is rarely described. Perhaps this is because records of bargaining are not easily come by; it is at least equally the result of disciplinary focus on the outcomes. Economic historians from the history side make a great deal more effort to find diaries and other written records of who said what to whom and when than do economic historians from the economics side.

The last question asks how the reader/student would go about gathering data and doing research on haggling. A clever student is not likely to suggest observation of haggling in process; the payoff would appear to come from understanding the characteristics of potential hagglers (preferences, valuations of time, relative power) and understanding the consequences, given those characteristics.

Economists do, however, appear to treat something very like the process of higgling when they deal with strategic uncertainty in game theory. Strategic uncertainty requires evaluation of and reaction to others involved in a transaction, and it is this kind of uncertainty that characterizes higgling. Consider, for example, a case of bidding (as described in Hirshleifer and Riley 1992). Description of strategy begins with a known valuation placed upon the good in question by each participant, and a specified order of bidding. The question about process is then a question about strategy of response, given the first move.

Now contrast that treatment of process with the treatment accorded by anthropologists. The first impression is that anthropologists give a lot more attention to process. Closer reading indicates that just as economists do, they too treat selected, disciplinarily defined, aspects of process.[4] It is possible to find process descriptions:

> West describes a long and complicated ritual of trading in which men engage in lengthy verbal sparring and bantering; disparagement of the partners's goods, and "brags" regarding one's own goods; numerous offers, refusals, and counteroffers; and [often] recountings of "famous" local trades. A man is admired for trading victories, and even for deception of his trading partner, if he has only concealed or evaded reference to flaws in articles offered. Deception must follow rigid rules. To lie directly is to "cheat."[5]

4. It is worth noting here that neither anthropologists nor economists, nor even those economic historians who practice modern cliometrics, deal well with change in human response to markets and other economic phenomena. What Schabas (this volume) describes as Hume's depiction of man "as a variable creature" who adapts, albeit slowly, to changes in socioeconomic condition is a view that is poorly integrated into either discipline.

5. This is from West 1945 as cited by Halperin (1990, 53). West's book is a highly self-conscious effort to describe a community in the United States as anthropologists described communities elsewhere in the world; this makes for an interesting treatment of the economy of "Plainville." It would have been even more interesting if West had described a less peripheral community. That anthropologists doing unto the United States as they have done unto others tend—even today—to focus on peripheral communities reveals the extent to which anthropological tools are thought to be inappropriate for study of central aspects of our economy and society.

This is a description of process—a description of actual higgling and haggling. However, anthropologists are more likely to offer descriptions of marketplaces and of the higgling therein in a limited set of terms—such as the tribal or national status of participants (Bohannan and Bohannan 1968, 149; Humphrey 1992, 119), physical arrangements (Bohannan and Bohannan, 149; Halperin 1990, 92–102), social status (Bohannan and Bohannan, 150–51)—or in terms of the specific questions underlying the study. Halperin, for example, classifies participants and their strategies according to degree of reliance on flea markets (extensive, regular, or peripheral).

In the anthropological treatment the process of market transacting is a process of social interaction, of interaction between groups classified by measures of status interesting to anthropologists. This has important consequences for understanding higgling; but before I turn to discussion of those consequences, another obvious contrast between the two disciplines should be addressed.

Individuals: Stylized, Real, and Other

Anthropologists appear to write about people. Jane and Larry Rogers trade in the Redside Market. They have a ten-year-old son. Jane has fourteen siblings. Et cetera. Economists write about stylized individuals. In the bidding process that Hirshleifer and Riley (1992) use to illustrate game strategy, "Alex" and "Bev" bid against each other. Their only characteristics are the values that they place on the tiara for which they are bidding. These "individuals" are "economic persons" conceived as Knight's "slot machines" (see Emmett, this volume). It would seem that this difference in the treatment of individuals is sufficient to account for differences in the treatment of market transactors. However, the difference is not as simple and straightforward as it seems, for there has long been tension in both disciplines between the two, apparently irreconcilable, concepts of humans.

Anthropologists (and sociologists) became concerned during the 1950s and 1960s that their focus on individuals was more apparent than real. The concern was that people were perceived as such culture-bound creatures that there was no room in analysis for strategy, for self-seeking behavior, for decision making. What would have looked to most economists like an excessive focus on individuals—as opposed to system characteristics—became suspect for its lack of reality in portraying individuals as conniving and self-seeking. The focus on individuals became suspect for leaving out what anthropologists of that era began to think of as one of the most universal of individual human characteristics. From this concern there developed, in the early 1960s, a series of rancorous exchanges between the "substantivists"—who appeared to be defending the anthropological status quo (even though, oddly enough, several were trained economists)—and the "formalists" (almost all anthropologists), who advocated adoption of the formal methods of decision modeling used in neoclassical economics.[6]

The formalists shared the legitimate concern that by classifying individuals according to tribal, residential, family, or other status, they overlooked the importance of the universally present human capacity to employ strategy in action. And what better place to look for ways to describe, analyze, and incorporate such strategy than neoclassical microeconomic theory? That is, it seemed to many anthropologists that the stylized individuals of economic analysis were more fully rounded than their own apparently real people. As enthusiasm for use of this theory grew, the substantivists who cautioned that such theory had serious shortcomings for anthropological application appeared to be saying that people outside the nonindustrialized nations were somehow different—perhaps less rational, less self-seeking, less given to strategy. After all, the formalists reasoned, since several of those who argued most vigorously for the substantivist position were economists—and must therefore believe that the microeconomic theory of choice was useful in the industrialized world (an untrue assumption about many of the substantivists)—they would argue its inapplicability elsewhere only if they thought that people were different in the nonindustrial world.

As I wrote (1980), the following syllogism was adopted:

1. All people choose and all are rational.
2. Microeconomic theory is *the* theory of rational choice.
3. Therefore, microeconomic theory must be useful for describing and analyzing all social systems.

Aided and abetted by happily imperialistic economists (Hirshleifer 1985) and by social scientists in other disciplines who were following somewhat the same course of action (for discussion see Mayhew 1989), many

---

6. For the classic statement in sociology see Wrong 1961. For the major sources in anthropology see the references given in Mayhew 1980.

anthropologists sought to wed their "real" people with the "stylized" strategists of microeconomics.

It was not a happy or long-lasting marriage; the reason why is perhaps more interesting than the outcome. When anthropologists attempted to use the tools of microeconomic theory, they found that they could say very little that was of interest within their discipline. Ortiz, for instance, an anthropologist strongly sympathetic to the formalists and dedicated to a focus on strategy, studied the behavior of Colombian peasants, doing so (in part) to show how economically rational they were. She reports that one farmer replied impatiently to her questions about his planting by saying that "he really could not tell me how many stems of manioc he was going to plant, because he stopped planting when he could see he had enough" (1967, 196). Ortiz concluded that the farmer was certainly rational and observed that we should not expect constantly conscious awareness of choice. She treated the farmer's behavior and his explanation as consequences of following a pattern chosen rationally at some earlier time. What she did thereby was return to the classical anthropological paradigm in which the origin—the assumed *strategically chosen* pattern of planting—was relegated to an unobservable past. From this past a cultural pattern emerged and was followed. Ortiz kept the description of that pattern of planting as the central focus of her analysis but added an assertion of strategic choosing and rationality; the underlying paradigm remained the same.[7]

Even though the fundamental paradigm was not substantially changed in anthropology, the formalist-substantivist dispute did make obvious once again an old issue in anthropology and the social sciences in general: an emphasis on culture as explaining how human behavior limits the importance given individual rationality and creativity in social analysis (Stocking 1968).

Economists have not experienced a ferocious methodological debate to match the formalist-substantivist debate since the *Methodenstreit* of the last century, and the majority of economists remain secure in use of the stylized "Alexes" and "Bevs." However, the same issue of how to merge analysis grounded in recognition of human rationality and cun-

---

7. This paragraph largely reiterates my statement in Mayhew 1989, 330. The formalist-substantivist debate in economic anthropology was too complicated to be fully and adequately described here. For excellent discussion of some of the larger issues involved see Stocking 1968 and Sahlins 1972.

ning with analysis based on recognition of the importance of inherited cultural patterns of behavior has reappeared in economic discourse.[8] The issue is an old one in institutional economics, so much so that it was a major point on which John R. Commons (1934, 657) criticized Veblen. In the "New Institutional Economics," and in questions raised by the assumptions of game theory itself about the role of norms, conventions, and institutions (Sugden 1989; Elster 1989), the old questions (in new form) about how to describe individuals are being asked again. Even so, the contrast between the individual of anthropological analysis and the individual of economic analysis remains great. Common *homo economicus* remains a creature, much like Alex and Bev, whose important characteristics are cunning and rationality, self-interest and immaculately conceived tastes and preferences that remain prior to analysis.

Higgling in Two Disciplines

Differences between disciplinary models of individuals are not the only source of disparity in treatment of higgling. As economists have not spent much time writing about higgling, in part because most exchanges in modern, Western, industrialized nations *can* in fact take place with little or no verbal exchange, the differences are not, however, always so clearly revealed. It is in marketplaces such as those described in the economic development literature of the 1950s and 1960s that higgling has occasionally surfaced for economists. When it did, economists noted, as did anthropologists and others, that people (very often women) sold and purchased small quantities of goods in marketplaces. They often did so for what appeared to be a very small economic payoff despite considerable higgling. When such behavior was observed it was most often labeled "noneconomic" and accounted for as "marketplace sociability." This was an explanation easily drawn from a wide range of literature. For example, Bohannan and Dalton (1965, 10) support their conclusions about Africa by quoting Henri Pirenne, who wrote about ninth-century Europe:

---

8. For discussion see Rutherford, this volume and 1989; Mayhew 1989; Samuels 1990; Coats 1990. And, for an excellent solution of the issue, see the statement by Clark and Pinch, this volume: "It is not that norms mechanistically govern these transactions but rather that pitchers as skilled patter merchants play upon or exploit such norms—in the language of social theory norms both constrain and *enable*" (emphasis theirs). They cite Anthony Giddens as a social theorist who has struggled successfully with the same issue in sociology.

The large number of markets might seem at first sight to contradict the commercial paralysis of the age. . . . But their number is itself proof of their insignificance. . . . The nature of the business transacted appears quite clearly from the fact that people sold *per deneratas,* that is to say, by quantities not exceeding a few pence in value. In short, the utility of these small assemblies was limited to satisfying that instinct of sociability which is inherent in all men.

It seems reasonable that much higgling, whether in ninth-century Europe or twentieth-century Africa, can be treated as a consumption good in and of itself. The flea market as Sunday entertainment fits the mold well, as does the patter of Clark and Pinch's pitchers (this volume).

Treatment of higgling as social rather than economic also comes easily because although we economists talk a lot about markets, we say little about what happens in marketplaces. Buyers and sellers respond to prices. Where do those prices come from? From the market. How? With rapid communication and long-standing processes and procedures for making and taking prices, these questions seem of little importance. But in places where most output is agricultural—and not therefore easily controlled for quantity and quality, and where marketing may be peripheral to the livelihood and therefore small in scale—the making of markets is observable and important. The Jamaican higglers that Mintz describes buy a few yams, a little corn from small-scale farmers who "depend on the sale of at least some items for money . . . [but are] unwilling to invest the time and energy necessary to go to market" (1974, 220). They sell their accumulated but still small quantities in marketplaces and are part of "a highly complex network of individuals . . . [in which] a myriad series of interpersonal relationships link traders with each other, and with the farmers and consumers who stand at each end of the chains of intermediation" (219). The discussions that give these traders their name—higglers—are the market in action.

In the economics of modern industrial nations the market in action is described in highly stylized fashion, so much so that the higgling (discussion of price, quantities, and qualities) is well hidden from view and perhaps does not occur at all. The actors are characterized in terms of market power (monopolistic firms, oligopolies, price-takers, price-makers), strategies (risk-averse, risk-neutral, profit-maximizing), stage of use (producers, intermediate users, final users), and so on. Any possible higgling is equally stylized in the terms of game theory, or is ignored.

In part this lack of emphasis on process is a consequence of lack of activity of the kind that gave rise to the higgling in the markets that anthropologists (and some development economists) describe. As noted, most exchanges in modern, Western, industrialized nations take place with little or no verbal exchange and do so because they can. Goods are standardized not only at the wholesale level, but also for retail sale. The mail order catalogs that developed in the United States in the nineteenth century were major vendors of standardized goods.[9] In the late twentieth century we have a wide range of specialized shop-by-mail opportunities. And even where face-to-face contact continues, in the supermarket and other modern retail establishments with their packaged and marked wares for retail sale, goods need only be passed through a checkout machine while clerk and buyer largely ignore each other.

It is tempting to suggest that the absence of attention to higgling by economists is simply, therefore, a consequence of what has happened in modern industrial economies. With standardization and routinization, so that prices are known to both buyers and sellers (for the importance of this see both Brown, this volume; and Clark and Pinch, this volume), prices do seem to emerge from market processes not observable in any marketplace and may with some justice be described as reflecting impersonal forces. In this view, the difference in the treatment of higgling between economics and anthropology stems in part from different conceptions of the individual, but largely from successful attempts by the two disciplines to deal accurately with very different kinds of economic processes. It is possible to argue that it was change in the societies described by anthropologists—the increased commercialization, standardization, and modernization that came with economic development—that led the formalists to reject what they perceived to be the old anthropological view of humans as cultural puppets. In like manner it can be argued that economic thought has developed as it has in this century because of the faceless and impersonal trading that characterizes so much of our distribution.

This is, however, a flawed interpretation. Anthropologists also write more about higgling because higgling may be about important matters other than price. Higgling may be about quantities and qualities where

---

9. Chandler describes the importance of standardization in the development of the modern commodity dealer, the wholesale jobber, department stores, mail order houses, and chain stores in his chapter "Mass Distribution" in *The Visible Hand* (1977).

standardization is lacking; it can also be a serious social process. This is why Uchendu objects to the view that higgling is only entertainment: "Haggling is not the bizarre institution which it appears at first sight. It is engaged in neither for entertainment nor for fun" (1967, 47). Where transactions—movements of goods—are guided in important ways by considerations of kinship, place of residence, and hierarchical status, what appears to be higgling may well be social sorting. Consider again the case of northeastern Nepal:

> The person arriving to trade is a visitor, the person *in situ* the host, known as the "owner" (*bdag po*). In return for the protection and hospitality offered by the host, the visitor is supposed to make the greater concession in bargaining, which in effect means, after due negotiation, accepting the going rate in that place. The situation is reversed when the host goes to trade on the visitor's territory. (Humphrey, 1992, 119)

According to Humphrey the local rates, where they exist—as they do for regularly traded goods—are locally determined as part of a complex village economy. The bargaining, the negotiations that appear to be higgling, surrounding the rates are about quantity and quality (and implicitly, therefore, about price), but they are also part of a complex social arrangement between two groups of neighboring people.

For anthropologists for whom the disciplinary questions are questions about varying social arrangements across cultures, descriptions of higgling become the source of information about who trades what with whom and when. It is possible—as the work of many of the formalists in economic anthropology shows—to translate the patterns of other economies into the language that we use to describe our own economic patterns. It would be possible, in other words, to translate the bargaining among the Tibetans and the Lhomi much as I translated Halperin's description of Redside Market into the language of economics. What is missed is the detail that is more than "color"; it is the substance of the anthropological description. That people are Tibetans or Lhomi, old or young, strangers or not, uncles, priests, or whatever is the focus of interest.

While such "detail" does not enter most economic analysis, perhaps it should. Although the list of trader characteristics important in most anthropological studies is not one that would add to understanding of most markets with which economists deal, attributes other than price, quantity, and (standard) qualities of goods might. Those who sell, and particularly those who sell or try to sell in international markets, think that characteristics such as nationality are important.[10] So, also, do those economists who, along with Williamson, recognize the importance of the many and varied arrangements that fall between the extremes of market and hierarchy.[11]

What is most important, however, is that the anthropological approach is based upon the proposition that by studying (in the pure anthropological case, by observing) higgling defined as the process of arriving at the conditions of exchange, characteristics important but not known to the analyst prior to observation may be discovered. The nationality of traders, trust based on past trades, and manner of presentation are among characteristics that might be important in processes of interest to economists. It is easy to see how such characteristics affect large and long-lasting contracts such as those to build bespoke ports or turnkey projects; it is more difficult but probably more important to understand how they may also affect trading that we more easily treat in the standard stylized manner.

It is, however, difficult for economists to follow the anthropological approach. The standard practice, as already noted, is for economists (following the practice outlined implicitly in Hemenway's primer for beginning students) to focus on preconditions and outcomes, and the possible set of preconditions and outcomes is severely limited by the models used. Leonard (this volume) may be correct in thinking that experimental economics will open the range of characteristics to be incorporated into economic analysis. Until that happens the anthropological approach will remain difficult to follow, for as Brown notes (this volume), the dominant approach in economics has long been to consider the characteristics that manifest themselves in the process of transacting, as opposed to those which are independent of the process itself, as relatively unimportant.

The actors who engage in the stylized higgling of most economic analysis are so stylized that it is very difficult to vary their character, their goals, or their strategies, and they are so stylized because it has

10. For example, see Levitt 1993 on the "globalization of markets." Though Levitt stresses the increased standardization of products in international markets, he also describes, as in the case of SmithKline Beecham's successful introduction of a decongestant (Contac 600) into Japanese markets, the importance of "daily contacts with the wholesalers and key retailers," even though that is in violation of common marketing practice in this country.

11. On this see Williamson 1985; for an excellent survey of the literature on "enduring relationships between legally separate economic units" see Dietrich 1992.

not seemed important to most economists to consider other aspects of their being. Economists bound Alex's and Bev's rationality, cause them to suffer dissonance and otherwise tamper with their faculties, but do not make them fully social beings. However, deductive reasoning about stylized market participants produces stylized results. The advantage of the anthropological approach is that the characteristics of market participants deemed important for full description of market processes form an open-ended list. If economists were to use a similarly open-ended list, higgling just might become apparent and more important, even to economists who never stray from the modern industrial world.

Conclusion

Differences between transactors and their markets as described in anthropology and in economics stem in part from objective differences in degree of standardization of products and routinization of the exchanges made. Important differences also exist because anthropologists, unlike economists, are interested in the process of arriving at the terms of exchange, because of what that process may reveal about the social structure and social status of the traders. For economists the process of exchange is unimportant, because it is assumed that only a very limited range of characteristics of traders are of importance, and these characteristics are not dependent upon the exchange process itself—they are in place before, and remain unchanged by, the exchange. Were economists to adopt an anthropological approach to the study of modern markets— were they to employ an open-ended list of characteristics that affect market processes—something very like higgling might be revealed to be of importance yet. However, the protocols of economic analysis, both as they have derived from the evolution of modern industrial economies and in their Western preconceptions about the economy, make the adoption of an anthropological perspective revolutionary and therefore extraordinarily difficult to achieve.

Appendix: Questions from Hemenway's (1993) Chapter on Haggling

1. Do you expect to find haggling over airplane tickets? Doctor fees? Christmas trees? Used books? Banquet speaker salaries? Explain. Might it matter who the buyer is (e.g., an individual or a large corporation)?

2. "The market for television advertising time is elaborately organized. While

networks have posted rate cards, negotiated agreements are the rule on *major sales*. An advertiser can get a better deal if he risks waiting to buy until a week or two before show time" (Richard E. Caves and Marc J. Roberts, *Regulating the Product* [Cambridge, Mass: Ballinger Publishing Company, 1975], 104). Comment. Might you have predicted this situation?

3. What factors determine whether buyer or seller normally sets the price? Does it matter who does?

4. Should the federal government be willing to haggle about its employees' wages? Should it negotiate or haggle over its purchases of paper clips? Of roads? Of spaceships?

5. Is haggling more a cultural or an economic phenomenon? Knowing just economic information but little about the social aspects of the nation, could you predict the amount of haggling and where it is likely to occur?

6. "Never look a gift horse in the mouth." Relate to gifts. Relate to haggling.

7. If other consumers haggle in a particular market, does this affect whether or not you will? Why?

8. How would you go about gathering data and doing empirical research on haggling?

[Reprinted by permission of University Press of America.]

References

Bohannan, Paul, and Laura Bohannan. 1968. *Tiv Economy*. London: Longmans, Green.

Bohannan, Paul, and George Dalton. 1965. Introduction. In *Markets in Africa*. Anchor Natural History Library. New York: Doubleday.

Brown, Vivienne. 1994. Higgling: The Language of Markets in Economic Discourse. See De Marchi and Morgan 1994.

Chandler, Alfred D. 1977. *The Visible Hand*. Cambridge: Harvard University Press.

Clark, Colin, and Trevor Pinch. 1994. The Interactional Study of Exchange Relationships: An Analysis of Patter Merchants at Work on Street Markets. See De Marchi and Morgan.

Coats, A. W. 1990. Confrontation in Toronto: Reactions to the "Old" versus "New" Institutionalism Sessions. *Review of Political Economy* 2.1:87–93.

Commons, J. R. 1934. *Institutional Economics*. New York: Macmillan.

De Marchi, Neil, and Mary S. Morgan, eds. 1994. *Higgling: Transactors and Their Markets in the History of Economics*. HOPE 26, special issue. Durham: Duke University Press.

Dietrich, Michael. 1992. The Economics of Quasi-Integration. Paper presented at the Sixth Malvern Political Economy Conference.

Elster, Jon. 1989. Social Norms and Economic Theory. *Journal of Economic Perspectives* 3.4:99–117.

Emmett, Ross B. 1994. Maximizers versus Good Sports: Frank Knight's Curious Understanding of Exchange Behavior. See De Marchi and Morgan 1994.

Forget, Evelyn. 1994. Disequilibrium Trade as a Metaphor for Social Disorder in the Work of Jean-Baptiste Say. See De Marchi and Morgan 1994.

Halperin, Rohda H. 1990. *The Livelihood of Kin*. Austin: University of Texas Press.

Hemenway, David. 1993. *Prices and Choices*. 3d ed. Lanham, Md., New York, and London: University Press of America.

Hirschleifer, Jack. 1985. The Expanding Domain of Economics. *American Economic Review* 75:53–68.

Hirshleifer, Jack, and John G. Riley. 1992. *The Analytics of Uncertainty and Information*. Cambridge: Cambridge University Press.

Humphrey, Caroline. 1992. Fair Dealing, Just Rewards: The Ethics of Barter in North-East Nepal. In *Barter, Exchange and Value,* by Caroline Humphrey and Stephen Hugh-Jones. Cambridge: Cambridge University Press.

Knoedler, Janet. 1993. Early Examples of User-Based Industrial Research. *Business and Economic History* 22.1:285–94.

Leonard, Robert. 1994. Laboratory Strife: Higgling as Experimental Science in Economics and Social Psychology. See De Marchi and Morgan.

Levitt, Theodore. 1993. The Globalization of Markets. In *Readings in International Business,* edited by Robert Z. Aliber and Reid W. Click. Cambridge: MIT Press.

Lowry, S. Todd. 1994. The Market as a Distributive and Allocative System: Its Legal, Ethical, and Analytical Evolution. See De Marchi and Morgan 1994.

Mayhew, Anne. 1980. Atomistic and Cultural Analyses in Economic Anthropology: An Old Argument Repeated. In *Institutional Economics: Essays in Honor of Allan G. Gruchy,* edited by John Adams. Boston, The Hague, and London: Martinus Nijhoff.

———. 1989. Contrasting Origins of the Two Institutionalisms: The Social Science Context. *Review of Political Economy* 1.3:319–33.

Mintz, Sidney W. 1974. *Caribbean Transformations*. Chicago: Aldine.

Ortiz, Sutti. 1967. The Structure of Decision-Making among Indians of Colombia. In *Themes in Economic Anthropology,* edited by Raymond Firth. London: Tavistock.

Rutherford, Malcolm. 1989. What Is Wrong with the New Institutionalist Economics (and Is Still Wrong with the Old)? *Review of Political Economy* 1:299–318.

———. 1994. Predatory Practices or Reasonable Values? American Institutionalists on the Nature of Market Transactions. See De Marchi and Morgan 1994.

Samuels, Warren. 1990. The Old versus the New Institutionalism. *Review of Political Economy* 2.1:83–86.

Sahlins, Marshall. 1972. *Stone Age Economics*. Chicago: Aldine.

Schabas, Margaret. 1994. Market Contracts in the Age of Hume. See De Marchi and Morgan 1994.

Stocking, George W., Jr. 1968. *Race, Culture and Evolution*. New York: Free Press.

Sugden, Robert. 1989. Spontaneous Order. *Journal of Economic Perspectives* 3.4:85–97.

Tax, Sol. 1953. *Penny Capitalism*. Chicago: University of Chicago Press.

Uchendu, Victor C. 1967. Some Principles of Haggling in Peasant Markets. *Economic Development and Cultural Change* 16.1:37–50.

Veblen, Thorstein. 1975. *The Theory of Business Enterprise*. Clifton, N.J.: Augustus M. Kelley.

West, James. 1945. *Plainville, U.S.A.* New York: Columbia University Press.

Williamson, Oliver. 1985. *The Economic Institutions of Capitalism: Firms, Markets, Relational Contracting*. New York: Free Press.

Wrong, D. H. 1961. The Oversocialized Conception of Man in Modern Society. *American Sociological Review* 26:283–93.

Tit for Tat: Concepts of Exchange, Higgling, and Barter in Two Episodes in the History of Economic Anthropology

Philip Mirowski

This essay, really little more than two extracts from a larger history, is an oblique plea to change our impressions of what it means to write a history of economic thought. I have in the past had recourse to histories of physics and mathematics in order to attempt to expand our horizons of explanation of how we have arrived at our *fin-de-siècle* nexus; but in many ways those moves were easier, both because histories of those sciences were already the province of an active community of historians, and also because I could take it for granted those fields of endeavor represented the pinnacle of what economists would consider as intellectual triumphs relevant to their concerns. The case of economic anthropology stands in stark contrast, though it also is equally absent from standard histories of economic "thought." With a few notable exceptions, neglect of anthropology is nearly ubiquitous in economics, often accompanied by convictions that it has little or nothing to offer the modern social scientist. On the contrary, I will eventually seek to claim that the bulk of the really perceptive discussions of such concepts as the gift, exchange, barter, higgling, and money have taken place outside the self-identified language community of economists, and was instead frequently located amongst those who called themselves economic anthropologists or economic sociologists. It will be largely a twentieth-century story and, curiously enough, one that, to my limited knowledge, has never before been written down anywhere. The present essay, describing two intersections of the anthropologists Bronislaw Malinowski and Marshall Sahlins with the economic orthodoxies of their time, is the first installment on this promissory note.

There are three reasons to restrict the focus to these two prominent figures in anthropology, to the neglect of such other giants as Karl Marx, Henry Maine, Raymond Firth, Karl Polanyi, Mary Douglas, Maurice Godelier, Clifford Geertz, Steve Gudeman, and many others I have left out of the account. First off, I should like to suggest that Malinowski and Sahlins prosecuted one relatively coherent account of barter, exchange, higgling, and value which stood as a viable alternative to the economic orthodoxies of their time; and moreover, this was recognized by contemporaries. Second, these two figures betray an ambivalence about the sustained development of their economic theories which I find very difficult to explain (and will beg the reader's indulgence because I fail to do so here), but which does begin to raise the question of why it is anthropology has yet to mount a more serious challenge to economists' definitions of the objects of their affections. Third, this focus exemplifies a genre of history to which I have become devoted, namely, narratives where one intellectual discipline comes to shape the concepts and methods of another largely through a set of unintended consequences, a dynamic which ends up revealing much about the structure of our own culture, the web of signs and events in which we are all enmeshed.

Natural Exchange in the Primitive's Mirror

> Let us suppose that two men who otherwise engage in no "social relation"—for example, two uncivilized men of different races, or a European who encounters a native in darkest Africa—meet and "exchange" two objects. We are inclined to think that a mere description of what can be observed during this exchange—muscular movements and, if some words were spoken, the sounds of which, so to say, constitute the "material" of the behaviour—would in no sense comprehend the "essence" of what happens. This is quite correct. The "essence" of what happens is constituted by the "meaning" which the two parties ascribe to their observable behaviour, a meaning which regulates the course of their future conduct. Without this meaning, we are inclined to say, an "exchange" is neither empirically possible nor conceptually imaginable. (Max Weber, quoted in Oakes 1977, 24)

George Stocking has said that we should look to German Historicism, and not just British utilitarianism, in order to understand the early history of anthropology (Geertz 1991, 609). This certainly is a sine qua non for the writing of a history of economic anthropology. One survey of the nascent field at the turn of the last century (Köcke 1979) traces a lineage from Karl Bücher, Wilhelm Koppers, and Max Schmidt through to Richard Thurnwald, documenting their influence on such eminent figures as Malinowski, Polanyi, Herskovits, and Sahlins. A similar lineage could readily be traced from the same initial point of departure across the French border, through Durkheim's approach to economic sociology in the *Année sociologique* group, to Marcel Mauss and thence to Mary Douglas (Lukes 1973).

The impetus for this whole line of inquiry appears to have been the tendency of German Historicists to reject Adam Smith's brand of conjectural anthropology, especially with regard to a supposedly innate tendency to truck and barter, as well as their need to posit an initial placeholder category in order to anchor their various stage theories of economic development. Historians of economics will be familiar with the Marxian construct of "primitive communism" in the march of historical materialism; but in the German-language community, there was more fascination with Bruno Hildebrand's postulation of the primitive moneyless economy; with Max Weber's classification of types of societies by types of money, from Ornament to Use to Clothing to Tokens; and with Karl Bücher's assertion of a thoroughly pre-economic phase of autarkic individuals dominated by the bare struggle for survival.

In the late nineteenth-century context, such initial primitive economic formations lost in the mists of time were all too readily equated with contemporary "primitive" societies on the fringes of European imperialist expansion. Indeed, the clear coincidence of the initiation of this German literature on primitive economies so close on the heels of the German "rush for colonies" at the end of the nineteenth century has not yet been explored, although there is beginning to be a more general literature in the history of anthropology researching the links between colonial expansion and the birth of the discipline (Stocking 1991). In such an environment, descriptions of non-Western economic practices were thought to have myriad implications for the validity of the "abstract" British approach to political economy, the legitimacy of contending Historicist stage theories, and the meaning of progress in the development of economic institutions. Much of this discourse revolved around an elaborate play upon the concepts of "nature" and the "natural."

The German Historicists often sought to set themselves apart from British political economy by counterposing a "cultural" or national economy to the natural-law theorizing so characteristic of Smith and Ricardo. Whereas the English were content to look round their study or up their high street in order to observe the operations of Nature, the German Historicists felt oppressed by the weight of Culture and History in their own situation, presuming therefore that the empirical manifestation of Natural Economy could only be observed in the thoroughly inaccessible past. By shifting the premises of the Natural to contemporary "savages," a novel method of attack upon British precepts could be mounted. One could raise various counterexamples to *homo economicus* from the ethnographic reports and then assert that the Nature of the British did not resemble the Nature found in the bush. This is indeed the standard trope of all the early writings in economic anthropology, up to and including that of Malinowski and Mauss.

The first attempt at a synthesis of ethnographic reports into a characterization of primitive economies seems to have been the one by the economic historian Karl Bücher in his *Industrial Evolution* (1901). The characterization was crude and sketchy, primarily because Bücher wanted to maintain that the "savage" was a "pre-economic man," in the sense that accoutrements of civilization such as forward-looking work, valuation of things, accumulation of wealth, and the transmission of culture were purportedly absent. All that obtained was a rudimentary sort of "domestic economy" consisting of an individualistic search for food and an incipient sexual division of labor. This "definition" of the "savage" as the complete negation of civilization is of course little better than Smith's own performance, and we should not normally pay it any attention, except that it seems to have mobilized the entire next generation of anthropologists with an economic bent to refute it. Bücher's taxonomy was criticized by the first generation of participant observers such as Koppers, Schmidt, and Thurnwald, as well as Marxists such as Luxemburg and Kautsky (Köcke 1979). More interestingly, the very first article on economic anthropology in the *Economic Journal* was constructed around an attack on Bücher. There Bronislaw Malinowski wrote:

> His conclusions are, in my opinion, a failure. . . . Bücher comes to the conclusion that the savages—he includes among them races as highly developed as the Polynesians—have no economic organization, and that they are in a pre-economic stage. . . . In savage societies national economy certainly does not exist, if we mean by the term a system of free competitive exchange of goods and services, with the interplay of supply and demand determining value and regulating all economic life. . . . Instead we find a state of affairs where production, exchange

and consumption are socially organized and regulated by custom, and where a special system of traditional economic values governs their activities and spurs them on to efforts. (1921, 1, 2, 15)

What is remarkable about that article is its keen strategic sense of audience. Malinowski sought to retail his proposed economic anthropology to the British economists as a vigorous counterattack upon German Historicism,[1] even though an overriding theme of the ethnography of the Trobriand Islanders and their now-famous Kula ring (described below) was a doggedly detailed critique of Marshallian price theory and utilitarianism, one clearly informed by Historicist tenets. Indeed, the Kula is not even described in the *EJ* article, an event all the more odd when one realizes that Malinowski himself regarded its description as the ethnographic finding most relevant to economists—or, as he put it, "The Kula is the highest and most dramatic expression of the native's conception of value" (1922, 176)—and, further, that it had already appeared in the anthropological journal *Man* the year before.

Two other major German anthropologists who responded to Bücher were Max Schmidt and Richard Thurnwald. The relevance of their work for our present narrative lies in the fact that both felt that conventional approaches to conceptualizing exchange were unavailing when it came to understanding "primitive economies." Schmidt was dissatisfied with the idea that generic exchange somehow reconciled rivals to their own self-interested schemes, insisting rather that alternative exchange strategies were associated with differing regimes of communal provisioning, competitive interaction, or hostile confrontation. The irony for Schmidt was that pure communism and pure hostility were both reportedly marked by the absence of higgling: in the communal case, allocations were fixed by fiat, whereas dealings with hostile strangers were conducted through "silent barter," or the leaving of goods in an isolated spot where the others were free to take and deposit anything they wished in return.

Thurnwald went even further in his synthetic work *The Economics of Primitive Communities* (1932). In an extended meditation upon the pitfalls of applying Western notions of the economic to other cultures, he insisted that while some form of trade or barter could be found in each and every known "primitive society," the goods involved were "related

---

1. A species of attack always welcome in the incipient Marshallian orthodoxy. See Mirowski 1993, on Edgeworth; and Kadish 1989.

to many other sides of life besides the economic one, and are affected by the connexion of the object with supernatural powers and forces. . . . This excludes the possibility of regarding economic possessions from a one-sided rationalistic point of view. . . . All observation of primitive peoples teaches us that the social motive, the desire for exceptional position in the group, has outweighed the economic motive" ([1932] 1965, 176, 177, 179).[2] Far from precluding the option of a general theory of exchange, Thurnwald instead suggested that various implied symmetries in the social organization, such as lineage branches in kinship systems, could actually be used to account for observed barter relations. "The idea of requital, like that of remuneration, appears to be one of the original reactions of mankind" (141). Beyond such hints, he did not manage to spell out how such a theory would work; but many of the protagonists in our subsequent narrative would come to regard his observations as prescient.

The conduit for these German Historicist concerns into the British context was Bronislaw Malinowski, a Pole whose first thesis was written on Mach's principle of the economy of thought, who had studied with Wundt in Leipzig, and who had attended Bücher's lectures there.[3] After spending much of World War I in ethnographic field work in Australia and Papua New Guinea, he obtained a readership at the London School of Economics and published *Argonauts of the Western Pacific* (1922), the book George Stocking (1991, 50) calls "the most literary and most romantic of his ethnographies." Notwithstanding everything else that *Argonauts* represents to the Western anthropological community, it is treated by economic anthropologists writing in English in much the same manner that economists treat their Adam Smith: he wasn't actually the first, but he is the one upon whom they have founded their origin myths and to whom they return for inspiration time and time again.

As Sir James Frazer wrote in his introduction to *Argonauts*, "In the present treatise Dr. Malinowski is mainly concerned with what at first sight might seem a purely economic activity of the Trobriand Islanders."

---

2. As one of his arguments against imposing standard economic categories (in this case the allocation of scarce resources), Thurnwald (180) cites various forms of "wasteful" behavior in various tribes. Perhaps unbeknownst to him, this argument had already been used against neoclassical theory in the American context in Thorstein Veblen's *Theory of the Leisure Class*.

3. Fechner/Wundt/Nietzsche influences upon British neoclassicism are discussed in Mirowski 1993. Some biographical sources on Malinowski are Stocking 1992 and Symmons-Symonolewicz 1958–60.

But the real purpose of the book was to call into question the orthodox notions of "economic activity" through description of a set of practices now universally referred to as "the Kula." There is still vigorous dissension over what the Kula actually is and was, as opposed to what Malinowski says it was[4]—a controversy which we shall bypass here. Instead, let us consider a brief outline of the Received View of the Kula, paraphrasing Leach (1983, 1–4). The main aspect of the Kula is the clockwise circulation of necklaces around a ring of islands in the Solomon Sea, in exchange for armshells which circulate anticlockwise around the same ring; both classes of "exchangeables" derive most of their value from having participated in the Kula, since they have few other uses, are system-communal property and cannot be privately owned, and in any event cannot be kept very long, or exchanged for anything else, even unilaterally (no shells for shells or necklaces for necklaces). The value of both necklaces and armshells is dependent upon their past history of exchanges in the Kula, accumulating value with augmented lineages; the shell-for-necklace exchange is structured according to a principle of reciprocity between lifelong male Kula partners. The transactors may solicit particular shells from partners by means of preliminary gifts of other items; but it is strictly forbidden that any haggling take place with Kula partners, while reciprocity is never simultaneous but always delayed, usually from one ceremonial canoe expedition to another. A fair amount of more conventional "utilitarian" trade accompanies Kula expeditions; but Kula partners do not engage in this kind of trade with each other.

Malinowski was in no sense the "discoverer" of the Kula; but he was the one who had the foresight and imagination to draw out its astringent implications for Western conceptions of "primitive economics" and its relationship to Western economics. The key, as he admitted later, was Thurnwald's stress upon symmetry and reciprocity (Köcke 1979, 157). "The whole tribal life," he wrote, "is permeated by a constant give and take; . . . every ceremony, every legal and customary act is done to the accompaniment of gift and counter-gift; . . . wealth, taken and given, is one of the main instruments of social organization, of the power of the chief, of the bonds of kinship, and of relationship in law" (Malinowski 1922, 167). So far, there seems nothing slated to perturb your average Marshallian economist; but then the analysis took a sharply critical turn:

4. For examples of such arguments see Leach and Leach 1983; Weiner 1992; Gell, in Humphrey and Hugh-Jones 1992.

Value is not the result of utility and rarity intellectually compounded, but is the result of a sentiment grown round things, which, though satisfying human needs, are capable of evoking emotions. The value of manufactured objects of use must also be explained through man's emotional nature, and not by reference to his logical construction of utilitarian views . . . In almost all forms of exchange in the Trobriands, there is not even a trace of gain, nor is there any reason for looking at it from the purely utilitarian or economic standpoint, since there is no enhancement of mutual utility through exchange. Thus, it is quite a usual thing in the Trobriands for a type of transaction to take place in which A gives 20 baskets of yams to B, receiving for it a small polished blade, only to have the whole transaction reversed in a few weeks' time. . . . A calculating cold egotism [tends to] ignore the fundamental human impulse to display, to share, to bestow. They ignore the deep tendency to create social ties through the exchange of gifts. (172, 175)

Now, from Carlyle's epithet of "pig philosophy" onward, British economists had become quite inured to the moral critique of a calculus of self-interest; but this was something else altogether. What Malinowski asserted was that Western conceptions of exchange were too blinkered and narrow-gauged and therefore incapable of encompassing such seeming counterexamples as the Kula. (Again, provisionally, we pass on the question whether in fact the Kula can be successfully subsumed under a utilitarian framework.) What economics had left out of the picture, to its detriment, was the existence of the *gift*. The notion of a single generic form of exchange must be relinquished:

[For] although there exist forms of barter pure and simple, there are so many transitions and gradations between that and simple gift, that it is impossible to draw any fixed line between trade on the one hand, and exchange of gifts on the other. . . . In order to deal with these facts correctly it is necessary to give a complete survey of all forms of payment or present. In this survey there will be at one end the extreme case of pure gift, that is, an offering for which nothing is given in return. Then . . . there come forms of exchange, where more or less strict equivalence is observed, arriving finally at real barter. (176)

There follows (177–93) a detailed description of this continuum and how certain structures of social relations cause "exchanges" to fall

Something for nothing	Balanced exchange	Pure trade
0	1	∞

Figure 1 Value of Object Received / Value of Object Tendered

within certain subsets of the continuum. The entire latticework is predicated upon a well-defined interpersonal value principle, which Malinowski realized is in large part what must be theorized and justified all along the continuum. Under certain extreme and rare circumstances, such as those located at the far left side of the continuum (see figure 1), the one salient aspect of gift behavior is the expression of a lack of concern over (and often an explicit prohibition of any interest in) the value principle. Approaching the middle of the continuum, value equivalence can be handled by a number of external structures, ranging from the most prosaic in the format of exact identity in all relevant physical respects of the objects exchanged, all the way to an external imposition of an interpersonal evaluation by a third party. The Kula is situated at this locus. Movement from left to right also tends to display a decreasingly elastic time frame for the performance of reciprocity, with time elapsed deemed irrelevant for the pure gift, but increasingly taken into account as part of the terms of the bargain with pure trade.

What does *not* happen until we are quite far along the right side of the continuum is the explicit constitution of the value principle by means of the activity of *haggling*. Indeed, only well toward that extreme righthand position was it culturally permissible to express publicly an interest in the goods in question. So the Marshallian economist's notion of exchange, with its windowless monads emanating a fixed individual psychological desire, pitted in free competitive barter against its rivalrous but similarly opaque opposite number, with market clearing, mysteriously static *ceteris paribus* conditions, and all the rest, occupied a severely diminished landscape in the larger social schema. The farther towards the righthand situation of mutual benefit, the more modern the surrounding context—"absence of ceremonial, absence of magic, absence of special partnership" (190)—the less likely was there anyone available to fit into the relevant social categories which sanctioned that type of exchange. Instead the distribution of types of exchange along the continuum were to be predicated upon the local kinship structures: "The first type of gifts . . . take place in the relationship between husband and wife, and in that between parents and children . . . the obligatory ones, given without systematic repayment, are associated with relationship-in-law, mainly, though the chief's tributes also belong in this class. If we drew up a scheme of sociological relations, each type of them would be defined by a special class of economic duties" (191). Of course, Malinowski did not go so far as to draw up this scheme; but the outline sketch of the theory was clear enough.

Just in case the reader had missed the theoretical import of the story of the Kula, distracted as it were by the exoticism of the ethnography, Malinowski made it a point to stress the target doctrine of the work in his final summation. He deplores

> the conception of a rational being who wants nothing but to satisfy his simplest needs and does it according to the economic principle of least effort. . . . [He] has nothing but his material advantage of a purely utilitarian type at heart. Now I hope whatever the meaning of the Kula might be for Ethnology, for the general science of culture, the meaning of the Kula will consist in being instrumental to dispel such crude, rationalistic conceptions of primitive mankind, and to induce both the speculator and the observer to deepen the analysis of economic facts. (516)

Given this clarity of purpose, it is amazing to observe astute economic anthropologists of a later vintage disparage Malinowski for that which he was most concerned to combat. See, for instance, Parry (1985, 454), who accuses him of "the tendency to see exchanges as essentially dyadic transactions between self-interested individuals, and as premissed on some kind of balance; the tendency to play down supernatural sanctions, and total contempt for questions of origin." Or Weiner (1992, 31): "Malinowski . . . never resolved for himself whether Trobrianders represented the alter ego or the antithesis of Western *Homo economicus*." Or, more germane to our next section, Marshall Sahlins: "The overriding sense of Malinowski's project was to reduce all manner of seemingly bizarre customs . . . to practical (read biological) values" (1976, 74). This construction of their progenitor may have numerous causes; and confronting them may help us in the future to understand the curious twists and turns of the subsequent evolution of economic anthropology.

The first source of the loss of credibility is derived from Malinowski's own peregrinations. For various reasons which we have yet to plumb, Malinowski implicitly repudiated part of his theory in his next book, *Crime and Custom in Savage Society* (1926, 40). There he relinquished the concept of a pure gift[5] but, by so doing in a distressingly unacknowledged manner, left his continuum without an anchor, attenuating the side of the taxonomy that served most as contrasting with standard utilitarian construction of exchange. Furthermore, he seemingly lost interest in economics after *Argonauts,* moving increasingly towards Freudianism and a Spenglerian disdain for modern science in the 1930s. One adds the qualifier "seemingly" because he had embarked upon one further project, on Mexican peasant markets, just prior to his death in 1942; it was only published in Spanish in 1957, and in English in 1982. This final product did not display his characteristic theoretical panache. Thus the progenitor of economic anthropology shot his progeny in the foot, and then left it to fend for itself.

The second reason for modern ambivalence regarding Malinowski is his apparent reconciliation to utilitarianism later in life, not through economics, but rather through a species of behavioralist determinism. One observes this in his later programmatic utterances, such as in his entry on "culture" for the *Encyclopaedia of the Social Sciences:* "Moral motivation when viewed empirically consists in a disposition of the nervous system and of the whole organism to follow within given circumstances a line of behavior dictated by inner constraint which is due neither to innate impulses nor yet to obvious gains or utilities. The inner constraint is the result of gradual training of the organism within a definite set of cultural conditions" (1931, 623). This reconciliation is even more evident in the posthumously published work on Mexican peasant markets (Malinowski and de la Fuente 1982), which does not once make use of the continuum in figure 1. "Many of those who might criticize Malinowski's functionalism are nevertheless satisfied with its essential counterposition of personal interests and social order. It is true that Malinowski

---

5. "When, however, I describe the category of offerings as Pure Gifts and place under this heading the gifts of husband to wife and father to children, I am obviously committing a mistake. I have fallen then, in fact, into the error exposed above, of tearing the act out of its context, of not taking a sufficiently long view of the chain of transactions. . . . [Footnote:] I had written the above paragraph before I saw M. Mauss's strictures, which substantially agreed with my own" (1926, 40–41).

was among the first anthropologists to deny the generality of 'economic man.' But was this not simply to give the same concept even greater scope?" (Sahlins 1976, 86).

Then there is the third aspect of Malinowski's work, its early symbiotic relationship to its colonial sponsors. A case can be made that the young Polish ethnographer with no disciplinary support and few academic prospects needed to choose a topic of research which would be regarded as useful by the colonial authorities that funded it; thus it is no accident that he acknowledged that colonial fiscal policies might be "strengthened by an appreciation of the 'psychology of the gift' which, if appropriately considered, would make it possible to introduce taxation without hurting native feelings" (Stocking 1991, 53). What initially was a calculated attempt to nurture bases of support for the fledgling discipline would later be something to disparage with a revulsion commensurate with any really important excrement taboo. So Malinowski is an ambivalent figure in our narrative, which explains some of the problem. But that's not the whole of it.

The question of the relationship of the continuum in figure 1 to orthodox Western economic theory is perhaps more important for understanding subsequent events. I think a case can be made that Malinowski had a fairly good idea of the outlines of Marshallian theory when he wrote *Argonauts,* perhaps even better than many of those who followed him in the field of economic anthropology. But context matters, so it will become increasingly important as historians to be very precise in our historical references to orthodox neoclassical economics. As I have explained elsewhere, Marshallian economics is characterized by its conflation of classical and neoclassical value theories: the first conceives of value as some entity embodied in the good, the second as a virtual field of preferences filling an a priori commodity space.[6] The differences in the two methods of modeling value have myriad profound implications for the treatment of time, money, higgling and price dynamics, disequilibrium, differential forms of market adjustment, and so on. Most critically, the substance and field versions of value theory treat "equivalent exchange" entirely differently.

In the classical substance theory, equilibrium exchange is always characterized by swaps of equivalent embodied-value magnitudes; profit

---

6. The contradictions involved in Marshall's attempts to reconcile the substance and field theories of value are discussed in Mirowski 1989 and 1991b.

only arises in production, or in disequilibrium arbitrage during a period of flows of investment between employments. In the neoclassical field theory, on the other hand, people are only motivated to exchange goods because they individually value them differently, and the role of arbitrage is to enforce the "law of one price," rendering quoted price parametric to the individual trader. In neither case does higgling play more than a subsidiary role, since the determinants of price are fixed prior to any activity by some natural or invariant cause. In orthodox neoclassicism, even the activity of arbitrage is itself presumed to have mysteriously happened before the fact of the calculation of equilibrium prices.

Most of this tended to get lost in the Marshallian tradition, summarily lumped together and then discarded under the rubric of "partial equilibrium." This confusion within the British economic orthodoxy made it more difficult to get a bead on what it was that Malinowski intended to counterpose to his own account, and I believe this shows up at various junctures in *Argonauts*. For instance, in one passage he comes very close to a proto–labor theory of value (172–73), but then in a footnote backs away from the question of the origins of value, fearing that he may have already gone too far in the direction of orthodox Western economics. When modern anthropologists stumble across such passages, they are inclined less to inquire into the context than to pronounce a pox on all Western theories. This too may have something to do with the modern disdain for Malinowski's theorizing.

And then, finally, there is the other landmark text of the decade, Mauss's *Essai sur le don* (1925). If Malinowski is now treated as the inadvertent utilitarian, the Trojan Horse of Western economics, then Mauss becomes the hero, the champion of a fully cultural theory sensitive to the native's point of view, the true opponent of Western economics. But just as in the previous case, there is something faintly rank and fusty about this assessment, since the most widely cited lesson of *Essai* among anthropologists is that there is no such thing as a pure gift, a tidy bit of utilitarian wisdom if there ever was one. I propose an alternative reading, building upon the commentary of Parry (1985). Briefly, Mauss can be read as a very good example of German Historicist economics, albeit with a strong whiff of Durkheim on the central role of the sacred. Situated in the French context, where at that time no version of neoclassical economics was deemed worthy of attention, Mauss had no developed tradition of price theory to oppose, and therefore he had no desire to make any contribution to an alternative theory of value. Nevertheless, as would any self-respecting historicist, he also portrayed his work as opposed to the blinkered economic orthodoxy of the time, so it will be of interest to see just how this was done.

It is apparent that *Essai* was written in response to reading Malinowski: "We have repeatedly pointed out how this economy of gift-exchange fails to conform to the principles of so-called natural economy or utilitarianism. . . . We add our own observations to those of Malinowski who devoted a whole work to ousting the prevalent doctrines on primitive economics" (Mauss [1925] 1954, 69). But there is also a rejection of Malinowski's attempt to categorize types of exchanges by degrees of interest or disinterest: "There is a series of rights and duties about consuming and repaying existing side by side with rights and duties about giving and receiving. The pattern of symmetrical and reciprocal rights is not difficult to understand if we realize that it is first and foremost a pattern of spiritual bonds between things which are to some extent parts of persons, and persons and groups to behave in some measure as if they were things" (11). This thingification of people and personification of things was a central thesis of Durkheim and Mauss's classic work on cognitive anthropology, *Primitive Classification*.[7] Throughout, it will be helpful to keep in mind that unlike Malinowski, Mauss was not a practitioner of the method of participant observation, but rather a representative of that older form of historicism that digested vast quantities of ethnographies and histories of others, hoping to distill out the dynamic essence of social laws.

On the whole, Mauss rejected Malinowski's stress on reciprocity as an organizing principle for a general theory of economics. It seems the motivation behind this position was the conviction that Malinowski did not adequately recognize that the distinction between things and persons was eminently a modern one. Resorting to philology, the history of ancient law, and ethnographies and histories of Western Europe, Mauss argued that gifts were actually a species of aggression: "To give is to show one's superiority, to show that one is something more and higher, that one is *magister*. To accept without returning or repaying more is to face subordination, to become a client and subservient" ([1925] 1954, 72). But Mauss claimed that what enforces the counter-gift is not so

---

7. The original source on the Durkheim/Mauss thesis is translated as Durkheim and Mauss 1963. This thesis, augmented by the writings of Mary Douglas, has been used in my own work (1989) to help explain the allure of physical metaphors in modern neoclassical economics.

much utilitarian calculation as the fact that the object handed over is imbued with the personality of the giver; in a sense it is the giver incarnate, looming over the life of the receiver. In redeeming it he redeems himself. Interest and disinterest are strangely intermingled, all colored by an animism and anthropomorphism that Mauss would like to implicate in the origins of capitalist trade and credit, the Durkheimian religious origin of economic value.

We have here a standard Historicist trope of an organically unified Garden of Eden in which there was no gift, no market, or no economy; it has been degraded in the interim into a cacophany of individualist pleadings and false dichotomies: gift/trade, disinterest/interest, society/individual, person/thing. Thus it seems that Sahlins's later characterization of Mauss's *Essai* as "a kind of social contract for the primitives" (1972, 169) is a curiously violent inversion of its original context. (Sahlins did later implicitly repudiate this reading, 1976, 109.) As Parry writes (1985, 458), "While Mauss is generally represented as telling us *in fact* the gift is never free, what I think he is really telling us is how *we* acquired a *theory* that it should never be [free]."

It should now be apparent that unlike Malinowski, Mauss was intent upon providing a theory of the historical obfuscation of the nature of exchange; he did not seem interested in providing a theory of primitive exchange per se and most emphatically declined the option of a theory of value. Hence his strictures against utilitarianism rang a little hollow; and there was no attempt actively to confront the economists. Nevertheless Mauss can be seen as (inadvertently) encouraging a species of antitheoretical bias amongst economic anthropologists, even though he ransacked ancient histories and ethnographies alike as though they were indifferently substitutable reports on a single "primitive" economic structure. Just about all that the two founding documents of economic anthropology had in common was an explicit disavowal of utilitarianism and an attempt to appropriate the term "gift" for the fledgling discipline.

Sahlins and the Revival of Theory

The most important theorist of gift and exchange in economic anthropology since Malinowski and Mauss is Marshall Sahlins (b. 1930; Ph.D. Columbia, 1954). Sahlins has undergone two or three sharp reversals in fundamental philosophical underpinnings in his career, so there is a danger of rendering his thought as much more continuous and self-consistent than it may actually have been, in the interests of narrative coherence. However, with respect to his middle period, when concern with economic anthropology was at its apogee, his trajectory might be summarized as having begun at Columbia with both Karl Polanyi and Karl Marx (through the intermediary of the members of the Mundial Upheaval Society; see Murphy 1991); becoming deflected for a time by his close contact with Leslie White at the University of Michigan; and then to be briefly captured in orbit around French structuralism, and Lévi-Strauss in particular.

The Polanyites in the 1950s and 1960s formed one of the primary nuclei of resistance to neoclassical economics in economic history and economic anthropology in the United States, to such an extent that the controversy between the "substantivists" (Polanyites) and the "formalists" (Marshallian neoclassicals) would require its own historical narrative.[8] Suffice it to say that at an early stage Sahlins's major opus *Stone Age Economics* was intended as a defense and vindication of the work of Karl Polanyi and George Dalton. This motivation was obscured in the final published text because of the omission of an introduction, which was, however, published in an obscure outlet (Sahlins 1969). Perhaps it was omitted because it was more revealing as documenting Sahlins's vain struggles to reconcile Leslie White and Karl Polanyi than as serving to usher the student into the anthropological theory of exchange.

The connection to White's own paradoxes over Nature and Culture has been noted in the anthropological literature (Barrett 1989). Leslie White was a most perplexing theorist, on the one hand championing evolutionary narratives of progress, even to the point of repeatedly suggesting an energy theory of value; and, on the other hand, upholding the more orthodox Boasian notions of "culture" as a self-sufficient explanatory principle, with all the trappings of cultural relativism which it implies. Sahlins himself trafficked in the former sorts of explanations earlier in his career: "General progress also occurs in culture, and it can be absolutely, objectively, and nonmoralistically ascertained. . . . In culture, as

---

8. See Mayhew, this volume; Polanyi-Levitt 1990. A separate reading of this episode is available as an unpublished paper from the present author. The importance of this episode in Sahlins's career is unaccountably neglected in the secondary literature on his work. Its significance is both highlighted and rendered problematic by a statement Sahlins made to me in a personal interview on 28 May 1993: "The formalist/substantivist controversy is over because the substantivists won." A more conventional interpretation is that both sides of the controversy collapsed in exhaustion.

in life, thermodynamic accomplishment is fundamental to progress. . . . A people may adopt a technological innovation that theoretically might double output, but instead, they only work half as long (twice as efficiently) as they used to. . . . Progress is not the inevitable outcome of efficiency" (Sahlins, in Sahlins and Service 1960, 27, 33, 34). It seems that sometime in the 1960s he came to appreciate the tensions in touting an absolute science of evolutionary energetics while privileging anthropology as the sympathetic understanding of alien cultures.[9] He seemed to perceive the test case for the rectification of this contradiction between Culture and Nature to be (at least initially) economic anthropology, and the instrument of clarification to be the structuralism of Lévi-Strauss.

As early as 1960 he enlisted in the ranks of those opposed to any form of reconciliation with economists: "Primitive economic behavior is largely an aspect of kinship behavior, and is therefore organized by means completely different from capitalist production and market transactions. The inference is clear: the whole of modern economic theory . . . fails to apply to primitive economies" (quoted in Firth 1967, 78). In his central contribution to economic anthropology, *Stone Age Economics* (1972), he summarized the history of economic anthropology as follows:

> If the problem in the beginning was the "naive anthropology" of Economics, today it is the "naive economics" of Anthropology. . . . It is a choice between the perspective of Business, for the formalist method must consider the primitive economies as underdeveloped versions of our own, and a culturalist study that as a matter of principle does honor to different societies for what they are. . . . The attempt in the end is to bring the anthropological perspective to bear on the traditional work of microeconomics, the explanation of exchange value. (xi, xii)

What sets *Stone Age Economics* apart from other treatises in the history of economic anthropology is that it mounts a sustained, coherent (though not impregnable!) critique of orthodox economics, combined

---

9. It may not be amiss here to indicate that Sahlins then became a persistent critic of the "Naturalism" of orthodox economic theory. Given that neoclassical economics was itself derived fairly directly from the mid-nineteenth-century energetics movement (Mirowski 1989), one might observe that it takes one to know one; and his strident rejection of neoclassicism is also a rejection of his own earlier career. One can also observe that the pivotal text, "The Original Affluent Society," is a fairly neat inversion of his own energeticist example of 1960 (quoted above).

with the outlines of an alternative theory of exchange, all supplemented with an impressive range of ethnographic illustrations, without once ever lapsing into the more familiar catalogue or laundry list of exotic, idiosyncratic phenomena. For this reason alone it merits extended summary; but beyond that, I also argue that it stands as the first analytic clarification of Malinowski's original attempt to theorize trade as a continuum of reciprocities. The book is essentially divided into three movements: a description of what Sahlins calls "the domestic mode of production" (chapters 1–3); a Hobbesian reading of Mauss's essay on the gift (chapter 4); and finally, an outline of a theory of "primitive exchange" (chapters 5–6). Most of these chapters were first published elsewhere between 1965 and 1968, and one should regard them as being roughly of that vintage.

The first section, on "the original affluent society," garnered the most attention in reviews and in the subsequent anthropology literature; but in retrospect, it was the least original of the three movements (Bird-David 1992). Sahlins wittily began, "If economics is the dismal science, then the study of hunting and gathering economies must be its most advanced branch." He then chose to invert the standard image of the savage, haggard and worn, pressed close to subsistence by rudimentary knowledge, technology, and organization, by replacing it with the "Zen road to affluence": material plenty and leisure with a low standard of living. Now the cliché of the "lazy savage" has a long heritage in Western discourse; and there was already, by that time, a literature which purported to explain the phenomenon from a rough neoclassical vantage point, ranging from Chayanov (here favorably cited) to W. A. Lewis (not cited). Sahlins wanted to turn the truculent native thesis against the neoclassicals—labor was not a scarce factor, no one was optimizing— but also wanted to subvert the standard Marxian materialism by claiming that in the ambit of the "domestic mode of production," culture ruled production norms and not vice versa.

He asserted that cultural classification, and not labor exploitation, was the major instrument of social differentiation, and that "as an *economic* rule, there is no class of landed paupers in primitive society. If expropriation occurs it is accidental to the mode of production itself" (1972, 93). He seemed to think that Marx could be used to help to distinguish "production for use" from "production for exchange" (84); but this misconstrues the purposes to which the distinction is put in Marx. What prevents all of this from collapsing into a rosy *Gemeinschaft* is what

Sahlins dubs the anti-surplus principle. If there is surfeit, then production is curtailed and it is given away. It is the gifts themselves that are the instrument of exploitation: "Gifts make slaves, the Eskimos say. . . . The economic relation of giver/receiver is the political relation of leader/follower" (133). This, of course, provides the transitional links to the other movements of the book. "A great proportion of primitive exchange, much more than our own traffic, has as its decisive function . . . the material flow [which] underwrites or initiates social relations" (186).

The second movement provides a very curious reading of Mauss on the gift as a kind of "social contract for the primitives": "The gift is the primitive way of achieving the peace that in civil society is secured by the State. Where in the traditional view the contract was a form of political exchange, Mauss saw exchange as a form of political contract" (169). There is an elaborate discussion of the meaning of the Maori term *hau* and an assertion that "a society in which [there is] freedom to gain at the other's expense is not envisioned by [their] relations and forms of exchange. Therein lies the moral of the old Maori's economic fable" (162). But how can Hobbes's Warre of all against all be so readily repressed by a paltry bunch of *things?* "If Mauss, like Marx, concentrated singularly on the anthropomorphic qualities of the things exchanged, rather than the [thinglike?] qualities of the people, it was because each saw in the transactions respectively at issue a determinate form and epoch of alienation: mystic alienation of the donor in primitive reciprocity, alienation of human social labor in commodity production" (181). This somewhat strained attempt to marry Marx and Mauss, followed immediately by a favorable citation of Lévi-Strauss, is less interesting as an *explication de texte* than as an indication of how Sahlins conceived of the possibility of integrating the symbolic order with the material/economic order at this juncture. For what he asserts about Hobbes is what he will assert about his own theory: "Natural law is established only by artificial Power; and Reason enfranchised only by Authority" (179). Far from denying aggression and duplicity, Sahlins willingly participates in the hallowed Western tradition of regarding exchange as a means of harnessing them; but here exchange will not be deemed the mediated expression of natural scarcities or fixed rational desires, but rather an intercalated structure of reciprocal signs, which operate according to their own self-sufficient set of rules. Abstract personal property is not sufficient to bring about order out of self-interest, because property itself is an expression of the variant cultural codes.

The third section culminates in Sahlins's own version of a theory of primitive exchange. Given his previous strictures on the lack of centrality of production, it follows that the main function of exchange will not be the material provisioning of basic needs: it "is less involved than modern exchange in the acquisition of means of production, more involved with the redistribution of finished goods through the community. The bias is that of an economy in which food holds a commanding position" (187). But food, as anyone who has read their Lévi-Strauss knows, is good to think with. Sounding more like Polanyi than Lévi-Strauss here, Sahlins divides primitive exchange into centralized redistribution and reciprocity, and then claims that for the latter "it is precisely through scrutiny of departures from balanced exchange that one glimpses the interplay between reciprocity, social relations, and material circumstances" (190).

In effect this was a revival of Malinowski's continuum of types of reciprocities, but now informed by an important article of Alvin Gouldner's of 1960 on the norm of reciprocity in social thought. Gouldner had by that era become a scathing critic of Talcott Parsons and his functionalist program in sociology; in "The Norm of Reciprocity" he noted that the very idea of a "functional" social structure presupposed some implicit norm of reciprocity. When encountering structures which at first seemed bereft of all rationale because nothing was being tendered in exchange for some benefit bestowed, "the empirical problem became one of unearthing the hidden contributions by a seeming survival, and thereby showing that it is not in fact functionless. . . . The early functionalists neglected the fact that a survival is only a limiting case of a larger class of social phenomena, namely . . . functional reciprocity [which] is *not equal*" (Gouldner 1973, 232–33). The sociologists were not alone in this presumption, as Sahlins discerned. Most of orthodox economics simply presumed an individually ingrained norm of reciprocity, a single-valued index of equivalence, and a general prevalence of an objective balance of interests. When confronted with exotic practices like the Kula or the potlatch, they would immediately set about searching for the "hidden" interests or implicit exchanges which would "restore" the balance. (This is still the standard Chicago move in Gary Becker–style "sociology" and its offshoots.)

Gouldner countered that this imposition of "equivalence" actually equivocates between some kind of concrete identity (tit for tit) and "value equivalence" (tit for tat), which introduced all manner of qualifications and confusions as to the meaning and interpretation of equivalence. The key to understanding social theory was to realize (1) that the equivalence class or principle was socially constructed, and therefore contingent; (2) that any "demand for exact equality would place an impossible burden even on actors highly motivated to comply with the reciprocity norm" (257); and (3) that there are plenty of good reasons for the social actors not to maintain pure equivalence in their quotidian transactions, even when under the sway of a norm of reciprocity.

In a later essay Gouldner elaborated upon this last point. For instance, he suggested that widespread procrastination in reciprocation of good turns may serve as a social stabilizing device, since behavior in the intervening period is governed by the further norm that one should do no harm to those who have done you a favor. Or else, a norm of benificence may arise so that the rich and powerful can explicitly dramatize that they are not simply operating within the conventional norm of reciprocity. Or, in a market society, "the recipient self that seeks something for nothing is therefore powerless to modify the conditions of his existence. Indeed, he often advocates and seeks something for nothing *because* he has nothing to give for what he wants. . . . Maturity is the recognition of the necessity for the thingification of the self" (270). Here we observe a rather poignant inversion of Mauss, in the form of an assertion that the separation of personality from the thing exchanged is itself an artifact of the market imperative that one must sell oneself as a thing—an impersonal provider of saleable items or services—in order to survive in the marketplace. All in all, Gouldner's great insight was to insist that a norm of unbalanced reciprocity was an inescapable and necessary complement of any zero-sum game, that is, of any socially reified structure of equivalence. As we all know, the drawback of a zero-sum game is the awareness on the part of all players that what I will win, you must lose: "If the zero-sum game predicates that the relationship among the players is in the nature of a *contest*, the norm of reciprocity . . . defines the relationship among players as an *exchange*" (293).

Sahlins's contribution in this regard was an attempt to specify how the continuum from generalized reciprocity (putative altruism) to balanced reciprocity (tit for tat) to negative reciprocity (getting something for nothing with impunity) could become jointly constituted within the ambit of a single society, so that any future economic anthropology would not be able to regard exchange ratios as expressive of any single condition of primal scarcity or operation of a generic "supply and de-

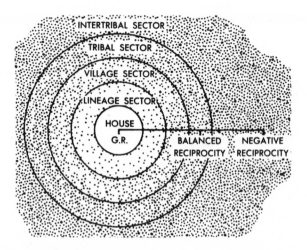

Figure 2 Sahlins's schema of reciprocity and distance (1972, 199). Reprinted by permission.

mand." The key, as was perhaps to be expected of one of the authors of the fourfold schema of band, tribe, chiefdom, and state (Sahlins 1972) and the enthusiast for Lévi-Strauss, was a correlation of position on the reciprocity continuum with "distance" defined in lineage and political terms. Sahlins himself summarized this idea with a schematic drawing, reproduced here as figure 2.

The theory was largely captured by the following statement on the continuum: "Reciprocity is inclined toward the generalized pole by close kinship, toward the negative extreme in proportion to kinship difference. . . . Exchange may be contingent on genealogical distance . . . or it may hinge on segmentary distance, or descent group status" (196–97). As is readily apparent, this was not a universal theory for all seasons and societies and circumstances, if only because there remained so much free play in defining the locally relevant metrics; but that does not even begin to exhaust the potential indeterminacy of the variables involved. As Sahlins readily admitted, "Simply to demonstrate that the character of reciprocity is contingent upon social distance . . . is not to traffic in ultimate explanation, nor yet to specify when exchanges will in fact take place. A systematic relation between reciprocity and sociability in itself does not say when, or even to what extent, the relation will come into play" (202). So this schema tended to sport the Achilles' heel of all such structuralist theories, namely, its inability to handle anything but the most static of situations. Given Gouldner's point about the necessity of flexibility of timing in reciprocal response, this might be regarded as a drawback. It also raised problems with the adequate conceptualization of possible divergences of de facto from customary rates of exchange, a problem which, to his credit, Sahlins readily conceded (280ff.).

Nevertheless this schema provided a vehicle for organizing many of the disparate caveats and observations on the "economic" voiced by anthropologists throughout their history. The treatment of higgling is simply the foremost of these concerns. In this scheme, incalculable charity, and not haggling, begins at home, while balanced reciprocity tends to assume a quotidian customary character only infrequently punctuated by bargaining or fine tuning of exchange ratios. It is only when one is dealing with the truly foreign that higgling is permissible; and there this is sanctioned as much by the inscrutability of their own equivalence classes as by the desire to take advantage of them. Once trade relations have become regularized, pressures ensue to move back towards the center of the continuum, in order to demonstrate some renunciation of hostile intent (220). The character of the goods transacted may also enter into consideration here, with foodstuffs less likely to be found at the far outside rings of the continuum (215). Primitive versions of money tend to be located towards the center of the continuum, since they are the reification of an equivalence constantly threatened by shifts to the left or the right due to the very instability of the notion of equivalence. Primitive monies are themselves a kind of surrogate political device, tending to be located in situations with "a marked incidence of balanced exchange in peripheral social sectors" (227).

Hence, in a way we do not find in Polanyi, we have in Sahlins a sustained argument for the existence of qualitatively different forms of exchange "embedded" in a continuum of differing social structures. Instead of mixing and matching various proportions of reciprocity, redistribution, and market forms, as was the case with Polanyi, we now have a rationale for regarding all exchange systems as some manifestation of a particular realization of a continuum of reciprocities, since "pooling is an organization of reciprocities, a system of reciprocities" (188), that is, just another system of signs. But nevertheless the question must still be asked: Does Sahlins provide us with a General Theory of

Exchange to rival those found in economics? Does it manage to subsume barter, money payments, silent trade, and the more familiar haggling of the bazaar under a single rubric? It seems this bothered Sahlins himself, since the last chapter of *Stone Age Economics* is devoted to a meditation as to whether this schema displaces more conventional supply and demand notions.

Central to Sahlins's schematic is the analytical ability to array reciprocities along some single-valued continuum—in other words, to subject reciprocity to calculation—but this is precisely one of the major objections raised against a "primitive economy" from the very beginning of the subdiscipline. In a footnote, Sahlins recognizes the problem as one of a *theory of value:*

> I do not attempt here a general theory of value. The principal concern is exchange value. By the "exchange value" of a good (A), I mean the quantity of other goods received in return for it (B, C, etc.). . . . It remains to be seen whether this "exchange value" approximates the Ricardian-Marxist "value," the average social labor embodied in the product. . . . "Price" is reserved for exchange value in money terms. (277–78)

This admission, relegated to the outer margins of his text, inadvertently reveals one of the major weaknesses of *Stone Age Economics.* There is, of course, the ambivalent relation to Marx; but there is also something deeper, something about a rupture between prior understandings of reciprocity and those of Sahlins. Earlier writers such as Thurnwald and Malinowski had suggested that reciprocity could stand as an apt organizing principle in primitive economies precisely because they were based upon other structures which independently displayed some kind of symmetry, be they kinship relations, tribal hierarchies, or whatever. The central thrust of this observation was that calculations we might think are required for allocational decisions would be replaced by local orderings inherent in the structures: in more modern jargon, say, kinship would serve as a computing device (a Turing machine?) which mimicked quantitative economic calculations without any explicit algebra. The problem in Sahlins's work is that he reverses this logic: he takes the quantitative relation of equivalence as a given and correlates the extent of reciprocity with the "social distance" along kinship or other axes. Because of this reversal, he cannot claim to propose a rival theory of value; and in our opinion, agnosticism with regard to value theory greases the slippery slope to orthodox neoclassicism.[10]

The bitter fruits of agnosticism surface whenever Sahlins considers what it would be like to situate a concrete exchange situation somewhere in his schema. We have already mentioned his distress that there could be divergence between de facto and customary rates of exchange. But there is also the revealing passage concerning how one might judge whether a specific exchange was balanced or one-sided: "the assessment of 'sidedness' can be supplemented by empirical criteria in addition to those of immediacy and material equivalence: the initial transfer may be voluntary, involuntary, prescribed, contracted; the return freely bestowed, exacted, or dunned; the exchange haggled or not, the subject of accounting or not" (193). Here the argument threatens to become trapped in a vicious circle from which it might never emerge: initially social structure explained extent of balance explained extent of higgling and so on; but now the inability to judge independently the extent of balance suggests that higgling determines social structure, etc. In order for the ethnographer to enter at any point of the "structure" and infer the implied collateral relationships, there must exist an invariance in the social sphere, a kind of preexistent order which plays itself out in a fixed repertoire of exchanges. Therefore, and rather ironically, higgling occupies a tenuous role in this theory, just as it does in neoclassicism.

In his last chapter Sahlins conflates the presence of haggling over exchange ratios with the operation of "supply and demand," which is simply an error in understanding how prices are "set" in either Marshall or Walras, although one perfectly pardonable given the litany of appeals to "perfect competition" in the neoclassical literature. The reason he does so is that he would like to claim that in primitive economies, "a supply-demand imbalance is resolved by pressure on the trade partners rather than exchange rates" (311). But given our observations above, this cannot do the work expected of it. If the continuum of quantitative balance does not possess a separate integrity, then it is the kinship or other social structures which must supply the invariant along which an outcome can be judged balanced or unbalanced; however, if

---

10. There have been some subsequent attempts to rethink this problem of the nature of the equivalence classes and then suggest a proper formalization. In this regard see Hage and Harary 1991; Mirowski 1991a.

the social ties themselves are disturbed by movements in "supply and demand," then "structures" cannot provide the requisite symmetry in order to underwrite any allocational order. The ultimate irony is that the reason haggling has no place in neoclassicism is that it disrupts any path-independent notion of equilibrium.[11] Here the problem is nearly identical: if higgling itself alters the network of trade partners, then there is no continuum of balance which anchors reciprocity.

There are one or two passages which suggest that Sahlins appreciated the severity of the problem. In one place he claims there is no evidence in any primitive economy that members of a trading party ever bid or haggle for the custom of their opposite numbers (298); but then, the precise way that social trading networks adjust to disruption is left dangling, unexplained. One might just reiterate that this is exemplary of the sort of historical change that structuralism seems impotent to explicate.[12] The problem arises again in the description of completely nonintersecting spheres of exchange (277). And then there is the extremely revealing passage (307–8): "Everything depends on the meaning and practice of that capital principle, 'generosity.' But the meaning is ethnographically uncertain, and therein lies the major weakness of our theory. . . . Those who bring a certain good to the exchange are related to it primarily in terms of labor value, the real effort required to produce it, while those to whom the good is tendered appreciate it primarily as a use value. . . . In many respects the opposite of market competition, the etiquette of primitive trade may conduct by a different route to a similar result." I think this loss of nerve, coming so late in the text after such an admirably sustained and stunningly synoptic theoretical foray, reveals nothing so much as the inherent inability to break away from Western economic tradition without a real innovation with regard to the theory of value.

The trajectory of the narrative in *Stone Age Economics* raises naggingly insistent questions about the entire project of an economic anthropology, questions that become even more important as the practice of ethnography itself has come into question in the anthropological community. Rather than further engage the theoretical conundrums raised by exchange, gift, reciprocity, higgling, and money, it seems contempo-

11. This is discussed in Mirowski 1989 and 1993.

12. This impasse may help explain Sahlins's subsequent repudiation of his attempts to produce general theories (economic or otherwise) out of ethnographic materials and tendency instead to plump for a species of historicism in anthropology. On his later position see Sahlins 1985 and 1992.

rary anthropologists have tended to regard the very project of theorizing a subset of social experience as an illegitimate totalizing move, a disguised form of the persistent colonial imperative to dominate the Other. The work of such anthropologists as Steve Gudeman, Clifford Geertz, James Clifford, George Marcus (and, although he might deny it, Sahlins himself) increasingly displays the acid influence of postmodernism upon the self-image of economic anthropology. This is yet another reason for historians of economics to take note; for there has not as yet been any parallel development in the community of economists. Although the speciality of economic anthropology may once have been beholden to developments in economics, it is now much more shaped by the imperatives of the self-conscious humanities.

I thank John Lodewijks, Anne Mayhew, James Ferguson, Marshall Sahlins, Gilberto Lima, Mary Morgan, and Neil De Marchi for conversations and comments. When one stumbles upon a largely unexplored continent, travelers' tales inevitably precede systematic ethnography. I hope this offering will be accepted in that spirit.

References

Armstrong, W. 1924. Rossel Island Money. *Economic Journal* 34:423–29.

Barrett, Richard. 1989. The Paradoxical Anthropology of Leslie White. *American Anthropologist* 91:986–99.

Bird-David, N. 1992. Beyond the Original Affluent Society. *Current Anthropology* 33:25–47.

Douglas, Mary. 1973. *Natural Symbols*. London: Barrie & Jenkins.

——. 1982. *In the Active Voice*. London: Routledge & Kegan Paul.

——. 1986. *How Institutions Think*. Syracuse: Syracuse University Press.

Durkheim, Emile, and Marcel Mauss. 1963. *Primitive Classification*. Chicago: University of Chicago Press.

Eribon, Didier. 1991. *Conversations with Claude Lévi-Strauss*. Chicago: University of Chicago Press.

Ferguson, James. 1988. Cultural Exchange. *Cultural Anthropology* 3:488–513.

Firth, Raymond, ed. 1967. *Themes in Economic Anthropology*. London: Tavistock.

Foster, Robert. 1989. Value without Equivalence: Exchange and Replacement in a Melanesian Society. *Man* 25:54–69.

Friedland, R., and A. Robertson, eds. 1990. *Beyond the Marketplace*. New York: Aldine de Gruyter.

Geertz, Clifford. 1973. *The Interpretation of Cultures*. New York: Norton.

——. 1991. Interview. *Current Anthropology* 32:603–13.

Gouldner, Alvin. 1973. *For Sociology*. New York: Basic Books.

Hage, Per, and Frank Harary. 1991. *Exchange in Oceana*, Oxford: Clarendon Press.

Hart, Keith. 1982. On Commoditization. In *From Craft to Industry*, edited by E. Goody. New York: Cambridge University Press.

Hayes, E., and T. Hayes, eds. 1970. *Claude Lévi-Strauss: The Anthropologist as Hero*, Cambridge: MIT Press.

Humphrey, C., and S. Hugh-Jones, eds. 1992. *Barter, Exchange, and Value*, Cambridge: Cambridge University Press.

Jarvie, Ian. 1989. Recent Work in the History of Anthropology and Its Historiographic Problems. *Philosophy of the Social Sciences* 19:345–75.

Kadish, Alon. 1989. *Historians, Economists, and Economic History*, London: Routledge.

Keynes, John Maynard. 1930. *Treatise on Money*, London: Macmillan.

Knight, Frank. 1941. Anthropology and Economics. *Journal of Political Economy* 49:247–68. (Rejoinder, by M. Herskovits, 49:269–78.)

Köcke, Jasper. 1979. Some Early Contributions to Economic Anthropology. *Research in Economic Anthropology* 2:119–67.

Leach, Edmund. 1970. *Claude Lévi-Strauss*, New York: Viking.

Leach, J., and E. Leach, eds. 1983. *The Kula: New Perspectives on Massim Exchange*, Cambridge: Cambridge University Press.

LeClair, E., and H. Schneider, eds. 1968. *Economic Anthropology: Readings in Theory and Analysis*, New York: Holt Reinhart.

Lévi-Strauss, Claude. 1963. *Structural Anthropology*, New York: Basic Books.

Lukes, Steven. 1973. *Emile Durkheim*, London: Penguin.

Malinowski, Bronislaw. 1921. Primitive Economics of the Trobriand Islanders. *Economic Journal* 31:1–16.

———. 1922. *Argonauts of the Western Pacific*, London: Routledge.

———. 1926. *Crime and Custom in Savage Society*, New York: Harcourt Brace.

———. 1931. Culture. In *Encyclopaedia of the Social Sciences*, 4:621–46. New York: Macmillan.

Malinowski, Bronislaw, and J. de la Fuente. 1982. *The Economics of a Mexican Market System*. London: Routledge.

Mauss, Marcel. [1925] 1954. *The Gift*. London: Cohen & West.

———. [1925] 1990. *The Gift*. New York: Norton.

Mayhew, Anne. 1994. Transactors and Their Markets in Two Disciplines. In *Higgling: Transactors and Their Markets in the History of Economics*, edited by Neil De Marchi and Mary S. Morgan. *HOPE* 26, special issue. Durham: Duke University Press.

Mirowski, Philip. 1989. *More Heat than Light*, New York: Cambridge University Press.

———. 1991a. Postmodernism and the Social Theory of Value. *Journal of Post-Keynesian Economics* 13:565–82.

———. 1991b. Smooth Operator. In *Alfred Marshall in Retrospect*, edited by Rita Tullberg. Cheltenham: Edward Elgar.

————. 1993. *Edgeworth on Chance, Economic Hazard and Statistics*. Totowa, N.J.: Rowman & Littlefield.

Moggeridge, Donald. 1992. *John Maynard Keynes*. London: Routledge.

Murphy, Robert. 1991. Anthropology at Columbia. *Dialectical Anthropology* 16:65–81.

Oakes, Guy. 1977. The *Verstehen* Thesis and the Foundations of Max Weber's Methodology. *History and Theory* 16:11–29.

Parry, Jonathan. 1985. *The Gift*, the Indian Gift, and the "Indian Gift." *Man* 21:453–73.

Parry, J., and M. Bloch, eds. 1989. *Money and the Morality of Exchange*. Cambridge: Cambridge University Press.

Polanyi-Levitt, Kari, ed. 1990. *The Life and Work of Karl Polanyi*. Montreal: Black Rose.

Sahlins, Marshall. 1969. Economic Anthropology and Anthropological Economics. *Social Science Information* 8.5:13–33.

————. 1972. *Stone Age Economics*. Chicago: Aldine.

————. 1976. *Culture and Practical Reason*. Chicago: University of Chicago Press.

————. 1981. *Historical Metaphors and Mythical Realities*. Ann Arbor: University of Michigan Press.

————. 1985. *Islands of History*. Chicago: University of Chicago Press.

————. 1988. Cosmologies of Capitalism. *Proceedings of the British Academy* 74:1–51.

————. 1992. Economics of Develop-man in the Pacific. *Anthropology and Aesthetics* 22:12–25.

Sahlins, Marshall, and P. Kirsch. 1992. *Anahulu*, Vol. 1. Chicago: University of Chicago Press.

Sahlins, Marshall, and E. Service, eds. 1960. *Evolution and Culture*. Ann Arbor: University of Michigan Press.

Schneider, Harold. 1974. *Economic Man*. New York: Free Press.

Seddon, David, ed. 1978. *Relations of Production*. London: Cass.

Simmel, Georg. [1907] 1990. *The Philosophy of Money*, 2d ed. London: Routledge & Kegan Paul.

Stocking, George. 1987. *Victorian Anthropology*. New York: Free Press.

————. 1992. *The Ethnographer's Magic*. Madison: University of Wisconsin Press.

————, ed. 1991. *History of Anthropology*, Vol. 7, *Colonial Situations*. Madison: University of Wisconsin Press.

Symmons-Symonolewicz, K. 1958–60. Bronislaw Malinowski. *Polish Review* 3:55–76, 4:17–45, 5:53–65.

Temple, R. C. 1899. The Beginnings of Currency. *Journal of the Anthropological Institute* 29:00–00.

Thomas, Nicholas. 1991. *Entangled Objects*. Cambridge: Harvard University Press.

Thurnwald, Richard. [1932] 1965. *Economics in Primitive Communities*. Oxford: Oxford University Press.

Vincent, Joan. 1990. *Anthropology and Politics*. Tucson: University of Arizona Press.

Weiner, Annette. 1992. *Inalienable Possessions*. Berkeley and Los Angeles: University of California Press.

Weintraub, E. R. 1991. *Stabilizing Dynamics*. New York: Cambridge University Press.

Wittgenstein, Ludwig. 1979. *Remarks on Frazer's Golden Bough*. Atlantic Highlands: Humanities Press.

Zelizer, Viviana. 1989. The Social Meaning of Money: Special Monies. *American Journal of Sociology* 95:342–77.

Laboratory Strife:
Higgling as Experimental Science
in Economics and Social Psychology

Robert J. Leonard

"How much do I want, sir?"

"Yes. Give it a name. We won't haggle."

He pursed his lips.

"I'm afraid," he said, having unpursed them, "I couldn't do it as cheap as I'd like, sir. . . . I'd have to make it twenty pounds."

I was relieved. I had been expecting something higher. He, too, seemed to feel that he had erred on the side of moderation, for he immediately added:

"Or, rather, thirty."

"Thirty!"

"Thirty, sir."

"Let's haggle," I said.

But when I suggested twenty-five, a nicer looking sort of number than thirty, he shook his grey head regretfully, and he haggled better than me, so that eventually we settled on thirty-five. It wasn't one of my better haggling days.—P. G. Wodehouse, *Aunts Aren't Gentlemen*

It could well be argued that in this delightful vignette concerning his protagonist, Bertie Wooster, Wodehouse captures the richness, unpredictability, and contingence of the layman's notion of "haggling."[1] Two parties confront each other to make a deal, settle on a price, make an exchange. The outcome, as is known by all who have ever found themselves duped by a huckster, seems to be as much a function of persuasion, rhetorical skill, style, and perhaps even one's mood on the day,

1. Or, for the purposes of this volume, "higgling." The *Oxford English Dictionary* makes no essential distinction between the two terms. To "higgle" is to "cavil as to terms; esp. to stickle for petty advantages in bargaining; to chaffer"; to "haggle" is to "cavil, wrangle, dispute as to terms, esp. to make difficulties in settling a bargain."

as it is of any purely "economic" factors such as cost or utility: at the heart of the matter, as no less than Donald Trump has reminded us, is the "*art* of the deal."[2] It should come as no surprise, therefore, that so human a situation, replete with features of motivation, communication, and interpersonal interaction should, in addition to attracting the interest of economists, also command the attention of social psychologists. In this essay I consider how both have dealt with the phenomenon.

In what follows I examine the two-person bargaining situation as it has emerged and developed in both the experimental economic and psychological literatures since the late 1950s. In its formative stages, economic experimentation was intimately linked to—indeed grew out of—sister experimentation in psychology; but the two subsequently became quite divorced. My purpose is to show how the "same" type of interaction has been perceived differently in the two domains, something which has contributed to a certain tension between the two. My main thesis is that despite strenuous and ingenious efforts to do so, economic experimenters have never quite managed to keep the psychological/cultural genie in the bottle.

Section 1 looks at early experiments in two-person bargaining, focusing on the seminal work on bilateral monopoly by Siegel and Fouraker. Explicitly straddling the fields of economics and psychology, this effort was seen as an interdisciplinary breakthrough in the late 1950s, and Siegel and Fouraker's *Bargaining and Group Decision Making* (1960) became something of a classic. Section 2 considers subsequent work based on axiomatic solutions to two-person bargaining, following in the cooperative game-theoretic tradition of Nash (1950a). The most accelerated and sustained effort in this area has been by Alvin Roth, beginning in 1979. Along with Vernon Smith and Charles Plott—who have been primarily concerned with different experimental markets concerning many buyers/many sellers, auctions, and public goods—Roth is an architect of what has become a veritable experimental revolution in neoclassical microeconomics.[3] Section 3 considers an experimental sequence gener-

2. See Trump and Schwartz 1987.

3. As Plott (1991) points out, from an annual handful in the early 1970s, the number of papers published has grown, two decades later, to one hundred. Similarly, experiments are no longer confined to Purdue or Illinois, but carried out in dozens of centers in North America and also in England and Germany. And this geographical spread is now being reflected in the nature of the experiments themselves (see Roth et al. 1991).

ated by another game-theoretic bargaining solution, that of Rubinstein (1982). As opposed to the axiomatic approach, which, broadly speaking, focuses on the coherence of the *solution*, Rubinstein's strategic approach considers the bargaining *process* itself, treating it in the context of a noncooperative game. The rather pointed predictions generated by the latter have given rise to a series of experiments, and an associated round of healthy interpretative controversy, currently being played out in the columns of the *American Economic Review* and elsewhere. Section 4 provides an overview of how two-person bargaining has been analyzed in the field of experimental social psychology over a broadly similar period. Its contrast with the utility approach in economics provides a window on interdisciplinary difference, tension, and conflict. These and other elements are brought together in discussion in section 5.

1. Early Experiments in Two-Person Bargaining

The current experimental movement in economics took root in the United States during the mid-1950s. The obvious salient historical features include von Neumann and Morgenstern's (1944) transformation of economic theory with their game-theoretic approach to economic choice, and the impetus and direction this work gave to research in economics, political science, decision theory, and related areas. Related to this was a changed intellectual environment in which "avant garde" interdisciplinary work in game theory, cybernetics, and decision theory was actively encouraged with the support of military budgets.[4] In the context of the Cold War, it was imperative that proper choices be made, and doing this required that they be understood in modern "scientific" terms. And as similar scientific dictates were obeyed regardless of where one stood politically in these matters, the *Journal of Conflict Resolution* provided an outlet for the same. Because it was "in the air," because of the *Zeitgeist*, several other individuals, often working independently of each other, were led, "as if by some invisible hand," to consider testing economic theories in the laboratory, as opposed to in the "field": thus Smith (1991a, 783 n. 1) points to Chamberlin at Harvard, Hoggatt

---

4. Thus some of the earliest economic experiments began as informal games at RAND in Santa Monica. See Flood, and Kalisch et al., in Thrall, Coombs, and Davis 1954. For discussion of this theory-institution nexus see Leonard 1991, 1992, and Mirowski 1991, 1992.

at Berkeley, Sauermann and Selten in Germany, Shubik at Yale, Siegel and Fouraker at Pennsylvania State, and Friedman also at Yale (see also Smith 1992).[5]

The experiments of interest to us here are those which I interpret as coming closest to higgling: those concerned with bilateral monopoly or, more generally, the two-person bargaining game. As experiments, they are invariably designed to test some hypotheses generated by economic theory, although, in the case of Siegel and Fouraker (1960), a more eclectic attempt is made to account for psychological influences. In what follows, I consider the Siegel and Fouraker experiments, which were concerned with testing various pre-game-theoretic theories of bilateral monopoly.

The various outcomes possible in a situation of bilateral monopoly can be summarized as shown in figure 1. Theories can be divided into those in which only quantity is determinate, and those in which *both* price and quantity are determinate. Theories that yield only a prediction about quantity (Stigler 1952; Fellner 1949) uniformly suggest that the Pareto-optimal, joint-profit-maximizing quantity, Qm, will be chosen, whereas price remains indeterminate. In Fellner's (1949) case, just where the chosen price will lie between the buyer's maximal and seller's minimal prices, P1 and P2 respectively, will depend on such noneconomic factors as toughness in bargaining and the ability to inflict and absorb losses in the event of a stalemate. Theories predicting *both* price and quantity differ depending on institutional structure. Pigou (1908) suggests that given equal bargaining strength, the most likely outcome, though inconclusive, is equal division of maximum joint profits, the outcome also predicted by Nash (1950a).[6]

Siegel and Fouraker's experiments are "an attempt to employ the methods of experimental social psychology in the study of behavior which has been considered in the theoretical province of economics" (1960, 72). They are designed to test various hypotheses concerning the choice of the profit-maximizing quantity Qm, and then the division of

5. Referring to Purdue, Smith (1991a, 154) also emphasizes his and his colleagues' general dissatisfaction both with their graduate training at Harvard, Chicago, and elsewhere and with "the state of economic knowledge," as well as the stimulative role of such individualists as the Purdue economist Em Weiler and the psychologist Sydney Siegel. Smith met Siegel at Stanford in 1961, six weeks before Weiler's untimely death.

6. Assuming both risk neutrality on the part of both players and that money rewards can be equated with utility.

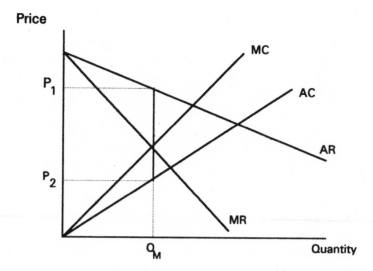

Figure 1

the payoffs, in a laboratory setting with individuals designated as buyers and sellers. The key elements of their experimental procedure can be summarized as follows.[7] The players were physically separated, and the only form of communication permitted was the passing of written bids (a price and quantity pair), done through an intermediary. The authors say this had the desired effect of eliminating

> certain variables which may well be important in bargaining—variables connected with interpersonal perceptions, prejudices, incompatibilities, etc. It is our belief that such variables should either be systematically studied or controlled in experimentation on bargaining. It cannot be assumed, as has often been done, that such variables may simply be neglected. We have chosen to control these variables at this stage of our research program, with the intention of manipulating and studying them systematically in future studies. (23)

The information provided took the form of isoprofit sheets showing the profit yielded by various price–quantity combinations. In the situation of incomplete–incomplete information, each player had information about his own possibilities only; in complete–complete information,

7. See Siegel and Fouraker 1960, 18–23, for the finer detail.

each had both isoprofit sheets; in the intermediate complete–incomplete case, only one side had full information. The opening bidder was chosen randomly, and participants were *explicitly* reminded that as they were to keep their earnings, it was in their personal interest to maximize profits.

The main result of the experiments, with regard to the *quantity* chosen, was a tendency for players to choose the Pareto-optimal, joint-profit-maximizing quantity, Qm. This became even more marked when the amount of *information* was increased, or when *discrimination* was heightened, that is, when the profit differential between Qm and other quantities was widened or, alternatively, when the cost of not choosing Qm was increased.

With regard to division of the surplus, several hypotheses were tested. The first of these concerned the predictions of the price chosen. Fouraker (1957) predicted that the equilibrium price would be that given by the intersection of the buyer's marginal cost and seller's marginal revenue functions. Fellner (1949), on the other hand, predicted that the outcome would be determined by bargaining power: if that was assumed to be randomly distributed among the players, the observed prices should be distributed around the equal-division midpoint price. The experiments, conducted under conditions of incomplete information, showed Fellner's prediction to be superior, in that the mean price observed was not significantly different from the midpoint.

The second hypothesis tested concerning the price chosen was that increased information to the bargainers should reduce the disparity in payoffs among any pair. Comparing the three different informational settings, Siegel and Fouraker did not reject this hypothesis: more information about one's opponent increases convergence towards the equal-division price. The next step was to control for a psychological variable, which they believed to have an influence on the observed division, the level of aspiration, which refers to "the goal-striving behavior of an individual when he is presented with a task whose outcome can be measured on an achievement scale. The person's level of aspiration is the particular achievement goal for which he strives" (1960, 61). The idea is that when only one player's expectation is deliberately increased, that player can be expected to achieve a greater proportion of the payoff. The authors manipulated players' aspiration levels by ascribing them target levels of profit, above which a chance of further gains would be given. All bargaining was conducted under incomplete information, and, not surprisingly perhaps, the mean profit levels were found to be greater for higher-aspiration players. Siegel and Fouraker concluded that "traditional economic forces cannot be depended on to yield an adequate explanation of the prices arrived at in bilateral monopoly bargaining" (69) and that "levels of aspiration of the subjects appeared to be a major determinant of the differential payoff and thus of price, especially in the contracts negotiated under incomplete information" (76).

The punchline of Siegel and Fouraker's study is that the aspiration level seems to be the "central determinant of the outcome of bargaining negotiations" (99). Further research, they suggest, should be directed towards examining the effect of manipulated aspiration levels on agreement, and the dynamics of increased interpersonal communication. In a later study (Fouraker and Siegel 1963) they undertook to test Bowley's (1928) price-leadership model, allowing the seller to act as price leader and the buyer to follow with a quantity bid. In this model the equilibrium outcome, for normal linear functions, is a quantity *lower* than the joint-profit-maximizing one, and a price which gives between two-thirds and all of the profits to the price-leading buyer. The Bowley solution, therefore, is not an element of the Pareto-optimal set.

The 1963 study examined the price-leadership model under various conditions concerning information, negotiation practices, and the possibility of an equal division of payoffs. In particular, complete information, where both sides know each other's isoprofit tables, insofar as it identifies Pareto-improving non-Bowley solutions to both parties, is believed not to favor the Bowley outcome. The negotiation practices permitted were the single transaction, where each side made one bid; and the repeated transaction, where each side could counterbid for a total of nineteen transactions before reaching an agreement. Finally, the cost and revenue functions were manipulated to allow the Bowley solution to yield equal payoffs.[8] The principal findings of this series of experiments were that the Bowley point is favored when it yields an equal-division payoff, when the players have single-shot bids, or when players are incompletely informed. But the possibility of repeated bidding, the possession of complete information, and the coincidence of the equal-split payoff with the Pareto point all yield a movement away from the Bowley point toward the Pareto. Taking a closer look at bidding behavior and

8. Fouraker and Siegel 1963, 19n. note that while a price can always be found which yields an equal division of the maximized joint profits, this can be hidden in experiments by offering discrete prices only and allowing no interpolation. They also add that isoprofit tables which yield an equal payoff at the Bowley solution imply nonlinearity of the underlying functions.

interviewing players about their choices, Fouraker and Siegel concluded that the move away from self-interested Bowley behavior towards joint-profit maximization ultimately depends on various extraexperimental psychological attributes. These include the players' cooperative or rival-rous nature, their levels of aspiration, and their willingness and ability to use the bidding mechanism to send signals to their opponents.

I have reviewed Siegel and Fouraker's experiments in some detail not only because they constitute a landmark in the experimental economics literature but also because they indicate the *interdisciplinary setting* in which early bargaining experiments first emerged. While these experiments were meant to test various economic models, they were also intended to explicitly reveal the shortcomings of such models and suggest where recourse might usefully be made to psychology: hence the incorporation of the "aspiration level." What the authors had in mind was a marriage of economics and psychology made in the laboratory. What happened subsequently, I claim, was the effective displacement or squeezing-out of explicit psychological considerations from economic experiments on bargaining. This happened when experimentation became oriented toward testing game-theoretic bargaining solutions. The latter fall into two categories: the axiomatic type, based on the cooperative solution given by Nash (1950a); and the strategic approach, stemming from the independent work of Stahl (1972) and Rubinstein (1982), both of whom derived a similar noncooperative solution based on subgame perfect equilibrium.

2. The Axiomatic Approach

In 1950 Nash developed a model of the bargaining game (1950a) which has had a profound impact on both theory and experiment ever since. His contribution may be seen as following the game-theoretic approach developed by von Neumann and Morgenstern (1944),[9] and together with two further articles (Nash 1950b, 1951) it marks the conceptual division of games into cooperative and noncooperative types.[10] His approach is to

9. It is convenient to understand Nash's work as stemming from that of von Neumann and Morgenstern, but greater independence can be claimed for Nash than is apparent. See Leonard 1994.

10. In what follows, the reader should not confuse the "Nash solution" (1950a), which refers to the bargaining game under immediate discussion, with the "Nash equilibrium" (1950b), which refers to the noncooperative game and forms the basis of subgame perfect equilibrium used in the strategic approach discussed below in section 3.

model the game as a pair (S, d), where S denotes the feasible expected utility payoffs to the players, and $d = (d_1, d_2)$ denotes the disagreement point.[11] Should they come to an agreement, players achieve a point $x = (x_1, x_2)$ in S: in the absence of agreement, players get d_1 and d_2, respectively. In addition to making certain regularity assumptions about S, Nash assumes that it is *known* by each player: that is, there is complete information. The question therefore is: what point in S will be chosen as a solution by the two players? The solution that Nash offers, $f(S, d)$, stems from a consideration of the "reasonable" (mathematical) properties that it should have, rather than any consideration of the process by which that solution will be reached. The properties in question are:

1. *Pareto optimality:* players will put themselves on the Pareto frontier.
2. *Symmetry:* if the game treats players equally, then so should the solution.
3. *Independence of irrelevant alternatives:* if (S, d) and (T, d) are bargaining games such that S contains T, then if $f(S, d)$ is an element of T, $f(S, d) = f(T, d)$.
4. *Independence of equivalent utility representations:* also called independence of positive linear transformations of the payoffs, this specifies that what matters for the solution is the *ranking* each player attributes to his own alternatives. *Thus neither the levels of utility nor interpersonal comparisons of those levels are important.*

Nash proved that given the above assumptions, the only solution satisfying them is F, that which maximizes the *product of the utility gains* to the players relative to their disagreement payoff. And in addition to satisfying the above required properties, this satisfies the property of strong individual rationality, in that it always yields each player a positive gain over the disagreement point. Various modifications of this solution have been made by relaxing one or more of these four assumptions initially made by Nash (1950a). For example, Raiffa (1953) relaxes the third, and offers a solution which maximizes the product of the players' gains, subject to the restriction that the actual gains are in proportion to the agents' maximum potential gains.

Over the succeeding years a series of experiments have been designed, ostensibly to test the properties of Nash's solution or to test its predictive power against alternatives such as Raiffa's. Nydegger and Owen (1975),

---

11. Throughout this section I draw on Roth and Malouf 1979.

for example, conducted an experiment in which bargaining was done face-to-face by pairs seated at a table, and it was assumed that utility would be synonymous with monetary payoffs. They found that all of the properties were satisfied except that of independence of equivalent representations. Even when the Nash solution dictated that they should not have, players *persistently* chose the equal division outcome, which indicated that interpersonal comparison of the monetary payoffs, and hence utility, matter. Another experiment, by Rapoport, Frenkel, and Perner (1977), reached a similar principal conclusion: the outcome is *not* invariant to positive linear transformations of the payoffs: that is, interpersonal comparisons matter. Roth and Malouf note that in other experiments with stricter communication possibilities, the main result was that "the outcome of bargaining is heavily influenced by various salient outcomes involving interpersonal comparisons, and . . . there is a strong tendency for agreements to be closer to an equal division than would be predicted by Nash's solution. . . . [But given] the fact that the game-theoretic models under consideration are stated in terms of utility rather than monetary payoffs, the question arises whether the experimentally observed comparisons involve money only, or whether they involve comparisons of the players' utility in some deeper way" (1979, 581–82). In other words, to the extent that the experiments above did not properly isolate the features deemed relevant by the theory, they cannot be considered a proper test of the theory.

Therefore, in order to measure the expected utility of the bargainers, Roth and Malouf (1979) devised the *binary lottery game,* in which, rather than bargaining over direct money payoffs, players bargain over the distribution of lottery tickets. Each player i faces a lottery between a small and a large prize. The proportion of tickets "won" by each player in the bargain determines his probability of winning his large prize: thus if player 1 gets 60 percent of the tickets, he has a 60 percent chance of winning his large prize, leaving player 2 a 40 percent chance of winning his (player 2's) large prize. Since von Neumann–Morgenstern utility is determined only up to a positive linear transformation, there is no loss of generality in setting the utility of the small prize at zero and that of the large prize at 1, for both players, thus permitting us to identify the utility of each player's lottery with his probability of winning his large prize. A bargain over lottery tickets thus becomes a bargain over utility.[12]

12. See Roth and Malouf 1979, 585–86; Roth 1988, 978.

This ingenious structure facilitates a distinction in the information each player possesses about his opponent: if he has *partial* information, he knows only the value of his own prize, whereas if he has *full* information, he knows both his own prize *and* his opponent's. With this structure, Roth and his collaborators began a series of experiments to examine the robustness of the Nash solution under various informational, reputational, and timing conditions.

These experiments shared a similar basic procedure. Opponents were physically isolated from each other and communicated anonymously through a computer network. The information transmitted was monitored so that no forbidden messages (concerning the identity of the players, for example, or the value of their monetary prizes) could be sent. In many cases, a deadline was set beyond which the disagreement outcome would be imposed. What emerged from this sequence of strictly controlled experiments is again suggestive of the *inadequacy* of the Nash solution as a predictor of behavior in two-person bargaining. The perceived inadequacy takes two forms: variables that the theory deems unimportant *do* matter; and the effect of a variable that the theory predicts to be important remains insignificant. Let us consider each of these in turn.

In Roth and Malouf's (1979) experiments, in situations of partial information—that is, where each player knows only his own prize—the Nash solution, which yields equal division of the tickets, seems to predict well. Once players know each other's money prizes, however, the distribution of outcomes changes radically, with the mean falling closer to the division offering equal expected value.[13] Interpersonal comparison of expected money payoffs affects the outcome, contrary to the Nash prediction.

Roth and his colleagues (1981) further modified the informational arrangements by slightly altering the experimental procedure: subjects played a binary lottery game for prizes expressed in terms of an intermediate commodity, "chips." The number of chips in each player's prize might be different. Furthermore, these chips had a monetary value, which again might be different for each player. Thus three informational conditions were possible. In each case, the player knows the number of chips in his prize and their monetary value. What varies is the degree of

13. In fact the distribution becomes bimodal, centering on both the Nash solution and equal division of expected payoff.

information he has about his opponent: (high) he knows both the number of his opponent's chips and their monetary value; (intermediate) he knows the number of those chips but not their monetary value; (low) he knows neither the number of those chips nor their monetary value.

The results of the experiment suggest that in both the low and the high information condition, the findings of the previous experiments are replicated: when bargaining with low information, each player tends to get an equal share of the tickets, as predicted by the Nash solution; when playing with high information, each gets tickets in proportion to the monetary value of their prizes, in other words, equal expected monetary payoff, as before in contradiction of the Nash solution. The main contribution of this experiment, however, concerns the case of intermediate information, where players bargained over prizes denominated in chips whose value to the opponent is unknown: players tended to agree on 50 percent of the tickets each *regardless* of the number of chips in their respective prizes. Roth and his team concluded that this confirmed a "sociological hypothesis" about bargaining. Higglers will tend to settle on the focal point of "fair allocation," that is, equal expected value of rewards, when the prizes are expressed in terms of "familiar quantities," namely, quantities to which social conventions apply, such as money. Once one is dealing in terms of some unfamiliar quantity such as chips, social norms concerning fair division are no longer binding.

In another examination of what Roth (1987a) has called the "fine structure of shared information," Roth and Murnighan (1982) considered the effect of the degree to which common knowledge, or *information about information,* is shared by the two participants. The nub of the matter concerns the distinction between (1) situations in which players simply have private information, and do not know what their opponent knows, and (2) situations in which it is *common knowledge* that players have particular information. The experimental games involved lotteries over money prizes, and varied both the opponents' relative prizes ($5 and $20) and the degree of common knowledge. Players were allowed to transmit any information they wished in the course of the game, except their identity.

The main conclusions were as follows. First, only when the $5 player knew both prizes did the equal expected payoff become a focal point.[14]

14. Again, in cases where the equal division payoff was relevant, the observed distribution was bimodal, with focal points at both the Nash solution and the equal division of expected payoff.

Once a player knew that his prize was smaller, he pushed for a larger share of the tickets. Second, the extent to which information structure was common knowledge primarily reduced the frequency of disagreements. Say, for example, that the $5 player knew both prizes and the $20 player did not. If the $5 player did not *know* that the $20 player knew only his own prize, then he ($5) could not determine whether the latter's skepticism about his own claims to have a small prize was simply a bargaining ploy or not. If, on the other hand, there were common knowledge, then the $5 player, *knowing* that the $20 player knew only his own prize, would be more persistent in the face of the latter's skepticism.

In Roth and Schoumaker's (1983) experiment, the purpose was to examine the effect of players' *expectations* about winning on the outcome of the game. In this experiment, played with unequal money prizes, the players were divided into three groups. Twenty-five trials were played, each time with a different partner from the same group, and the players always had unequal prizes. The first fifteen trials, however, were put to special use. In two of the groups, instead of playing a partner, each player bargained with a computer. The latter was programmed to bring about agreement only on the Nash solution (50 percent of the tickets to each) for one group, and the equal expected value agreement (in this case 20 percent–80 percent) for the other. The third group played each other throughout, as a control experiment. The classical game-theoretic hypothesis is that expectations do not matter: the solution for each game depends on the set of feasible utility payoffs and the strategic possibilities. What was found, however, was that the patterns established in the first fifteen trials persisted in the remaining ten, when the players in each group were let play each other. The expectations of the players could be successfully "programmed" so as to induce them to play a particular way. Those who had been programmed to play the Nash solution continued to do so, and those who had been trained to expect 80–20 continued to do so. The control group, which (as in other experiments) displayed a bimodal distribution centering on the two focal points in question, maintained such a distribution for the duration of the entire game. Implicitly echoing Siegel and Fouraker's discussion of the "aspiration level," Roth and Schoumaker concluded that "it may be necessary to incorporate the expectations of the bargainers into any description (or definition) of equilibrium outcomes" (371).

The above sequence of experiments, beginning with Roth and Malouf's (1979), all point to the weaknesses of the standard axiomatic theory of bargaining. In a remarkably consistent manner, variables deemed unimportant by the theory were seen to be significant. These include interpersonal comparison of money payoffs, the extent to which knowledge is common or not, and the expectations the players carry with them into the game. "As such," says Roth (1987b, 34), "the experimental results demonstrate that these theories have serious shortcomings." [15] On reviewing the series of experiments, Roth (1988, 983) noted further that most experiments imposed a *deadline*, after which the bargainers would get their disagreement outcome. Not only was the frequency of disagreements nonnegligible, but the concentration of agreements near the deadline was extraordinary. Indeed agreements were often made within *seconds* of the deadline! Thus, in addition to indicating the weakness of the theory, the experiments suggest new directions in which the theory might be modified, which, in turn, has stimulated further work, and so the cycle continues. A further study (Roth, Murnighan, and Schoumaker 1988) manipulated the deadline further and revealed its robustness as an experimental phenomenon; but the authors called for further experimentation to help modify the theory.

3. The Strategic Approach

One conclusion of the experiments centered on the axiomatic model described above was that, in practice, *time* seems to matter in reaching an agreement in two-person bargaining situations. The second, game-theoretic approach, considered in this section, explicitly takes time into account. The strategic approach is based on the independent contributions of Stahl (1972) and Rubinstein (1982). Whereas Nash (1950a) considered the "reasonable" features that a bargaining solution should have and uncovered the solution that fits those requirements, the present approach takes account of the strategic possibilities that the players face in the problem of how to divide the pie, or share the surplus. Unlike the Nash solution, which pays no explicit attention to the *process* of reach-

---

15. A further experiment (Murnighan et al. 1986) attempts to examine the impact of a factor that the theory suggests *is* important; risk aversion. According to the theory, risk aversion is disadvantageous in bargaining except when there is a positive risk of winning a prize that is less than the disagreement outcome. Having measured the risk aversion of individual players by having them make various risky choices, they found that risk-averse players do better in such situations, but that the effect is weak relative to the focal point effects. They conclude that more research on risk is needed.

ing the rational outcome, the Stahl/Rubinstein theory is based on the consideration of process, in a stylized, albeit elegant, manner.

Players have a finite number of periods, T, to reach agreement about how to divide a sum of money, k.[16] It is a model of sequential offers, each player making an offer in every second period, beginning with player 1 in the first period, and the game ending if the offer in any period is accepted. Time is economically valuable in that players have either positive discount rates, or a fixed cost of bargaining each period. A player i with discount factor ∂_i receives utility of $(\partial_i)^t x$ if he accepts an offer of x in period t. If the offer in the last period is refused, then each player receives 0. Thus time is limited, and costly in that the pie diminishes with time. The equilibrium solution applied here is that of subgame *perfect equilibrium:* the player to go first considers what would happen should he reach the final period and, reasoning by backward induction, formulates an optimal decision to be taken in period 1.[17] The offer in the final period is an ultimatum, in that the alternative for both players is zero payoff. The person j making the last-period offer, therefore, can guarantee himself as near to whole pie, K, as makes no difference.[18] In the next-to-last period, therefore, j will want an offer of at least $\partial_j K$ if he is to agree. The most player i can guarantee himself, therefore, in the next-to-last period, is $K(1 - \partial_j)$. If j wants to secure an agreement in the third-from-last period, therefore, he must offer at least $\partial_i K(1 - \partial_j)$ to i. And so, continuing the process and working backward to the first period, the player to go first can see the minimum he must offer if agreement is to be reached straight away. Depending on the parameters of the model in question, the equilibrium division predicted may be quite imbalanced indeed. These sharp predictions, in addition to the strong assumptions made about rationality and the use of backward induction, make the strategic approach interesting from an experimental point of view, and it too has duly been thrust into the laboratory.

Güth, Schmittberger, and Schwarz (1982) considered the above model in the context of an "ultimatum game," a one-period game in which player 1 makes an offer, and either agreement is reached, or each receives

16. The present account draws on Roth 1988, 984.

17. Subgame perfect equilibrium, a refinement of the Nash (1950b) noncooperative equilibrium, due to Selten (1975), ensures that the strategy chosen remains optimal at all possible subgames of the complete game.

18. The players can ensure themselves $(K - \varepsilon)$, which approaches K if payoffs are continuously divisible.

the disagreement payoff of zero. The perfect equilibrium prediction for this game is that player 1 demands, and receives, virtually 100 percent of the sum to be divided. The experiments show, however, that the average demand made was less than 70 percent, and 20 percent of all offers were rejected. And when player 1 was judged by his opponent to be offering "too little," the latter often punished by refusing to agree. Thus, for the ultimatum game at least, the strategic model appears to be a rather poor predictor.

In response to the above, researchers at the London School of Economics (Binmore, Shaked, and Sutton 1985) conducted an experiment in which a two-period game was played. The "pie" diminished from 100 pence in period 1 to 25 pence in period 2. The perfect equilibrium in this game was an opening demand in the range of 74 to 76 pence by player 1, with player 2 accepting a demand of 74 pence or less. The results showed that the modal demand was 50 pence, with 15 percent of all offers being rejected. Again, the strategic model performed poorly: players seemed to prefer to play "fairly" rather than "strategically." The authors, however, also implemented a second game, in which player 2 of the first game was allowed to make the opening offer. In this game there was a marked shift in the opening offers towards the perfect equilibrium. In the authors' view, these players had obviously learned the structure of the game and had learned to "play 'like a game theorist'." rather than "play fair" (1179).

The Germans responded (Güth and Tietz 1988) with a further set of two-stage games in which they varied the discount rate faced by pairs of players. Again, the opening offers were much closer to equal division than to the perfect equilibrium prediction, leading the authors to reject the Binmore team's (1985) support of "gamesmanship": "the game theoretic solution has nearly no predictive power" (quoted in Roth 1988, 986).

Colleagues at Princeton (Neelin, Sonnenschein, and Spiegel 1988) extended the experimental coverage to games of 2, 3, and 5 periods. They found that the Stahl/Rubinstein division was "strongly controverted" and that, instead of offering an equal split, player 1, in the first round, tended to offer player 2 the value of the entire sum for the second round; that is, player 1 offered player 2 the most that player 2 could possibly hope were he to go into the next round. It was concluded that this behavior showed strong regularity across games and was robust to variations in both experience and the amounts at stake; the authors thus rejected "both the Stahl/Rubinstein theory and the equal-split model" (829).

In a somewhat strange response, Binmore and his team (1988) replied that game theory is unlikely to be a good predictor of laboratory behavior if subjects lack the incentives to invest in learning or to pay attention. In the "real economic world," however, such incentives and opportunities are present. The authors then pointed to the psychological literature that exists on the subject of how people bargain in the laboratory and suggested that psychological "equity theory provides a good explanation of a great deal of laboratory behavior" (837). In addition, the idea of focal points, while too "hydra-headed to properly deserve being called 'theories' " (838) had been too often replicated in laboratories to be ignored. Finally, in the context of equity theory, they cast doubt on the Neelin experiment, pointing out that it was conducted using intermediate microeconomics students, who therefore " 'knew' a priori that optimizing behavior was expected of them" (838). In conclusion, they did suggest that the Neelin experiment offers an example of bounded rationality in simple bargaining games.

The "experiment to end all experiments" concerning the strategic approach is reported by Ochs and Roth (1989). Here the authors hoped to test not just the point-predicting capability of the perfect equilibrium model—rather weak by all accounts to date—but also the *qualitative* power of the model, that is, its ability to predict directional shifts in the observed outcome in response to changes in the experimental parameters, such as independent variation of the individual players' discount rates. Their results were striking and concerned both observed opening offers and rejected opening offers. With regard to opening offers, the perfect equilibrium model "not only fails as a point predictor of observed behavior, it also fails to account for observed qualitative differences" (361). Only in one experimental setting was the perfect equilibrium offer within two standard errors of the observed mean, and the mean observed offers were uniformly closer to the equal division payoff than to the perfect equilibrium. Furthermore, the response of observed opening offers to changes in parameters was significantly different from that predicted by the theory. As for rejected opening offers, the findings were even more striking. Recall that the theory predicts that there will be *no* rejected opening offers: in fact, 16 percent of opening offers were rejected in this experiment. On top of this, player 2, in the second period, in 81 percent of cases, responded by demanding *less* than he had just refused in the first period! Given the theory's prediction that player 2 should demand at least as much as he has just rejected, such counterdemands appear irrational, or, more plausibly, suggest that player 2's utility is not measured by monetary payoff alone. Ochs and Roth thus concluded that "the high frequency of disadvantageous counterproposals makes it inappropriate to continue to interpret the monetary payoffs to the bargainers as being equivalent to their utility payoffs" (362).

They also examined (in the same 1989 article) data from several of the other strategic experiments (Neelin, Sonnenschein, and Spiegel 1988; Binmore, Shaked, and Sutton 1985) to see whether the phenomenon of disadvantageous counterproposals was simply an artifact of their own experiment. However, these others too revealed a strikingly similar pattern of initial rejections followed by disadvantageous counteroffers.[19] Ochs and Roth suggest that the "unobserved element in the bargainers' utility function may have a component related to the perceived 'fairness' of a proposal" (365). However,

> the sensitivity of these ideas [about fairness] to specific contexts could well mean that the differences in experimental environments, subject pools, and instructions employed could have much larger effects than would be anticipated if bargainers' own monetary payoffs were the only determinant of their utility. (379)

> Bargaining is a complex social phenomenon, which gives bargainers systematic motivations distinct from simple income maximization. This means that special care must be taken in designing, conducting, and interpreting bargaining experiments . . . [and] some cautious appraisal of how particular bargaining processes and environments might influence bargainers' utilities seems called for. (380)

4. Meanwhile, among the Psychologists . . .

The analysis of bargaining has received no less attention in the domain of social psychology than it has in economics. As suggested at the out-

---

19. The Güth and Tietz (1987) experiment is not strictly comparable, since there a disadvantageous counterproposal automatically led to the disagreement outcome. However, even in that experiment, Ochs and Roth point out, of the seventeen first-period refusals, six were followed by disadvantageous counterproposals, even though player 2 knew that this would automatically count as disagreement!

set, what one perceives as interesting in a typical two-person exchange situation depends on one's perspective, and once one breaks away from the confines of utility theory, the possibilities become enormous. In what follows, I outline this embarrassment of experimental riches and, in the process, perhaps convey why economists have been loath to dispense with utility-based models.

The revolution in psychological experimental research on bargaining situations seems to have peaked before that in economics, with the bulk of experiments being performed between the late 1950s and the late 1970s, many of them being reported in such venues as the *Journal of Experimental Social Psychology* and the *Journal of Personality and Social Psychology*. Literally hundreds of experiments have been carried out, examining negotiation and bargaining among groups of two or more persons. Many of these adopted frameworks—such as the Prisoner's Dilemma, group games of coalition formation, or adaptations of matrix games such as Deutsch and Krauss's (1960) trucking transport game— that are not germane to the present study. These either involve more than two players or lack the opportunity for (even limited) interactive negotiation.[20] There remain several hundred experiments, however, which give freer rein to subjects in their bid to reach agreements and examine their behavior from a variety of psychological perspectives.

In their survey of such experiments Chertkoff and Esser (1976) group the psychological theoretical approaches into those which focus on bargaining *outcomes* and those concerned with evaluating the bargaining *process*.[21] The former are dominated by equity theory, which "emphasizes people's desire to achieve fair outcomes in social exchange" (466), whether in order to maintain one's relationship with one's opponent, or because of the pressure of social norms or conventions, transgression of which induces feelings of guilt. Such norms manifest themselves as mutually suggestive "focal points" (Schelling 1963). Approaches to process include face-saving theory (one's readiness to make concessions will be limited by one's concern for public appearance or reputation); attributional analysis (personality characteristics of the bargainers, such as toughness or perceptions of each other's toughness, will influence their approach to bargaining); and level of aspiration theory (the expectations element, discussed above in section 1).

20. See Rubin and Brown 1975 for a review of these experiments.
21. In what follows, I draw freely on their review.

Because experiments designed to test specific psychological theories are rare, the results may often be interpreted from the perspective of several theories. The following survey focuses on the principal categories of psychological factors seen to influence bargaining outcomes in the psychological literature. I summarize them briefly.

General bargaining dispositions. "Tougher bargaining occurs by people high in Dogmatism, people with feelings of internal Locus of Control, and people with a competitive orientation when competition means personal strength" (Chertkoff and Esser 1976, 470).

Payoff system. The position of the zero profit point or the *minimum necessary share* will influence a bargainer's resistance to make concessions, as will time pressure, the cost of no agreement, threat capacity, and the size of payoffs.

Social relationship with the opponent. Bargainers tend to be more cooperative when the social relationship between them is positive or when concern for the interests of the opponent is increased. In one experiment (Dorris 1972) subjects were asked to sell a set of coins to actual coin dealers. In each case, the subject told the dealer that the coins were an inheritance and that he had no idea of their value. One set of subjects used a moral appeal, claiming that the money was needed for textbooks and that they had been sent by somebody who had assured them the dealer was fair. The other subjects used no such appeal. Subjects using the moral appeal secured a better deal.

Social relationship with significant others. Those bargaining on behalf of others tend to be more competitive than nonrepresentatives, and increase competitiveness when subject to monitoring by their constituents. Similarly, directives from the experimenter encouraging self-interest are likely to induce competitive behavior.

Situational factors. Drawing on bargaining manuals written by experienced negotiators, Chertkoff and Esser cite the influence of physical aspects of the bargaining situation. It is better to negotiate on home ground; but if on neutral territory, "choose a place with colorful rooms and pleasant surroundings" (479). Such conditions tend to induce cooperative behavior and may also reduce the urgency of reaching agreement. Similarly, when taking a seat, avoid the small chair and always choose the head of the table!

Bargaining strategy. Not to be confused with strategy in the game-theoretic sense, this concerns the personal characteristics brought to bear in negotiating. Toughness helps in bargaining, but one can go too far: intransigence may prove excessive when negotiations are deadlocked.

Toughness is most successful when it is interpreted by one's opponent as stemming not from excessive greed, but from economic necessity.

Confronted with results of such heterogeneity and generality, Chertkoff and Esser meekly conclude that "the theoretical conceptions are often so general that any result can be interpreted as supportive of a theory." They call for "theories of greater specificity and precision and research of greater theoretical relevance" (483).

5. Discussion

As we consider the evidence presented above, the reasonably narrowly defined phenomenon of the two-person bargain appears sufficiently rich to support a multiplicity of perspectives. The economist reading Wodehouse will likely see in it the hint of a "focal point," in that twenty-five is "a nicer looking sort of number than thirty," as well as the suggestion of a "disadvantageous counteroffer" in Bertie's acceptance of thirty-five when he was seemingly prepared to go no higher than thirty. Bertie's utility function presents an interesting challenge if he is to be retained as a rational maximizer. The psychologist, on the other hand, will see Bertie as someone who, lacking "toughness" or an "internal locus of control," seems to regard bargaining as a last resort, and who may also have been swayed by the suggestion that the high price is due to forces beyond the other fellow's control: after all, he "couldn't do it as cheap as [he'd] like."

Because of their willingness to work with a very large number of different theories, psychologists' explanations of bargaining behavior have tended to be diffuse and context-dependent. In the absence of an overarching theoretical structure, the heterogeneity of experiments is reflected in the heterogeneity of conclusions. In this regard, psychologists resemble the anthropologists discussed by Mayhew (this volume) in that they are concerned with process and are willing to entertain an open-ended list of factors. Such a stance, however, is anathema to neoclassical economics, which places greater emphasis on a precisely stated, albeit predictively inadequate, utility theory. Psychologists, on the other hand, abhor the narrowness of their neoclassical neighbors. As Morley and Stephenson remarked in 1977: "Sufficient at least has been done to ensure that economists will in future pay respect to behavioural as well as economic principles in their . . . accounts of bargaining processes" (46). That being said, the number of bargaining experiments in psychology does seem to have fallen dramatically since the early 1980s. Some of the researchers conducting the game-theoretic experiments discussed above are themselves psychologists. Is it possible that some psychologists, at least, have been attracted by the theoretical coherence of game-theoretic bargaining in face of the relative "fuzziness" of their own domain?

The experimental sequence in economics, however, suggests that bargaining remains less than hermetically sealed from the psychological and cultural influences which theories based on utility maximization have difficulty incorporating. Although the earliest experiments by Siegel and Fouraker were concerned to reconcile the psychological and narrowly economic approaches, the axiomatic solution of Nash represents a deliberate idealization of rationality, a theory-dictated squeezing-out of psychology and culture. But experiments on the Nash solution uniformly reveal that considerations surrounding the interpersonal comparison of wealth matter crucially to the outcome, steering players towards equal expected monetary gains. On the other hand, when bargaining is in terms of chips of unknown value, the equal-split focal point loses its attraction, for reasons that remain unclear. This set of observations seems to resonate with the concerns of two other papers in this volume. The concurrence on the equal-expected-monetary-gain outcome is clearly linked to Lowry's discussion of focal points; the curiously diminished importance of the equal-split result when the prize is determined in chips of unknown value is tied to Hutter's discussion of the symbolic importance of money. Once again, this suggests that an understanding of the historical development and internalization of these social norms will be necessary for any reconciliation of theory and experiment. The same experiments also suggest the importance of both the degree to which knowledge is shared and the conditioning of the players' expectations, variables which again point towards both social and psychological influences.

The strategic approach, too, constitutes a strong idealization of what it means to be rational, and the related experimental work is duly controversial and the subject of current debate. In an attempt to reconcile the model of strategic utility maximization with the disadvantageous counteroffers and other unpredicted regularities observed, Ochs and Roth (1989) conclude by suggesting that the utility function might be modified to incorporate distributional concerns, that is, the individual's ideas about fairness.[22] This tampering with the utility function drew a

---

22. The authors acknowledge that this could heighten the importance of the particular experimental environment or the subjects chosen.

sharp response from Güth and Tietz (1990), who "strictly reject the idea [of including] results of analysing a social decision problem into the utility functions of the interacting agents. Utility functions are an instrument of describing individual characteristics needed to define a social decision problem. Furthermore, all our experiences from ultimatum bargaining experiments indicate that subjects do not 'maximize' but are guided by sometimes conflicting behavioral norms. . . . The utility approach necessarily neglects the dynamic nature of the intellectual process which subjects apply to derive their decision behavior" (440).

And so the debate continues. A recent article by Bolton (1991) puts flesh on Ochs and Roth's (1989) suggested modification of the utility function, and concludes that money and the desire for fair treatment of oneself (that is, relative money) should both appear in the utility function. This, he argues, will suffice to rehabilitate the perfect equilibrium model. Another (Roth et al. 1991) investigates the basic strategic equilibrium model in four different cultural settings: Israel, Japan, the United States, and Yugoslavia. Again the model was found to predict outcomes quite poorly; the various nationalities are seen to settle on different average divisions of the "pie." The authors believe that what matters is what each group *perceives* to constitute a reasonable offer, and that this is primarily determined by *cultural* factors (such as nationality, in their own experiment).

Conclusion

In a recent response to the question "Will economics become an experimental science?" the Caltech experimentalist Charles Plott answered in the affirmative: "The profession has tasted the devil's brew, the use of experimental methods, and likes it" (1991, 918). It is not that field research will disappear, he says; "economies found in the wild" will remain important, but researchers will also rely on the laboratory to help isolate the principles governing economic behavior.

As we consider the sequence of research on bargaining described above, the mainstream profession certainly has taken the bait. Such work is increasing in prominence, but the meaning of "isolating the governing principles" seems somewhat unclear. It could be argued that the most significant accomplishment here has been the confirmation of the theory's predictive inadequacy. And in revealing those weaknesses, experiments have forced economists to acknowledge the influence on bargaining of factors, psychological and cultural, which cannot easily be accommodated in the framework of rational maximization. Critics of the narrow rationality embodied in neoclassical economics and game theory have long called for the introduction of such influences into economics. It is somewhat ironic that it has fallen to *laboratory* practice, of all possible phenomena, to induce a renewed emphasis on such factors.

For helpful criticism and comments, I thank the participants in the conference "Higgling: Markets and Their Transactors in the History of Economic Thought," held at Duke University in March 1993; an anonymous referee; and the editors of this special issue of *HOPE.* I am also grateful to the Comité d'Aide Financière aux Chercheurs of the Université de Québec, Montréal, who supported the research for this paper.

References

Binmore, K., A. Shaked, and J. Sutton. 1985. Testing Noncooperative Bargaining Theory: A Preliminary Study. *American Economic Review* 75.5:1178–80.

———. 1988. A Further Test of Noncooperative Bargaining Theory: Reply. *American Economic Review* 78.4:837–39.

Bolton, Gary E. 1991. A Comparative Model of Bargaining: Theory and Evidence. *American Economic Review* 81.5:1096–1136.

Bowley, A. L. 1928. On Bilateral Monopoly. *Economic Journal* 38:651–59.

Chertkoff, Jerome, and James Esser. 1976. A Review of Experiments in Explicit Bargaining. *Journal of Experimental Social Psychology* 12:464–86.

Contini, Bruno. 1968. The Value of Time in Bargaining Negotiations: Some Experimental Evidence. *American Economic Review* 58:374–93.

Crawford, Vincent. 1990. Explicit Communication and Bargaining Outcomes. *American Economic Review* 80.2:213–19.

Cross, John G. 1969. *The Economics of Bargaining.* New York: Basic Books.

Deutsch, M., and R. M. Krauss. 1960. The Effect of Threat upon Interpersonal Bargaining. *Journal of Abnormal and Social Psychology* 61:181–89.

Dorris, J. W. 1972. Reactions to Unconditional Cooperation: A Field Study Emphasizing Variables Neglected in Laboratory Research. *Journal of Personality and Social Psychology* 22:387–97.

Fellner, W. 1949. *Competition among the Few.* New York: Knopf.

Flood, M. M. 1954. Game-Learning Theory and Some Decision-Making Experiments. In Thrall, Coombs, and Davis 1954, 139–58.

Fouraker, Lawrence. 1957. Professor Fellner's Bilateral Monopoly Theory. *Southern Economic Journal* 24:182–89.

Fouraker, Lawrence, and Sidney Siegel. 1963. *Bargaining Behavior.* New York: McGraw-Hill.

Güth, Werner, R. Schmittberger, and B. Schwarz. 1982. An Experimental Analysis of Ultimatum Bargaining. *Journal of Economic Behavior and Organizations* 3:367–88.

Güth, Werner, and Reinhard Tietz. 1988. Ultimatum Bargaining for a Shrinking Cake: An Experimental Analysis. In *Bounded Rational Behavior in Experimental Games and Markets,* edited by R. Tietz, W. Albers, and R. Selten. Berlin: Springer.

———. 1990. Ultimatum Bargaining Behavior: A Survey and Comparison of Experimental Results. *Journal of Economic Psychology* 11:417–49.

Hoffman, E., and M. Spitzer. 1982. The Coase Theorem: Some Experimental Tests. *Journal of Law and Economics* 25:73–98.

Hutter, Michael. 1994. Higgling with Money: German Contributions between 1900 and 1945. In *Higgling: Transactors and Their Markets in the History of Economics,* edited by Neil De Marchi and Mary S. Morgan. *HOPE* 26, special issue. Durham: Duke University Press.

Kalisch, G. K., J. W. Milnor, J. F. Nash, and E. D. Nering. 1954. Some Experimental *n*-Person Games. In Thrall, Coombs, and Davis 1954, 301–27.

Komorita, S. S., and David A. Kravitz. 1979. The Effects of Alternatives in Bargaining. *Journal of Experimental Social Psychology* 15:147–57.

Leonard, Robert J. 1991. War as a Simple Economic Problem. In *Economics and National Security: A History of Their Interaction,* edited by Craufurd D. Goodwin, 261–83. *HOPE* 23, special issue. Durham: Duke University Press.

———. 1992. Creating a Context for Game Theory. In *Essays in the History of Game Theory,* edited by E. Roy Weintraub. *HOPE* 24, special issue. Durham: Duke University Press.

———. 1994. Reading Cournot, Reading Nash. *Economic Journal* 104:492–511.

Lowry, S. Todd. 1994. The Market as a Distributive and Allocative System: Its Legal, Ethical, and Analytical Evolution. In *Higgling: Transactors and Their Markets in the History of Economics,* edited by Neil De Marchi and Mary S. Morgan. *HOPE* 26, special issue. Durham: Duke University Press.

Malouf, Michael W. K., and Alvin E. Roth. 1981. Disagreement in Bargaining. *Journal of Conflict Resolution* 25:329–48.

Mirowski, Philip. 1991. When Games Grow Deadly Serious. In *Economics and National Security: A History of Their Interaction,* edited by Craufurd D. Goodwin, 227–55. *HOPE* 23, special issue. Durham: Duke University Press.

———. 1992. What Were von Neumann and Morgenstern Trying to Accomplish? In *The History of Game Theory,* edited by E. Roy Weintraub, 113–47. *HOPE* 24, special issue. Durham: Duke University Press.

Morley, Ian, and Geoffrey Stephenson. 1977. *The Social Psychology of Bargaining.* London: George Allen & Unwin.

Murnighan, J. K., A. E. Roth, and F. Schoumaker. 1986. Risk Aversion in Bargaining: An Experimental Study. University of Montreal, mimeo (revised).

Nash, John F., Jr. 1950a. The Bargaining Problem. *Econometrica* 28:155–62.

———. 1950b. Equilibrium Points in *p*-Person Games. *Proceedings of the National Academy of Sciences* (U.S.) 36:48–49.

———. 1951. Non-cooperative Games. *Annals of Mathematics* 54.2:286–95.

Neelin, J., H. Sonnenschein, and M. Spiegel. 1988. A Further Test of Noncooperative Bargaining Theory: Comment. *American Economic Review* 78.4:824–35.

Nydegger, R. V., and G. Owen. 1975. Two-Person Bargaining: An Experimental Test of the Nash Axioms. *International Journal of Game Theory* 3:239–49.

Ochs, Jack, and Alvin E. Roth. 1989. An Experimental Study of Sequential Bargaining. *American Economic Review* 79.3:355–84.

Pigou, A. C. 1908. *The Economics of Welfare*. London: Macmillan.

Plott, Charles R. 1991. Will Economics Become an Experimental Science? *Southern Economic Journal* 57.4:901–19.

Raiffa, Howard. 1953. Arbitration Schemes for Generalized Two-Person Games. In *Contributions to the Theory of Games*, 2, edited by H. W. Kuhn and A. W. Tucker. *Annals of Mathematics Studies* 28. Princeton: Princeton University Press.

Rapoport, Anatol. 1974a. Testing Nash's Solution in the Cooperative Game. In Rapoport 1974b, 103–15.

———, ed. 1974b. *Game Theory as a Theory of Conflict Resolution*. Dordrecht: Reidel.

Rapoport, A., O. Frenkel, and J. Perner. 1977. Experiments with Cooperative 2×2 Games. *Theory and Decision* 8:67–82.

Roth, Alvin E. 1986. Laboratory Experimentation in Economics. *Economics and Philosophy* 2:245–73.

———. 1987a. Bargaining Phenomena and Bargaining Theory. In Roth 1987b, 14–41.

———. 1987b. *Laboratory Experimentation in Economics*. Cambridge: Cambridge University Press.

———. 1988. Laboratory Experimentation in Economics: A Methodological Overview. *Economic Journal* 98 (December): 974–1031.

Roth, Alvin E., and Michael W. K. Malouf. 1979. Game-Theoretic Models and the Role of Information in Bargaining. *Psychological Review* 86.6:574–94.

Roth, Alvin E., Michael W. K. Malouf, and J. K. Murnighan. 1981. Sociological versus Strategic Factors in Bargaining. *Journal of Economic Behavior and Organization* 2:153–77.

Roth, Alvin E., and Keith Murnighan. 1982. The Role of Information in Bargaining: An Experimental Study. *Econometrica* 50.5:1123–42.

Roth, Alvin E., J. Keith Murnighan, and Françoise Schoumaker. 1988. The Deadline Effect in Bargaining: Some Experimental Evidence. *American Economic Review* 78.4:806–23.

Roth, Alvin E., and Françoise Schoumaker. 1983. Expectations and Reputations in Bargaining: An Experimental Study. *American Economic Review* 73.3:362–72.

Roth, Alvin E., Vesna Prasnikar, Masahiro Okuno-Fujiwara, and Shmuel Zamir. 1991. Bargaining and Market Behavior in Jerusalem, Ljubljana, Pittsburgh, and Tokyo: An Experimental Study. *American Economic Review* 81.5:1068–95.

Rubin, Jeffrey, and Bert Brown. 1975. *The Social Psychology of Bargaining and Negotiation*. New York: Academic Press.

Rubinstein, Ariel. 1982. Perfect Equilibrium in a Bargaining Model. *Econometrica* 50.1:97–109.

Schelling, T. 1960, 1963. *The Strategy of Conflict.* Cambridge: Harvard University Press.

Selten, R. 1975. Reexamination of the Perfectness Concept for Equilibrium Points in Extensive Games. *International Journal of Game Theory* 4.1:25–55.

Siegel, Sidney, and Lawrence Fouraker. 1960. *Bargaining and Group Decision Making.* New York: McGraw-Hill.

Smith, Vernon. 1991a. Experimental Economics at Purdue. In Smith 1991d, 154–58.

——. 1991b. Theory, Experiment and Economics. In Smith 1991d, 783–801.

——. 1991c. Experimental Economics: Behavioral Lessons for Microeconomic Theory and Policy. In Smith 1991d, 802–12.

——. 1991d. *Papers in Experimental Economics.* Cambridge: Cambridge University Press.

——. 1992. Game Theory and Experimental Economics: Beginnings and Early Influences. In *Essays in the History of Game Theory,* edited by E. Roy Weintraub. *HOPE* 24, special issue. Durham: Duke University Press.

Stahl, Ingolf. 1972. *Bargaining Theory.* Stockholm: Economic Research Institute.

Stigler, G. 1952. *The Theory of Price.* New York: Macmillan.

Stone, Jeremy J. 1958. An Experiment in Bargaining Games. *Econometrica* 26.2 (April): 286–96.

Thrall, R. M., C. H. Coombs, and R. L. Davis, eds. 1954. *Decision Processes.* New York: Wiley.

Trump, Donald, with Tony Schwartz. 1987. *Trump: The Art of the Deal.* New York: Warner Books.

von Neumann, J., and O. Morgenstern. 1944. *The Theory of Games and Economic Behavior.* Princeton: Princeton University Press.

The Interactional Study of Exchange Relationships: An Analysis of Patter Merchants at Work on Street Markets

Colin Clark and Trevor Pinch

In this essay we describe a variety of the sales techniques employed by a special group of market sellers known as pitchers. We compare and contrast the strategies used with those encountered in "higgling" as well as in more orthodox retailing environments.

Pitchers are to be found largely on British and other European markets. They employ an extended patter or sales spiel full of humor and audience participation to sell to a crowd, en masse, at a fixed point in the sale. The goods sold include china and glass pots, towels and bedding, meat, perfumes, jewelry, and toys. Pitchers are the original patter merchants.

Pitchers have a long and colorful history, complete with their own traditions and argot. In Victorian times most goods on street markets were sold by pitching. Today, when market regulations place restrictions on the activities of pitchers, usually only the occasional pitcher can be found on regular markets.[1] "Demonstrators" who work inside large department stores and fairs selling highly portable mechanical gadgets also employ a similar form of sales patter. Sometimes "fly pitchers" can be found on street corners using compressed forms of a pitching spiel.

Since 1985 we have been engaged in a study of the rhetorical and interactional skills that pitchers use to sell. Our research methods have included video and audio recording (sometimes with two cameras present), still photography, observation, interviewing, and participant observation. We have collected more than sixty hours of video recordings of

1. Market authorities hold that the large crowds that pitchers attract block narrow alleyways in and around markets.

pitchers from a variety of markets throughout England, and, to a lesser extent, France, the Netherlands, and the United States. Our data corpus includes instances of the same pitchers selling different types of goods, different pitchers selling the same goods, and the same pitchers selling both the same and different goods in different locales.

Our interest, as sociologists, has primarily been in the pitchers' communicative and interactional skills. This has involved documenting and analyzing issues such as the sorts of rhetorical devices effective in this form of selling, the methods pitchers use to attract and hold the attention of a large crowd, the role of humor in pitching, and so on. Our analysis is informed by the work of interactional sociologists such as Goffman (1955) and to a lesser extent by ethnomethodology and conversational analysis (Heritage 1984; Pinch and Clark 1986; Clark and Pinch 1988, 1993). The present essay focuses on one systemic feature of pitching—how an obligation to buy is instilled in an audience—and is based upon part of a book we are writing about pitching (Clark and Pinch 1993).

Why should historians of economics and others who study "higgling" be interested in pitching? We think the reason is simple. Pitching is a particularly apposite form of economic exchange to study, because (unlike in most economic transactions) the seller makes explicit why the buyer should participate in the exchange. In most normal buying and selling in retail settings verbal exchanges are perfunctory. They simply mark a request for the exchange to take place, what the prices are, and so on. However, in pitching the *verbal exchanges are the key to understanding the economic exchanges.* Pitching is a discursive context in which persuasion is to the fore. Here the salespeople work with the assumption that goods do not sell themselves; rather, the prospective customers have to be persuaded to buy those goods. Pitchers make explicit a variety of reasons why customers should buy goods at a particular price. These verbal strategies can be inspected to appreciate how bargains are constituted and sales are managed in this context (Pinch and Clark 1986).

Higgling is another form of economic exchange which prima facie should be amenable to study by the methods of interactional sociology. This is because higgling is accomplished primarily through the use of verbal means. Again we can expect that many of the considerations which govern the exchange will be made explicit by both parties in the course of their negotiations. In other words, inspection of "higgling" transactions should reveal the systematic communicative and interactional skills employed.

Higgling, however, has one feature which makes it appear to be rather different from pitching. While pitching involves selling to a whole group of potential customers, most higgling is conducted on a one-to-one basis. This difference may, however, be only a matter of degree. In a way pitching can be viewed as a special case of higgling where the pitcher acts as the seller and plays the part of a substitute buyer at the same time. In other words, the pitcher speaks for both parties and builds into the routine all possible buyer objections and how they might be overcome. Rather than both parties' negotiating the price, as in higgling, the pitcher runs through a set of possible prices that a "fictional" buyer might pay. The pitching spiel is designed to provide potential buyers with *all* the information they might need to make a purchasing decision. There is no need for individuals in the audience to talk with the pitcher, let alone negotiate.

Thus in pitching the interaction is much more one-sided; the pitcher is always in the driver's seat. The pitchers initiate the sales and set the initial parameters within which this form of transaction is to be conducted.[2] By and large the pitchers address the audience in general. When they do initiate interactions with individual members of the audience, they demand simple minimal responses and ask leading questions which can then be restated by the pitcher for the benefit of the audience as a whole.[3] Having a crowd of shoppers looking on and/or also willing to buy goods is of course the main difference between pitching and higgling.

The one-sided nature of pitching, where the pitcher acts as both buyer and seller, makes pitching an ideal research site to study interactional features of economic exchanges.[4] Thus we start off our analysis with pitching. In the latter part of our discussion we draw more specific comparisons between pitching, higgling, and retail selling in general.

2. This can include the physical setting for the interaction, whereby the pitcher stands above the audience on a raised, brightly lit stall and with the aid of a microphone and loudspeaker has the power to repackage audience responses for the benefit of the audience at large, who can neither see nor hear everything.

3. This does not mean that the audience are dopes or "suckers." The audience can themselves employ resistance strategies: see Clark and Pinch 1993.

4. The advantages of studying pitching over higgling resemble the type of advantages gained in the field of conversation analysis by turning to the study of rhetoric. For example, Atkinson (1984) and Heritage and Greatbach (1986) have studied political rhetoric, where the response of the audience is essentially a binary one: they either applaud or they do not. This has enabled the researchers to elucidate in a particularly clear-cut way the rhetorical devices which are effective in eliciting applause from audiences, and it serves as a way of determining the persuasiveness of the rhetoric.

Obligations and Crowd Behavior in Pitching

For a sales pitch to have any chance of mass sales success, an audience of prospective customers (known collectively as "the edge") has to be attracted to the market stall. This is one of the hardest tasks in pitching. The main difficulty seems to be that people are reluctant to stop at a pitching stall because they construe that the very act of stopping and standing to listen to a pitcher places them under some form of obligation. Pitchers employ special techniques in order both to attract an edge and overcome such reluctance.

One way to "build an edge" is known as the "pull-up." Here an individual passerby is simply stopped by the pitcher's asking a question. As one trader told us: "Getting them to stop is definitely the most difficult thing. You start off by asking a passerby a question. For instance, 'What is this made of?' So you ask them something and put the product in front of them so they've got to answer you and stop. If you ask them a question they don't know what it is to do with. And then [laughing] . . . they realize." The pull-up helps overcome others' reluctance to stop. If there is already someone standing at the stall, potential customers feel easier about stopping themselves.

Another technique to get people to overcome their reluctance to stop is known as the "blind start." The pitcher simply starts to shout about the dramatic bargains that will be on offer later in the sale. As people come within earshot they invariably stop and listen. Various features of the goods are described and extolled in short, catchy, appetizing sound bites which summarize the upcoming sales offer. The following examples are typical:[5]

> P: It'll be the *best* deal for *cash,* you'll find *anywhere.* And we'll give you more value for money now, in the *next* two *minutes,* than them shops and stores will give you *there* in two *years.*

> P: In fact, the man who owns this stock, he's in Spain with my wife right now. An' what he's doing to my wife right now, I'm gonna do to his business. *Now watch.*

> P: Ah'll tell you something. *Whoever* comes in possession, of a pair

5. In all of the transcripts, P is the Pitcher, A is a member of the Audience, and PC is a member of the Pitch Crew (i.e., an assistant). Italicized talk is that which is spoken louder. Words in upper-case lettering indicate shouting.

> of these, at the *ridiculous* amount of money I'm gonna charge you
> today, never mind a *customer,* you'll be a *friend for life.*

What is likely to follow is made crystal clear. Anyone who cares to stop at the stall is soon likely to receive the chance of obtaining a major, if not unparalleled, bargain. Because each of these summary phrases lasts, at most, only a couple of seconds, every member of the public who passes within hearing range of the stall has the opportunity to listen to (and be persuaded to stop by) at least one self-contained segment of sales patter.

To further overcome people's reluctance to stop, pitchers avert their eyes from the individuals who gather. Also, the "out of the ordinary" claims made during the "blind start" provide people with a reason to overcome their reluctance.

Yet another strategy is known as "knocking out." Rather than simply extolling the exceptional bargains that will be offered in the forthcoming sale, pitchers actually start a preliminary sale of goods at extremely low prices:

> P: This is Loctite glue—little bits of odds and sods that I get from
>   time to time. It's ninety pence *each.* There's one, two, three of
>   them. *Go on, there's* four, *there's* five, *there's half a dozen of*
>   *them.* Somebody give me a POUND the price of *one.* Here you
>   are. [Gives bags to PC]
> PC: [To a buyer] Got your pound?
> P: In fact COME BACK. What did I say? *A pound the price o' one?*
>   Here you are, let's be bloody fair with them. *It's Christmas.*
>   Ninety-nine pence each, there's six in a bag an' I said a pound.
>   [BANG] I'll take FIFTY PENCE to get them out of the road.

The goods that are sold during "knocking out" function as loss leaders. They are usually small items such as tea towels, playing cards, or (as in the example above) tubes of glue. Passersby are attracted to the stall when their expectations about what something is worth are dramatically subverted by a pitcher's actually selling that item at a much reduced price.

Sometimes an accomplice of the pitcher (known as a "rick") will pose surreptitiously as an audience member to make it easier for people to stop at the stall. All this person has to do is stand at the stall—his (or her) presence alone seems to attract other passersby. The imitative nature of stopping behavior is familiar to most market traders. As one demonstrator told us: "Sometimes I'll have a walk round the market and I'll stand talking to another grafter who's also taking a break. So I stand right up in front of his joint [stall] and we'll be talking about having a drink or whatever. All of a sudden we'll have two people standing behind me."

A pitcher who is not satisfied with the number of people who have gathered at the stall may then capitalize upon these imitative processes in attempting to build an "execution pitch," that is, a crowd of the size that would, as tradition holds, turn up to watch public executions. To build such a large crowd (with at least fifty customers) the pitcher uses the audience who have already congregated at the sales site as unwitting accomplices in attracting additional people to the stall. For example:

P: Ladies an' gentlemen, the *next* time, [CLAP] I clap my hands like that, the FIRST few buyers [P raises his right hand] to have their hands in the air like that can have one of them bath towels. I want *no* cheatin'. NOT three p., NOT two p., NOT for a penny (. . .) when I *clap* my hands, I'm watching who's first I'll be the judge and I'll be the jury, it's the end of the day. NOT three p. or two p., not for a penny, *who could,* make use of any one of them bath towels today? [CLAP]

As: [Many hands rise]

P: For twenty pound?

As: [LAUGHTER] [The vast majority who have raised their arms rapidly lower them]

P: *I'm only joking.* You ought to have seen your face—*your* hands then. *Your* hands went *like that* [P rapidly raises his hand] and bloody *like that.* [P rapidly lowers his hand] Ey?

As: [LAUGHTER]

The commotion and positive responsiveness that the pitcher generates in the audience attracts additional passersby. The audience act as unpaid opinion leaders to provide proof to passersby that it is worth stopping at the stall.

A retired pitcher explained why this technique is so effective: "This is how Dickey used to work. The forks [hands] go up. So now you say 'Not quick enough—put 'em down.' 'Raise your hands,' he'd shout, 'UP–DOWN–UP.' Now, people over the other end of the market would see them lifting and lowering their arms, and they'd come over to see what's going on. That way you get an even bigger edge still."

Even when a crowd has gathered, its constituents do so in such a way as to indicate their reluctance to be placed under an obligation. Often a "no man's land" opens up between the front of the audience and the pitching stall. Pitchers explicitly request the audience to move closer, or use techniques such as throwing cheap items into the no man's land, to entice people nearer the stall:

> P: If you'd like to be in the sale, can you plase do me a simple favour and take one step forward. *Thank you.* Will you *all* move in towards the stall because I want now to give everybody the same chance. I don't want people saying "*Aye,* he's only serving his friends, *aye,* he's only serving her 'cos he's *married* to her." I want *everybody* to have the *same equal opportunity.*

> P: Can you come a bit closer, look? If you stand any further away he'll [PC] 'ave to 'ave a motorbike to come an' deliver the *bloody* stuff.

> P: *Move in. Move right in.* The closer you get to me, love, is the closest you'll get to heaven.

Responsiveness

The difficulties that pitchers face in obtaining any form of responsiveness from individuals in their audiences should not be underestimated. In the last analysis, achieving the one form of reaction that pitchers desire most—a buying response—depends upon their having already received other forms of buying-implicative responses at earlier points in the sale.

People do not want to be "put on the spot." This reluctance hinders the pitcher's attempts to establish credibility with the audience and eventually to obtain commitments (and sales) from them. Pitchers usually want people in the audience to take part in the sale, whether by confirming that the goods are worth buying, that the price stated on a box is the correct one, or that the towels on offer are thick and soft to the touch. Yet even in these apparently simple tasks, individuals in the audience can show great reluctance in speaking with pitchers. To help overcome this, at the start of the sale, the pitcher may make audience responsiveness a condition for receiving bargains:

> P: [Talking to his assistant about the crowd that have gathered at the stall] Ay-up, we've got the dumb lot in.
> As: [Laughter]

P: Before I do these [a set of glass decanters], 'ere, there's an odd dinner service there, one of you buy that one. Five, four, three, one of you, [BANG] *two quid*, who's havin' that one out the way?

A: [A hand is raised]

P: 'Ere, ah'll tell you what, because he [the hand-raiser] said yes, [BANG] charge 'im fifty pence for the bugger. Now then—

As: [Laughter and appreciative commotion]

P: Charge 'im fifty pence 'cos I'm in a good mood. Has anybody got any children?

As: Yes.

P: *That's it!* They're talking to me now, look. [BANG] *Hey,* ah'll tell you what. Ah'll tell you what I've got here—*oh,* by the way, before I do them, can anybody catch?

As: [No response]

P: *Can you catch?*

As: [Many hands rise, many shouts of YES]

P: *Catch that bugger.* 'Ere y'are, [hands over goods] because you talked to me. Somebody say "Thank you."

As: [Shouts of THANK YOU]

P: [Hands over goods] 'Ere y'are, catch that bugger. Now then, somebody else say thank you.

As: [Shouts of THANK YOU]

Pitchers sometimes offer deals where the actual selling price of the goods is posited as being conditional upon the strength of the audience's responsiveness and participation.

P: Ah'll *say* to you *once,* who could use a case o' chicken? The more 'ands that go up the cheaper ah'll be. If I get *twenty* 'ands up I've got another ten in the fridge, so the more 'ands that go up the cheaper ah'll be.

P: Forget about the money because its Xmas, forget about the price and the more hands I see the cheaper they will be. Who might be interested in a set if we can do a deal? You might, you might, you might, you might. *Say yes,* You might.

As with all pitching sales, however, the price is set in advance by the pitcher, and in cases such as those above it is highly unlikely that the audience interest that is displayed materially affects the final selling price. However, the audience are given a direct incentive to respond and in this case to cooperate with each other—thus increasing the likelihood of the pitcher's obtaining mass sales.

Getting Individual Responses

The easiest way for a pitcher to get around the reluctance of certain members of the audience to respond is to talk only to those people who are most likely to speak in return. This is one reason why pitchers use humor. They can monitor the laughter to see who laughs first or the loudest. The person who does so is most likely to respond and respond positively when addressed. Pitchers invariably select someone in the audience who exhibits a suggestible demeanor (known as "clocking the divvy").

Yet when someone is asked to respond to a direct question from the pitcher, the work that the pitcher has undertaken to obtain that response will be wasted if it is inaudible to the rest of the audience. Individuals, when addressed, are more likely to nod their heads than open their mouths. This can give an impression of disinterest. One means of resolving this difficulty is for the pitcher to pose the question in such a way that even a nod can be taken as a confirmation. More specifically, pitchers tend to ask individuals in the audience to confirm rather than to state the price. To maximize the number of people in the audience who hear these confirmations, pitchers will repeat the responses or, if the response is nonverbal, will acknowledge it in the affirmative—for instance, by saying "thank you," as in the following sequence. The pitcher is selling sets of perfume:

> P: *Now watch.* To go with it, look at this. I'll put on top, look, World of Beauty's "Number Five." Now this one retails, in all the stores, look, from World of Beauty—
> [P thrusts an advert under the nose of someone in the audience]
> P: It's exactly six pounds, am I right, love?
> A: [Nods]
> P: Thank you.

To offset any audience suspicions that it is a confederate that has been chosen to respond, pitchers may ask two or three individuals at any one time.

Pitchers may also exaggerate the type of responsiveness supplied, in order both to compensate for any reluctance displayed and to ensure that the rest of the crowd hear a positive response:

> P: Have you felt the quality of those towels, love? Go on, have a feel, you're nearest to me.
> [P holds the towel out so that A can feel it]
> A: [Tentatively and self-consciously feels the towel]
> P: Don't wear them out, will you?
> As: [Laughter]

In a large crowd the majority of the audience will not be able to either hear an endorsement or see anyone examining the goods. They will only be able to hear the pitcher's own analysis of what is going on. With these strategies the audience are thus left with the impression that the person's opinion of the goods was an overwhelmingly positive one.

Sometimes a pitcher may even do what many shoppers appear to fear most—put an individual member of the audience "on the spot." In the following case a pitcher suddenly suspends his patter to harangue an individual (and her mother) standing among the audience:

> P: Ah you buyin' or spyin'?
> [Silence]
> A1: Spyin'.
> A2: Er, spyin'.
> P: Well *Blake* got fifteen years for spyin', can you go—can you go spy round there, you schmuck?
> As: [Laughter]
> P: *Go on. Off you go.* Anybody else want a lot? Ah wa—ah want *buyers,* not spyers.
> [A1 and A2 leave]

By playing upon people's fear of public embarrassment (although, as usual, with a degree of humor—the joke above refers to the famous Soviet spy George Blake) the pitcher may intimidate other individuals in the audience into realizing the implications of their listener status— being obliged to be buyers. In such cases pitchers always pick out people who, they infer, are not likely to buy (such as people who have stood at the stall for a time without displaying any signs of interest or making a purchase).

Obligation to Buy and "Nailing"

It should now be clear that some audience members feel that standing in the crowd places them under some form of obligation to buy. To enhance prospects for obtaining mass sales, pitchers will try and make this obligation more apparent and, therefore, more ineluctable. They do this with a strategy known as "nailing," which places audience members under an obligation to buy before they know the final selling price of the goods on offer. Such strategies "nail" the feet of the edge to the sales site, so that the prospect of mass sales is dramatically enhanced when the final price is announced. In the sequence of sales described below, the audience are placed under a more and more irresistible obligation to buy. In the final case that we examine—the "proviso"—the audience are nailed and obligated by *accepting* the goods before knowing exactly what their final price will be.

Back-Nailing

The following sale is somewhat unusual in that it occurs between a pitcher and only two members of his audience. The pitcher has just finished selling several china vase sets for £2 each to the large crowd gathered at the stall. Everybody who wanted the vases has already purchased one. Or so it seems. The pitcher is now about to attempt to obtain more sales of the same sets of vases from that same audience. He does this by revising the sales offer and by promising to sell the "last two sets" for less than their original price of £2:[6]

> P: An' 'oo's gonna buy the other one an' ah'll make the buggers cheaper than two quid? Come on?
> [No response]
> P: Come on?
> [No response]
> P: *'oo's gonna buy the other set?*
> [Pause]
> [Al raises hand]
> P: Lady here. An' 'oo 's 'avin' the very—
> [A2 raises hand]

6. The halfpence coin was still legal tender when we recorded this routine.

P: Gentleman there. Knock 'em all the profit off. [BANG] One ninety-nine an' a 'alf. Now then, 'ere y'are.
[P throws the goods down to PC. These goods are then exchanged for money from A1 and A2.]

As: [Laughter]

P: There wasn't a lot of—there wasn't a lot of profit on them, ah'll tell you now.

As: [Laughter]

Upon hearing the offer to sell the vase sets at a price that is lower than £2, two more members of the audience have raised their hands indicating a willingness to buy. Rather than the substantial reduction they no doubt expected, the new selling price turns out to be £1.99½—a reduction of a mere halfpence. Despite this least possible reduction, these two people willingly buy the vases.

By not stating precisely what his final price will be and by persuading two people to commit themselves to buy the goods at a lower but un-specified price, the pitcher has managed to do two things. First, he has been able to sell two additional vases that otherwise would not have been sold. Second, he has been able to sell these vases at essentially the same price he had originally charged.

The main issue of interest here is, why do these people accept the goods and not complain? The first thing to note is that the pitcher has in fact formally fulfilled all his obligations. He *has* actually gone cheaper than £2, and if challenged, he can always maintain that the profit on this particular line was indeed only half a pence. More importantly, by *not* going significantly cheaper he has not risked the ire of all those who have paid the full £2 for the vases (such people were still standing in the audience). Indeed, he has done the very opposite: he has got them to laugh at the misfortune of the two buyers. And by doing so he has created conditions whereby those two individuals are pressured to treat their experience as something which can be "laughed off."

This procedure of "back-nailing"—a remedial sales strategy used to sell a few more of the same goods—is rather exceptional. In fact, the amount of money pitchers take from conducting this type of sale hardly covers the cost of their time and effort. Pitchers are more likely to use back-nailing to get the audience to laugh and to maintain a con-vivial mood that will be conducive to attracting additional customers and keeping customers at the stall for the next sale.

Back-nailing will not work as a mass selling strategy, because it plays off the audience who have already purchased the goods at the higher price against individuals seeking an even cheaper bargain. There are, however, other forms of "nailing" which can be used to produce mass sales.

Getting the Forks Up

Probably the most common way that pitchers attempt to obtain purchase-implicative commitments from the audience is by "getting the forks up." Members of the audience are asked to raise a hand (a "fork") if they would be interested in the goods on sale—provided that the pitcher makes the price cheaper. In the following sequence the pitcher is selling sets of five pens:

> P: Ah won't charge you five ninety-five, ah WON'T charge you three
> ninety-five or one ninety-five, in fact ah'm not even chargin' look,
> a pound and ten pence for all the five of 'em. Now 'oo can use
> 'em if ah go a bit lower than a pound ten pence? Raise an 'and?
> As: [Many hands rise]
> P: [Counting the hands] One, two, three, four. AH CAN ONLY DO
> IT FOR SO MANY. Five, six, seven, eight, nine, anybody at the
> back? Ten, eleven. Here's what ah'll do with you. FIRST come
> first served. ALL the five of 'em, you must 'ave fifteen pounds'
> worth of pens, [CLAP] ah'll take a pound the whole jolly lot.

Unlike in back-nailing, the hand-raising members of the audience above have not expressed an explicit intention to buy. The pitcher has merely asked who can *use* the pens? The raised hands can be taken more as a display of interest in the goods than a firm commitment to purchase. Nevertheless, the question " 'oo can use 'em if ah go a bit lower than a pound ten pence?" does seem to entail some commitment to buy the goods as the pitcher has referred to a specific purchasing price. Certainly, those people who raise their hands at these junctures treat this as in some way obliging them to buy—they nearly always do buy.

The pitcher's offer to go "a *bit lower* than a pound ten pence" is much more specific than the offer in the vase sale to go "*cheaper than* two quid." A "bit lower" does not promise the possibility of much further price reduction. Because pitchers usually round off their prices to the nearest pound ("level and silly money"), the audience can guess that £1 will be the final price. Indeed some members of the audience can be seen to be waving pound notes (still legal tender when this film was shot) in the air. Thus, unlike with the vase sale, the pitcher, when he announces the final price, does not have to deal with having misled the audience.[7]

The display of interest the pitcher has obtained not only obligates those who have raised a hand, it also helps persuade others at the stall to buy and furthermore serves to attract additional people to the stall. The positive responsiveness is particularly evident in the extract above because people are holding *money* in their hands.

A smart pitcher will try and turn the public expression of "interest" in the goods into a more explicit commitment. One way of doing this is to point out each person who has raised a hand, thereby affirming in public the individual's interest and obligation. The pitcher above does this when he counts out each of the individual hand-raisers in turn ("one two, three," etc.).

Bag-Nailing

Sometimes when people have expressed an interest in the goods by raising their hands, but *before* the announcement of the selling price, pitchers will then provide them with bags (or wrapping paper, and the like). In the following example the pitcher is attempting to sell sets of four different perfumes for £3.

> P: Now 'oo can use all the four of 'em, for the purposes of the advertisement, they've got to be cleared cheaply an' quickly. 'oo can use all the four of 'em, twenty-three pounds worth, at less than three fifty, raise an arm?
> As: [Many hands rise]
> P: Anybody else? Now as—[to PC] Now listen, Rick, the first eighteen people wi' their 'and in the air, will you please step forward. Now look, give every one of these people with their 'and in the air a carrier. Ah'm givin' out eighteen carriers an' that's it.

The question that the pitcher puts to the audience is designed to encourage everyone who has even a remote interest in the goods to respond ("who *can* use . . . them? . . . at less than three fifty, raise an arm"). By

---

7. The pitcher also appeals to scarcity to get more hands up. He says that he can only "do it for so many," implying that the stock is about to run out and that if people don't get their hands up they may miss out on the sale. (Creating scarcity is frequently used at other stages in pitching routines; see Pinch and Clark 1986; Clark and Pinch 1993.)

handing over carrier bags to these interested parties, he has transformed the display of *interest* (hand raising), in effect, into something more ineluctable: an expression of *intent* to purchase the perfume. The receipt of a bag implies that ownership of the goods is imminent. The pitcher does nothing to indicate that taking the bags is anything other than completely straightforward—it is not a problem. Instead of asking the audience if they mind accepting the bags, he simply instructs an assistant to give them to those people who have raised their hands.

Also, the pitcher again exploits the imitative basis of buying behavior to attract additional people to the stall and convince ditherers to buy. The protracted process[8] of handing over and accepting these bags clearly demonstrates the existence of "willing" buyers to others in the crowd as well as to passersby. It is not only the goods which will soon be bagged, but also the shoppers themselves!

The "Proviso"

Although essentially similar to bag-nailing, the "proviso" is a more explicit form of obligation and also more dramatic in its outcome. Now people not only raise their hands and take a bag, they also take the goods themselves—and all well before they know the final selling price of the goods! Because this technique is of necessity somewhat elaborate and time consuming, it is usually reserved for more expensive goods (in 1985 prices, those over £5). The routine gets its name from the pitcher's original sales offer, which is posited as being conditional upon the pitcher's reducing the price (for example, "Providing I make the goods cheaper than . . ."). In the following example the pitcher is selling sets of towels:

> P: An' ah'll put it to you like this. *Providin'* this morning, that I make any set that's caught your eye, a *lot* less than Marks an' Spencers' price of twenty pound, this morning, [CLAP] *providing* I make them a *hell of a lot less* than twelve quid a set, an' when ah say a LOT less, ah DON'T mean fifty pence or a pound or two, I Mean a HELL of a lot less than twelve quid, [CLAP] is there any lady or gentleman listenin' to me at the moment, who fancies a set of these, if I make them a *lot* cheaper? Now if you do, *don't* show me any money. I *'aven't* asked you for any money. If you've

---

8. These displays can be prolonged because they occur *before* the final price announcement.

seen a set you like, [CLAP] can you just show me a sign here, please?

As: [Many hands rise]

P: *You 'ave, darlin'; you 'ave, madam; you 'ave, sir; you 'ave, sir; you have, you have, you have, an' so have you.* Well, *everybody* has, now just a second.

Again the offer to sell is phrased in such a way that people in the audience can take it as merely asking for an expression of interest (for example, who "fancies a set" "if you've seen a set you like"). Also, as the pitcher does not explicitly ask to see any money, the audience are encouraged to draw the impression that the pitcher is simply conducting an opinion poll about the towels, rather than trying to sell them. But as in the sales described above, even such innocent questions are loaded, because they are attached to the proviso. In other words, the towels people "like" or "fancy" are towels which are going to be sold below a certain price. Expressing an interest at this stage already starts the process of nailing. As in previous examples, the pitcher publicly confirms the displays of interest by pointing out the people who have raised their hands.

The pitcher now prepares to hand out the "nailer." In this case it is not merely a bag, but the goods themselves. But these goods are not initially handed out to everyone who has raised a hand. Because of the greater risk taken in actually handing out the goods, the pitcher, rather than giving them out to everyone, chooses one audience member. Again, this person is selected as being likely to produce an enthusiastic and positive response ("clocking the divvy"). In other words, the pitcher uses opinion leadership (or, more correctly, *an* opinion leader) to manage the difficult transition from displaying an interest to accepting the goods:

[A has raised her hand.]

P: Now just a second, darlin', can ah speak to you?

A: Yes.

P: Ah won't embarrass you, just a minute, love, which colour do you like best?

A: [Points to a set of towels]

P: You like the burgundy. Now just a minute. Ah'm gonna ask this lady one question. Then ah'll serve *everybody*. [. . .] Darlin', would you say at twelve quid that was fair value for your money?

A: Aye.

P: *Yes?* If I make them a lot cheaper, you won't get annoyed, will you?

A: [Small shake of head]

P: 'Cos if you swear at me ah'll bloody swear back. Ah know all the words. Listen, ah'm gonna put those into a bag, ah hope you're all watchin' this. Ah'm gonna give them to you now, but you've got a very nice surprise in store for you. Okay, darlin'?

A: [No answer]

P: Don't look so bloody worried.

A: [Nervous laugh]

   [P hands over the goods to A.]

The key things to notice in this exchange are how the pitcher gently leads the shopper into the commitment and also how he repackages her responses. Rather than simply "fancying" or "liking" a set, she is asked to express a *preference* for a particular color. The pitcher asks her an understated leading question concerning the bargain status of the goods. By the time the pitcher has finished with her, it seems as if the woman has bought the goods, although nowhere along the line has she been explicitly asked if she wants to buy them or indicated, herself, that she wants the towels. That the goods are wrapped when they are handed over further confirms their status as goods which have been purchased.

The strategic advantage of all this one-to-one interaction to the pitcher is that he is able to publicly display to other hand-raising audience members that the first and only person he has spoken to is willing to take the towels. As he remarks, "I hope you are all watching this." Rather than immediately handing out the remaining towel sets, the pitcher then exploits his earlier success by showing that despite the interest at this price he will go lower. This is designed to be the "clincher" for those who have not been fully convinced by the endorsement of the individual who has just accepted the towels:

P: That lady's got the first set. Now listen. Just a minute. There's one gone, ah'd like to make it into twenty. For the people who can't decide, I'm gonna do it for you. At the next price I stop at, they cost more money, seven or eight years ago. Ah'm showin' you the *best*. You *can't buy better*. They *cost twenty*, ah've just been offered twelve. Another hint, [CLAP] ah won' even charge you ten pound a set. I am *still* coming cheaper. An' they've *all* got that *money back guarantee*. *In other words*, you can't lose. Ah'll say that *once more* to let the penny drop. [CLAP] At *less than* a tenna, a set today, *who else* wants a set, now, let me see? *Everybody.* Ah thought so. What colour would you like, darlin'?

[P then hands out the towel bales.]

Here the pitcher uses the familiar strategy of representing the earlier interest *he* has solicited from the woman as having been a firm bid of £12 ("I've been offered twelve"). By lowering the price even more (although he still hasn't said what his final price will be), he is able to present the bargain as being a still better bargain. When it comes to giving out more towel sets, he has little trouble in getting most of the audience to accept them.

Only after having handed out the wrapped goods does the pitcher announce the selling price:

P: This is the price, for the two bath, the two hand, there's twenty pounds' worth there, mine's a silly price, but it's marvellous value for your money. Not twenty, [CLAP] ah want nine ninety-five a set. OK?

The final price of £9.95 is strategically contrasted with the alleged worth of the whole set of towels (£20), not with the immediately preceding price of £10. Despite the minimal reduction, the work the pitcher has already done is enough to ensure that most people who have towels in their possession do in fact pay up.[9]

The success of the proviso, like all the nailing techniques, rests upon people's treating their responses to the pitcher as having obligated them to buy. The beauty of this technique, from the pitcher's viewpoint, is that it places the onus on the "buyers" to return goods already in their possession, rather than simply having to make a purchasing decision. The decision has in effect been made for them.

Nailing the edge—with forks, bags, or more dramatically, with the goods themselves—is a repertoire of well-established techniques employed by pitchers to obtain mass sales. Each of the techniques we have examined in turn is more complex, and more explicitly obligating than the previous one, yet all share the same basic elements of incrementally

9. The proviso is a highly successful technique for mass sales. Very occasionally some members of the audience will return the goods (known as "jebbing out"). And sometimes audience members will try to walk away with the goods without paying. In such sales the pitch crew often move to the rear of the audience, to ensure that everyone does pay.

converting a public expression of interest into a commitment to buy. Perhaps the most extreme example of nailing is an illegal fraud routine known as the "mock auction," in which members of the audience actually part with their money before knowing exactly what the price is, or even what goods they are about to receive (see Clark and Pinch 1992 for details).

Everyday Buying and Selling

It is probably clear by now that pitching differs from most other forms of retailing. In everyday shopping it is usually buyers who initiate transactions, by expressing an intent to purchase (for example, by taking goods to a counter or checkout). Buyers are also likely to be fully cognizant of the exact selling price of the goods before initiating the sales transaction. Prices are usually marked on the goods, and the shopper who doesn't know the price will usually ask before making a purchase.

Everyday shopping transactions also involve obligations on the part of both buyers and sellers. The sales staff, for instance, are under an obligation to sell goods at their designated price (and certainly not at more than that price), and to hand over the goods if they receive the requisite money from buyers. If a sales assistant announces that the goods have suddenly increased in price, or just pockets the money without handing over the goods, a primary obligation on the seller's part will have been broken, and the customer would have a right to feel aggrieved. Similarly, buyers are under some obligation both to pay for and to accept goods that they have indicated a wish to buy. One only has to think of the embarrassment caused when a buyer discovers lack of available funds to pay, or when, at the last moment, after the goods are wrapped and in the sales assistant's hands, the buyer decides the purchase is unwanted after all.

Another common characteristic of everyday shopping activity is that the act of handing over the money and receiving the goods usually happens at the same time as, or very soon after, the buyer has indicated a desire to purchase. Finally, and perhaps most importantly, in everyday shopping situations, although these obligations are *tacit* (unlike in pitching, where they are brought out into the open), buyers and sellers are all aware of their different obligations. What is going on is made as unambiguous as possible.

Unlike in pitching, most such buying and selling is carried out one-on-one. If obligations are brought out or broken, it is usually a private matter between the seller and the buyer. Unlike in pitching, there is no crowd to act as witnesses and, in some ways, executioners.

Sales Transactions in Pitching

The most dramatic difference between pitching and retail selling is the presence of a large crowd of buyers and potential witnesses to the transaction. Also, unlike in ordinary buying and selling, it is the seller who initiates the transaction. Furthermore, as we have seen, the buyer is persuaded to express some form of purchasing-implicative commitment without knowing precisely what the actual selling price will be. The expressed intent to buy the goods and the moment of exchange are separated, thus enabling the pitcher to manage the sale prospectively, turning expressions of interest into expressions of intent, and then into actual purchases.

Finally, in pitching, the obligations which the parties have to meet are often strategically ambiguous, and the implications of the information provided—especially by the pitcher—are somewhat equivocal. Thus, as we have remarked, it is not clear exactly whether standing in a crowd is itself a form of obligation, and how much further obligation is entailed by such actions as raising a hand, taking a bag, or taking the wrapped goods. Although people who participate in pitching sales often treat such actions as signifying obligations, the norms underlying such obligations are not as well institutionalized as in ordinary transactions. Also, the information provided by the pitchers is equivocal. The final price is not clearly stated but is merely hinted at or promised in terms of "going cheaper," etc. By contrast, the information provided by the buyers is rather unequivocal. People either raise a hand, take a bag, etc., or they do not. In this respect, because the pitcher has initiated the transaction, the pitcher has an advantage: the pitcher can demand unequivocal responses of the audience, but the audience cannot demand unequivocal prices from the pitcher. And, of course, throughout, the pitcher uses the crowd "for support."

All of these features enable the pitcher to accomplish the sales quest to great effect. Unlike in everyday shopping, where the shopper initiates the transaction, it is the pitcher who is in the driver's seat from the very start. This control enables the pitcher to separate the point of purchase from the first expressed interest, and incrementally to instill a sense of obligation into the audience. As we have seen, pitchers may first encourage an audience to be responsive before going on to use one or more of a set of nailing techniques which enable them to reconstitute responses as being more and more ineluctable obligations to buy. Although the pitcher does not force the audience to buy, the audience themselves retrospectively deem their positive responsiveness as having committed them to a purchase.

It is precisely the ambiguity over what social norms underpin transactions in this retail setting which enables the pitcher recurrently to gain the upper hand. Some norms are unambiguous. For example, as in normal retail settings, the pitcher, once having clearly announced a price, has to stand by that price and hand the goods over. Even in these unorthodox sales, if pitchers did not fulfill these sorts of obligations, problems inevitably would arise. The norms of ordinary buying also help explain pitchers' success. It seems that the buyers, although in an unorthodox situation where the seller has initiated the transaction, respond by following the normal rules of buying. For instance, they take it that they are under some obligation to buy those goods in which they have expressed an interest.

The central point of analytical interest here is that through their rhetorical and interactional skills pitchers are able to exploit the normative considerations that underpin everyday economic exchanges. It is not that norms mechanistically govern these transactions but, rather, that pitchers as skilled patter merchants play upon or capitalize upon such norms. In the language of social theory, norms both *constrain* and *enable* (Giddens 1976).

Higgling

As our research has not been on higgling per se, our comments here are mainly schematic. Pitching, as we remarked earlier, can be seen as a special case of higgling: it is, in a way, higgling by means of soliloquy. The pitcher acts out in his or her spiel a "fictional" higgling transaction. It is as if pitchers have thought through in advance all the problems which higglers might encounter and have tried to devise a set of solutions to these problems. Even the familiar decrease in price of the goods on offer in pitching mirrors the descending price structure to be found in higgling.

Higgling is thus like pitching in that both involve price uncertainty.

In pitching, however, the price uncertainty is only shared by the buyers, because the pitcher works with a prefigured final price. Although in higgling, sellers and buyers might have a final price in mind, the actual price set depends upon the negotiating skills of both parties.

Higgling transactions are evidently conducted within an environment where normative constraints apply.[10] For example, a seller who refuses to come down at all from the initial asking price will likely have breached some normative consideration as to how such transactions are to be conducted. Similarly, the buyer who makes a ludicrously low initial offer and then refuses to go higher is equally likely to have broken some norm. Such normative constraints might, of course, be breached simply out of ignorance or naïveté. For example, a buyer unfamiliar with bartering (say, a British tourist visiting an African market for the first time) may accept the first price suggested by the seller at face value—and either buy at that price (to the delight of the seller) or else walk off, complaining about the high price.

Let us assume, for the moment, that there *are* norms underlying such transactions and that we have delineated them.[11] Even so, these norms will not be sufficient to fully account for and explain what transpires, because, as in pitching, there remains the possibility (perhaps even the necessity) that one or both parties may try to exploit the norms. Each party may explicitly appeal to normative constraints in order to try outmaneuvering the other, to get the other to change position. This is evident in the following excerpt from a bartering exchange recorded on the streets of New Delhi. The seller (S) is selling a chess set to a buyer, a tourist (T):

> S: This is for real, good quality, I'll show you, this is much better, this real real wood, sandalwood, nice pocket chess, play in trains or (starrund woods?) cheap and best.
>
> T: No thanks.
>
> 5 S: Try it, automatic, my grandfather manufactures.
>
> T: Your grandfather?
>
> S: Yes, my house, 160 Falleen, born in Delhi, we are lucky, very hard working, car, friends, always wearing jeans. This is

10. What these norms are and how they vary from culture to culture and context to context have yet to be elucidated, although anthropologists such as Malinowski and others have made a start on this important topic: see also Mirowski, this volume.

11. See Schabas, this volume, for an account of the commitments and contracts that underlie higgling.

sandalwood, ebony wood. . . . one hundred and sixty-eight,
10   one hundred and eighty, twenty percent discount morning sale,
no business today.

T: No, it's too much.

S: How much?

T: Um, twenty.

15 S: Sorry sir?

T: Twenty.

S: I say one hundred eighty, you say twenty, how can it be? This
is very last, small fortune last week, I say hundred eighty you
20   say twenty, how can we deal? This is one hundred percent
sandalwood. One hundred, one hundred for this. You like?
How much for this? Don't make joke price. This is nice, this,
again open like this [demonstrates chess set], twenty-four-
hour making, sir, show price three hundred, four hundred
rupees price, I sell wholesale price, one piece is making one
25   piece sell.

T: Twenty for that.

S: How can this be, sir? Very bad, this is too bad, very last, one
hundred fifty I give you, cost price.

T: Naugh.

30 S: Sir, very last, how much do you want to give?

T: I said twenty.

S: You don't want to buy at any price, you don't want to buy at
any price.

T: Orright, how much do you sell for?

35 S: I give you for a hundred and thirty, sir.

T: One hundred and thirty?

S: Yes.

T: No.

40 S: [Shows different chess set] This is rosewood, sir, one hundred,
for mango wood, I don't mind for this.

T: No, it's too much.

S: How much do you want to give? Tell me a good price.

T: For this?

S: Yes.

45 S: How much do you give, how much do you want to give?

T: No. I said thirty.

S: How much?

T: Thirty.

S: [Laughing] Joking price. Make no profit . . . one hundred.
50 One hundred for you.

T: I go back down here now [waving seller away].

S: One hundred, half price.

T: One hundred, half price, no, no.

55 S: One hundred, I said one hundred eighty, now one hundred,
nobody beats this price, cheap. No profit.

T: Forty, forty.

S: No, you are joking, sir.

T: No.

60 S: I said I not make profit, I am poor man. How much is last
price? Last price is how much?

T: No, forty is my last price.

S: Not even very good, I give you two, I take one hundred fifty.
Wholesale price. I give to somebody else, I go home.

S: How much you give for two pieces? For you small gift.

65 T: Urrrh. For two, sixty.

S: You know one hundred and fifty, one hundred and fifty, three
hundred, two hundred, for fixed profit, very small price I
charge.
I sell you for two hundred. You say one for forty, how you say
70 two for sixty?

T: Because I'm buying more.

S: Too late, how much for one?

T: No, I'm not interested anymore.

S: How much is last price for one?

75 T: For one? I said forty.

S: Okay, last deal on that price ninety.

T: Ninety? For one, I said forty.

S: Okay, last deal on that price is ninety.

T: Ninety.

80 S: Ninety.

T: No. [leaving]

S: Alright I sell you half price, I sell one hundred and eighty, I say
ninety, half price, this is sandalwood, ivory, this is costly wood.

85 T: No. I wouldn't pay ninety for that.

S: How about this?

T: No. No, I'll leave it.

S: Okay, how much is last price?

S: Thirty or forty, that's your forty, that's my ninety.

90 T: No, forty is my last price.

S: Compromise, how much?

T: No, forty is my last price.

S: Compromise. Come on, last price.

T: I want to take a photograph.

95 S: How much is last price? Very nice sandalwood.

T: Forty.

S: Sandalwood, I make a loss.

T: You make a loss.

S: Not cost. Really.

100 T: No, leave it. Forty is my last price. It's up to you. . . .
[long pause]

T: Okay, I'll give you fifty.

S: What?

T: I'll give you fifty, okay?

105 S: Okay.

T: I'll take a picture of you and I'll give you fifty. Okay?

S: One hundred and fifty.

T: No, fifty for one, I won't take that one too.

S: Two pieces.

110 T: No, no. I'll just take the one. Okay?

S: Okay. [Sells chess set for 50 rupees]

At several points the seller dismisses the price offered by the buyer as a "joke" price. This occurs when the price offered by the buyer is 20 rupees (line 21), again at 30 rupees (line 49) and again at 40 rupees (line 57). The chess set is eventually sold for 50 rupees. That T's price of 40 rupees is only 10 rupees off the final selling price suggests that the offer at that point is, in fact, taken seriously by S. We have no way of knowing whether the buyer has in fact infringed the ways these negotiations are conducted, or whether the seller is constituting this normative infraction solely for the purposes of getting a better offer. Like obligations in pitching, it would seem that such norms and obligations are used to attempt to constrain the other party in such a way as to try and gain an advantage for one party.

Just as we have argued with respect to the negotiations which take place during telephone selling (Clark, Pinch, and Drew 1993), it would seem that many notions in higgling are amenable to interactional analysis. Higgling can be viewed as a transaction where each party is striving resolutely to gain an advantage over the other. The buyer wants the cheapest deal possible; likewise the seller wants to charge as much as possible. The resources to be used in such bargaining situations are largely interactional: what the goods are claimed to be worth, what is a fair price, and so on. Furthermore, because the negotiations have a sequential character, with each verbally stated position being explicitly on the table, there is an element of ritualistic brinkmanship involved (as at line 32 above). When the buyer says "last offer," is the buyer serious or not? If the buyer makes another offer after the "last offer," how much credibility will the buyer lose? It would seem that once a prior position is stated explicitly, it can be held by the other party to commit that person to *maintain* that position (as at lines 69 and 70, where S challenges T as to how he can say "two for sixty" when he has already said "one for forty"). Similarly, how much can the seller afford to reduce the initial price without displaying weakness, losing credibility, and opening the floodgates to a much lower price?

It would seem, prima facie from the above transcript, that worth and price are negotiated locally; that is, the outcome in some significant way depends on the negotiating skills of the two parties. The seller can proclaim how much the goods are normally on sale for (lines 23, 24), how much the price has been reduced for the special circumstances of this sale (54, 55), can extol the virtues of the goods (1, 2, 19–20, 23), cite personal history for added legitimacy (7, 8), say that the price is the "last deal" (76), and threaten to leave (63). The buyer, on the other hand, can likewise threaten to leave (81), or offer a "last price" (92), and so on. But such claims are negotiating stances: whether they are treated as believable and persuasive depends not so much on the proffered information per se as on its subsequent treatment by the other party in the local context of the negotiation itself. Although we have not attempted a detailed analysis here, we feel encouraged that a social-interactional analysis of higgling is feasible. The way forward is to make recordings and conduct analyses of naturally occurring higgling in a variety of different contexts.

Conclusion

Our comparison between pitching and both retail selling and higgling has revealed a number of interesting similarities and differences (see table 1 for a summary). Perhaps the biggest difference is between retail selling,

Table 1 The Principal Features of Pitching, Higgling, and Everyday Shopping

	Market pitching	Higgling	Everyday shopping
People involved in the transaction	Transactions occur between one seller and a number of different buyers. The sale is coordinated in such a way that many people buy at a single fixed point.	The transaction usually takes place on a "one-to-one" basis between an individual buyer and seller.	The transaction usually takes place on a "one-to-one" basis between an individual buyer and seller.
Instigation of the transaction	The exchange is initiated by the seller.	There is no special onus on who instigates the transaction. It can be initiated by a buyer approaching a vendor or by a seller attracting the attention and interest of a buyer.	The actual transaction typically is initiated by buyers.
Knowledge of selling price and intent to purchase	Buyers express an intent to purchase before knowing the exact selling price. They do this en masse, and their intentions are witnessed by the rest of the crowd that have gathered at the stall.	Neither the buyer or seller is fully aware of what the agreed sales price will be. An intent to purchase is usually made by the buyer when entering into the negotiation but, unlike in the context of pitching, such an intention is not expressed before a crowd and, hence, is relatively less binding.	The buyer is fully aware of the requisite selling price *before* an intent to purchase is expressed.

Placement of expression of intent and moment of exchange	An expression of "intent" is solicited before the moment of exchange takes place. In each of the (progressively more ineluctable) forms of obligating we have documented—from "forks up" to "the proviso"—the expression of intent is displaced further and further back from the selling price announcement and the moment of exchange.	These two points are separated, as in the context of pitching, but, unlike in both pitching and retail selling, there is a radical uncertainty as to whether an exchange will occur at all. The threat to curtail the exchange (by the seller refusing to sell or the buyer walking away) is often one of the main resources used in the negotiation by both parties.	The moment of exchange co-occurs with (or happens very shortly after) the intent to purchase has been made by the buyer. In other words, the seller usually does not strategically attempt to invert these two points.
Nature of obligations and information	The obligations entailed are somewhat unclear and the information provided can, at least initially, be equivocal—especially that provided by the pitcher. The buyers' expression of intent and the ensuing obligations are expressed publicly and are witnessed by the pitcher and other members of the crowd.	As in pitching, the types of obligations that both parties are under is unclear and potential obligations can be solicited in order to try to get the other party to change his position. However, unlike in pitching, the private "one-to-one" nature of the transaction makes the obligations relatively less binding. There is radical uncertainty as to the information provided by both parties, especially as to what price	The obligations are largely tacit, but both buyers and sellers are aware of each others' obligations and provide unambiguous information so as to make their intentions apparent and therefore unequivocal.

—Continued

Table 1 Continued

Market pitching	Higgling	Everyday shopping
	the seller will sell the goods for and how much the buyer will agree to pay. It can be advantageous for both parties to present information in an equivocal fashion.	

where prices are known in advance to both parties, and pitching and higgling, where there is some uncertainty as to what the price of goods will be. This uncertainty over the price (in the case of pitching, for buyers only) and the concomitant uncertainty as to the rules and procedures whereby an agreed-upon price will be settled allows the transaction to be conducted in such a way that its outcome depends on the interactional skills and finesse of the parties involved. Perhaps the major difference between pitching and higgling is the presence in pitching of a mass of shoppers who participate in the sale. This crowd of both onlookers and active buyers is important because it reinforces the intentions and obligations which the pitcher has solicited from individual members of the audience. In these circumstances individuals seem to take it upon themselves to treat their expressed intentions as obligations to buy.

Our whole approach to studying exchange relations in situ seems to be radically different from the understanding of markets, selling, and buying within the discipline of economics. We hope that this fine-grained study of naturally occurring sales and negotiating transactions has thrown some additional light upon the way in which the economic order is crucially influenced and underpinned by the sociolinguistic "interactional order."[12]

References

Atkinson, J. M. 1984. *Our Masters' Voices: The Language and Body Language of Politics*. London: Methuen.

Brown, V. 1994. Higgling: The Language of Markets in Economic Discourse. In *Higgling: Transactors and Their Markets in the History of Economics*, edited by Neil De Marchi and Mary S. Morgan. *HOPE* 26, special issue. Durham: Duke University Press.

Clark, C., and T. J. Pinch. 1988. Micro-Sociology and Micro-Economics: Selling by Social Control. In *Structures and Actions*, edited by N. Fielding. Beverly Hills and London: Sage.

———. 1992. The Anatomy of a Deception: Fraud and Finesse in the Mock Auction Sales Con. *Qualitative Sociology* 15:151–75.

———. 1993. The Hard Sell. Book-length typescript.

Clark, C., T. J. Pinch, and P. Drew. 1993. Managing Customer Objections in Real-Life Sales Negotiations. Typescript.

Giddens, A. 1976. *New Rules of Sociological Method*. London: Hutchinson.

12. See Brown, this volume, and Klamer and McCloskey 1993 for the importance of language to studying market activity.

Goffman, E. 1955. On Face-Work: An Analysis of Ritual Elements in Social Inter-action. *Psychiatry* 18:213–31.

———. 1959. *The Presentation of Self in Everyday Life*. New York: Doubleday Anchor.

Heritage, J. 1984. *Garfinkel and Ethnomethodology*. Cambridge: Polity.

Heritage, J., and D. Greatbach. 1986. Generating Applause: A Study of Rhetoric and Response at Party Political Conferences. *American Journal of Sociology* 92:110–57.

Klamer, A., and D. McCloskey. 1993. Talk Is Not Cheap. Paper presented at the Duke University conference on Higgling.

Mirowski, P. 1994. Tit for Tat: Concepts of Exchange, Higgling, and Barter in the History of Economic Anthropology. In *Higgling: Transactors and Their Markets in the History of Economics,* edited by Neil De Marchi and Mary S. Morgan. *HOPE* 26, special issue. Durham: Duke University Press.

Mulkay, M., C. Clark, and T. J. Pinch. 1993. Laughter and the Profit Motive: The Use of Humor in a Photographic Shop. *Humor* 6.2:163–93.

Pinch, T. J., and C. Clark. 1986. The Hard Sell: "Patter Merchanting" and the (Re)Production and Local Management of Economic Reasoning in the Sales Routines of Market Pitchers. *Sociology* 20:169–91.

Schabas, M. 1994. Market Contracts in the Age of Hume. In *Higgling: Transactors and Their Markets in the History of Economics,* edited by Neil De Marchi and Mary S. Morgan. *HOPE* 26, special issue. Durham: Duke University Press.

Smith, C. W. 1989. *Auctions: The Social Construction of Value*. London: Harvester Wheatsheaf.

Index

Contributors

Vivienne Brown teaches economics at the Open University in the United Kingdom. She is currently interested in the implications of contemporary literary theory for the development of economic discourse and has just completed *Adam Smith's Discourse: Canonicity, Commerce and Conscience* (1994).

Colin Clark is a sociologist and is currently working as a professor of marketing at the Ecole Supérieure de Commerce de Rennes in France. His main research concerns the study of the rhetoric and interpersonal negotiation strategies people use to persuade and control others in everyday interactional situations. He is presently studying video recordings of real-life sales interactions in an attempt to document the various social rules and communicative skills that influence and underpin these types of "economic" transactions.

Neil De Marchi is professor of economics at Duke University. He is editor of a volume entitled *Non-Natural Social Science: Reflecting on the Enterprise of "More Heat than Light"* (1993) and is currently working on the art markets of the Netherlands in the seventeenth century.

Ross B. Emmett is associate professor of economics at Augustana University College in Canada. His current research project is a study of Frank Knight's changing relations with social science in the United States from the mid-1930s to the 1970s.

Evelyn Forget is an associate professor of economics at the University of Manitoba. She spends most of her time trying to leave Winnipeg for Paris, to continue her ongoing research on "The Political Economy of Jean-Baptiste Say."

Paul Harrison is a Ph.D. student at Duke University. His dissertation examines stock market price regularities from eighteenth- and twentieth-century series.

Michael Hutter is professor of economics and chair of the Department of Business Administration and Economics at Witten/Herdecke University. His major fields of research are cultural economics and the theory of money and financial institutions.

Michael S. Lawlor is associate professor of economics at Wake Forest University. He is currently at work on a book on the historical context of Keynes's *General Theory*.

Robert J. Leonard is assistant professor of economics at the Université du Québec, Montréal. He is interested in the history of contemporary economics and is currently completing a book on von Neumann, Morgenstern, and the history of game theory (*In the Spirit of Exact Science*, forthcoming).

S. Todd Lowry is professor of economics and administration at Washington and Lee University. His publications include *Pre-Classical Economic Thought: From the Greeks to the Scottish Enlightenment* (editor, 1987), *The Archaeology of Economic Ideas: The Classical Greek Tradition* (1987), and volumes 7 and 8 of *Perspectives on the History of Economic Thought* (1992).

Anne Mayhew is professor of economics at the University of Tennessee, Knoxville, and is editor of *The Journal of Economic Issues*.

Philip Mirowski is Carl Koch Professor of Economics and the History and Philosophy of Science at the University of Notre Dame. His books include *More Heat than Light* (1989), *Against Mechanism* (1988), and an edited volume, *Natural Images in Economics: Markets Read in Tooth and Claw* (1994).

Mary S. Morgan is professor in history and philosophy of economics at the University of Amsterdam and lecturer in economic history at the London School of Economics. She is author of *The History of Econometric Ideas* (1990) and is currently working on the history of American economics.

Trevor Pinch is professor in the Department of Science and Technology Studies at Cornell University. He has served on the faculty at Bath University and York University in England and has been a visiting research fellow at the University of Twente in The Netherlands. His primary research interest is in science and technology studies. He is also interested in interactional sociology.

Malcolm Rutherford is professor and chair of the Department of Economics at the University of Victoria in Canada. He has written extensively on the American institutionalist tradition and is author of *Institutions in Economics: The Old and the New Institutionalism* (1994).

Margaret Schabas is associate professor of philosophy at York University in Toronto. She is the author of numerous articles as well as *A World Ruled by Number: William Stanley Jevons and the Rise of Mathematical Economics* (1990).

Michael V. White is senior lecturer in economics at Monash University in Australia. His published research has been principally concerned with the work of W. S. Jevons.